THE FLETCHER JONES FOUNDATION
HUMANITIES IMPRINT

The Fletcher Jones Foundation has endowed this imprint to foster
innovative and enduring scholarship in the humanities.

The publisher and the University of California Press Foundation gratefully acknowledge the generous support of the Fletcher Jones Foundation Imprint in Humanities.

The Anthropology of Sport

The Anthropology of Sport

BODIES, BORDERS, BIOPOLITICS

*Niko Besnier, Susan Brownell,
and Thomas F. Carter*

UNIVERSITY OF CALIFORNIA PRESS

University of California Press, one of the most distinguished university presses in the United States, enriches lives around the world by advancing scholarship in the humanities, social sciences, and natural sciences. Its activities are supported by the UC Press Foundation and by philanthropic contributions from individuals and institutions. For more information, visit www.ucpress.edu.

University of California Press
Oakland, California

Library of Congress Cataloging-in-Publication Data

Names: Besnier, Niko, author. | Brownell, Susan, author. | Carter, Thomas F., 1967– author.
Title: The anthropology of sport : bodies, borders, biopolitics / Niko Besnier, Susan Brownell, and Thomas F. Carter.
Description: Oakland, California : University of California Press, [2018] | Includes bibliographical references and index. | Identifiers: LCCN 2017023360 (print) | LCCN 2017026172 (ebook) | ISBN 9780520963818 (ebook) | ISBN 9780520289000 (cloth : alk. paper) | ISBN 9780520289017 (pbk. : alk. paper)
Subjects: LCSH: Sports—Anthropological aspects.
Classification: LCC GV706.2 (ebook) | LCC GV706.2 .B48 2018 (print) | DDC 306.4/83—dc23
LC record available at https://lccn.loc.gov/2017023360

Manufactured in the United States of America

26 25 24 23 22 21 20 19 18 17
10 9 8 7 6 5 4 3 2 1

CONTENTS

ILLUSTRATIONS

ACKNOWLEDGMENTS

Niko Besnier's work on this book was financed by an Advanced Grant from the European Research Council under the European Union's Seventh Framework Program (Grant Agreement 295769) for a project titled "Globalization, Sport and the Precarity of Masculinity" (GLOBALSPORT). He is particularly grateful for the input of the project's members (in alphabetical order): Paweł Banaś, Domenica Gisella Calabrò, Sebastián Fuentes, Daniel Guinness, Mark Hann, Adnan Hossain, Uroš Kovač, Michael K. Peters, and Douglas Kwaw Koi Thompson. He wrote segments of the book while benefiting from guest professorships at the Programme interdisciplinaire de recherche en sciences du sport et du mouvement humain at the Université de Toulouse III Paul Sabatier, the Département des sciences sociales at the École normale supérieure in Paris, the Department of Social Anthropology at the University of Manchester, and the School of Humanities and Social Sciences at La Trobe University. He holds a debt to all research participants who consented to share their lives during his fieldwork on sport in Tonga, Fiji, Japan, France, and the United Kingdom. He is grateful for his lifelong friendship and collaboration with Susan Brownell and for Mahmoud abd-el-Wahed's continued support during this project and beyond.

Susan Brownell would like to thank Niko Besnier for conceptualizing and spearheading this book, as well as for his unswerving emotional and professional support. She would also like to acknowledge the people and institutions who enabled and financially supported the research of three decades on which this book draws. The Centre for Olympic Studies at Beijing Sport University facilitated numerous stays in Beijing, and her colleagues and collaborators contributed enormously to her knowledge of Chinese sport, especially Ren Hai and Wang Fang. The year that she spent there up to and including the

Beijing 2008 Olympic Games was funded by a Senior Research Award from the US Fulbright Commission. As a member of the Grant Selection Committee of the International Olympic Committee's (IOC) Olympic Studies Centre (OSC), she also benefited from the support of the OSC, which over a decade paid for a dozen trips to Lausanne, Switzerland, and an additional trip to conduct interviews. In particular, she would like to thank Nuria Puig, head of University Relations. Multiple invitations from the International Olympic Academy (IOA) enabled many trips to Greece and an entrée into the global network of Olympic education. She would like to thank Konstantinos Georgiadis, honorary dean of the IOA, for putting her name forward for those invitations. The University of Missouri Research Board funded her 2004 conference on the Anthropology Days and Olympic Games held in conjunction with the 1904 St. Louis world's fair. A gift from the Costamare shipping company funded three international symposia from 2007 to 2008, titled "From Athens to Beijing: West Meets East in the Olympic Games," which she organized with Michael Cosmopoulos, Hellenic Government–Karakas Foundation Chair of Greek Studies at the University of Missouri–St. Louis (UMSL). Grants from the UMSL College of Arts and Sciences and from International Studies and Programs funded multiple trips to Lausanne and Beijing and covered fieldwork at the 2012 Nemean Games Revival in Greece and the Rio 2016 Olympics. Three influential figures in the Olympic Movement were generous enough to spend hours sharing their knowledge and experiences with her; she owes a profound debt to all of them for teaching her about not only sports but also leadership in times of crisis, resilience under attack, and perseverance in pursuit of one's grander visions–even if it takes half a century to achieve them. They are He Zhenliang, China's first IOC member; his wife, Liang Lijuan; and Hein Verbruggen, former president of Union cycliste internationale and SportAccord, and chair of the IOC's Coordination Commission for the Beijing Olympic Games.

Thomas Carter would like to recognize the dozens of people who have provided support while he was involved in this project, people of whom there are too many to identify individually. The Institute of Iberian and Latin American Studies at the University of New Mexico provided early support for fieldwork in Cuba and elsewhere in the 1990s. The British Academy funded fieldwork in the mid-2000s in Havana, and the International Sociology of Sport Association, by virtue of his organizing its international congress held in Havana in 2011, provided funds for multiple trips to Cuba in 2009–11. The Climbing Higher initiative and a sabbatical leave provided by the University of Brighton allowed him to further develop numerous ideas that fed into this book. His colleagues at the Centre of Sport, Tourism and Leisure Studies have been excellent sounding boards and critical voices in recent years, and their pointed critiques are always appreciated. Last, but certainly not least, he thanks his family for their support and understanding over the years, during long absences and difficult silences.

We thank the three reviewers of the book proposal, William Kelly, Alan Klein, and an anonymous scholar; the three reviewers on the draft manuscript, Joseph Alter, Alan Klein, and Stanley Thangaraj, for their particularly constructive comments; and Jean-Charles Basson, Christine Mennesson, Gillian Evans, and Mani Mitchell for their comments on specific chapters. We are grateful to Reed Malcolm, acquisition editor at the University of California Press, for his trust in us, and to Pablo Morales for his outstanding copyediting.

Introduction

FEW ACTIVITIES IN THE LIVES of ordinary people around the world bring together physicality, emotions, politics, money, and morality as dramatically as sport. Whether in Brazil's huge soccer stadiums or in China's parks, on baseball diamonds in Cuba or rugby fields in Fiji, or in wrestling arenas in Senegal, human beings test their physical limits, invest remarkable amounts of emotional energy, bet money, perform witchcraft, ingest substances, and display what they think is important in life. Sport plays a tremendously important role in setting boundaries between groups, contesting them, defining what is normal and what is extraordinary, and entangling the everyday lives of ordinary people with the state, the nation, and the world. Thus, while sport is easy to dismiss as an inconsequential aspect of our lives, on closer inspection it emerges as a microcosm of what life is about. To borrow a phrase from Émile Durkheim, one of the founders of the modern social sciences, sport provides a window on "the serious life."[1]

A particularly intriguing aspect of sport is that it fuses experiences that are otherwise considered contradictory, such as playfulness and seriousness, leisure and work, individualism and collectivism, pleasure and violence, hierarchy and equality, morality and corruption. These tensions are found with remarkable predictability in very different parts of the world and at radically different times in history. Even in the ancient world, sport evoked themes that resonate with people today. For example, in the Mayan and Aztec empires of Mesoamerica prior to the Spanish conquest, ball games were clearly a family affair, as seen in a delightful clay model from Nayarit, Mexico, dating from circa 100 BCE–250 CE, showing spectators, including women with their arms around children, leaning out from their seats above to look down into the ball court (figure 1). But the games also had a deeply political

FIGURE 1. Model of ball game with spectators, Nayarit, Mexico, ca. 100 BCE–250 CE (Yale University Art Gallery).

quality, since rulers in carved-stone murals donned a ballplayer's hip pads and headdress as if the equipment indicated fitness to rule, and human sacrifices were conducted together with the games. The Olympic Games held in ancient Greece from the eighth century BCE brought together athletes representing city-states that were often at war with each other outside the sacred Olympic sanctuary, but laws and an athlete's oath protected the games from political interference, even while the plazas between the competition spaces were crowded with statues and monuments commemorating the victory of city-states over each other in battle.

While today we might see sparks of recognition across vastly different cultural and historical contexts, sport also takes on very different meanings depending on where and when it is practiced. To continue with the example of ancient Mesoamerican ball games, they were at times so violent that being hit by the hard rubber ball could prove fatal, and there is evidence to suggest that players were sacrificed after games. In contrast, in most (if not all) sports as they are practiced today, violence is constrained so that, when death occurs, it is viewed as a tragic accident rather than an integral part of the sport, even in sporting activities that involve considerable danger, such as mixed martial arts, boxing, and bobsled. Moreover, a specific sport may be played according to the same rules everywhere but differ in how it is played, who plays it, and how people assess it. Soccer in contemporary US society is largely associated with either the white middle class or Hispanic minorities, whereas in Argentina it is the rough sport of the masses, one that the upper-middle classes are keen to keep at a distance. In other words, sport is embedded in a tension between universalism, as it draws its significance from abilities shared by all, or nearly all, human bodies, and particularism, as those abilities are not interpreted and shaped in the same way in all places and at all times. That people's lives are organized in fundamentally similar ways around the world but also determined by specific contexts is a fundamental recognition in anthropology, and thus the discipline is particularly well suited to shed light on the nature of sport as both a universal and a particular human activity.

THE CONCEPT OF SPORT

What is sport? As conventionally understood, sport is an invention dating back to mid-nineteenth century Britain. As we will elaborate later in this book, sport also emerged in other places and at other times, but these sporting forms either have disappeared or have been marginalized by the global spread of the particular type of sport that emerged almost two hundred years ago in the British Isles. Before their encounter with British—and later American—sports, most world languages did not possess a term defining a unified category of competitive athletic activities that distinguish a winner from others. The ancient Greeks labeled their Olympic and Panhellenic games as *agones,* "contests," a category that also included music, debate, and other activities. In English, the term *sport* first occurs in 1863 in the narrow sense of an athletic activity regulated by rules.[2] The modern concept of sport appeared at the same time as the concept of the sports record, a reflection of the centrality of modern technologies of measurement and record keeping in sports (even sports that do not time or measure the performances still utilize sports fields and equipment made with standardized measurements, something that the ancient Greeks, for example, never did). One of the earliest usages of the word *record* in the sense of a best-ever measured performance occurred in an 1868 training manual for track and field.[3] The word *sport,* along with the set of activities that it labels, was frequently adopted into languages spoken around the world, and in many languages it refers solely to Western-style sports and is simply a borrowing from English or another European language.

Although sport is often described as a celebration of what makes us who we are as human beings—as in the International Olympic Committee's Celebrate Humanity publicity campaign launched in 2004—competitive sports organized by rules with clear winners and losers are not human universals. Both the historical and anthropological evidence hints at why this is so: the uncertain outcome of a competition that is run by egalitarian rules sits uncomfortably in hierarchical societies, in which elders and elites prefer to control the outcome of contests to reinforce their own status, and in which no one on either end of the social ladder wants to risk what might happen if a sports contest challenges the position of the elites. In societies that value harmony, the preferred result may be a tied game. In ritual settings, there may be a preference for an outcome that serves the purpose of the ritual, such as letting guests win or honoring the gods.

All this means that we must be cautious about identifying certain activities as sport and be reflexive about what it means to perform such identification, because granting an activity the status of "sport"—as well as denying it this status—is laden with cultural and political assumptions. A good example is the ongoing tension in the international sports world about which sports should be included in the Olympic Games program: judo was first contested as an exhibition sport in 1964, when Japan first hosted the Summer Games, but wushu, or Chinese martial arts, did not make it into the program at the Beijing 2008 Olympics, despite heavy pressure from China. What underlies these decisions is not any essential trait that delimits sports from nonsports but rather power differences that determine who decides, in what political context, according to what criteria, and for what ends.

In this book, we refrain from imposing necessary or sufficient conditions on what counts as sport, such as the centrality of competition, since competition may be overshadowed by other, more pressing concerns in many sportlike activities around the world. The Waiwai on the Guyana-Brazil border, for example, hold archery rituals during which each male member of a village aims to shoot an arrow at a target in a generally jovial and festive atmosphere, but there is no winner or loser, since these events are symbolic performances of masculinity as a category rather than as a focus of competition.[4] Similarly, in the 1950s, the Gahuku-Gama of the Papua New Guinea Highlands had reconfigured rugby as a substitute for intertribal feuding and held games that ended when elders of the opposing groups agreed that a tie had been reached.[5]

Thus, rather than engaging in debates over whether chess, cockfighting, video games, and bodybuilding are "really" sports, we find it more productive to include a broad spectrum of physical exercises and competitive activities in our analysis while being mindful of the Western-centered historical processes that ultimately led to some of them being classified as "sport," while others were excluded. We pay attention to efforts by advocates who would like to see certain activities included in international sports events or in alternative events designed to counter the hegemony of events such as the Olympic Games or the FIFA World Cup. We generally take an encompassing definition of sport, paying particular attention to what brackets it off from other activities of everyday life, how it is characterized locally, how it is understood by others, and how it is positioned against the mainstream activities recognized internationally as "sport."

SPORT IN ANTHROPOLOGY

One of the most distinctive characteristics of sociocultural anthropology, since Bronislaw Malinowski's foundational work in the 1910s and 1920s, has been its grounding in ethnography—the personal, long-term, and in-depth engagement with the people whose lives the researcher seeks to understand. The central role of intensive fieldwork has weakened considerably in the last decades of the twentieth century, for a number of reasons. One is that ethnography has been claimed by multiple other disciplines, including sociology, cultural studies, media studies, and so on. Some currents in sociology, such as the Chicago school, already appropriated ethnographic methods back in the 1930s and 1940s; cultural studies, particularly under the foundational influence of the Birmingham school, brought ethnography to what was until then the study of high culture (particularly literature) and used it to democratize the scope of its interests to include "popular culture," from fashion to shopping to television programs. Many anthropologists have reacted with some suspicion to the characterization as "ethnography" of television viewing and off-the-cuff interviews with people the researcher knows very little about. But the fact remains that ethnography is no longer the exclusive purview of the discipline.

Another reason that the marriage of anthropology and ethnography has experienced stress in recent decades is the realization, spearheaded by postcolonial scholarship, that knowledge production is never innocent of politics, particularly in contexts that are already suffused with power and inequality. This placed a damper on anthropologists' faith in their ability to describe social and cultural facts in a neutral manner and resulted in calls for a shift to ethnography as an intersubjective and self-reflexive enterprise.[6] Furthermore, in the ensuing decades, anthropologically informed ethnography underwent major transformations with the advent of, for example, multisited ethnography associated with the analysis of global flows, and digital ethnography and the ethnography of social media, in which the ethnographer's engagement is no longer based on in-body copresence.[7]

The preoccupation with globalization and multisited research in the first decades of the new millennium highlighted the value of sport in the effort to develop new research methodologies. The challenge for ethnography in today's globalizing world is that it is the most microscale of all the social science research methods, so it has been difficult for anthropologists to figure out how to "scale it up" to account for macroscale global processes. The ethnography of sport has proved to be an excellent method for taking on this challenge, because at one end it concerns minute bodily actions, while at the other end these actions are linked into a worldwide sports system that operates hand in glove with ambitious government officials, powerful multinational corporations, international media conglomerates, and the global culture industry. Sport offers a particularly productive context to conduct a multiscalar analysis of the contemporary world, analysis in which "local, regional, national, pan-regional and global are not separate levels of analysis but are part of mutually constituting institutional and personal networks of unequal power within which people both with and without migrant histories live their lives."[8] In short, it is possible to trace the pathways of power starting from the bodies of athletes on faraway training fields, following them as they cross multiple boundaries to compete or migrate to training centers with better opportunities, and finally arriving at the very center of the global political economy. Michel Foucault used the term biopower to capture this polymorphous nature of power, which does not stop at the limits of the state but continues flowing into class, gender, ethnicity, and other kinds of power difference, eventually permeating everyday body practices. Biopolitics refers to the politics of biopower, the control of bodies through the regulation of family, health, sexuality, birth, death—and, we might add, sports and exercise.[9] It is this capacity of sport to traverse social scales that explains the subtitle of this book—Bodies, Borders, Biopolitics.

In today's neoliberal world order, sport tends to follow the path of capital, and in so doing it leaves behind a tracing for anthropologists to see, making visible the often-hidden workings of powerful people, institutions, and social networks. Sport ethnography shows the workings of power across the multiple temporal and spatial scales of ethnography. By connecting everyday life to seemingly unrelated areas, it expands the horizons of ethnography without losing the focus on concrete ethnographic stories grounded in local settings. Sport mega-events provide particularly focused sites for conducting the ethnography of the global system because of the way in which leading politicians and CEOs, major media, and celebrities gather there, while the world's largest television and Internet audiences tune in.

Because the three authors of this book are particularly interested in the intellectual endeavor of linking the local with the global, this book tends to focus on sports that are connected with the global sports system. We have given more attention to soccer, rugby, cricket, baseball, the Olympic Games, and the FIFA Soccer World Cup than to local, indigenous, "traditional" sports, for example. At the same time, it will be abundantly clear that we are mindful of the ever-changing relationship between activities that are "inside" and "outside" the world system, a relationship that mirrors the more general tension between tradition and modernity that is a central issue (perhaps *the* central issue) in these fast-changing times.

As anthropologists, we continue to find that the intense and localized engagement required by ethnography bestows a quality on anthropological analyses that is largely absent in other disciplines. A distinctly anthropological approach, with its specific research methods, theoretical frameworks, and holistic thinking, can utilize insights from the constitution of sport as human action to illuminate important social issues in a way that no other discipline can.

But therein lies the catch. Other disciplines, particularly sociology and history, have had a much longer and more extensive history of engagement with sport as a topic than anthropology, as witnessed in the fact that a number of journals are dedicated to the sociology and history of sport, while no journal is dedicated exclusively to the anthropology of sport. Of course, the existence of journals focused on sport does risk isolating it from larger concerns, and indeed many of the other disciplinary journals end up being largely engaged in descriptive "butterfly collecting," to use anthropologist Edmund Leach's caustic phrase.[10]

As we will elaborate in chapter 1, sport has occupied an ambiguous place in the history of anthropology. On the one hand, some of the most classic works in the discipline concerned sporting or sport-like activities; we are thinking of Clifford Geertz's classic analysis of the Balinese cockfight and the ethnographic documentary *Trobriand Cricket,* both of which are staples

FIGURE 2. A young Senegalese wrestler strikes a pose before his fight, in a sport that showcases the tension between tradition and modernity (Dakar, June 2014/Niko Besnier).

of introductory courses in anthropology wherever the discipline is taught.[11] In a more recent yet little-recognized event, in 1987, the Korean anthropologist Kang Shin-pyo, working with the American scholar John MacAloon, invited a large number of prominent theorists in different disciplines to an international conference, including anthropologists Roberto DaMatta, Edith Turner, Marshall Sahlins, Ulf Hannerz, and Arjun Appadurai. Pierre Bourdieu contributed a paper but did not attend the conference.[12] It seemed that these theorists benefited from firsthand observation of a sport megaevent in the making, since they produced influential articles out of the papers first presented there.[13] The anthropology of sport was finally receiving the attention of leading thinkers, but it was not until two decades later that the disciplinary mainstream, aided by developments in sport history and sociology, caught up with the approaches outlined by these scholars.

Today, sport has gained considerable legitimacy as a serious topic in the discipline, although there remains a need for more ethnographically informed work, particularly on topics that frame sport and sport-like activities within questions of central importance to the discipline. In this book, we emphasize insights from scholars whose methods and theoretical concerns are anthropological, but we find it necessary to rely on works in other disciplines, such as sociology, history, and sport studies, as well as quality journalism, on topics that could also be productively subjected to anthropological analysis, even though this analysis has yet to happen. In such cases, we will attempt to highlight the unique contribution that could be made by an anthropological approach that asks different questions and explores different kinds of links between sport and other categories of human existence.

This book draws on our own decades of experiences as athletes and as organizers, practitioners, and spectators of sport. It also draws on our decades of ethnographic research on all five continents. Niko Besnier has conducted fieldwork in the Pacific Islands (Tuvalu, Tonga, and Fiji), Japan, and the United States, and when he directed the European Research Council project on athlete migrations in 2012–17, his research became increasingly unmoored from any local setting. Susan Brownell is employed in the United States and specializes in China, but she has also done participant observation in Greece, the United States, and at the headquarters of the International Olympic Committee in Switzerland. Brownell and Besnier attended the Rio 2016 Olympics and wrote a series of essays for *Sapiens: Anthropology/Everything Human,* a then-newly launched e-zine for the discipline of anthropology.[14] Thomas Carter is employed in the United Kingdom and specializes in Cuba and

Northern Ireland, but he has also done ethnographic fieldwork in the United States, Ecuador, and Wales. Between the three of them, the authors draw on ethnography and written sources in seven languages: Mandarin Chinese, English, French, Fijian, German, Tongan, and Spanish—with a little Greek, Japanese, and Portuguese thrown in for good measure. In addition to our long-term ethnographic research, in this book we have included snippets of personal experience where they provide a more concrete and personal example to illustrate broader issues.

We recognize that some contexts and topics may be difficult or impossible to research ethnographically for practical reasons, such as the world of top-level athletes in the major sports, athletes whose celebrity status is carefully guarded by retinues of agents, managers, lawyers, coaches, and other minders who may make ethnography impossible. We nevertheless see an anthropological approach as shedding a unique light on sport, and a focus on sport as contributing novel ideas to anthropology. We thus see this book as pivoting between critically assessing the state of the field of sport anthropology on the one hand, and outlining a program for future exploration on the other.

ONE

Sport, Anthropology, and History

SPORT HAS OCCUPIED A TENUOUS position in anthropology since the late nineteenth and early twentieth centuries. Until the new millennium, there was no "sport anthropology"—that is, a critical mass of scholars who focused on the topic and recognized the relevance of one another's work. There was instead only a small number of anthropologists who studied sport. There was no journal of sport anthropology, no international association, and no section or interest group of the American Anthropological Association. In 1974 a handful of interdisciplinary scholars mobilized around the concept of play and established the Association for the Anthropological Study of Play. This led to the publication in 1985 of *The Anthropology of Sport* by Kendall Blanchard and Alyce Cheska, the first—and for another decade and a half, the only—attempt to define the field. When anthropologists made excursions into the topic, they did so as part of their interest in certain theoretical paradigms or broader issues and then moved on to other topics. With a few notable exceptions, sport was not recognized as a topic that led to major theoretical breakthroughs in the discipline, unlike topics considered more central, such as religion, social class, and nationalism. Thus, this chapter is not a history of the anthropology of sport so much as an overview of those moments when sport received anthropologists' attention. Any attempt to generalize about the "state of the field" runs into the problem that the anthropology of sport was not a unified field that underwent a clear theoretical development but rather one that drafted off the winds of leading topics in the broader discipline as they shifted over time.

By the time anthropology began to emerge as a discipline and discover sport, there was already a body of scholarship on ancient sports loaded with heavy Western-centric baggage. As the Industrial Revolution brought distant peoples into closer contact, a cultural geography of the world began to cohere among both Western academics and their popular audience, a geography in which the primary categories were "Western civilization" and its heirs, "Orientals" (with the primary focus on Europe's closest cultural and military rival, the Ottoman Empire), and "savages" (everyone else). Before the late nineteenth century, there was only one form of elite (and, of course, male) education in the West, and that was one focused on the Greek and Roman classics. Oriental studies emerged in the late eighteenth century to study the Orientals, and the discipline of anthropology emerged in the mid-nineteenth century to study the savages. The West's studies of Oriental and savage Others helped to strengthen a shared identity among educated men who had received a classical education and believed themselves to represent the attainments of "Western civilization."[1]

This shared identity emerged in an era when the old social order based on monarchs and the Catholic Church was collapsing, and in its place the system of modern nation-states was arising. The remaking of the social order was accompanied by some of history's most brutal wars. Classically educated elite men noted the parallel between warring ancient Greek city-states and warring modern nation-states. They knew that, in antiquity, athletic games had been important forums for interstate diplomacy, and so they conceived of reviving the ancient Olympic Games to solve the political ills of their times. Perhaps the first call to revive the ancient Olympic Games appeared in 1790 in France, where the foundational thinkers of the French Revolution had linked sports with ancient Greek democracy.[2]

In 1875 the largest archaeological excavation to that point was undertaken at the site of the Olympic Games in Ancient Olympia, Greece. It was led by Ernst Curtius, a professor of classical archaeology at the University of Berlin, and funded by German emperor Wilhelm I. Archaeology had become a tool of the Western powers, which sought not only to extend their control over physical territories through colonialism and imperialism but also to exert symbolic control over the past by claiming the most spectacular archaeological sites. Governments and wealthy elites funded expeditions in search of archaeological and ethnological artifacts. At a time when millions of artifacts were expatriated to Western museums to symbolize the commitment to civilization and progress claimed by their possessors, the excavation at Olympia was unusual in that Curtius negotiated an arrangement with the Greek government in which all artifacts except for selected duplicates would remain in Greece.[3] Curtius was perhaps the first to see ancient Greek sports and games as emblematic of the restless, competitive spirit that made Westerners the masters of history and everyone else their subjects, or so he claimed. Curtius and prominent classicists who followed him asserted that the ancient Greeks valued competition more than any other peoples, that their competitive spirit ("agonal spirit," after the Greek *agon*, "contest") was a defining feature of "Western civilization," and that this spirit explained why the Greeks invented democracy and why the heirs of their tradition would inevitably shape the course of world history. The Olympic Games were said to be the quintessential expression of this competitive spirit.[4]

The wider neoclassical revival, in which archaeology played a key role, formed the context in which the first modern Olympic Games were founded in 1896, spearheaded by Pierre de Coubertin, a classically educated French aristocrat. For the next two decades, the Olympics served as the original world championships for a number of sports, cementing the link between modern sports, democracy, and Western colonial and imperial supremacy.

In the realm of sport, the past weighs especially heavily on the present because of the way in which history has been used to legitimize different kinds of sporting practice. These processes of legitimization were part of large-scale dynamics whereby a particular construction of history served to justify the power of certain regions of the world over others. But as anthropologist Eric Wolf demonstrated in his Marxist-inspired opus *Europe and the People without History,* the world, including its seemingly isolated regions, has in fact been deeply interconnected through trade and other dynamics since 1400 CE.[5] He argued that Western intellectual traditions viewed Europeans (the "people with history") as the driving force of historical change, and "primitive" societies (the "people without history") as pristine, unchanging survivals from the past. Wolf advocated a new global anthropology to overturn Western-centric history, insisting that world history had always consisted of a two-way interaction between the Western and non-Western areas of the world. If scholars properly recognized the interconnections between the world's peoples, their works would demonstrate that "the global processes set in motion by European expansion constitute their history as well."[6]

To this day the International Olympic Committee still claims that ancient Greek humanistic "Olympic values" underpin the modern Olympic

Movement.[7] Contemporary Olympic sports are given a mythical attachment to the ancient history of "Western civilization," which is supposed to be located in ancient Greece rather than in other logically possible locations, even though ancient Greece was a crossroads of many cultures both "eastern" and "western," which was a major source of its vitality. In fact, the ancient Olympic Games emerged as an institution at the end of the eighth century BCE, a period of increasing interactions among the civilizations of the eastern Mediterranean and Near East. This is known as the "Orientalizing period" because of the large number of motifs in Greek art borrowed from the then more developed states of Syria, Assyria, Phoenicia, Israel, and Egypt. The Greeks came to be maritime traders with colonies throughout the Mediterranean, where Greeks not only interacted with their Others but also were occasionally ruled by them. From the sixth to the fourth century BCE, the Greeks' main Other was the huge Persian Empire, stretching from what is today northeastern Greece to the Indus valley in India. These interactions funneled cultural influences back toward the mainland, with the quadrennial gathering of freeborn Greek athletes at Olympia acting as a centripetal force to pull in new ideas and practices. In antiquity, as in the modern era, "sporting cultures traveled by trade and colonization, as well as by conquest and empire."[8]

In the classical era, the Olympic Games provided a common ground for warring city-states, helping to create a unifying Hellenic identity. In the end they were patronized by Macedonian and Roman conquerors to display their power as well as their admiration of Hellenic culture. In fact, the Olympic Games reached their grandest scale not in the era of city-states but in that of the Romans, when participation was no longer limited only to freeborn Greeks, and all the best athletes of the Mediterranean could compete. Integration into a much larger empire disseminated Hellenic art, culture, and ideals to a much broader segment of the world's populace.

Given the Olympic Movement's romantic linking of the modern Olympic Games to the ancient ones, it is not surprising that both the scholarly and popular imaginations have tended to draw a direct line from the ancient Egyptians to the ancient Greeks to the Roman Empire to British and American sport and finally to contemporary global sport.[9] That the complexities of the archaeological record from millennia ago are frequently simplified is not surprising, since the ambiguous nature of the evidence allows historians and archaeologists considerable leeway in their interpretations— which, more often than not, have been shaped by their own assumptions.

FIGURE 3. The Nemean Games Revival in 2012, showing ancient *hysplex* starting mechanism and starting pose, with coauthor Susan Brownell fourth from left (Ancient Nemea, June 23, 2012/Susan Brownell).

While they focus on the Greco-Roman era, they are largely informed by very modern concerns: nudity, athletic events, athletic ideals, games in society, women, athletes, education, and the relationships among sport, spectacle, political power, professionalism, and nationalism. These discussions are not just dull descriptions of material remains; rather they increasingly attempt to draw a connection between the silent arenas of the past and the roar of contemporary sport. In so doing, more recent works are invoking cognitive archaeology's material engagement theory, which considers the minds of the maker and user of archaeological objects as integral to an understanding of the physical object.[10] Recent works by historians of the ancient world have combined literary criticism with contextual historical analysis to provide some of the most informative and illuminating analyses of ancient sport.[11]

For example, Stephen Miller has utilized a unique ethnographic tool to aid his analysis of ancient sports—reenactments. The "revival" of the ancient Nemean Games that he initiated after two decades of excavations at the site has become a quadrennial event attracting hundreds of competitors, many from other countries (figure 3). Miller's reconstruction of the preparation, organization, and operation of the Nemean Games allowed him to make experimental archaeological observations about spectators, lane markers, and the benefits of olive oil to capture the spectacular environment of an athletics event. He also addressed how the *hysplex,* a kind of starting gate, was used to ensure fair starts to races.[12] Susan Brownell personally experienced the *hysplex* when she won her age group in the *stade* (length of stadium sprint) in the 2012 Nemean Games revival—wearing a tunic, running barefoot, and anointed with olive oil.[13]

"THE PEOPLE WITHOUT SPORT HISTORY"

That sport was practiced by other civilizations besides the Greeks and Romans has not gained nearly as much attention from scholars. In much of the archaeology of sport, it is virtually impossible to move beyond the Mediterranean world, widely assumed to have served as the cradle of Western civilization. Like a long line of historians of ancient sport before him, Nigel Crowther in his 2010 book *Sport in Ancient Times* provided only brief chapters on China, Japan, and Korea and did not engage at all with South Asian sport.[14] He did acknowledge Mesoamerican civilizations, but not the North American areas of Cahokia, the Southeast, and Great Lakes city-states, where early forms of stickball games were apparently played.[15]

One of the enduring legacies of nineteenth-century biases has been the continued life of the idea that the ancient Greek concept of *agon* is a defining feature of Western civilization from the Greeks until today. The notion that a cultural focus on contests was unique to the ancient Greeks is still accepted today to some degree by prominent classical scholars.[16] One of the few scholars to dissent with the stereotype of Western competitiveness was Johan Huizinga (1872–1945), a Dutch medieval historian and author of a foundational theory of play. Impressed by French sinologist Marcel Granet's interpretation of ancient Chinese culture, he argued that "the agonistic principle plays a part in the development of Chinese civilization far more significant even than agon in the Hellenic world."[17] Huizinga was decades ahead of his time; his contributions to the study of play will be discussed below.

In the late nineteenth and early twentieth centuries, Germany had been the world center for classicism, and much of the leading scholarship on ancient sports in the classical world had come out of its universities. In the wake of Germany's romantic and ultimately catastrophic obsession with ancient Greece and "Aryan civilization," postwar German scholars were most incisive in criticizing the omission of non-Western cultures from the history of ancient sports. One was Wolfgang Decker, who demonstrated for the first time that Egypt had a rich sports tradition before Greece (nineteenth-century classicists considered Egypt an "Oriental civilization"). Another,

Ingomar Weiler, criticized classicists' fixation on the Greek pursuit of individual excellence—expressed in Homer's proverb *Aien aristeuein,* "Ever to excel"—arguing that it played a role in racist scholarship that denied the existence of competition and sport among non-Aryan races.[18]

Henning Eichberg was the only scholar to enter into the debate from an anthropological perspective. A German scholar based in Denmark since 1982 and trained in history and sociology, he conducted fieldwork on sports in Indonesia and Libya. He sharply criticized what he considered to be neocolonialism in sport studies, observing that "by thinking in terms of an 'absence' one tends to reproduce the colonial inequality on a new level: modern sport remains the measure—the others 'don't have it yet.'"[19]

However, almost none of these works have been translated into English, except for a few of Eichberg's essays.[20] As a result, the question of Western-centrism in ancient sport history has not been seriously taken up by anglophone scholars; furthermore, while the subfield of classical sport history has borrowed many anthropological theories, few trained anthropologists have published in the field. The history of Greek and Roman sports as a whole could benefit from closer collaboration with anthropologists.

GAMES, SPORT, AND ANTHROPOLOGY IN THE VICTORIAN CULTURE OF DISPLAY

Anthropology emerged in this context, and much of its early history was intertwined with classicism and classical archaeology. Thus, US-based archaeologists sought to find spectacular sites in the Americas that could produce artifacts to rival those dug out of the classical sites that had already been claimed by Europeans. The disciplinary divide between classical and anthropological archaeologists remains today. Moreover, both classical and anthropological archaeology were intertwined with the growth of mass popular culture. P. T. Barnum is often considered the originator of "popular culture," commodified entertainment ventures that earn their profit by attracting very large and not particularly educated audiences who pay small admission fees. Opened in New York in 1841, Barnum's American Museum (which was not a museum in today's understanding of the word) displayed ethnological artifacts along with exotic animals, historical artifacts, paintings and sculptures, waxworks, freak shows, and other curiosities, drawing the idea from the Enlightenment-era "cabinet of curiosities" but making it available for mass consumption. After his museum burned to the ground in 1870, Barnum took his first circus on the road.[21] In the United Kingdom, a Victorian "culture of display" emerged through newly created public museums. The Great Exhibition of the Works of Industry of all Nations in London in 1851, often referred to as the Crystal Palace Exhibition, was the first exposition that aspired to be international, kicking off the fashion of "world's fairs."[22] In the early years of anthropology the novel institutions of museums and world's fairs provided the financial underpinning for professional positions. Circuses and world's fairs mixed Greco-Roman reenactments such as chariot races, gladiator contests, and wild-animal shows with boxing contests, equestrian and rodeo performances, and acrobatic performances, as well as displays of humans from Asia, Africa, and North America who occasionally engaged in sport-like activities.

Building on the circus tradition, in 1883 William F. Cody, or Buffalo Bill, invented the Wild West show, reenactments of battles fought against Indians on the American frontier or in the imperialist expansion into Mexico and around the world. The shows included riding, roping, shooting, and dramatic narratives, and advertisements claimed that the performers included army scouts, soldiers, cowboys, and Indians who had taken part in the actual events. Wild West shows provided employment for many "show Indians" who otherwise would have been stuck on the reservations. They were wildly popular in the United States and Europe, and they helped forge the imagined cowboy-and-Indian past that became an important element in American national identity. Moreover, Indian schools trained their pupils in sports in an attempt to guide their assimilation and took them on tours to compete against Euro-American schools.[23] The vexed relationship between Indians and sports boiled up in the twentieth century when activists began to protest the use of Indian symbols as mascots for sports teams, arguing that they expressed white infatuation with Indian stereotypes combined with an unwillingness actually to understand Indian culture. A lawsuit against the Washington Redskins football team claimed that its name violated the law against using pejorative names in trademarks, but the judgment against the team was overturned on appeal.[24] Clearly, in the realm of sport symbolism, some non-Indians are just as attached to fictional Indians who live in an imaginary past as are some non-Greeks to fictional ancient Greeks and their imaginary Olympian past. These fictions are part of the great symbolic systems that give meaning to the times in which we live—in ways that are often problematic for disadvantaged populations.

At the 1893 world's fair in Chicago, Stewart Culin, one of the founders of the American Anthropological Association (established in 1902), organized an exhibition of world games. This was an extension of his interest in games that resulted in more than a dozen articles and two books on the subject published between 1889 and 1925.[25] Culin linked games primarily with religious beliefs and divination practices. He was also interested in using the similarity of games from distant parts of the world as proof for cultural diffusion—for example, finding evidence that "the higher culture of the New World had its source in Asia." In addition, he found these similarities to be proof of the "psychological unity" of the human race, that is, that all human minds share a set of similar fundamental capacities, an idea with roots in Enlightenment-era philosophy that became a central tenet of anthropology thanks to the influence of Adolf Bastian and his student Franz Boas (see chapter 3).[26]

Culin's encyclopedic work on games did not, however, extend into the realm of sport. The only sports displays by natives at the Chicago world's fair occurred when the revenues were not on pace to repay the financial backers, and so in an attempt to attract paying spectators, boat races and swim meets were arranged between the Zulus, South American Indians, Dahomeans, and Turks inhabiting the re-created "ethnological" villages along the carnivalesque strip of attractions outside the fairgrounds.[27]

From the discipline's very beginnings, anthropologists paid much more attention to the games played by people around the world than to sports. However, for a long time, the study of games was little more than the cataloging of equipment and rules, and they were often regarded as children's pastimes. It was not until the 1970s that greater analytic thought was given to attributing a significant social role to those games, as we discuss below.

Perhaps the most interesting convergence of anthropology and sport occurred at the world's fair in St. Louis in 1904, when native sports were incorporated into the "scientific" investigations undertaken by WJ McGee, director of the exposition's Division of Anthropology.[28] McGee had just been forced out of the position he had held since 1893 as ethnologist in charge of the Bureau of American Ethnology, but he had become the first president of the newly formed American Anthropological Association in 1902, confirming his status as the most powerful man in American ethnology. He responded to a challenge from James Sullivan, head of the fair's Division of Physical Education and organizer of the third modern Olympic Games held in conjunction with the fair, on the question of whether "savages" were

FIGURE 4. "Spear throwing contest of Igorrote Warriors" (original caption; the preferred spelling today is *Igorot*). Philippine Reservation, Department of Anthropology, 1904 world's fair (Louisiana Purchase Exposition: St. Louis World's Fair Albums. Jesse Tarbox Beals, from the Missouri History Museum collections).

athletically superior to civilized men. McGee agreed to organize the natives on display in St. Louis to take part in sports events so that their performances could be measured and compared with those of the athletes who would take part in the Olympics. As ridiculous as this seems today, McGee was somehow able to conceive that it was sound scientific methodology to line up a group of "natives" from around the world, explain the rules to them in English (which many of them did not understand), and then measure and time their performances in running races, high jump, broad jump, shotput, javelin, baseball throwing, tug-of-war, and pole climbing for comparison with the best-trained athletes in the United States (figure 4). The event, called Anthropology Days, was enough of a failure as a scientific experiment that no academic reports were ever published on it, but this did not stop McGee from organizing a second event one month later in an attempt to generate more revenue, having concluded that the fair organizers had not given the first event enough publicity to attract the numbers of paying spectators that he had expected. For the second event the participants were provided with some advance training and with interpreters who spoke their languages; they also performed wearing "native" dress. About thirty thousand spectators attended, of whom almost three thousand paid ten to twenty-five cents to sit in the bleachers erected for the occasion. While McGee claimed that the performances improved, no record remains, and again no academic paper was ever published.[29]

MESOAMERICAN AND NORTH AMERICAN SPORT IN ANTHROPOLOGICAL ARCHAEOLOGY

Sport also appeared on the radar screen of anthropological archaeologists. With the excavation of the great ball court at the Mayan center Chichén Itzá in 1923, archaeologists had their equivalent of the ancient Greek games. It is in Mesoamerica where archaeological evidence for sport's central spectacular role is apparent due to the durability of the stone-built Olmec, Aztec, and Mayan architecture. Ball courts as old as thirty-six hundred years and rubber balls as old as thirty-five hundred years have been excavated. Murals depicting contests and rulers adorn important architectural structures. The ball court was formed by high walls in the shape of an I. Balls were made of solid rubber weighing up to nine pounds. Rubber trees being indigenous to South America, early Spanish observers were astounded by the bouncing balls and wondered whether they were animated by spirits. Spectators watched from above as two teams of two to four players tried to score points by keeping the ball in play by hitting it only with their hips. Blows from the fast and heavy balls could cause severe bruising and even be fatal, so players wore protective headgear and large hip pads. Rulers were often depicted wearing the iconic ballplayer dress, demonstrating the game's role in reinforcing political authority. Some ball courts also had two stone rings protruding from the center of the long wall, sometimes nearly twenty feet from the ground. Sending a ball through the ring, which must have been a rare event, may have resulted in immediate victory.[30]

The evident grandeur and scale of Mesoamerican ball games rivaled the circus spectacles of Rome or Byzantium. The Mesoamerican ball game clearly played a central role in the display of theocratic authority and social hierarchy, as evidenced by the spatial architecture, urban planning, various art forms, murals, ceramic figurines, stone statues of ballplayers, and myths and legends recounting the sporting prowess of gods and heroes. Ball games appear to have played a pivotal role in the transition from relative social and political egalitarianism to a rank-based society, in which hereditary leaders claimed divine origins and controlled the labor of others. Prehistoric statuettes depict men of chiefly rank wearing ball game protective gear, and the Mayan cosmological text Popol Vuh describes the creation of the world as a ball game that pits mortals against gods. Ball games and the attendant activities played an instrumental role in establishing early forms of government. Sport for the ancient inhabitants of the region was serious business.[31] (The link with Mesoamerican cosmology is further described in chapter 3.) While ball courts were a common feature of central plazas in Aztec and Mayan cities, they were actually widespread and found among such cultures as the Hohokam culture in what is now Arizona.[32]

Other sports in North America also played significant social roles. One such sport was chunkey, in which a contestant tossed a smooth stone disc several inches in diameter so that it rolled across the ground, and then he and his opponent tried to hit it by throwing long poles up to eight feet in length. It was typically the occasion for gambling. Archaeologists have found evidence of this sport spread throughout much of Mississippi valley and the Southeast. One scholar has argued that envoys from Cahokia, a ritual center near present-day St. Louis, carried chunkey stones in one hand and war clubs in the other as they traveled into the Midwest, South, and Plains seeking political alliances and eventually establishing a region-wide Pax Cahokiana.[33] The spatial organization of mounds, state houses, or pyramids fronted by an open plaza in settlements throughout the US Southeast, the Mississippi valley, and Mexico is suggestive of the importance of spectacle in those settings.[34] Without asserting any causal relationship, we may conclude that sport played a central role in the emergence of complex societies in North America and Mesoamerica, given that these societies all engaged in sport-related spectacles, chunkey, stickball, or ball games. The degradable materials of North American settlements have left behind less evidence, but wherever found, the sports associated with these spaces demonstrate the same links among spectacle, athleticism, and political power.

Archaeology contributes a great many things to our understanding of early complex societies but does not help us to understand sport outside the practices of the more powerful elites. The archaeology of sport lacks sources on informal sports and games, which may have been a popular part of everyday life. Instead, the focus is on the links among politics and sport, state formation, and the practices of the elite. In contrast with Mesoamerican civilizations, those of the Mediterranean appear not to have embraced team sports, according to the archaeological record: the Panhellenic Games, the Roman circuses, and Byzantine races emphasized mano a mano competition and individual achievement. Apparently, city fathers did not believe that ball playing prepared citizens of these societies for any meaningful civic responsibilities. What is evident, then, is that sport can take numerous forms even as its apparent singular purpose, the linking of sport to sociopolitical power, cuts across the diverse range of sport found in antiquity.

RETHINKING ROMAN SPORT

As a legacy of their link to Western colonialism and imperialism, most popular and historical writings about the evolution of modern sport follow a historical narrative that reflects, if not wholly reproduces, the dominant narrative of modernity, demonstrating the inevitable progress of modern sport out of its antiquarian forms. This ideological linkage does not reflect the values, organization, or structures of sport as it was then, but mirrors the core beliefs about humanity, the world, and civilization in the scholar's own era.[35] Despite presumptions about the uniqueness of modern sport, the politics of pageantry, spectacle, and celebrity making seem to have crossed the centuries when we consider the ancient Greek games and the various entertainments of the Roman and Byzantine Empires. In earlier interpretations of archaeological remains, the "progress" and "civilizing" discourses of sport were seen to be confirmed by various archaeological findings, heavily influencing our understandings of antiquarian sport, most especially in the Panhellenic world and of the Olympic Games in particular.[36] Much more recently, these assumptions have been scrutinized critically in a large body of works rethinking the role of sport and other spectacles held in grandiose spaces of stadiums, amphitheaters, and plazas in reinforcing the political legitimacy of rulers and the state.[37]

Continuing a bias from the early founders of Christianity, who demonized Roman spectacles with legends of martyred Christians, nineteenth-century classicists produced a positive stereotype of Greek sports and a negative stereotype of Roman sports: Greek sports were characterized as admirable, pure, participatory, amateur, noble, and uplifting; Roman spectacles were decadent, vulgar, spectatory, professional, sadistic, and debasing.[38] Coubertin subscribed to this stereotype, and that was why he insisted that Olympic Games should be awarded to a host *city* rather than a *country,* imitating the status of the Greek city-state as the main political unit; this remains the case today, although most people are not aware of it (on this point, Olympic Games differ from FIFA World Cups, which are awarded to countries). In an era when European nation-states were threatening to gobble up each other and parcel out other continents between themselves in the process, Coubertin stated that there was a "latent eliminatory conflict" between the principle of the Roman state and that of the Greek city, and he feared that the future favored the Roman state, while he himself preferred the Greek city.[39]

It was not until the 1980s that scholars started "taking the Greeks down from their pedestals and raising the Romans from their ruins."[40] The purported "amateur ideal" of ancient Greek sports, which had been much cited by, in particular, British elites wishing to exclude laborers from their sports, was overturned when David Young documented that ancient Greek athletes were well-remunerated professionals. Similarly, the purported exclusion of women from sports was invalidated when it was revealed that contests for women in honor of Zeus's wife, Hera, had been held at the Olympic complex.[41] Not surprisingly, both of these facts were rediscovered by scholars when the reality of elite sports had changed: it was an open secret that star Olympic athletes were clandestine professionals, and by then women had achieved a modicum of acceptance in sport. It is interesting that more accurate scholarship followed the emergence of new social practices rather than preceding them, so that it appears that sportspeople forced scholars to remove their blinders and not the other way around.

In the new millennium, scholarship on Roman sports utilizing anthropological perspectives on rituals, cultural performances, and gift exchange revealed that Roman sports were embedded in social, economic, and political structures in complex ways.[42] Gladiator combat was not as brutal as Hollywood would have us believe, although it still surpassed the threshold of tolerance of the contemporary world. It is interesting to point out the variation in thresholds of tolerance across cultures: while the Romans eventually embraced Greek athletics, they had to overcome initial resistance because of the association of Greek sports with homosexuality, and they never embraced athletic nudity. The Roman masculine ideal, unlike the Greek, was somewhat prudish and paranoid about effeminacy, so spectators who delighted in watching men slaughter each other would have been offended by male nudity. Gladiators were, paradoxically, both admired for their quintessential masculinity, exemplified in their physical prowess and acceptance of death, and held in contempt for their low social status. Most were non-Roman prisoners of war, and they were assigned specific kinds of armor and weapons that signaled "barbarian" ethnic identities. There was no "Roman type" because that would have risked the defeat of a gladiator representing Rome by a barbarian, and gladiator shows were about glorifying Roman martial prowess.

Gladiators were enslaved to private owners who supplied them with food, medical attention, training facilities, and a trainer. Even if they earned their freedom, they were permanent outsiders classified as *infamia,* a status that included actors, criminals, debtors, prostitutes, and gravediggers, all of whom had restricted legal rights. In the Republic of the third century BCE to the first century CE, gladiator contests were organized by a producer, an elite man who presented them as a "gift" to his constituents in order to win their support. He financed the show and contracted the gladiator troupe. Combat was not uncontrolled slaughter; rather it was highly choreographed and overseen by two referees. Fights were brief and ended when one fighter acknowledged defeat by dropping his weapon and raising his finger (a gesture adopted from the Greek mixed martial art *pankration).* The referee made sure that the victor stood back and awaited a decision from the spectators, who signaled either a reprieve by a closed fist or two figures pointing out, or death by thumbs turned toward the throat and shouts of "Kill him!" The crowd's reaction was based on the quality of the fight and the fame of the fighter. The final decision was indicated by a gesture from the producer, who sat in the stands and assessed the crowd's reaction. He could defy the crowd, but that would controvert the purpose of the event, which was to display his generosity and gain their support. If he saved a gladiator, they might feel he was being cheap: producers were reluctant to give the thumbs-down because every gladiator represented a substantial financial investment—some contracts even specified a rental fee of eighty sesterces if the gladiator survived, but a compensation of 4,000 sesterces if he was killed or maimed. A gladiator could be worth more than the annual salary of a Roman soldier (about 12,000 sesterces), despite price-control regulations. Between 20 and 50 percent of fights ended in a death, with the rate increasing from the first to third centuries. A gladiator who survived three years was released from the arena, and after five years he was granted full freedom. Free Roman citizens were not supposed to fight in gladiator games, but the fact that some did (including one emperor, Commodus) is indicated by repeated imperial decrees trying to stop them;

they were unpaid and were not stigmatized by *infamia*. Women very occasionally became gladiators who fought other women or beasts.[43]

Arena games were so integral to politics that Augustus took greater control of them as he strove to turn the Republic into an empire with himself as emperor and "father of the country" from 27 BCE onward.[44] He regulated games held in Rome to ensure that rivals could not organize games to gain popular support: gladiator schools were moved under imperial sponsorship, limits were set on shows that magistrates could produce while in office, and the state provided the funding so that magistrates could not buy supporters with extravagance. Augustus himself was featured as the producer in centralized games that reinforced his authority. In Rome gladiator games were the grand finale to a day of performances in the Colosseum provided free of charge to as many as fifty thousand spectators.

Chariot racing was the most popular sport from early Rome into the Byzantine Empire, with the number of races reaching an average of one every five or six days in the fourth century CE.[45] At its peak, the Circus Maximus held one hundred and fifty thousand spectators. Males and females intermixed in the stands, offering opportunities for courtship. The sport was organized by circus factions, privately owned and operated businesses that owned the chariots, charioteers (slaves of mostly Greek or Hellenistic origin), horses, stables, and equipment. *Factiones* also was the label for the spectators who wore different colors associated with their faction to distinguish themselves in the stands, and whose frequently zealous support was aided by massive betting. The lives of the charioteers (and probably those of the horses) were often short because of the danger of crashing, either from bumping into other chariots (which was allowed) or crashing into the barrier or turn posts. However, they received a portion of the prize money, and so, if they survived long enough, they could purchase their freedom. When the Republic became an empire, the emperors took control of the arena itself, but the factions continued to organize the sport in a kind of public-private partnership until the third century CE. The bodily presence of the emperor at the events was symbolically very important, not least because this was an occasion when organized protests by the citizenry demanding food or tax relief were normally (but not always) tolerated, providing a vent for public discontent.

The rethinking of Roman sport gives us much food for thought about modern sport. Too many elements are uncomfortably familiar. Sports celebrities from outsider ethnic backgrounds were regarded with simultaneous admiration, contempt, and fear; they possessed limited legal rights, were

owned by private groups of wealthy male elites, and were sometimes eroti-
cized by elite women. Their condition is far too similar to the status of black
and African athletes in contemporary sport (discussed in chapters 2, 4, and
8). As the early Christian writer Tertullian put it with disgust, "The perver-
sity of it! They love whom they lower; they despise whom they approve; the
art they glorify, the artist they disgrace."[46]

The use of sports in local politics by elite owners who hosted games to win
popular support for their political ambitions is hauntingly similar to today's
professional sports clubs—although increasingly the elites who own them are
no longer locally based but members of transnational networks, making
them less responsive to their local fan base. The incorporation of state-
sponsored sport spectacles into the rituals of the state echoes the link of sport
with modern nationalism (discussed in chapter 7) and the political symbolism attributed to sport mega-events today (chapters 6). Clearly, one can hear
echoes across the millennia indicating that sports are a significant tactic of
power in whatever form they take. Another lesson is that although the inspiring ideals of the ancient Olympic Games may be more present in the popular
imagination today, the social, political, and economic organization of contemporary sports has more in common with Roman sports—as much as we
might prefer not to think about it.

THE ANTHROPOLOGY OF PLAY

The abundant evidence of the presence of sport in ancient cultures demonstrates that sport as an activity (as opposed to a cultural concept) is not a
modern invention or even an invention of Western civilization. Yet it is not
a human universal, either, because it clearly varies according to the particular
historical, social, and political contexts in which it is practiced. While sport
as it is defined today is not universal, play, a human activity that is central to
the emergence and organization of most sport, appears to be a human universal motivated by biological, and thus pan-human, imperatives.

In other species, prey and predators engage in play, albeit not together
(although some predators use prey to play). Pronghorn fawns engage in fast
running interspersed with twists and leaps. Their play strengthens the skills
required to evade predators. Those that play more have a greater chance of
surviving their first month than those that do not play as much. Similarly,
wolf cubs' main form of play is mock predation, which helps them develop

the individual and social skills required for hunting in packs. Play tones muscles, builds coordination, hones skills useful in hunting, and helps young wolves establish their place in the pack hierarchy. But that does not explain why adult wolves also play. For wolves, humans, or any other social creature among which play has been observed, the rules are the same: if a participant becomes too aggressive, play ceases abruptly. One cannot play with a partner one cannot trust. For any living being whose livelihood and survival depends on a social group, a solid foundation of trust is critical.[47] Understood in this manner, play emerges as an inherently biological condition in which a set of actions is set off from the other contexts of life. Play is adaptive in that, through it, the young learn the requisite skills and knowledge required for survival, and it helps to maintain social cohesion among the grown members of a social group. Play is thus biologically important, but it is also one aspect of human life in which the biological and the cultural are intertwined. Why human beings engage in play—and by extension, games and sport—is much more complex than a simple manifestation of a biological imperative.

In 1930, New Zealander anthropologist Raymond Firth published a classic analysis of a dart match on the isolated Polynesian island of Tikopia in the Solomon Islands. His analysis moved the focus from the material aspects to the social functions of games, in step with the search for "function" that dominated British anthropology at the time. Firth proposed that "sport as an integral feature in the life of many primitive peoples, offers a number of problems for investigation. Some of these are concerned with questions of organization, of the nature of the factors which differentiate a vague play activity from a regularly established game with clearly defined procedure, hemmed in on every side by rules of strong sanction."[48] He went on to explore motivations and emotions, physiological patterns, and the activity's overall relationship to the rest of life, especially religious affairs, economics, and aesthetics. Nevertheless, the article reproduces the rigid view, later developed by Roger Caillois (discussed below), that games are activities rooted in play, culturally sequestered, and consequence-free.

In his foundational *Homo Ludens,* Johan Huizinga suggested not only that play is primary to and a necessary (though not sufficient) condition of the generation of culture, but also that culture exists as a form of play only because it presupposes the understanding that it is "enclosed within certain bounds freely accepted."[49] Play then is not so much an activity separate from the world but a disposition toward the world. As a creative force, play marks the agent as ready to improvise and practically equipped to act, successfully or not, amid novel circumstances. This disposition acknowledges that a being may affect events, but its agency is not confined to its intent or measured by it. Rather, play allows for unintended consequences.

In *Man, Play, and Games,* French scholar Roger Caillois challenged Huizinga's emphasis on competition in play, recognizing that it was only one of a range of values that could be attributed to play.[50] In particular, he divided play into four discrete categories of games along a continuum of two poles between utterly open fantasy *(paidia)* and strictly controlled efforts, skills, and knowledge *(ludus)*. Those four categories recognize the difference between games of skill *(agon)* and games of chance *(alea)* as well as taking on pretense (mimicry) and altered perceptions *(ilinx)*. While play informs all these categories, Caillois surmised that modern sport arose out of a combination of both *agon* and *alea,* and this is where he disagreed with Huizinga. Caillois also argued that gambling is a game "like a combat in which equality of chances is artificially created, in order that adversaries should confront each other under ideal conditions, susceptible of giving precise and incontestable value to the winner's triumph." For Caillois, gambling is a game of chance, particular to humanity, based on luck with specific kinds of risk that shape a distinctly human form of play.[51] Huizinga insisted that gambling was the corruption of play, in which "fatality" should not be involved.[52]

A growing focus on the creative force that is play developed in anthropology to challenge the materialism that prevailed at the time. Whether a game was essentially a social activity and enabled a winner to triumph was not a problem for Caillois. He considered that play is best described by six core characteristics: it is free, or not obligatory; it is separate from the routine of life, occupying its own time and space; its outcomes are uncertain, thus requiring human initiative; it is unproductive, in that it creates no wealth and ends as it begins; it is governed by rules that suspend ordinary laws and behaviors and that players must follow; and it involves make-believe that confirms for players the existence of imagined realities that may be set against "real life."[53]

One of the most creative minds of the twentieth century, Gregory Bateson, saw the need to completely rethink play after observing two young monkeys at the San Francisco Zoo unequivocally "playing, i.e., engaged in an interactive sequence of which the unit actions or signals were similar to but not the same as those of combat."[54] He realized that play could occur only if the monkeys were capable of "metacommunication"—communication about communication. In this case the monkeys were engaging in behaviors that looked like combat, but they had somehow communicated the message "This is play." The paradox of play was that a playful nip denotes a vicious bite—that is, an action that is play denotes an action that is not play. This meant that the animals were communicating about something that did not exist (the vicious bite) and were capable of distinguishing metacommunicative frames—in this case, play from not-play.[55] If animals were capable of such complex mental constructs, then how much more complex must be humans' mental constructs, that is, their "fantasies"? Bateson proposed that human rituals were a similar type of meta-communicative frame. Humans are capable of a further paradox in which metacommunication about a symbol denoting something that does not exist indicates that the symbol is nonetheless real; he used as an example the fact that men will die to save a flag, signaling that the flag is a "metaphor that is meant."[56] John MacAloon later incorporated Bateson's notion of metacom-munication into his theory of performance frames, as we discuss in chapter 6.

As mentioned above, the Association for the Anthropological Study of Play served as a takeoff point for the development of the anthropology of sport. It produced ten annual conference proceedings in the 1970s and 1980s. However, the number of anthropologists in the association decreased over time, and in 1987 the word "Anthropological" was dropped from the name of the organization; the reborn series, "Play and Culture Studies," continues to the present.[57]

Despite Caillois's attempt, definitions of play and game remained open to debate. A 1976 review article pulled together the existing studies of children's play to outline the state of a fragmented field in which there was "clearly no single agreed-upon definition, classification, or metaphor/reduction of play available."[58] It described four approaches in ethnographies of children's play. The first saw play as form of socialization through role-playing and mimicry. Various forms of play were presumed to be differences based on culture rather than in biological makeup. The second focused on children's play, especially in relation to its material culture—games and toys—at the expense of the social processes of play. The third examined children's play from a psychologi-cal standpoint in which play revealed anxieties and fears. The fourth treated play as essentially a trivial activity barely warranting notice despite its acknowledged human universality.

One scholar who attempted to provide an anthropological definition of play was Edward Norbeck.[59] Drawing on the work of Huizinga, as almost all scholars investigating play do, he proposed that play is never imposed by physical necessity. Instead, a person engages in play because the activity is intrinsically rewarding, not because the activity is a means to some end outside the activity. Play is separate from what one considers "real" life, although within its own boundaries, it can proceed with the utmost seriousness. But Norbeck's efforts make it abundantly clear that play is one of the more difficult behaviors to pin down precisely because of its amorphous, ambiguous contexts of engagement. No firm definition of play has emerged since the mid-1970s despite regular, recurrent anthropological research on the topic.

Play's freedom, its "bracketing" from everyday life, and its independence from material interest makes it appear antithetical to all that is held dear in modern capitalist society. The "escapist" potential of play rests on the idea that individuals in a leisure-based modernity are "free" to play.[60] The obligation to spend leisure time "wisely," however, is not a human universal but a specific cultural norm rooted in capitalism.[61] Nevertheless, Huizinga clearly separated play from work, arguing that modern sport is not play because it is rooted in industrial capitalism and thus embroiled in material concerns. The regimentation and systematization of modern sport have pushed it away from the playful disposition: "The spirit of the professional is no longer the true play-spirit; it is lacking in spontaneity and carelessness."[62] The tightly scripted spectacles and regimented labor found in sport do nothing for humanity. Thus, for Huizinga, sport has nothing to do with play, though playful elements can unintentionally emerge during sporting activities.

Yet to play a game is to embrace a specific cultural framework that reinterprets the context in a new, and often comprehensive, system of meaning. Games are specialized activities composed of symbolic packets of play, as both Huizinga and Caillois contend. The rules of any game coordinate the terms of engagement and help participants reach a conclusion or a moment of disengagement. In this way games provide play with circumscribed, often linear, qualities that play outside of a game might otherwise lack. Players may grow tired or bored, or may otherwise wish to quit the game even as each player is normatively expected to finish it; they are encouraged to complete the game by its very structure. This structure orders time and space, helping turn "mere behavior" into a bounded and complete "event." A game has a beginning and an end, which bracket it from other activities and encourage distinctive behaviors that alleviate the drudgery of life while simultaneously confirming the salience of that everyday world. Elsewhere, these same insights became important in ritual theory, as we will discuss in chapter 6.

The assumption that play is trivial has dominated the general attitude toward play in the discipline of anthropology and spilled over into its attitude toward sport. While children's play has been treated as an object of anthropological inquiry, adults' play typically has not, although online games and other forms of Internet play have attracted some recent ethnographic attention.[63]

RITUAL, TRADITION, AND MODERNITY IN SPORT

The realization that sport is not play still leaves open the question of what sport is and what anthropology can contribute to an understanding of it. In the 1970s historians began to assert that the modern, Western conception of sport is unique in world history and fundamentally different from the "traditional" sports of historical and non-Western peoples. One aspect of the debate was the attempt to identify which criteria should be used to define a sport as "modern." An area of sustained inquiry was the concept of the sports record as a best-ever, measured performance.

Historian Allen Guttmann's paradigm-changing *From Ritual to Record: The Nature of Modern Sports* argued that "traditional," premodern sports had a ritual character that disappeared with the emergence of industrial society and was replaced by an emphasis on achievement, as manifested in sports records.[64] Although there was no causal relationship between them, modern sports developed at the same time as industrial capitalism; both were driven by the scientific revolution of the seventeenth century and the mathematical discoveries of the eighteenth century. The emergence of modern sports manifested the development of an empirical, experimental, mathematical worldview.[65] In refusing to declare a causal relationship between an industrial economy and sports, Guttmann disagreed with Marxist historians who argued that modern sports arose along with capitalism because they facilitated the capitalist exploitation of workers by keeping the workers fit and docile (Guttmann was located, after all, on the capitalist side of the Cold War).[66]

Challenged by Guttmann, later researchers found sports record keeping in other cultures and epochs, leading some to argue that sports records are not a distinctly modern practice.[67] Even if a preoccupation with record keeping and quantification per se is not modern, what *is* decidedly modern is a bureaucratic system designed to keep records on local, national, and global scales. At this point, an anthropological contribution to the discussion might help resolve its current impasse—we need to better understand who keeps records, why, and whose power interests records serve.

Henning Eichberg agreed that sports records involved capitalist-style production—the "c-g-s production" of centimeters, grams, and seconds—but he disagreed with Guttmann's unilinear evolutionary scheme ("from ritual to record"), arguing that although modern sports fetishize the production of records, the ritual aspects of sport continue to flourish in the modern context—modern sports are a "ritual of the record." Borrowing from Michel Foucault's concept of the "epistemic break," he eschewed the search for the "origins" of sport, before it "evolved" into its modern form, preferring to see a historical discontinuity between the seventeenth and eighteenth centuries, when one configuration of space, time, and interpersonal relations gave way to another. Before the break, a person's social place was determined by an ascribed status contained within a bounded hierarchy; after the break, a person's social place was based on "achievement" in an open economy oriented toward productivity. The "from ritual to record" theory continues to be a topic of heated debate and still has its adherents.

The notion of "traditional sport" in much of the sport studies literature effectively presupposed a temporal distance between the secular, "rational," contemporary practices of modern sport and the premodern, "irrational" practices of traditional sport, which were said to be based on superstition, religious belief, and other nonscientific ways of understanding the body, what it means to be human, and humanity's place in the cosmos. The label "traditional sport" implies that the activity is not "civilized," not secular, and not scientific. In effect, these are physical activities and embodied practices embedded in a worldview that differs from the modern, secular rationality inherited from Western Enlightenment. Implicit in this perspective is the unilinear evolution and belief in inevitable progress and constant improvement of humanity that so drove the Enlightenment and the concomitant expansion of European power.

VICTOR TURNER'S RITUAL THEORY

In a completely independent effort in the same time frame, Max Gluckman and his student Victor Turner were developing a new brand of ritual theory that, like Guttmann's, subscribed to the then-prevailing modernization theory, which held that there are clear differences between "traditional" and "modern" societies. Guttmann and Turner were not aware of each other's work. Applications of ritual theory and the other theories that it inspired to sports events will be discussed in chapter 6.

Here we will observe that Turner incorporated some of the insights that came out of the works on play into his ritual theory. For him, the most creative human spaces were found along the margins or interstitial zones of social structure, frequently sites of frolic, play, and joking. The performative, display-oriented, or representative aspects of an event, most especially the symbolic presentations and re-presentations typically associated with "ritual," mingle with experience-oriented qualities central to "play." Turner was particularly interested in the highly focused and pleasurable mental state associated with play, which psychologist Mihaly Csikszentmihalyi labeled "flow."[68] Ritual shares with sport, theater, and other performative genres a playfulness from which new expressive possibilities of self-representation emerge, although play is constrained by conventions and rules. This returns us to the earlier points made by Huizinga and other theorists: play is that wholly voluntary, creative force in life that is not conscripted by social conventions. Play coalesces the emotional, cognitive, and moral dimensions of existence into sharp, distilled instances. Through such activities, human capacities are diversified and thickened, and societies are made stronger, and in that sense play deepens social life.

Play is, then, what Turner called (originally in reference to initiation rituals) a "liminal" activity, one that is both part of and removed from normative everyday life, in a "betwixt and between" state.[69] "The dominant genres of performance in societies at all levels of scale and complexity tend to be liminal phenomena. They are performed in privileged spaces and times, set off from the periods and areas reserved for work, food, and sleep."[70] The commonalities between play and ritual were clearly a significant concern for both Huizinga and Turner, although the two approached the same activities from different angles.

CLIFFORD GEERTZ'S "BALINESE COCKFIGHT"

Probably the most read article written by an anthropologist about a sport (if one considers its subject a sport) is Clifford Geertz's "Deep Play: Notes on the Balinese Cockfight."[71] While it was the product of the general intellectual milieu that included Bateson, Norbeck, Gluckman, and Turner, the article cited none of the key thinkers of the time other than Erving Goffman, the founding father of the symbolic interactionism school of sociology, which would have an important impact on the social sciences in years to come. Like

Geertz's work in general, it stands apart from the discipline, but its enduring appeal lies in his clever storytelling and compelling writing.

As widely read as the essay is, it is hard to pin down whether it imparted a legacy of a theory or method that other scholars could utilize. The opening of the essay narrates the abrupt breakup of a cockfight in rural Bali, an island of Indonesia, by a police raid and the need for everyone (including the anthropologist and his wife) to flee and hide because the Indonesian government considered cockfighting and gambling illegal. The article advanced the concept of "deep play," "play in which the stakes are so high that it is, from [a] utilitarian standpoint, irrational for men to engage in it at all."[72] The higher the status of the men involved, the deeper the play and the more interesting the cockfight to the spectators. The basic argument was that, in Bali, cockfighting and the betting practices around it were extremely important to Balinese men at the time of Geertz's fieldwork, even though the Indonesian government had outlawed it as a cruel, antimodern practice. The cockfight makes nothing happen, and thus it does not have a "function." It renders everyday experience comprehensible by removing the practical consequences of acts and objects. It makes those acts and objects meaningful; it displays social passions, but does not assuage or heighten them. Status is at stake, but only symbolically—a man might be momentarily affirmed or insulted, but his status will not actually be altered. For Geertz, cockfighting is "a story the Balinese tell themselves about themselves" (by which he really meant Balinese men). These metaphors have found some purchase in sport studies: sports as a mirror for society, an expression of a culture as a whole, a story that we tell ourselves about ourselves, or a text that the anthropologist strains to read and interpret.

Geertz's Balinese cockfight came to be the canonical exemplar of a particular kind of anthropology that held considerable sway in anthropology and other disciplines in the 1970s and 1980s, but it also came to represent all that was problematic with the approach it espoused. Criticism of the essay has implications for anthropological approaches to sport that were largely unexplored at the time. For example, in one of the trenchant critiques that Geertz's article provoked, William Roseberry outlined a number of theoretically consequential problems in Geertz's reading of the Balinese cockfight.[73] One is the fact that, despite the article's opening vignette depicting the police raid, the author ignored the power of the state in defining what counts as possible, legitimate, and important in people's lives. The state and its institutions have considerable effect on how sport is organized on a local level all over the world. Women, who are in charge of the marketplaces where men bring their animals to fight, are largely excluded from cockfights in Bali, and in fact their attempts to carefully monitor family finances are frequently turned upside down by husbands' and other male relatives' betting all the household income and savings to save face; Geertz's inattention to gender presages the general lack of concern about the marginalization of women and the way in which sport naturalizes masculinity in many societies of the world. Balinese men are known to lose their family savings in cockfight betting, yet for Geertz this is only a matter of saving face, and hence of symbolism, an interpretation he obviously did not check with Balinese women. We cannot ignore the implications that cockfights have for material concerns, in the same way that we must ask about the material implications of winning or losing in elite sport. Finally, history is completely absent from Geertz's reading of the Balinese cockfight, yet the practice had long been outlawed by the Dutch colonial administration, among others. This critique reminds us to look at history for an understanding of what we witness at the present moment, including the constitution of sport.

THE POSTMODERN TURN

In the 1980s cultural anthropology began to turn away from the kind of universalizing grand theories that had characterized most of the theory described earlier (with the exception of Geertz, who certainly did not offer a grand theory). A variety of theoretical approaches and topics entered the scene, providing new contexts in which sport could be situated—postcolonialism, postmodernism, feminism, the body, modernity, nationalism, the state, citizenship, transnationalism, globalization, and gender and sexuality. The new focus on globalization brought attention to the fact that the institutions that govern sport crosscut local, national, regional, international, and global structures in ways that highlight important theoretical issues.

In the 1990s, Alan Klein wrote three important ethnographies, which placed him at the forefront of the anthropology of sport for two reasons: he was the first anthropologist to systematically explore sport via the theories that had emerged since the 1980s, and he was the only anthropologist with such prolific output on sport. *Sugarball: The American Game, the Dominican Dream* (1991) examined issues of nationalism and resistance to US cultural imperialism in baseball, applying Antonio Gramsci's theories of hegemony and resistance; *Little Big Men* (1993) analyzed gender in bodybuilding; and *Baseball on the Border* (1997) developed an original theory of nationalism, which incorporated gender, based on fieldwork with a team that represented both Mexico and the United States.[74] Although he framed all these works within the cutting-edge paradigms in the discipline at the time, Klein's work failed to attract the attention from other anthropologists that it probably deserved. After years of being marginalized by his own discipline, he found an intellectual community in the North American Society for Sport Sociology (NASSS), which elected him president for 1998–99. The weak reception of this solid work might have been a measure of the degree of resistance to sport in the mainstream of the discipline. Many sport anthropologists have had no choice but to look toward interdisciplinary networks with sociologists, physical educators, and historians. Intellectually, this is not necessarily a bad thing, but the reality of academic politics meant that anthropologists lacked a power base in their own discipline. Klein continued to be prolific, writing three more books in the new millennium, one of which won 2015 Book of the Year from NASSS.[75]

The remainder of this book will take up the various themes and topics opened up by these developments without trying, as was common up until the 1990s, to fit sport into a one-size-fits-all conceptual frame. We will demonstrate the contribution that the study of sport can make to the theories and debates that have been central in the discipline since the 1990s, and we will also show how these theories and approaches provide new insights into sport.

Chapter 2 analyzes sport through the lens of postcolonial studies and anthropological critiques of colonialism. Chapter 3 examines the relationship between sport, health, and medicine, utilizing a perspective derived from critical science and technology studies. It points out that Western biomedicine shapes international sport in definite ways that are usually not questioned, and that there are other non-Western configurations of exercise and health that have a more holistic vision of the body and its connection with the natural environment. The chapter also discusses the future of the biomedical body as seen in futuristic sports medicine technologies such as genetic enhancement and high-tech prostheses.

Chapter 4 uses sport as a particularly rich field for elucidating the practice theory put forward by Pierre Bourdieu, since it helps makes visible the often-hidden mechanisms by which social class, ethnicity, and race are reproduced at the level of daily practice. Chapter 5 illustrates sport's value for feminist and anthropological critiques of sex, gender, and sexuality, demonstrating the culturally constructed nature of all of these—even in the realm of sport, which is popularly believed to separate men from women on the basis of biology.

Chapter 6 returns to the ritual theory of the 1970s and 1980s discussed briefly above, identifying the aspects of the theory that we now find outdated, while also finding aspects of the theory worth preserving. In particular, ritual theory is still being used by scholars to understand the world's two biggest sport mega-events—the Olympic Games and the FIFA World Cup in soccer. This chapter closes the circle with this chapter's discussion of ancient sport in its examination of mega-events as spectacles embedded in global economic, social, and political networks.[76]

Chapter 7 illustrates the multiple ways in which sports fit theories of nationalism that emerged in the 1980s and afterward, producing concepts such as the "invention of tradition" and "imagined community," and the recognition that gender and nationalism are thoroughly intertwined. Chapter 8 analyzes international and Olympic sports as a global system, showing that sports deserve to be considered in the growing number of approaches critical of various aspects of globalization, including North–South labor migration, the development aid sector, and the worldwide multiplication of nongovernmental organizations. The international sports system is also an excellent site for comprehending the growth of transnationalism since the end of the Cold War.

Sport is both a performance genre that exhibits qualities of play, liminality, and storytelling, and a unique nexus of the body, multiplex identities, and multilayered governance structures from local to global scales. Recognizing its complexity means acknowledging that no one theory can completely explain its nature and the enormous appeal it has for a broad variety of people around the globe. Placing sport at the center of anthropological theories reveals that while each theoretical approach may explain only a limited aspect of our world, taken as a whole they are starting to come together into a more complete explanatory framework than we had at our disposal in previous decades.

TWO

Sport, Colonialism, and Imperialism

IN THE 1980S ANTHROPOLOGISTS TURNED a critical eye toward the categories that had been so important in the effort to scientifically classify groups of human beings in the early years of the discipline—most prominently as "civilized" and "savage," "traditional" and "modern," "primitive" and "advanced." These contrasts are particularly salient in the context of imperialism and colonialism, two concepts that are closely related. Imperialism is an ideology that underpins the expansionary domination by one society over another by military conquest, economic dependency, or whatever practices may be employed. It is possible to have imperialism without having an official empire, as in the case of the United States since the late nineteenth century.[1] Imperialist ideology underpinned colonialism, one version of imperialist expansion in which a colonial power claims jurisdiction over a territory for the purpose of exploiting its people and resources for its benefit, which is commonly justified by the belief that the colonized are inferior and in need of civilizing by the colonizer. The British Empire was from the late eighteenth century the prime example of imperialism that went along with an official empire constituted by territories administered as colonies. Sport has played a central role in imperialism and colonialism, and vice versa. However, while the origin of European colonialism can arguably be placed at 1492, the year that Columbus crossed the Atlantic and launched the European colonization of the New World, sports did not become entangled with colonialism until the nineteenth century, in conjunction with Europe's Industrial Revolution, which was in turn made possible by colonialism.

Postcolonial studies is a field of scholarship focused on the enduring negative legacy of colonialism, even in a contemporary world that has supposedly undergone decolonization. In particular, postcolonial studies seeks to demonstrate that the knowledge that the West had developed about the peoples of the world did not have the objectivity that it was presumed to have; rather, it had been produced by institutions with a vested interest in justifying and promoting imperialism and colonialism. The foundational texts of postcolonial studies, authored by such thinkers as Frantz Fanon, Edward Said, Gayatri Spivak, and Homi Bhabha, are inspired by Marxism, feminism, psychoanalysis, postmodernism, and Michel Foucault's theories of power.[2]

Postcolonial scholars were particularly critical of anthropology as a discipline that had been implicated in the reproduction of colonial hierarchies. As anthropologist Nicholas Dirks noted, although colonial conquest was predicated on the power of superior arms, military organization, political power, and economic wealth, it was also "a cultural project of control. Colonial knowledge enabled colonial conquest and was produced by it; in certain important ways, culture was what colonialism was all about."[3] Anthropologists themselves gradually came to a self-critical realization of the role they had played in imperialism and colonialism. A landmark critique was Talal Asad's edited volume *Anthropology and the Colonial Encounter* (1973), but it was not until the 1980s that anthropologists began to fully engage with the postcolonial critique.[4] They came to realize that, while very few anthropologists actually contributed to the colonial enterprise, many had benefited from it, if only because colonial administrations authorized and facilitated their fieldwork.

One of the most influential postcolonial voices was the Trinidadian Marxist scholar C. L. R. James, whose autobiographical *Beyond a Boundary* (1963) focused on cricket in the Caribbean and is to this day widely admired both as sport history and as a critique of colonialism.[5] For James, West Indian cricketers challenged racialized colonial hierarchies by outperforming the British in the "imperial game." While they technically did not violate the rules of the game, West Indian cricketers used the sport as a way to challenge the received assumptions of the colonial elites. The fact that this book is a centerpiece of postcolonial studies is somewhat ironic because sport was otherwise a marginal topic in postcolonial studies, while historians who turned their attention to colonial sports in the 1980s did not frame their works in terms of postcolonialism.[6]

The postcolonial critique not only concerned the social and cultural structure of colonies but also shed a fresh critical light on historical developments that until then had been seen as evidence of the genius of the colonial metropoles. In particular, postcolonial critics demonstrated that the Industrial Revolution of Britain and northern Europe was predicated on the plundering by colonial powers of the resources of the colonized world, not least of which included human slaves, without which it could not have taken place. Even the very idea of national identity resulted from the responses of colonial elites who challenged the power of the imperial metropole, so the "nation" was, in effect, an idea derived from European ideals rather than from any formerly colonized group's self-identification.[7] Sport expressed political positions of all kinds in the formation of modern nation-states and national identities. In the distant, self-governing settler colonies of the antipodes, such as Australia and South Africa, cricket and rugby became "national" games through which people could identify and express their own emergent identities as, paradoxically, both British and something other than that of the "mother country." The development of sport illustrates that discourses of nationalism had to be formulated in accord with the logic of European ideas, reflecting the historical and continuing power relations among western Europe, North America, and the rest of the world.

THE HISTORICAL ROOTS OF THE INTERNATIONAL SPORTS SYSTEM

The physical activities that were the predecessors of modern sport had been organized by courts, municipal governments, academies, and universities. Because they were limited to local, face-to-face communities, there was no need for codified rules. This is often surprising today, when strict rules are widely considered to be a fundamental feature of the thing that we call sport. Even the ancient Greek Panhellenic Games, which moved around four different stadiums across the Hellenic world, had neither written rules nor standardized distances (nor, as previously discussed, did they keep any sports records other than numbers of wins by a single competitor).

Two concurrent, interrelated strands facilitated the emergence of an international sports system. The first was the writing of rules to facilitate competitions on a larger scale. In England, boxing was codified in 1743, cricket in 1744. Internationally, shooting and yachting were codified and regulated between 1800 and 1840. The International Football Association Board (IFAB) was formed in 1886 to standardize rules of play and coordinate relations between the national soccer associations in England, Scotland, Ireland, and Wales. Between 1840 and 1880, baseball, soccer, rugby, swimming, track and field, skiing, cycling, canoeing, soccer, tennis, badminton, and field hockey were codified and regulated. By 1900, twenty-two of the approximately thirty sports that had been or would become summer Olympic sports had written rules.[8]

The second strand was the rapid increase in the second half of the nineteenth century of voluntary associations as the form of organization utilized by the emerging industrial and colonial elites and middle class wherever they established themselves around the globe. Sports clubs began to replace the early-modern organizers of sports. The new sports organizations were part of the much larger phenomenon that escalated as modern means of transportation and communication connected people across increasingly longer distances, and sport was carried along with them. At first they were local, single-sport clubs. In England, the Jockey Club was formed in 1752, the Marylebone Cricket Club in 1787. In Germany, the Hamburg Turner Society was formed in 1816.

The interesting point about voluntary sport associations is that almost as soon as they appeared on the landscape, they began to be organized into a bigger, multilayer system that imitated the levels of the political structures that were emerging at the same time: local, national, (sometimes) regional, and international levels. The National Association of Base Ball Players was formed in 1857 in the United States, perhaps the world's first national-level association for a single sport. The German Turner Society was founded in 1860. England's Football Association was founded in 1863, the Rugby Football Union in 1871.

National associations for single sports were followed by associations for multiple sports. The British National Olympian Association was founded in 1865 to promote "Olympian" contests throughout Britain; today's British Olympic Association (established in 1905) is a continuation of it. The American Amateur Athletic Union was founded in 1888, the French Union des sociétés françaises de sports athlétiques in 1890.

The International Olympic Committee (IOC) was one of the several hundred international organizations founded between 1860 and 1910, an era that also saw the establishment of the Boy Scouts, Esperanto, the Red Cross, the Universal Postal Union, and the First and Second (workers') Internationals. Like the IOC, these organizations espoused universalistic ideals and described themselves as "movements."[9] The IOC was perhaps the first international organization to claim jurisdiction over multiple sports, and in any case it was one of the earliest international sports organizations. Logically, one might expect that after a critical mass of national organizations had been formed, they began to look across national borders for competitors and thus established an international organization to facilitate this task. But this was not the case. Rather, national and international organizations multiplied simultaneously. The formation of an international organization stimulated the formation of lower-level organizations by people wishing to join it. The history of national Olympic committees illustrates this point. The first three Olympic Games faced the daunting challenge of identifying a person and an address to which an invitation could be sent. Individuals represented sports clubs (or just showed up and competed), not countries. In response, the IOC began to request that countries form national Olympic committees to organize their participation, and the Athens 1906 Intercalary Games were the first at which national team members were selected by the national Olympic committees, and clubs and individuals could not submit entries. This immediately gave rise to the first nationalistic Olympic protest on the part of an Irish athlete, as related below. A second challenge for the Olympic Games was establishing common rules of play before the competitors arrived. International sports federations were formed to address that challenge.

The Fédération internationale de football association (FIFA) was founded in 1904 to coordinate competitions on the European continent. The (English) Football Association was not a founding member, but it joined FIFA shortly thereafter under an unusual arrangement that survives to this day: the FIFA statutes recognized the IFAB as the sport's rule-making body. With British soccer being such a powerhouse in itself, it frequently felt that it did not need FIFA: Britain withdrew from international competition and FIFA after World War I and did not become a full participant in FIFA until after World War II. In 1912 the International Association of Athletics Federations was established to govern the only other sport that rivals soccer in its worldwide reach—track and field, known in Europe as "athletics."[10] By 1914, fourteen international sports federations (known as IF's) had been established. They also began organizing their own world championships.[11]

The amazing speed with which the international sports system took shape provides a good picture of the rapid social changes engulfing the planet at the beginning of the twentieth century. The founding of the core organizations began with the IOC in 1894 and ended in 1914, just before the outbreak of World War I. While the organizations themselves have changed with the times—sometimes too slowly, as the corruption scandals in the IOC in 2000 and FIFA in 2015 demonstrate—the structure itself has hardly changed in the last century. Most sports fans may be shocked to know that many if not most of the associations that administer profitable sporting empires, including the IOC, FIFA, National Hockey League, Professional Golfers' Association of America, and Ladies Professional Golf Association, are incorporated as nonprofit organizations. In professional sports, member clubs and teams may be for-profit while the league office is not. Their tax-exempt status has become increasingly absurd in the twenty-first century and in the United States has come under examination by Congress, which is eyeing the massive revenues they would provide if their tax-exempt status were revoked.[12] In the United States, Major League Baseball gave up its tax-exempt status in 2007 and the National Football League in 2015. In the German soccer Bundesliga, clubs were legally required to be nonprofit until 2000. The British system has been unusual, since associations do not have legal status; as a result, clubs and leagues, such as the English Premier League (established in 1992), tend to be organized as limited-liability companies.

Moreover, an entire body of international sports law has arisen to reinforce the authority of these organizations worldwide. The IOC sits at its pinnacle, with the Court of Arbitration for Sport (CAS, established by the IOC in 1983) having ultimate authority in most instances, although appeals can be lodged in extreme cases with the Federal Supreme Court of Switzerland.[13] The laws can be enforced only because countries and organizations acquiesce to them for fear of being excluded from international sports competitions. International sports law is different from all other forms of international law in that it is "stateless." Most international legal regimes are based on treaties between sovereign states, but the sports system relies on agreements between nongovernmental international bodies (international sports federations, national Olympic committees, etc.). CAS is an arbitral tribunal, not a court, so its decisions are binding only on governments that agree to be bound by them.[14]

It is these unusual organizations and laws that make possible today's global sports system. The entire system is a product of Western history of the last two hundred years. The organizational forms depend upon the existence of a well-developed civil society autonomous from the state—a Western political structure that cannot be imposed wholesale on other societies, and it has proved difficult for non-Western and developing countries to fully implement the organizational system of nongovernmental, voluntary associations that is required by the IOC and FIFA. This has been particularly true in the former Eastern Bloc and today's China, North Korea, and Cuba, where there is limited freedom of assembly and little or no civil society in the conventional understanding of the term. The Chinese Olympic Committee, for example, is a false front for the benefit of the IOC; its members are almost all government employees of the State General Administration for Sport, but they have nominal appointments in the Olympic Committee and business cards that they give out to international sportspeople.

SPORT AND COLONIALISM

The international sports system provided a relatively stable structure that aided the dissemination of sports worldwide. Sport was deeply implicated in colonialism since its invention as a modern practice. When public school teachers and students of mid-nineteenth century Britain codified and regulated the physical activities that they would eventually call "modern sports," they probably did not anticipate that what they were inventing would become, in the course of its century-and-a-half-long history, the focus of some of the most intense human passions. To be sure, they were convinced that their invention—rationalized, institutionalized, and quintessentially modern—was yet further proof of their unflinching superiority, as men, as Christians, as white people, and as masters of the then largest empire on the planet. They codified sporting rules with the deep conviction that physical activity was in the service of God, country, and empire. Muscular Christianity, one of the most significant ideological forces in both the development of modern sport in Britain and its early globalization, was explicitly based on the convergence of masculinity, physical activity, asceticism, racial purity, and the white man's burden.[15] These "rational recreationist" and muscular Christian movements ostensibly set out to "save" and "civilize" the working classes and the impoverished at home as well as the colonial Others elsewhere in the world. The colonial project was also gendered: colonial agents used sport either to virilize colonial subjects whom they considered "degenerate" or, alternatively, to bring the "excessive" masculinity of others under colonial control.[16]

Sport served imperial, colonial, and "civilizing" purposes. Playing sports provided visible evidence of the superiority of the colonizers through their bodily comportment and their "civilized" values and norms of play. The reactions by the conquered, colonized, and otherwise "uncivilized" (i.e., non-Western) peoples were complicated, and sports in colonial contexts ended up sometimes serving to assimilate the natives, sometimes to dominate them outright, and sometimes to offer them a perfectly suited tool to resist and contest colonial power. Tactics of resistance at least challenged theories put forward by "evolutionarily more advanced" authorities. When colonial empires began to collapse after World War II, sport evolved from a tool of anti-imperialist resistance to nation-building exercises in postcolonial contexts in which it served to foster nationalist fervor.

The colonizers, anxious to re-create little corners of Britain, France, and North America throughout their empires, founded sports clubs in emulation of those that, by the turn of the twentieth century, had effloresced throughout Europe and North America. These clubs were voluntary associations run (in principle) by elected officers, a new kind of social organization that had sprung up in the wake of the collapse of the old aristocratic order. Sports clubs were governed by leading citizens, but the sports often provided a forum for the more serious function of the clubs, which was to reinforce elite social networks. While it was generally men who organized, played, and refereed the sports, other social events involving both genders were sometimes as important as the sports, including dances, receptions, and awards banquets, where women played a prominent role. In the metropole, one chief concern in the selection of club members was to admit only members of the appropriate social class; in the colonies, the concern was to ensure that the colonizer and the colonized would not mix in contexts other than those in which power hierarchies were abundantly clear. Thus the presence of the colonized in colonial sports clubs was limited to the attending staff and, in more progressive contexts, to local elites who had been properly inculcated with the ideals of the colonial power. At the same time, the class barriers that dictated who could join sports clubs in the mother country did not disappear in the colonial context, as the underbelly of colonial communities (e.g., colonials of working-class background, low-ranking soldiers, whites who had "gone native," *petits blancs*) were just as excluded from colonial elite clubs as working-class individuals were in metropolitan clubs. As was true of colonialism in general, the relations between colonists of different social rank were almost as tense and oppressive as the relations between the colonizer and the colonized, and the colonial project was hardly a unified one.[17]

The sports that predominate worldwide, measured by the number of participants and spectators, are all sports that imperial powers used in the nineteenth and early twentieth centuries to disseminate a particular ideology that projected their power and explicitly contributed to the colonization of non-European peoples: soccer, baseball, basketball, cricket, and rugby are all team sports that represented a specific ethos of how to comport oneself as a "civilized" or "modern" human being. That ethos has its roots firmly embedded in the hierarchical classifications of colonialism. Colonized peoples did not passively accept these sports and the ideologies in which they supposedly were grounded. Instead, like the colonizers, they used sport as a physically expressive critique of the Other.[18] Nevertheless, the global prevalence constitutes an important aspect of "cultural imperialism"—the historical colonization of much of the world by Western culture. The expansion of Euro-American sports into African, Asian, Australasian, and "other" American societies at the cost of indigenous sporting practices is a historical reflection of empire building, colonial expansion, economic dominance, and neocolonialism.[19] The sports that constitute the modern Olympics are the culmination of these broader processes; thus, there are only two sports of clearly non-Western origin on the summer Olympic program, namely judo (originally from Japan) and taekwondo (originally from Korea), and even these were not "traditional" sporting practices but indigenous sports reworked to fit the "modern" sports system in a complex cultural conjuncture.[20] All other Olympic sports are exclusively of European and North American origin.

Missing from the Olympic program are Chinese martial arts (wushu), South Asian *kabaddi,* and various Southeast Asian ball games, indigenous American ball games, and many others—many of whose supporters would very much like to have them added to the Olympic Games. One of us, Susan Brownell, observed the pent-up frustration that this topic generates in the Olympic system when she made a presentation titled "The Multicultural Nature of Modern Olympism" at the 2006 World Forum on Sport, Education and Culture, held in Beijing and organized by the IOC's Commission on Culture and Olympic Education. The topic had cleverly been assigned to her by the Chinese chair of the commission, He Zhenliang, and she did not realize its sensitivity. When the panel was concluded, a line of Asian and African audience members formed who wanted to give her their business cards in the hopes that she could take up the cause of *kabbadi, sepak takraw,* and other sports inside the IOC. Chinese people thanked her for mentioning wushu's exclusion from the Olympic Games. One audience member told her, "I never thought I would hear a speech like that inside the IOC." As nations outside the Western sports powers increasingly found their footing in global sports, they demanded that "their" sports be accorded international recognition. However, the continuing strength of the Western grip over the international sports system was evident in that China, even after emerging as a superpower, was unable to get wushu onto the official Olympic program despite intense pressure on the IOC. While in previous eras backroom politics had mainly dictated which sports were in and which were out, after 2001 a new process emphasized indicators such as numbers of countries with national associations in the sport, participation rates, and television audience sizes. The new system still favored sports of Western origin, leading to the addition of rugby sevens and golf to the 2016 Olympics. Skateboarding, surfing, sports climbing, and a third East Asian sport—karate, a Japanese martial art—were added to the 2020 Olympics, and baseball/softball were reinstated after being eliminated for the 2012 and 2016 games.

COLONIALISM AND THE DIFFUSION OF SPORT

Observing that "modern sports abetted the imperial expansion that carried them to the ends of the earth," historian Allen Guttmann gave the label "ludic diffusion" to the spread of games and sports throughout the world.[21] But he also argued that it would be too simple to view the spread of sports as a simple act of domination, because colonized people were often complicit in the process. The trajectory of two key British sports, cricket and soccer, and two key American sports, baseball and basketball, illustrates the variety of ways in which sports diffused throughout different parts of the world. According to the histories of individual sports outlined by Guttmann, cricket was the first modern British sport (the rules were codified in 1744) to reach other continents, as English colonists introduced it into the southern United States in the early 1700s and British sailors introduced it in Calcutta, India, in 1721. Soccer reached continental Europe when an Irish student introduced it in Melle, Belgium, in 1863, and British sailors introduced it to Buenos Aires, Argentina, in 1867. In the United States, Union soldiers during the Civil War took baseball from New England to the Midwest and South starting in 1860. Cuban students returning from the United States took it to Cuba in 1864, although there are also accounts of American sailors teaching Cuban dockworkers the sport as well. When Cuba's Ten Years' War for independence from Spain ended in 1878, Cuban elites who had supported the independence movement fled to the Dominican Republic, Puerto Rico, Venezuela, Colombia, and the Yucatán, bringing the sport with them to these countries. In 1873 an American teacher introduced baseball in Japan, and in 1882 railroad workers from the United States introduced it in northern Mexico. Invented in 1891, basketball was introduced to China a mere four years later by educators working for the Young Men's Christian Association (YMCA), an independent, nongovernmental organization that was designed to simultaneously promote sport and religion and that was grounded in the ideology of muscular Christianity; it also, as we will soon see, played an important role in spreading both sport and Christianity around the world. Chinese and Japanese students then brought basketball to Germany in 1927. American soldiers had brought the sport with them to France during the First World War.[22]

In the thirty-one examples of the diffusion of sports that Guttmann describes, teachers were the agents of the diffusion in six cases and students in seven. Most were students who had learned the sports abroad and brought them back to their home countries, although in one case students learned basketball in their home countries (China and Japan) and took it to Germany, where they were studying. In such cases, then, the question of "imperial dominance" is problematic. If the students had been forced to master the sports while studying abroad, they would have been unlikely to teach them to their friends in their homeland unless they enjoyed them. The fact is that people found sports "fun" and engaged in them for their own sake. This led Guttmann to discard the notion that the spread of sports was a form of imperialism. Instead, he argued that the process was a form of "hegemony," invoking a concept first developed by fascist-era Italian Marxist philosopher Antonio Gramsci, who defined it as the ideas, values, and common sense that serve to justify the control of dominant classes over society. Hegemony is a politically powerful tool because the dominated groups, for reasons of their own, endorse the dominant ideology even though it might be against their best interests.[23] Guttmann acknowledged that subordinates in many ways collaborated and were "complicit" in their own domination (if domination is indeed what is at stake), undermining simplistic models of absolute dominance and absolute submission.[24]

While Guttmann's point is well taken, it does not change the fact that the diffusion of sports took place in a general context of imperialism. Why did students study abroad, and why did they learn these particular sports and not others? Why, indeed, did they learn "sports" at all? To what degree did they really have a choice in the physical activities they learned and took back home? For example, the launching point for soccer's remarkable spread throughout the European continent was its inclusion in the curriculum of cosmopolitan private schools and polytechnics in Switzerland because British sports in general, and soccer in particular, helped to attract the sons of the

British capitalists who dominated the international economy. Thus the diffusion of soccer followed the trail of imperialist capital.[25]

Sport's capacity to attract people who by all rights should reject it as an imperialist imposition led John MacAloon to call sport an "empty form." By this he meant that sport can be decontextualized and emptied of its original (usually Western) meaning, enabling it to be "filled" again with local meanings. Sports constitute "intercultural spaces" for cultural interaction, and cultural differences are created during the process of integration.[26] However, whether this optimism about sport's shape-shifting capacity is shared outside the developed West is an open question; a dissenting view is held by the Chinese sport scholar Lu Yuanzhen, who argued that Western sport culture has, "like a lawnmower, mowed down the cultural diversity of world sport into neat and tidy rows."[27] In the encounter with "modern" sports, "folk" sports met various fates: they died out, as did Tutsi high-jumping, which we will describe at greater length in chapter 4; they were rationalized as modern sports but not quite accepted into the approved canon, as were Chinese martial arts; or they became the ground of resistance to colonial hegemony, as did wrestling in India and the Gaelic Games in Ireland.[28]

The colonial diffusion of sport was a key factor in whether particular sports became global while others were played in more limited geographic areas, and still others remained exclusively local. Thus sports that originated in nineteenth-century Britain or that were quickly adopted by other colonial powers (particularly France), such as soccer, are today played throughout the former British and French colonial empires and beyond. Rugby is also played in many parts of the world, although it is most visible as a feature of the "settler societies" of the former British Empire (South Africa, Australia, New Zealand, and, to a lesser extent, Canada) and societies of the Pacific Islands that experienced relatively mild forms of colonialism (Fiji, Tonga, and Samoa). Cricket is most prominent in South Asia and in the English-speaking Caribbean.

In contrast, the sports practiced in countries with a more limited and qualitatively different history of imperialist expansion, such as the United States, have more modest distribution: the spread of baseball, for example, mirrors the United States' historical sphere of influence in Central America, the Spanish-speaking Caribbean, Japan, Korea, the Philippines, and Taiwan.[29] And sports that originated in societies with no colonial history or a truncated history of colonialism were less likely to undergo global diffusion: one thinks of curling, originally practiced in Scotland, which has the added disadvantage of requiring ice, and hurling, a version of field hockey played in Ireland.[30] The German system of turner gymnastics never expanded much farther than the German-speaking countries of Europe and the German diaspora abroad, although this constituted a large population and global network until Germany's defeat in two world wars reduced its cultural influence worldwide.

While the introduction of sport to the colonies was a major force in the spread of sport throughout the world, paths of diffusion did not always respect the boundaries of particular colonial empires. Colonialism, of course, took the form of not only territorial annexation but also economic domination in parts of the world that were self-governing, and even where Britain did not plant its flag, its citizens did the work. For example, British migrants introduced soccer to Brazil, where it became a central focus of people's lives, even though there were no colonial ties between Britain and Brazil.[31] In the early decades of the twentieth century, British industrialists in Argentina controlled the commercial, industrial, and agricultural sectors of the country's economy and introduced British sports (soccer, rugby union, and polo), even though the country had been an independent nation since 1816 and was never part of the British Empire. While soccer eventually became the sport of the masses in that country, today rugby and polo retain the elite status that was associated with the expatriate clubs in the early twentieth century, and the exclusive clubs play a pivotal role in the social, cultural, and economic reproduction of the elite classes.[32]

A darker reality underpinned the colonizer's romantic project of civilizing the colonized through sport. Contests between people of color and white Europeans or North Americans were seen as demonstrations of racial and civilizational superiority, a topic that would remain highly charged until embarrassingly recent times. In several instances, anthropologists became complicit in these unfortunate projects. One of them was Anthropology Days at the 1904 St. Louis world's fair, described in the previous chapter. When nonwhites proved to have superior sporting abilities, they were found to be profoundly problematic, as was Jesse Owens, who, in the aftermath of his extraordinary performance in athletics at the Berlin 1936 Summer Olympics, was shunned by not only Adolph Hitler, which was predictable, but also US president Franklin D. Roosevelt.[33]

The grip of colonial empires over the colonial subjects and their sports was tighter in Africa than elsewhere. A telling episode was the attempt by the first IOC member based in Africa, Angelo Bolonaki (or Bolonachi, as he was known in the IOC), to organize an African Games in 1925, following the success of the YMCA-organized Far Eastern Games (see discussion below) as well as the first Latin American Games in 1922. Actually, Bolonaki was not an indigenous African but a member of the large Greek migrant community settled in Alexandria. He was the IOC member in Egypt from 1910 until he switched his membership to Greece in 1932, amid the strengthening regional identity emerging in the Middle East and North Africa. Bolonaki's African Games plan alarmed the colonial authorities on the continent, who feared the nationalism that such an event might inspire and worried that the mixing of the races might subvert their authority. Bolonaki gained enough support from French and Italian officials to plan for an event to be held in Algiers in 1925, but the French eventually backed down and pressured the Italians to do the same. The date was pushed back and the site changed to Bolonaki's own Alexandria, but a few weeks before the opening, the British blocked the plans and persuaded the French to support them. Having observed the nationalist pride expressed at the Far Eastern Games, European IOC members concluded that the "spreading of the doctrine of International Sport" in Africa was "ill-advised."[34] Coubertin argued that victories of the "people in bondage" over the "dominant race" would not lead to rebellion, but colonial administrators were not convinced.[35]

An account of boxing in Salisbury, Southern Rhodesia (known as Zimbabwe after independence), in the late 1930s is particularly interesting because it was the object of a study by an anthropologist commissioned by the colonial authorities. Boxing had become popular around 1915, but apparently this had happened without any European encouragement. Rather, the British-trained local police who practiced boxing were held in high prestige, and locals began to imitate them. However, they reinterpreted the British form to suit their own cultural context. Bouts were short, few blows were exchanged, no one was ever knocked out, no points were awarded, there was no decisive result, and the boxers performed strutting dance moves when an opponent took a rest. The matches mystified Europeans who observed them. Boxing clubs were organized by ethnic groups, so matches often provoked interethnic fights among the spectators, who numbered up to two thousand. The authorities feared that boxing was serving as a vehicle for self-determination and "urban tribalism." They debated whether to ban boxing outright or try to control it. The anthropologist's report was commissioned to aid in the decision. After considerable debate, the authorities finally decided to regulate and control boxing.[36]

Particularly in sub-Saharan Africa, the authorities strongly suppressed the formation of sports clubs by and for the locals, and, because of their concern with maintaining proper social distance between whites and blacks, they largely excluded people of color from their sports clubs until the 1930s. It was not until 1922 that the first sport association for black players in Africa, the Football Association of Kenya, was founded. In the following decade, sports clubs for black Africans finally began appearing.[37] Yet South Africa and Egypt were the only African countries that competed regularly in Olympic Games until after World War II. Outstanding African athletes from other countries represented the colonial metropole.

BRITISH COLONIALISM AND SPORT

Throughout the British Empire, a primary purpose of upper-class education was to train men of character through games, an ideology that has been called the "British games ethic." The headmasters of the elite public schools

> held that games were at the heart of the educational process. And these men were merely the more active, the more public, and more visible representatives of a widespread cult. And, as equally convinced imperialists, they had a view of national education that was not only national but also imperial. They saw it as their duty to give a lead to the imperial world.
>
> And they gave it. The outcome was a unique phenomenon: in the most bizarre locations could be found those potent symbols of pedagogic imperialism—football and cricket pitches.[38]

The British internationalized sport by exporting their cultural traditions and many of their games—older games such as cricket and newer games such as rugby—around the world to their colonies. The institutions of sport, which often fell under the control of educational and state-level bureaucracies, embodied core Victorian beliefs regarding civilized and modern behavior. As a tool for the training of future colonial administrators within the education system, first in England and then in other locations of the empire, sporting knowledge assimilated indigenous elites into the nuances of modernity, thereby paving the way for indirect rule in far-flung colonies. As a component of various modernizing projects, social reformers, nationalist ideologues, and others claimed that sport contributed to the overall health and fitness of the populace and, by extension, national well-being in Britain.

Among those aspects of life that became synonymous with the empire was the elitist "amateur" ideal, which was used to exclude manual laborers from the sports events organized by the elites, based on the reasoning that physical labor gave them an unfair advantage. Under pressure from the British, the IOC also adopted the amateur ideal, with the result that Olympic athletes were forbidden to receive pay for their sports until the late 1980s.

Key institutions for the colonial project were the colonial and mission schools where the children of the colonized enrolled. In the Massim area of the British New Guinea Protectorate at the end of the nineteenth century, educationalists and missionaries made pupils practice sport (cricket and soccer for the boys; badminton, croquet, and tennis for the girls), as well as physical drills, practical skills, and hygiene, in an attempt to dissipate the sexual energy that teachers and others attributed to them and found profoundly problematic.[39]

Even though it is no longer the most popular sport in the United Kingdom, cricket is the one sport that came to represent "Britishness," the British Empire, and all that typifies nineteenth-century colonialism. Clubs dedicated to the quintessential "imperial game" provided the social meeting grounds that reinforced imperial ideology and knit the empire together. The exclusivity of sports clubs was a powerful symbol of colonial domination. Originally played overseas by military officers, governors, and other colonial elites, cricket was believed to express a distinctively British morality and to impart the moral obligations involved in extending the benefits that were believed to accompany British rule. After touring India with the Oxford University Authentic team in 1903, Cecil Headlam wrote that British colonization had proceeded in three stages:

> First the hunter, the missionary and the merchant, next the soldier and the politician, and then the cricketer . . . of these civilizing influences, the last may, perhaps, be said to do the least harm. . . . Cricket unites, as in India, the rulers and the ruled. It also provides a moral training, an education in pluck and nerve, and self-restraint, far more valuable to the character of the ordinary native than the mere learning by heart of a play by Shakespeare.[40]

Similarly, Lord Harris, a former colonial administrator, suggested that cricket "has done more to consolidate the empire than any other influence."[41] Cricket and imperialism became mutually supporting ideological practices.[42] Cricket in the Victorian and Edwardian periods shaped how the white English perceived themselves and how they imagined that the world perceived them. Playing cricket, so it was said, encouraged moral qualities such as self-lessness, putting the interests of the team before one's enjoyment, accepting the decisions of umpires and captains without complaint, observing the spirit rather than the letter of its laws—all qualities that resonated with Christian ethics, what came to be called "fair play." Playing cricket was also believed to encourage nonwhites to accept the white English qualities of sportsmanship, which in turn would convince them of the beneficence of British rule. The symbolic discourse and embodiment on the pitch readily transferred to colonial life.

The social norms and meanings embedded in cricket changed over time and space as the sport moved from the colonial metropoles out to British colonies in the Caribbean, Africa, and Asia, and then back again as formerly colonized peoples migrated to the metropoles. As is true of sport in general, cricket had the potential to reinforce and disseminate countervailing and even contradictory messages. In colonial society, both the colonizer and the colonized used it as physically expressive critiques of each other, so that it was "really about the colonial quest of identity in the face of the colonizers' search for authority."[43] The colonizers and then the Indian elites used cricket to legitimize their position in the existing social hierarchy. Colonized peoples throughout the Caribbean demonstrated their own claims to national sovereignty and symbolically reversed power relationships, at least on the cricket pitch.[44]

The extent to which any sport served as an imperial tool for the colonizers is much more complex than most accounts of sports history admit to. Nowhere is this more apparent than in what is widely considered to be a classic in ethnographic filmmaking, as well as one of the best-documented examples of the appropriation of a world sport. *Trobriand Cricket: An Ingenious Response to Colonialism* (1973) is a documentary about the transformations that cricket underwent after Methodist missionaries introduced it at the turn of the twentieth century to Trobriand Islanders (in what was then New Guinea), who incorporated the sport into specifically local social and cultural practices.[45] The crowd-pleasing film has delighted generations of anthropology undergraduates, who have applauded Trobrianders' ability to turn an imperial game on its head, complete with body paints, sorcery, and erotically suggestive dancing, an aesthetic exoticism that the film depicts lavishly. One does like to see the underdog use the tools of discipline against the oppressors. However, critical analyses of the film have faulted it for romanticizing resistance and glossing over the fact that the film itself was deeply implicated in local politics, as it was used by one of the big men for his own political ambitions.[46]

While cricket served the interests of the British Empire, it also served as a site of resistance against British colonialism. In the British West Indies, for example, the population was primarily descended from Africans and South Asians who were transported to the various islands as slaves or indentured laborers after the indigenous Amerindians were wiped out within the first one hundred years of European occupation. There, cricket evolved from a pastime that colonial officials "played" while the rest of colonial populace spectated, to a "game" in which the masses participated at various levels, and ultimately to a "sport" that was a source of national pride and a business tool.[47] Over time, slaves, indentured laborers, and their descendants were incorporated into the sport, but only in highly restrictive roles. At first they were allowed to prepare pitches, and a few were permitted to bowl and retrieve batted balls during practice sessions. "Blacks were regarded as machines in the cane fields and no less so as providers of batting practice for White batsmen/colonizers."[48]

Nonwhite West Indians expressed resistance on the cricketing pitch and in the stands with behavior that "simply was not cricket," by aggressively bowling at a batsman's body or head, or by mocking athletes' actions and umpires' decisions.[49] Crowd hostility was more often heaped upon umpires than upon a poorly performing West Indian side, because the decisions against the local athletes were being enforced by an authority figure backed by the hated groups that were agents of colonial and, later, neocolonial power.[50]

Cricket was not a priority when the United Kingdom established its Indian empire in the eighteenth century or while it was consolidating its power in the nineteenth century. The education of the Indian elite did not explicitly include cricket.[51] When the British left India in 1947, cricket was still not yet the national sport, as field hockey and soccer were more popular in certain parts of the country, particularly among rural farmers and the working class, while cricket remained firmly a middle-class urban sport, especially in Mumbai.[52] It was only after independence that national pride coalesced around beating their former colonial masters. "To most Indians, the game now looks more Indian than English. They find it only natural that cricket arouses more passions in India than in England."[53]

With decolonization, cricket took on new meanings in India, Pakistan, and the West Indies. The notion that cricket is intrinsically British has evaporated, and the former colonies of the British Empire now regularly defeat their former colonial masters in the game that was previously used to

FIGURE 5. A beach cricket game on a lazy Sunday afternoon (Trinidad, May 2015/Adnan Hossain).

legitimate British rule.[54] However, in Trinidad and Tobago, as we will discuss in chapter 4, now that colonialism is a faint memory, cricket has been transformed into something different—a battleground for interethnic politics rather than a symbol of the colonial past.

US IMPERIALISM AND SPORT

Since the United States conceived of itself as a postcolony, it never labeled the territorial possessions that it acquired through war as "colonies" and governed largely by indirect rule. This devolved approach applied to sport: US sporting influence was not spread through colonial clubs and schools but through other channels. The YMCA was the major channel through which British and American sports were introduced into East Asia.

While it was founded in 1844 in London, it was the North American branch of the YMCA that became most active in East Asia by the end of the century in the general context of intense efforts by French, British, and American churches intent on converting millions of heathen souls. The

YMCA's first permanent office was opened in Japan in 1889, in China in 1895, and in Korea in 1899.

In Japan, the port city of Yokohama was created after the US commodore Matthew Perry arrived with a fleet of American warships in 1853 to demand that the Tokugawa shogunate open several ports for commerce. Foreign residents in Yokohama introduced European-style horse racing in 1862, rugby union in 1866, and cricket in 1868. It was also the takeoff point for the Japanese passion for baseball. In 1896 a team of Tokyo schoolboys resoundingly defeated the Yokohama Athletic Club, a team of foreigners that had rebuffed their request for a contest for five years before finally accepting it. The schoolboys' victory sent baseball on its way to becoming Japan's national sport. Yokohama continues to have a particularly "international" flavor to this day.[55] In China, Tianjin and Shanghai played a similar role. They were entry points for Western influence because they were important seaports with foreign-controlled territories ("concessions") that Western powers had wrested from the Qing dynasty when British troops had attacked the country in the Second Opium War in 1860.

The United States took control of the Philippines from the Spanish at the end of the Spanish-American War in 1898, and by 1902 it had quelled the Philippine struggle for independence. The colony became a launching point for regional efforts by the YMCA. Its strong presence explains the early incorporation of East Asia into the Olympic system. Because of the influence of the YMCA and the United States, the early emphasis was on Olympic sports and baseball, rather than soccer or cricket. The Far Eastern Championship Games in 1913 were the world's first regional games. Ten installments were held in Japan, China, and the Philippines up until 1934, when Japan's occupation of northeast China ended cooperation.

Elwood Brown, the physical director of the YMCA in Manila, envisioned that regional games would be a feeder system for the Olympic Games, a concept that secured the IOC's support. This idea galvanized the patriotism of East Asians who wanted to see their countries take their place among the dominant nations of the world, symbolized by hosting Olympics and winning medals. Over the next half century, many of East Asia's influential sports organizers were educated in missionary schools or sent to Springfield College in Massachusetts, where the YMCA trained its future administrators. These included Hyozo Omori, who introduced basketball and volleyball to Japan in 1908, and Dong Shouyi (Shou-yi Tung), who became an IOC member in the Republic of China in 1947.[56]

Kanō Jigorō became the IOC member in Japan in 1909, making him the first Asian and first non-European member. He was the creator of judo, which in 1964 became the first sport based outside the West to enter the Olympic Games. Kanō apparently anticipated that a sport perceived as too non-Western would not be accepted in the West, since, when speaking about judo before international audiences, he was careful to use scientific language and avoided references to Confucianism or Buddhism, to which he nevertheless referred when speaking Japanese.[57]

The West's intensive effort to create Christians through sport in East Asia resulted in sport becoming the context for the expression of regional rivalries, and the idea took root that hosting the Olympic Games and winning Olympic medals symbolized that a country stood as an equal among the dominant nations of the world. A YMCA annual report documented the first calls by patriots for Korea and China to host the Olympics in 1907.[58] When China finally achieved this goal in 2008, it was called the realization of China's "one hundred-year dream."

In short, Japan's passion for baseball and East Asia's passion for the Olympic Games are legacies of Western imperialism of the turn of the previous century. The introduction and trajectory of Western sports in East Asia differ from that of sports in the British Empire because China, Japan, and Korea were never fully colonized by Western powers. Sports were not part of the civilizing project of a colonial regime but a by-product of Christian missionizing. The official Chinese terminology describes China as a "semicolony" at this time, since part of its territory, in treaty ports and concessions, was under the control of the foreign powers, and the government did not possess full sovereignty. Many other areas of the world, such as the Philippines, occupied similar ambiguous positions, and semicolonies even existed inside Europe, as in the cases of Ireland and Greece, as discussed below. These gray zones were often sites for some of sport history's most interesting stories.

The YMCA was also active in the Caribbean basin, where it introduced various sports, while the US military, often in conjunction with it, consciously promoted baseball to inculcate US values and civilization.[59] Throughout the Caribbean, US occupation leaders encouraged youth to play baseball as a means to control their "heated passions" and presumably distract them from the idea of taking up arms in the hills. Thus James Sullivan, US minister to Santo Domingo, expounded that the American national game of baseball is being played and supported here with great enthusiasm. The remarkable effect of this outlet for the animal spirits of the young men is that they are leaving the plazas where they were in the habit of congregating and talking revolution and are resorting to the ball fields where they become wildly partisan each for his favorite team. The importance of this new interest to the young men in a little country . . . should not be minimized. It satisfies a craving in the nature of the people for exciting conflict and is a real substitute for the contest on the hill-sides with the rifles, if it could be fostered and made important by a league of teams in the various towns in the country. This well might be one factor in the salvation of the nation.[60]

But in fact baseball needed little encouragement from the United States. It had already acquired cultural and nationalist significance long before American military occupations, and Cubans themselves became exporters of the sport to other areas of Central and South America, as mentioned earlier. In Cuba and other Latin American locations where it was played, baseball long served as a means to challenge and beat the Americans, if only on the playing fields. Those symbolic victories on the diamonds fueled nationalist fervor across the Caribbean as well as where the Americans landed in Asia.

MUSCULAR CHRISTIANITY, THE YMCA, AND "MANLY LOVE"

In Europe and North America, sports were implicated in changing structures of gender and sexuality, as sport increasingly became a "male preserve" and was utilized as a means to build character and inculcate manliness through the British public school system and the North American YMCA.[61] In the former, this approach received strong inspiration from the ideology of muscular Christianity, to which a significant number of headmasters, teachers, and physical educators subscribed. As we saw earlier, muscular Christianity emphasized physical activity as a way of glorifying God and was a reaction against both cerebral and introverted forms of Protestantism that were in fashion at the time and that regarded indulgence in pleasure (particularly sexual), effete idleness, and luxury as sinful, believing that they were caused by the lack of masculine role models and the nefarious influence of women on boys and young men.[62] Muscular Christianity and the institutions that were founded on it came to play a pivotal role in cementing the conceptual connection among sport, manhood, and morality.

But they had other, unintended consequences. Placing boys and young men together also encouraged them to cultivate affective bonds with one another, which Victorian ideology not only allowed but also encouraged. Chaste same-sex love between equals could be expressed quite openly, frequently bordered on the romantic, and was viewed as superior to married love, which, in contrast to same-sex love, was not defined as egalitarian.[63] It drew on a very long tradition that valorized spiritual "manly love," including the Platonic classical tradition of ancient Greece and the European medieval tradition of chivalry (which itself had roots in Muslim Sufi mysticism). Men socialized in all-male institutions, fed on sport as evidence of their country's and race's immanent superiority, and were heterosexual but stuck in a protracted adolescence, favoring each other's company, marrying late, or remaining lifelong bachelors.[64] This ideology of masculinity was dominant in Victorian culture and for decades was an institutionalized and integral part of Victorian life.

It was only at the beginning of the 1880s that these relationships began to be suspected of having a sexual component. In Britain a moral panic emerged, fed by a series of scandals, and the Criminal Law Amendment Act of 1885, designed to make all forms of homosexuality illegal, heralded a new form of repression (Oscar Wilde was its most illustrious victim). In the United States the YMCA increasingly catered to the practical and spiritual needs of a growing population of young men migrating to cities for find work. It offered them housing in single-sex dormitories and a Christian environment that was an alternative to the church, which men at the time saw as increasingly falling under the problematic control of women.[65]

In the 1880s the YMCA launched a physical education program, which it conceived as playing an important role for the sex education of its patrons. But in 1890 it realized rather belatedly that the single-sex sports and housing facilities it provided were the perfect setting for the development of bonds between single young men that were not only affective but also sexual. The leadership became concerned with combating homosexuality, but the more it tried to control what took place within its institutions, the more it was confronted with evidence of the very practices it tried to regulate: "Perhaps the greatest tragedy of this story is that so much of the dynamism and power of the early YMCA flowed from the passionate commitments between men which were later denigrated and neglected as the YMCA sought to prove its heterosexuality."[66]

On both sides of the Atlantic, ideals of masculinity predicated on the practice of sport and the bonding between men were epitomized in such institutions as all-boys schools and the YMCA, which encouraged but also attempted to eradicate male homosexuality. The profound homophobia that characterizes the sports world in general, which we will discuss further in chapter 5, is anchored in this history of contradictions.

EUROPEAN DOMESTIC IMPERIALISM AND SPORT

It was not only non-Western peoples that were subjected to imperialist ambitions but also the inhabitants of the European periphery, and sport was implicated there as well in a complicated interplay of power and resistance.

Ireland was part of the British Empire for centuries. The Irish were more complicit in the British occupation and held a more privileged status in the empire than other colonized peoples, so the status of Ireland as a colony is somewhat debatable. Sport played and continues to play a significant role in the relationship between the Irish and the English on the one hand, and between Catholic and Protestant Irish on the other, accentuating the best and the worst of all. Ireland provides a paradigmatic example of sport both unifying and dividing a people along ethnonationalist lines, defined in Ireland as a contrast between "Catholics" and "Protestants," even though most Irish do not practice any religion. Which sports one played served as a marker of one's political loyalties, with "British" sports like cricket played almost exclusively by those whose identifications and identities were British or Protestant and who were seen by others as part of the imperial apparatus deployed to dominate the Irish.[67]

Rather than challenging the British by trying to beat them at their own game, Catholic and Republican Irish took a different tack, cultivating their own sports as distinct markers of national identity. They formed the Gaelic Athletics Association (GAA) with an explicit anti-British stance, actively preventing any association with such institutions as the Royal Irish Constabulary or the British Army, and prohibiting soccer or rugby at any GAA ground.[68]

Gaelic sports such as hurling and Gaelic football are today played almost exclusively in Ireland, although at the turn of the previous century they were popular among Irish migrants in the United States and were even included in the sports program of the 1904 St. Louis world's fair. GAA revived and developed them as part of a campaign to resist what Irish nationalists saw as the spread of British sports. Playing and supporting Gaelic sports became a way of demonstrating Irishness and part of the struggle against British domination in the late nineteenth and early twentieth centuries.[69] This is especially true in Northern Ireland, where education and sport have remained clear markers of sectarian division even after the 1998 Good Friday peace accord.[70] Catholics and Protestants have separate education systems, and the sports taught in those schools reflect the ethnoreligious identity of each "community." Catholics practice these Gaelic games in clubs and schools in explicit contrast to rugby union, cricket, and hockey, which are Protestant and Unionist sports. The only sport the groups play in common is soccer, though "mixed" clubs are the exception rather than the norm, and fans usually choose clubs and cheer on one national side based upon the same sectarian division.

One of the galvanizing events of the Irish struggle in the early twentieth century was the sport-related Croke Park massacre.[71] On November 21, 1920, Tipperary was to play Dublin in Gaelic football at Croke Park, the GAA's major stadium, before a crowd of five thousand spectators. The spectators were startled by a volley of shots fired from inside the turnstile entrances. Seeing armed and uniformed men enter the field and fire on the crowd, the spectators and athletes rushed for the far side of the park. Fourteen people were killed and dozens injured. Once the firing had been stopped, the security forces searched the remaining men in the crowd before letting them go. The military raiding party recovered one revolver, which a local householder testified had been thrown into his garden by a fleeing spectator. Two military courts of inquiry were held, but the British government suppressed their findings until 2000.

Gaelic Games, then, were not merely sports but an active political practice tied to colonial struggle and Irish identity, one that continues well into the twenty-first century. The GAA changed its constitution only in 2005 to allow other sports in Croke Park and other facilities because Landsdowne Road (now Aviva Stadium), the national rugby stadium, was under reconstruction. That amendment was to be in effect only until the refurbishment was complete. A subsequent vote by the GAA Central Council in 2009 relaxed the prohibition but did not change the exclusivity of Croke Park for "Irish sport." In ironic contrast, cricket and rugby union in postcolonial

Ireland are governed by bodies representing the entire island. Thus, cricket and rugby athletes represent Ireland no matter which state they are citizens of.

The Irish conflict extended into the Olympic Games. The first-ever political protest at the modern Olympic Games occurred at the 1906 Intercalary Olympic Games in Athens.[72] It was the first Olympics that had delegated to national Olympic committees the authority to select participants, and the British Olympic Council had monopolized the entries from Britain, requiring all athletes to register under "Great Britain." It was also the first Olympics at which national flags were hoisted for medal winners. Peter O'Connor, the silver medalist in the triple jump, climbed the flagpole waving the Irish flag to protest the Union Jack being raised for his ceremony. The IOC recognized the Olympic Council of Ireland (OCI) in 1924, but conflict over who could represent Ireland in the Olympics continued until the issue was resolved in 1952 by OCI president Lord Killanin: since citizens of Northern Ireland could carry either an Irish or a British passport, the athlete's passport would decide which Olympic committee he or she could represent. The diplomatic skill that Killanin demonstrated in resolving this issue resulted in his being elected IOC president in 1972.

Another "domestic colony" in Europe where sport played an important political role was Greece. From the fifteenth century until the start of the Greek rebellion in 1821, most of the territory occupied by today's Greece, the Hellenic Republic, was under the control of the Ottoman Empire, Europe's main political and cultural rival. The Greek revolution helped solidify stereotypes of East and West: Europeans saw it as a conflict between a youthful, European, and Christian civilization on a dynamic path to progress against an old, Oriental, and heathen civilization mired by decadence, corruption, and cruelty. With the help of Western powers, Greece gained independence in 1832, even though it had never been united under one flag previously, and Otto I, the son of Ludwig I of Bavaria, was installed as king in 1833. Concerned with maintaining the balance of power between them in the midst of the colonial quest to carve up the planet (known as the Great Game), the great powers (England, France, Bavaria, and Russia) determined the form of government the new state would have. Greece was on England's route to its eastern empire; it was also on Russia's route to the Mediterranean.

At that point, Greece had been part of the "Orient" for 1,426 years. The new state was constructed in accordance with Western models of nationalism, and the new Greek state called on all Greeks to think of themselves as descendants of the ancient Hellenes. However, Greece's relationship to its classical pagan past had to be reconciled with its near fifteen hundred years as the center of eastern Christianity. As Michael Herzfeld observed,

> The Greeks were constantly told, in the established tradition of imperial paternalism, to let their political elders and betters decide what parts of their present-day culture could be legitimately classified as "Greek."[73]

There was considerable ethnic and linguistic diversity within the country, and there were large populations of Greeks outside of Greece, only some of whom spoke Greek. Greece's political leaders pursued a policy of creating a single national culture called Hellenism in which the Olympic Games played an important role. Four Zappas Olympiads (named after their wealthy benefactor, Evangelos Zappas) were held in the second half of the nineteenth century, for which the ancient Panathenaic Stadium in Athens was excavated and restored. The language and rituals of the games were almost all inspired by ancient practices, even to the wearing of body stockings by the athletes to imitate ancient nudity.[74]

In 1894, Pierre de Coubertin invited two thousand international luminaries to an international congress in Paris, where they established plans to revive the ancient Olympics as a modern, international form. The first event would be held in Athens in 1896, and the first president of the IOC was the Greek writer Dimetrios Vikélas. In his speech before the congress on June 23, Vikélas argued the case for Athens by appealing to the romantic European view of Greece:

> In this moment, as the Olympic Games are negotiated, does not Greece have a certain right to see the premiere of their restoration take place on its soil? Do not forget, gentlemen, when you regard ancient Greece as your intellectual homeland, that we Greeks are in many ways directly descended from it. Therefore, if you are the grandchildren of our common ancestors, then we are their children.[75]

The first modern Olympic Games opened in Athens on March 25, 1896, the Greek Independence Day, and were successful. They attracted tens of thousands of spectators and teams from around Europe and North America. In this way, the Olympic Games, both ancient and modern, were written into the unilinear national history of modern Greece, which ideologically obliterated four centuries of Ottoman rule. They became an important way in which Greece shed its Oriental history and presented itself as a member of

Western civilization, a membership that has caused conflicts in its internal and external relations ever since. When Athens hosted the 2004 Olympics, one of the official slogans claimed that the games were "coming home."

DECOLONIZATION AND SPORT

At the center of colonialism are power relations, but as Foucault insists, power is "polymorphous," meaning that it is not simply the explicit and clearly identifiable suppression of one person or group by another but is, rather, at work everywhere, even when those in power or those who are dominated do not consciously recognize power relations. In a similar way, resistance is found everywhere, since both power and resistance are in constant tension with each other: "where there is power, there is resistance, and yet, or rather consequently, this resistance is never in a position of exteriority in relation to power," Foucault reminds us.[76] Sport was a perfect tool for the implementation of resistance against colonialism because it was unobtrusive and lay below the radar screen; it is a good example of the micropolitics of power practiced in an embodied "everyday form of resistance."[77]

It thus should not be surprising that sport played an important role in the decolonization that followed World War II, as former colonies began claiming independence and colonial powers were sometimes anxious to shed their less profitable colonies. When colonial hegemony began to crumble, sports clubs continued to serve the same functions for the new elites that they had served for the old. For example, in late nineteenth-century Cairo, Egypt, the British army of occupation, which had been sent to quell the uprising against the ruling pasha of Egypt and Sudan after the Anglo-Egyptian War in 1882, founded the Gezira Sporting Club. Its members were mostly British aristocrats, army officers, and upper-echelon government officials, with a few French and German citizens; Egyptians were a tiny minority, and almost all were pashas and beys (honorific titles bestowed upon elites). During the revolution of July 1952 against the British occupation, the government took control of the club and replaced its expatriate leadership with Egyptians. After the Suez crisis of 1956, the new elite replaced the old, both in Egyptian politics and in the Gezira sports club. It was, so to speak, new wine in an old bottle. The Gezira club remained the most prominent sports club in the Middle East from its inception to the present.[78] As Frantz Fanon, the "father" of postcolonial theory, would have predicted, power relations in the postcolonial world often mirror those of the colonial era, with the emergence, for example, of new elites who slipped into the roles formerly occupied by colonizers (the "new whites," as they are called in various parts of Africa).[79]

Decolonization from the 1950s to the end of the 1970s resulted in forty-eight new Asian and African nations establishing national Olympic committees following their independence. However, the Western-dominated organizations that governed international sport were slow to respond to the shift. When Indonesia hosted the 1962 Asian Games, the IOC withdrew its approval of the games at the last minute because athletes from the Republic of China (Taiwan) had been excluded from the games on the excuse that their identity cards had been lost in the mail. At that time, Indonesia was one of the few countries in the IOC that was friendly with the People's Republic of China, which had withdrawn from the IOC and from other major sports federations that recognized the Republic of China. The IOC threatened to ban any Asian Games competitors from the 1964 Olympics in Tokyo. Indonesian president Sukarno reacted with an attempt to organize an alternative Olympic Games for the newly independent and nonaligned nations, the Games of the New Emerging Forces (GANEFO). With substantial funding from China, the first GANEFO in Jakarta attracted three thousand athletes from fifty-one nations, including the Soviet Union, the People's Republic of China, recently independent colonies, and even some individual athletes from Europe. A coup d'état in Indonesia and the Cultural Revolution in the People's Republic prevented any subsequent GANEFO from taking place. In 1978 the People's Republic led a second attempt to break the West's death grip over international sports competitions. The Intergovernmental Committee for Physical Education and Sport was established under the UN Educational, Scientific and Cultural Organization. By this time it had become clear to IOC president Killanin that the IOC would have to accommodate the new world order. He pushed through the People's Republic's readmittance into the IOC in 1979.

Sport played an important role in decolonization processes in other, more subtle ways. In Morocco, for example, which was under French rule from 1912 to 1956 in the form of a protectorate (during which the sultan continued to hold some power), Moroccan men conscripted into the French military (particularly the all-Moroccan infantry battalions, the *tirailleurs marocains*) started training from the 1930s in long-distance running, a sport that the French colonists considered low class.[80] Since Morocco was under French rule, they had to run in the French elite competition system, which they came to dominate. While their accomplishments in international track-and-field competitions were represented in France as proof of the country's greatness as a colonial power, in the protectorate, nationalist leaders saw them as proof that Moroccans could compete quite effectively with the colonial power. After independence in 1956, the state invested considerable resources to promote long-distance running, identify promising children, and train talented athletes, and Morocco came to have the prominence in the sport it holds to this day. While numerous commentators continue to attribute Moroccans' sporting success to alleged physiological characteristics that make them particularly suited to the sport, this success is in fact the outcome of colonial prejudices, the forced conscription of colonized men into the metropole's military, and the astuteness of a state that saw in the sport a way of giving the country global visibility.

One of the last remnants of the old-style colonial order was eliminated thanks in part to activism in the realm of sport. African nations unified against the apartheid system in South Africa, resulting in its exclusion from the Olympic Games and FIFA from the 1960s to the early 1990s. Given the importance that white South Africans attached to sport, the boycott hit South Africa particularly hard. New Zealand shares a passion for rugby with white South Africans even while the nonwhite indigenous Māori minority plays a prominent role in the sport. When in 1981 the New Zealand government acquiesced to a boycott-breaking tour of the South African national team, the Springboks, it galvanized nationwide protests and left a lasting divisive effect.[81] Following the abolition of apartheid in 1994, South Africa's triumph in the 1995 Rugby World Cup ignited jubilation about the future that, it was hoped, would follow Nelson Mandela's victory in the country's first democratic election.

While rugby union was enmeshed with the colonial apartheid order in South Africa, it had a different valence in Fiji, a British colony from 1874 until 1970. During the colonial period, the sport was taught at selective colonial schools to boys and young men of chiefly rank and of part-European elite families. In the course of the twentieth century it trickled down the social hierarchy, largely through the vector of the army and the police, to eventually become the most important national sport, the object even of a national obsession. It is enmeshed with the ideology and structure of the country's social, political, gender, and religious organization, among both the politically and numerically dominant indigenous Fijians, as well as the country as a whole. It is played, however, only by indigenous Fijians and excludes the

FIGURE 6. Fijian boys learn to handle rugby balls from the earliest age (Suva, Fiji, February 2016/Niko Besnier).

descendants of late nineteenth-century and early twentieth-century immigrants from India, who currently constitute about 40 percent of the country's population.[82]

A few historical events stand out in the history of the sport in the country as key moments when the colonial or postcolonial outpost demonstrated its superiority over the colonial masters. In 1977 the Fijian national team beat the Lions, an elite supranational team composed of the best English, Welsh, Scottish, and Irish players, during their stopover on their way to New Zealand. This event was of momentous importance in the memories of those who were there, since very few teams from overseas, let alone such an important team from Britain, had visited the country. Fijians remember the event as a milestone in the country's international emergence in the world of the sport rather than as a victory against the former colonial power.

As we will elaborate further in chapter 8, since the 1980s, along with neighboring countries Tonga and Samoa, Fiji has become an exporter of rugby talent. Far from representing a postcolonial revenge against the colonizer, the sport is for Fijians a way of showcasing their country on the global scene. Rugby in Fiji thus represents a different alignment of sport with postcoloniality from that of, say, cricket in South Asia. One may speculate that

Fijians' experience of the colonial era did not provoke a backlash in the post-colonial era as it did in other parts of the British Empire because the remoteness of the colony, its relatively small size and modest resources, and the absence of settler colonialism from the colonial metropole (other than the indentured sugarcane workers that the British brought from India) made for more relaxed relations between colonizer and colonized. Furthermore, the entire edifice of the indigenous Fijian system was constructed in the nineteenth century with the support of the British strategies of inventing traditions and governing through indirect rule. If anyone has any postcolonial sensibilities in contemporary Fiji, it is Indo-Fijians, the descendants of indentured laborers and subsequent free migrants from South Asia.[83]

POSTCOLONIAL LEGACIES IN SPORT

Sport in a postcolonial context can take on a variety of configurations. In some postcolonies it may be a vehicle of postcolonial critique, as postcolonies appropriate colonial sports and turn them into nationalist emblems used to beat the former colonizers "at their own game." Baseball in Latin America challenged US supremacy; cricket in the West Indies and India marked their emergence from under the thumb of Britain. In other postcolonies, such as Fiji, sport was adapted to the local contexts without the resistant qualities found elsewhere. Nations that were subordinated to the Western colonial powers but never fully colonized were nevertheless drawn into the outer reaches of the inescapable vortex of colonialism. Baseball in Japan was a way of contesting US supremacy; the Far Eastern Championship Games symbolized East Asia's incorporation into the world system and resulted in the East Asian rivalry to host Olympic Games in the new millennium; and Greece's hosting of the modern Olympic Games bolstered its claim that it belonged to the cultural West.[84] In still other cases, there have been attempts to escape the clutches of colonialism altogether by setting up alternative sports systems, such as the Gaelic Athletic Association, which marked the separation of Ireland from Britain, or the Games of the New Emerging Forces, an attempt by developing countries to challenge Western control of international sports. If sport was an integral component of colonialism, then it should not be surprising that, half a century after most former colonies gained their independence, the legacy of colonialism is still evident in the shape of today's global sport.

THREE

Sport, Health, and the Environment

ANTHROPOLOGISTS WHO STUDY SPORT and medical anthropologists should have many overlapping interests, given their common concern with health and the human body. Modern medicine, physical education, and anthropology all emerged from the same roots in the mid- to late nineteenth century, and many early anthropologists were trained as physicians. Originally, the three disciplines shared a racial evolutionary paradigm and a research method—anthropometry (the measurement of the human body). However, when sport anthropology and medical anthropology emerged as discrete subfields several decades later, they had very little to do with each other.

Presumably, the main area of overlap should be physical exercise, which all major medical traditions since antiquity have recognized as one component of good health. The phrase *humoral medicine,* used to label the Greek and Islamic tradition, refers to the belief that bodily fluid (Latin: *humor*) flows throughout the body in different forms that interact with each other and with essences flowing through the environment. Types of medicine labeled "humoral" assume that the proper balance of bodily constituents creates good health, the balance is increased or depleted by nourishment and exertion, and the healthy body is in equilibrium with the natural environment. The Hippocratic, Galenic/Islamic, Mesoamerican, Indian, and Chinese medical traditions all subscribed to a holistic view of medicine that included diet, exercise, and the body's relationship to the natural environment, such as the seasons, the weather, winds, and water. In the West, however, exercise became largely marginalized from approaches to medicine that emerged in the late eighteenth century as a subfield of modern "science" (although it would be over one hundred years before it largely attained the standards considered "scientific" today). Here we will use the label *biomedicine* to describe this medical tradition.

The current disconnect between medical anthropology and sport anthropology is grounded in the history of medicine. Starting in the European Renaissance, holistic views of health were gradually pushed out of biomedicine, and by the mid-nineteenth century, elite university and government-controlled medicine largely replaced them with germ theory and quantitative methods, including anthropometry. These developments relegated holistic medicine in the West to marginalized, alternative traditions such as homeopathy and naturopathy—which, however, flourished in popular practice in some countries. The 1960s saw a reversal of this trend, with efforts to reconnect health, sport, and environment drawing on alternative medicine and non-Western traditions such as Indian and Chinese medicines. However, another trend moved in the opposite direction: in sports medicine, the biomedical approach to the body as an alienated, material object has sometimes been taken to extremes. Today's sports medicine provides a glimpse into the future of the body, with its emerging technologies such as genetic enhancement and prostheses that surpass the capabilities of the unaided human body.

MEDICAL ANTHROPOLOGY AND THE ANTHROPOLOGY OF SPORT: A NONRELATIONSHIP

Since the 1980s medical anthropology has grown into one of the largest specialties within sociocultural anthropology because of its links to the vast and well-funded field of medicine. However, medical anthropologists have almost completely ignored sport. The keyword "sport" calls up no articles in the digitized collection of the journal *Anthropology and Medicine,* 1988–2014. A search on "sport" in *Medical Anthropology Quarterly,* 1983–2016, turns up only one research article, which is about the role of horse-human relationships in the lives of fifty women who ride for pleasure.[1]

What explains the nonrelationship between medical anthropology and the anthropology of sport? Biomedicine focuses almost completely on the treatment of sick bodies, while sports are unquestionably practiced by living and mostly healthy bodies. Accomplished athletes are popularly seen as achieving a kind of bodily perfection, and great sports performances even seem to extend the abilities of healthy bodies to near-superhuman levels. Of course, many elite athletes are hardly paragons of physical perfection, given the negative effects of sports training on the body, and Paralympic sport challenges popular prejudices about physical disability—points to which we will return later. Nevertheless, until the past few decades, biomedicine had focused on illness rather than "wellness," largely excluding exercises and sports from its field of view.

Likewise, from the time it began to emerge as a subfield in the 1950s, medical anthropology was unified by a concern with medicine and illness rather than a theoretical vision. The three reviews of the subfield in the *Biennial Review of Anthropology* (later the *Annual Reviews of Anthropology*) from 1963 to 1974 illustrate this point. In 1963 the first review argued that medical anthropology was as significant as the anthropology of kinship, political structure, and economics because "concepts of health and disease involve basic sets of attitudes, life views, perceptions, cognitive systems, and action patterns."[2] Biological disease does not exist independently of the social environment, which affects and is affected by disease. However, it does not appear that the subfield embraced this view, because the second review in 1971 limited the definition of medical anthropology to inquiry into the processes that play a role when individuals or groups are affected by illness.[3] By 1974 the authors of the third and final review "failed to find a shared and conceptually-based view of the field" and therefore decided to concentrate on a content review of the research being conducted—and all the content that they reviewed concerned illness.[4] Although ethnomedicine, the study of local or folk medical knowledge and practices, had been a major area of inquiry since the beginning of anthropology, it too tended to focus on healing techniques, beliefs about healing, and traditional medications. Symbolic anthropologists have investigated healing in the context of trance and ritual, but they often sidestepped the realm of bodily health by focusing on the religious, political, and social context of ritual rather than physiology and anatomy. While ritual studies find common ground with sport studies when it comes to the ritual in sport, they have failed to establish a common ground with respect to physical health and healing.[5]

In short, medical anthropology, ethnomedicine, and studies of ritual healing have not systematically examined health, that is, the absence of illness. There is also the question of what "health" means cross-culturally. An anthropology of health should not impose Western biomedical concepts of health and sickness upon other cultures but rather should seek to establish local beliefs about health and medicine.[6] This type of approach could better embrace medicine, exercise, and sport within a larger framework.

The relationships among sport, exercise, health, medicine, and the environment take different configurations in different cultures. For example, in *Giorgias,* Plato has Socrates saying that there are two kinds of techniques for the care of the soul and the body. Politics is the art that cares for the soul, and then there is the "art that is the care of the body, of which I know no single name, but which may be described as having two divisions, one of them exercise, and the other medicine."[7] *Gymnastikos,* which we translate as "exercise," referred to physical activities that freemen practiced in the nude *(gymnia)* in *gymnasia,* the facilities where they worked out and also engaged in learned conversations. Plato might be referring to athletes in training or fitness-minded citizens, or more likely both. The passage indicates that Plato connected exercise with medicine, but it also demonstrates that, as in contemporary English, ancient Greeks had no single word for the care of the body. Exercise was so central to their culture that *gymnasia* were a symbol of Greek identity. Every town and city that considered itself Greek had a gymnasium, a fact that archaeologists have used to establish that an ancient city was culturally Greek. Physical exercise was considered good for the individual as well as for the collective because it ensured an ever-ready reserve of soldiers that could be called on in time of conflict, which was frequent.

The Western medical tradition was first codified in the Hippocratic corpus, the sixty texts attributed to Hippocrates (460–370 BCE) but now considered to have been written by multiple authors over one or two centuries. This set of texts systematized an even older tradition that saw health to be the result of a balance of four "juices" in the body, achieved by a proper relationship between intake in the form of nutrition and expenditure in the form of physical exertion. As Hippocrates put it, "For food and exercise ... work together to produce health."[8] The Hippocratic tradition became the basis of all codified medicine in ancient Greece, Rome, and the Islamic world and still had its proponents among educated doctors in the West well into the nineteenth century. It also continues to this day in the Unani medical tradition in India.

In accord with humoral medicine, the Hippocratic authors considered simple walking to be beneficial to health because it caused the flesh to heat up, and heat was necessary for digestive and other processes. Respiration and perspiration were good for the body in moderation. The Greeks admired fit bodies (one need only study Greek statues to see that their ideal was not entirely different from that of today's Hollywood); for those who wanted to slim down, the Hippocratic writers advised that the best exercise for losing weight was sprinting.[9] We do not know whether women had similar concerns: while there were athletic games for unmarried women, the surviving records mention systematic physical education and even athletic nudity for women only in Sparta, where the goal of such education was strengthening women's bodies for motherhood. It seems that other city-states did appreciate fit female bodies, since Spartan women were known for their beauty, and in one of Aristophanes's plays a character is praised for her beautiful skin, firm breasts, and physical strength, which she attributes to exercise.[10]

Sports, exercise, and diet should also be attuned to the seasons. The Hippocratic text *Regimen in Health* advised that winter was the appropriate season for running and wrestling, but in summer only a small amount of wrestling should be practiced, and the body should not be oiled (as was normal practice in winter) because it would melt the flesh too much. In summer, walking was the most appropriate exercise.[11] Excessive exercise and eating too much meat violated the ethical principle of "nothing in excess," so doctors wrote that professional athletes were not healthy.[12] A "perfect condition that is at its highest peak" was an extreme state that could not be sustained.[13] Doctors did not specialize in taking care of high-performance athletes—that was the job of professional athletic trainers. Their occupations sometimes clashed. The surviving medical texts largely represent the viewpoint of the doctors.

GALENIC MEDICINE AND EXERCISE

Galen of Pergamon (129–216 CE), a Greek physician in the Roman Empire, expanded on the Hippocratic corpus in hundreds of treatises. He sought to explain physiology in terms of the interaction of four humors (blood, phlegm, yellow bile, and black bile) with each other and with air and breath *(pneuma)*. He also saw the body as interconnected with the natural environment, advocating sunshine, fresh air, clean water, and a healthy diet. The ideas laid out in his treatises became the unquestionable "truth" in the Middle East, parts of India, and the West for over sixteen hundred years until biomedicine finally replaced humoral medicine.

Galen defined exercise as movement that was vigorous enough to cause a person to breathe faster. It could contribute to either health or disease based on how it was employed. It needed to be used in moderation: excess could put the humors into imbalance and result in disease. Sufficient exercise was necessary for healthy living by promoting bodily functions and processes.[14] However, based on his experience working for a time as a doctor to gladiators, he criticized sports because they violated the rule of "moderation in all things." Athletes "spend their lives in over-exercising, in over-eating, and over-sleeping like pigs." They are "in miserable pain," and when they stop competing, "most parts of their bodies become deformed." He believed that exercise with the "small ball" was better than running, horseback riding, jumping, throwing the discus, and boxing, because it did not involve danger.[15]

In sum, ancient Greeks considered physical exercise beneficial, even if it was somewhat strenuous. However, it does not appear that they imagined exercise *as medical treatment*. Rather, there was a difference—the Hippocratic corpus even calls it an opposition—between exercise in *gymnasia* and the arts of medicine oriented toward remedying sickness. In this respect, the Greek sport-health-medicine complex differed from other traditions that *did* incorporate a concept of medicinal exercise, such as Indian Ayurveda and Chinese medicine, discussed below.

THE BODY, ENVIRONMENT, AND COSMOS IN MESOAMERICAN BALL GAMES

Traditional medical systems throughout Mesoamerica at the time of the Spanish Conquest resembled Greek humoral medicine in that "heat" was a central concept. The Aztecs understood food, diseases, medicines, types of people—indeed, the whole universe—in terms of a hot-cold dichotomy. Scholars have debated whether the humoral system predates the Spanish Conquest or was in fact borrowed from the Galenic medicine of the Spanish invaders; most agree that at least part of it was indigenous since the earliest Spanish accounts mention it.[16] The three main humors (*tonalli*, "life force"; *teyolia*, "soul and intelligence"; and *ihiyotl*, "emotions and witchcraft") were associated with specific organs and were a microcosm of the forces of the universe. Good health depended on maintaining a balance between them, and moderation was the path to health.[17] Exercise heated up the *tonalli* and produced fatigue, while rest and drinking pulque (fermented agave juice) cooled it down. When the *tonalli* became hot, the belly and feet became cool, so Aztecs rubbed them with "hot" remedies such as tobacco. One Spanish account finds the sequence in which the Aztecs ordered rest and exercise to be "depraved" and possibly the work of the devil, because around the world "reasonable men" rested *after* exercise, while the Aztecs rested and drank pulque beforehand in order to gather their strength. The writer suspected that they were getting drunk in order to face the extensive compulsory work required of all men (work in their own fields, compulsory labor, long trips).[18] The Aztec medical tradition is well documented, and given its high level of development, it is logical to assume that athletes used medicines intended to enhance their performances and that battle medicine would also have been used for athletic injuries. However, the surviving accounts describe no such links. It is impossible to say whether this reflects a bias on the part of the Spanish chroniclers from the sixteenth to the eighteenth century or a lack of contemporary scholarship on connections between medicine and sport. Nor is it possible to say whether the Aztec medical system simply did not incorporate ball games. The last possibility seems unlikely in view of the political, economic, and cultural importance of the games.

Tonalli was derived from the sun and located in the heart, so human sacrifice that consisted of cutting out the victim's heart and sprinkling the blood on the earth constituted a ritual of renewal that returned life force to the sun and sustained the cycle of life and death. The sun must be fed blood and hearts in order to continue to exist and sustain the crops. Because both human sacrifice and ball court games were widespread and culturally important, many have assumed that the Aztecs sacrificed ball game players. However, there is no strong evidence for this practice. Furthermore, we do not know how the ball game linked humoral physiology with the cosmos. One can imagine that the heat of the *tonalli*/heart produced by the exertion of the game might share symbolism with the sacrifice of humans and the dedication of their hearts to the gods, but the sources do not spell out this interpretation.

In contrast, Mayan iconography on pottery, stone stelae, and murals depicts many images of human sacrifice by decapitation in the context of ball games, often accompanied by dismemberment, with some of the victims apparently ballplayers while others are war captives.[19] Although we do not have a good understanding of the concepts of health and body that might have underpinned the practice, we do know that ball games reenacted a charter myth recorded in the Mayan sacred book, the Popol Vuh. The ball games played by the Hero Twins, in which they defeat the Lords of the Underworld, who had killed and sacrificed their uncle and father, are commonly interpreted as a cosmological battle between life and death. Of the twelve Lords of the Underworld, eight personified disease and sickness with attractive names such as Flying Scab, Pus Demon, and Jaundice Demon. One pair of Lords attacked the blood; a second pair caused bodies to swell up; a third turned dead bodies into skeletons; a fourth caused people to die coughing up blood while out walking.[20] It thus seems likely that the Mayan ball game and associated human sacrifice were interpreted within a symbolic framework of health and disease that is, as yet, poorly understood.

FAST-FORWARD TO THE ENLIGHTENMENT

The biomedicine that emerged in the West during the Enlightenment departed from the humoral medical systems in ancient Greece and Rome, India, China, the Islamic world, and Mesoamerica. It located illnesses in bodies that had been removed from the contexts of everyday life and the natural environment. Having observed the importance of corpse dissection in the production of medical knowledge in Europe in the late eighteenth century, Michel Foucault went so far as to say that death played a central role in the emergence of bio-medicine. The study of corpses enabled a fundamental shift of perspective in which the human body could be seen as an inanimate, material object. The elaboration of medical knowledge over the next one hundred years correlated lists of symptoms with specific diseases, mapped the cause of disease onto organs and tissues, invented instruments to measure the workings of the body as if it were a machine (e.g., the stethoscope, blood pressure monitor), and applied chemistry to body fluids (e.g., blood and urine testing). Previously, sick people in Europe had been treated by the women of the family at home, considered the "natural" setting for disease. From the Enlightenment, professional male medical scientists began isolating patients in hospitals and were no longer interested in them as human beings with individual life histories. Biomedicine became focused on disease and death, which, according to Foucault, facilitated the emergence of new "rational" scientific discourse about the body that "unfolds endlessly in the void left by the absence of the gods."[21]

In the mid-seventeenth century, the term *antropometria* was first used to label an attempt to correlate the proportions of the body with disease.[22] By the late eighteenth century, Johann Friedrich Blumenbach (1752–1840) employed anthropometry in his 1775 text that became foundational to the discipline of anthropology, *De generis humani varietate nativa* (On the natural variety of mankind). The book was his MD thesis; he was the first in a line of physicians who contributed not only to the establishment of anthropology but also to the unfortunate development of the pseudoscience of race, which marred the early years of anthropology. He classified the world's peoples into five races (Caucasian/white, Mongolian/yellow, Malayan/brown, Ethiopian/black, American/red). Sadly, his categories still have a hold on the popular imagination today. By the end of the century, anthropometry had become a methodological obsession, used and misused in a wide array of fields, including anatomy, ethnology, criminology, physical education, and public health.

BIOMEDICINE ARRIVES AND EXERCISE EXITS IN THE NINETEENTH CENTURY

Anthropology shared fundamental epistemological assumptions with medicine. Physicians were at the forefront of encounters with the West's Others because colonial expansion into new territories exposed the agents of colonialism to new diseases such as malaria and cholera. "Tropical medicine" took shape as a specialty devoted to making Africa, Asia, the Caribbean, and the Americas habitable to European and American colonists. Colonial medicine was justified by stating that it was the responsibility of the colonizer to provide the natives with the best medical treatments for their diseases, but this rationale was probably less important than keeping the colonizers alive and preventing foreign diseases from being carried back to the motherland. As doctors went out onto other continents, they encountered indigenous peoples who piqued their interest. Being physicians, they were more focused on documenting physical difference than other forms of difference and contributed directly to the intellectual justification of imperialism.[23]

Physicians who contributed to ethnology and the anthropology of race included the Germans Philipp Franz von Siebold and Adolf Bastian. Siebold, the founder of Japanology, traveled between Japan, Korea, Sakhalin, and nearby islands in 1823–30.[24] Bastian became chief of ethnology at the Berlin Royal Museum in 1876, the first German scholar to hold a professional anthropology position. He later oversaw the building of a separate Royal Museum of Ethnology, completed in 1886, which continues today as the Ethnological Museum of Berlin. In 1885, Franz Boas, who would become the father of North American anthropology, became his assistant while he was preparing his habilitation (a degree that follows the PhD) in ethnology after having earned four years earlier a PhD in physics with a focus on geography.[25]

Histories of medicine often credit Rudolf Virchow (1821–1902) with finally overturning humoral medicine in the mid-1850s.[26] He is regarded as the founder of modern pathology (the study of the causes of diseases) due to his work in linking diseases to abnormalities in cells. He was the first to reject the theory of spontaneous generation and argue that all cells come from the division of other cells. He coined the term "social medicine," by which he meant that epidemics and disease are caused by poverty, an idea that medical anthropologist Paul Farmer would take up again a century later.[27] He was very radical and prescient on this point but, according to the precepts of basic science, wrong, because he never accepted that diseases can be caused by germs; he felt that the microorganisms observed in diseased tissue had just opportunistically taken advantage of degradation caused by poor living conditions. For his advocacy for the health of the poor and disadvantaged, he is considered a key figure in the development of public health.[28] He ardently opposed the racist theories that were then gaining credence and tried to debunk the existence of an Aryan race with a massive anthropometric study of German schoolchildren. His stance on race strongly influenced Boas, who carried his legacy to the New World, where he emigrated in 1892, and it became a cornerstone of Boas's legacy.[29]

Virchow was the leader of the change of course that sent biomedicine off onto a different trajectory from the two-thousand-year-old tradition of humoral medicine, taking the discipline of anthropology along with it. Over time, the approach to understanding difference became less benign than that of early physicians such as Siebold and Virchow. One of the conceptually bizarre results of Virchow's legacy was that the study of indigenous peoples was often incorporated into the discipline of pathology. As scientists sought to distinguish healthy from diseased bodies, they envisioned white Europeans as the standard of health and bodies that did not conform, including non-Western bodies, as pathological. Thus, teaching collections of wax models of diseased body parts and body parts preserved in glass containers also included "ethnological" busts, and books on pathology contained a section at the back about perfectly healthy non-Western peoples who nevertheless were seen as deviating from the white European standard. In the popular realm, freak shows could include misshapen Europeans as well as indigenous peoples.

Anthropologists were also involved in establishing the discipline of physical education because anthropometry was a shared research method. Anthropometry was embraced by the forerunner of today's American Alliance for Health, Physical Education, Recreation and Dance (established 1885), which counted among its founding members E. P. Thwing, president of the New York Academy of Anthropology.[30] From 1898 to 1904, Franz Boas was an associate editor of the association's journal, where his name sat oddly among the MDs and education specialists. In 1902, Boas became a member of the founding group of the American Anthropological Association and its first vice president. Frederick Skiff, director of the Chicago Field Museum of Natural History, became a member of the Amateur Athletic Union and the American Olympic Committee in the early twentieth century. Physical education and anthropology were nodes in what Foucault might have called a "power-knowledge complex," united by a shared ideology of evolutionary progress and a methodological faith in the quantification of the human body.[31] However, as the 1904 Anthropology Days (discussed in chapter 1) illustrate, ideology often trumped science. But Anthropology Days was an exception, as anthropologists did not generally focus on athletic performances. Another exception was an expedition to Rwanda in 1907 led by Adolf Friedrich, duke of Mecklenburg, who had studied anthropology. He became interested in a form of high-jumping practiced by the Tutsi, locally known as *gusimbuka urukiramende.* He organized and photographed a contest and recorded the best jump at the incredible height of 8 feet 2 ½ inches (2.5 meters).[32]

New forms of biomedical knowledge did not immediately lead to improvements in the medical therapies available to ordinary people. Galenic humoral medicine flourished because it offered remedies that were available through self-help, many of which, such as fresh air, were free (although probably not available to everyone). Galen's work underwent a revival in the first half of the nineteenth century, taken up by many authors writing about self-improvement, hygiene, and preventive medicine.[33] Having observed the injuries suffered by student and professional athletes, nineteenth-century physicians shared Galen's negative view of athletic sports.[34]

In the nineteenth century, tourism emerged as a form of consumption. A large segment was strongly motivated by considerations of health as Victorians traveled from urban areas to seaside resorts and natural mineral or hot springs for the invigoration of their constitutions by immersion in healthy air and water. These practices were in accordance with the concepts of naturopathy and hydrotherapy, which were then in vogue.[35] Naturopathy was developed in Germany and the United States by healers distrustful of the growing prominence of hospitals, pharmaceuticals, and specialist doctors. Frustrated by the inability of modern medicine to treat chronic diseases, they reached back to Hippocratic and Galenic sources to develop a theory that linked nature, metabolism, and ecology. Based on the Hippocratic elements of earth, air, fire (in the form of sunlight), and water, they advocated what they called nature cure in the belief that with the aid of nature and natural elements, the body could heal itself. Hydrotherapy (bath treatments), fasting to purge the body of "toxins," walking, and hiking in nature were important remedies.

At the start of the twentieth century, two developments finally severed the link between medicine and exercise. On the one hand, sports took a more prominent place in physical education taught in schools in Europe and North America, turning the focus on the athletically talented and away from the average youth. Muscular Christianity, which we discussed in chapter 2, gained momentum in the United States and the United Kingdom, and gymnastics in Germany and Scandinavia. Physical education was systematized, but the focus on sports limited its impact on the overall health of the public. However, with new discoveries in antibiotics, vaccinations, and antiseptic procedures, biomedicine finally had effective treatments for many common diseases, and it increasingly turned toward drugs and surgery, leaving behind Galenic humoral medicine. The connection between health and tourism weakened with the alienation of the body from the environment.

ANTHROPOMETRY REFUSES TO DIE

As early as 1893, Boas criticized the use of anthropometry in physical education, although he continued to teach a course in anthropometry at Columbia University, where he founded the first department of anthropology in North America. In the decades following the excesses of the 1904 world's fair in St. Louis, he led the development of a US brand of anthropology that was critical of evolutionary comparative methods and focused, instead, on culture. Sociocultural anthropology began to split away from physical (biological) anthropology.

While physical anthropologists rejected racist evolutionary theory, particularly after World War II, the application of anthropometry to simpleminded questions of racial, national, and sexual difference persisted in sport studies. Anthropometric comparisons of athletes were conducted at multiple Olympic Games starting in 1928. A study at the Helsinki 1952 Olympic Games was conducted by Ernst Jokl, an MD who was one of the founders of sports medicine. He collected massive amounts of statistics from the organizers, but the study ended up being of little use to scientists. The fact that he was a Jew who had fled Nazi Germany, and who should have known better, did not prevent him from calculating the relative success levels of "white," "yellow-brown," and "black" athletes.[36] Another study at the Rome 1960 Olympic measured forty-five characteristics, including cephalic length, diameters, and skinfolds on men from thirty-eight countries using a racial matrix that included Negroids, Mestizos, Mongoloids, and Caucasoids.[37]

The most ambitious attempt to study race at the Olympics took place at the Mexico City 1968 Olympics, when an interdisciplinary team collected information on 1,265 athletes from 92 countries, representing 30 percent of participating athletes. The team, led by a Mexican geneticist, an American biologist, and an American sport scientist, developed an extensive protocol to understand the genetic and anthropological characteristics of the biology of athletes to "benefit all humanity by providing a better understanding of human excellence and diversity."[38] They collected family information such as birth order, genetic information (DNA, blood groups and proteins, finger and palm prints, and taste sensitivity to PTC),[39] and comprehensive anthropometric measurements. This approach turned out to be a dead end. No scientific papers were presented from the results, and the book describing the research did not come out until 1974. Most of the results were inconclusive, and one reviewer of the book observed, "To the casual reader they may appear no more exciting than reading logarithm tables."[40]

The failure of the bad pseudoscience of race to produce useful conclusions out of anthropometric measurements did not hinder the use of sports performances in establishing racial hierarchies in the popular imagination. In an aptly titled book, *Darwin's Athletes,* historian John Hoberman demonstrated that the nineteenth-century interest in the quantification of race persists in contemporary sports because the fantasies that underlie racial stereotypes have not died out.[41] The nineteenth-century anxieties of white Europeans are still alive, and the popular stereotype about African athletic aptitude helps perpetuate archaic ideas about racial differences. "Indeed," he states, "the rise of the black athlete during our own century has revived nineteenth-century racial physiology in new and more scientific forms."[42]

NON-WESTERN CONFIGURATIONS

By the nineteenth century, the configuration of sports, exercise, and medicine in the West differed from that found in other major medical traditions that did not clearly separate exercise and medicine. In these traditions exercise may be a "truly healing art," and specific exercises may be prescribed to heal illnesses.[43] Anthropologists researching the highly developed medical traditions of India and China have pointed out the constructed nature of the Western dividing line. But anthropologist Joseph Alter, who conducted innovative research on traditional Indian wrestling and yoga, also criticized medical anthropologists for ignoring "physical fitness" as a facet of medicine and taking good health as a natural, biological given. He called on medical anthropologists to extend the same critical and relativistic approach to good health that they take toward illness, pain, and disease and to pay more attention to the cross-cultural differences in the ideals of health upon which medical systems and concepts of the body are founded.[44]

Alter coined the term *metaphysical fitness* to describe the fusion of medicine with metaphysics in Indian body culture, which combines "humoral body-building and cosmic self-improvement" into a set of techniques for holistic self-perfection. While the classical Ayurvedic texts offer little guidance on the topic of exercise and do not mention sports, Ayurvedic principles constitute a broader vision of health that practitioners have drawn on to interpret exercise and sports since the late nineteenth century.[45] Some passages that recommend walking for reducing fat and advise against pushing the body beyond its limits seem to have been borrowed from Galen. In Ayurvedic medicine the human body is composed of fluids, saps, elements, essences, and humors that constantly ebb and flow and interact. Metaphysical fitness is achieved by influencing the ebb and flow through daily health and hygiene regimens.[46]

The Ayurvedic theory of health that has developed in the last century is based on *pran* (subtle wind), a kind of energy or essence that pervades the body and flushes out the organs, opens up blocked channels, and detoxifies the body. *Pran* is taken into the body along with air, and by performing the right sequence of movements, one can channel it through *nadi* conduits that run through the body.[47] Metabolism is a process in which the digestion of food produces semen, which enhances physical strength and promotes digestion in men. Thus, traditional wrestlers eat a lot, and their virility is manifested in both strength and appetite.[48]

Yoga means "union," namely the union of self with the universal cosmic self and the transcendence of all things. As a philosophy, it dates back to 150–500 CE. In the first centuries CE, yoga was a philosophical tradition rather than a holistic medical system with associated exercise techniques. As is typical in shamanic traditions, the techniques were used by the healer, not the patient; yoga masters used the powers that they gained from esoteric practices to heal others, but yoga was not practiced by the sick in order to improve their own health or by the healthy to preserve it.[49] Its connection to nature and shamanism is evidenced by the many yoga *asanas,* or postures, named after animals: lion, cow, fish, peacock, rooster, tortoise, eagle, locust, crocodile, camel, cobra, and so on.

Despite its image as an authentic local tradition, even in the nineteenth century, Indian practitioners had global connections. Henry David Thoreau promoted yoga in the United States in conjunction with his interest in "transcendental meditation," and numerous gurus took it to the United States and Europe. In 1918, near Mumbai, a young man who later took the title Shri Yogendra reconceptualized yoga as a form of "physical education" explicable in terms of the scientific vocabulary of biochemistry, anatomy, and biology.[50] One year later he founded the Yoga Institute in New York.

Yoga became a symbol of Indian civilization associated with modernist nationalism, in large part due to promotion by Mahatma Gandhi, leader of India's struggle for independence. Gandhi saw the body and health as a key site where the impact of British colonialism had been felt, and he positioned yoga as an alternative to the class injustices of capitalist medicine.[51] Influenced by nature cure, he advocated a lifestyle that did not depend on (often costly) medical intervention but was in tune with a natural order of things. Both nature cure and yoga shared a holistic perspective that integrated the healthy body, the cosmos, and ecology. By the 1920s the system of government-supported yoga clinics and hospitals, which still exists today, was taking shape throughout India. In the 2010s, however, with the emergence of new forms of religious, ethnic, and class politics associated with the prime ministership of Narendra Modi, yoga had become a point of political contention: in 2015, the United Nations General Assembly, after being lobbied by Modi, declared an International Yoga Day, which many commentators saw as being embroiled in Hindu nationalism, which seeks to marginalize Muslims, Christians, and other citizens of India.[52]

Over the twentieth century, yoga became increasingly popular in both India and the West as an alternative to biomedicine, particularly for the cure of chronic diseases such as diabetes, asthma, and high blood pressure. Naturopathy and yoga developed into a singular medical system, and it is now virtually impossible to distinguish the two. *Asana* (exercises or postures), *kriya* (purification techniques), and *pranayama* (breathing exercises) are prescribed along with diet and baths, the mainstays of nature cure.[53]

Yoga's straightforward path to modernization and globalization contrasts with the path followed by traditional forms of exercise in China. After the Communist victory in 1949, the ruling Chinese Communist Party's legitimacy was based on the wholesale rejection of the "feudal" past, allowing only a politically fragile space for "traditional" exercises.

Like the Hippocratic corpus, early Chinese medical texts did not simply spell out a therapy for illness but prescribed an annual health regimen that adjusted personal hygiene, grooming, exercise, diet, sleep, and sexual intercourse to the four seasons. One such text is the painted silk *Daoyin Tu* (168 BCE), a "guiding and pulling chart" that is the earliest evidence of medical gymnastics. Most of the exercises depicted there involve stretching, bending, breathing, and the rhythmic squeezing and contracting of the muscles. Incredibly, it recommends one thousand repetitions in a day and, in one example, four thousand. As is found in yoga, many of the exercises are named after animals, as in the following examples:

Wild Duck Bathing. Interlock the hands behind the back and shake the head

Gibbon Hold. With the right hand hold the left foot. Raise the left hand, turning the back. Bend forward to left and right

Prostrate Deer. Raise the two hands, turning the back and bend forward as far as possible.[54]

The animal imitation in yoga and daoyin starkly contrasts with the Greek tradition: as much as Hippocrates and Galen saw the body as connected to the surrounding natural environment, there is no evidence of animal imitation in the Greek exercise tradition. This may have been because Greek humanism placed human beings above animals.[55] Also, unlike competitive sports in classical India and China, those in Greece were widely practiced among freemen, so that the moderate exercise of the average male citizen shaded into the excessive and unhealthy exercise of the trained athlete, perhaps making exercise less likely to be prescribed as medicine.

Throughout East Asia today, concepts of the body are still largely shaped by fundamentally different assumptions from those of Western biomedicine.[56] Like Ayurvedic *pran, qi* (*ki* in Japanese) flows throughout the environment in the form of winds, air, and positive or negative energy and is taken into the body through breathing. The early hours of dawn before the *yang* of daylight starts to gain its strength are considered to be the *yin* hours and are believed to be most beneficial for absorbing *qi*. Therefore parks throughout

FIGURE 7. Practicing tai chi on a river bank, Guilin, China, February 17, 2008 (Taiji Collection/© Wojtek Chodzko-Zajko).

China in the early morning are full of exercisers. The "soft" or "internal arts," such as tai chi *(taiji),* cultivate *qi* for good health (figure 7).

A few years after China's era of reform and opening up to the outside world was initiated (1978), a *qigong* craze swept across China. *Qigong* consists of very mild breathing-centered exercises designed to strengthen and properly channel the flow of *qi* throughout the body. The simplest technique, *jinggong* (quiet practice) involves standing with the arms slightly rounded and the fingertips close to each other and imagining that *qi* is flowing through the arms. Nancy Chen's ethnography in the 1980s and 1990s showed that *qigong* offered free means of cultivating health to Chinese urbanites who had lost their medical benefits with the dismantling of the welfare state. At the same time, it helped to fill the "moral vacuum" that appeared with the loss of faith in Communist ideology due to the catastrophic Cultural Revolution (1966–76), during which the Red Guard had violently attacked traditional cultural practices.[57] Although martial arts practices were not as harshly attacked as were religious practices, itinerant peddlers of medicine and healing who advertised their skills with martial arts displays disappeared during the Cultural Revolution. When *qigong* reemerged, the government attempted to regulate it by "scientizing" it and incorporating it into the state under a national association.

Despite this effort, the party, which distrusted anyone able to attract thousands of followers, arrested some of the most popular *qigong* masters in the late 1980s. In 1992, Li Hongzhi invented a new branch of *qigong,* Falun Gong, a mild exercise system combined with Buddhist-style beliefs about the Wheel of Dharma. He quickly accumulated millions of adherents all over China, including high-level government officials. After a brief period of official government support, things started to go sour, probably aided by the fact that Li became increasingly popular outside China and finally moved to the United States in 1995. The State Commission for Sports and Physical Education rejected Falun Gong's application for official sponsorship in 1996, judging it to be insufficiently scientific and excessively superstitious, and Falun Gong became illegal under the tight restrictions on freedom of assembly. In 1999 tens of thousands of Falun Gong practitioners held sit-down demonstrations in Beijing and other cities.[58] The party leadership responded with a harsh crackdown that has continued ever since, turning what seemed to be a simple exercise system into an international human rights issue.

However, it was only in the Western worldview that a set of meditational exercises seemed so innocuous. As this chapter has demonstrated, in other worldviews the body is a microcosm of the larger cosmos. In the Confucian worldview, the right to rule, the Mandate of Heaven, is granted and taken away from rulers by heaven. Still today, the government is believed to mediate between the body and the cosmos—and that is the sensitive point, because an unhealthy populace (and a polluted natural environment) can be interpreted as the government's failure to fulfill its duty and, ultimately, as the loss of the Mandate of Heaven. Thus, overly sensitive leaders interpret everyday health-preservation practices as political protests—and they are probably correct that the waves of popular exercise forms that have swept across China since the beginning of the era of reform reflected low levels of resistance.

The latest fad in the new millennium was *yangsheng* ("life cultivation" or "life nourishment"), which revolved around the idea of a healthy daily regimen and diet that maintains the proper harmony of *yin, yang,* and *qi* within the body and with the surrounding environment.[59] It was a free-form concept interpreted by its practitioners in multiple ways, ranging from mild forms of exercise such as walking and tai chi to practices not regarded as exercise in the West, such as calligraphy and the tea ceremony. Most practitioners were middle-aged or elderly women, though men and younger people also followed the trend. The most important factor behind the fad was the withdrawal of state-provided health care and the desire of people, particularly the elderly, to avoid incurring health care expenses. Other factors included China's aging population, the early retirement age (fifty-five for women, sixty for men), the end of socialist collective life, the lack of public spaces, and the bustle and chaos of urban life (particularly stressful for the large portion of the population that had migrated from the countryside in the last three decades).

THE TURN TO EXERCISE AND EASTERN MEDICINE IN THE WEST IN THE 1960S

In the industrial West, chronic diseases surpassed infectious diseases as the leading cause of death by the 1960s. Eastern medical traditions helped to fill the void left by the medical establishment's ambivalent attitude toward exercise and holistic health. In the context of the countercultural movement of the 1960s and 1970s, yoga became globally popular. One of us, Susan Brownell, recalls the way that elite track-and-field athletes training in California pushed forward the legitimation of alternative medical traditions by demanding the inclusion of chiropractors on US national teams at international competitions. At that time, the only remedy for back pain offered by biomedical doctors was surgery, which was usually career ending (the same was true of knee injuries before the dissemination of arthroscopy in the 1980s). Athletes looking for alternatives to surgery found chiropractors, and the effectiveness of their treatments was spread by word-of-mouth.

Perhaps pushed by the popular interest in holistic health, medical professionals in the United States turned their attention to exercise. In 1964 the US National Institutes of Health established a National Center for Chronic Disease Control, which began examining the relationship between physical activity and heart disease, as well as the incorporation of exercise science into public health.[60] However, the unit was closed when funding was diverted to the Vietnam War, and exercise was not taken up at the federal level again until 1983, when the Centers for Disease Control and Prevention (CDC) convened a group of experts to examine physical activity as an integral part of public health, culminating in the establishment of the National Center for Chronic Disease Prevention and Health Promotion in 1988. In the 1990s the CDC brought the American College of Sports Medicine into the conversation; the 1995 paper that they published was labeled a "paradigm change" in thinking about the importance of exercise for public health.[61]

In response to the American "obesity epidemic" of the late twentieth and early twenty-first centuries, exercise and diet returned to center place. However, "fat talk" gained considerable prominence because experts drew upon the enormous cultural authority of bioscience and biomedicine among the general public to speak in the name of "the truth," and few challenged their authority. In fact, the "war on fat" was based on a muddled and controversial science of obesity, exercise, and diet, but the pressure to come up with solutions led to formulaic pronouncements. It was not surprising that the war was largely being lost.[62]

While the focus on pathology is still at the center of biomedical practice, recent years have witnessed greater emphasis on what has come to be known as "wellness." Yet even wellness is phrased as "preventive medicine," demonstrating the teleological focus of biomedicine on sickness—we are all heading toward sickness, so we need to take measures to "prevent" it.

·

SPORT AND THE ENVIRONMENT

The backlashes against biomedicine of the late nineteenth century and the 1960s were echoed by "back to nature" movements in sport spaces. While most premodern sports were played outdoors, by the mid-nineteenth century indoor gymnasiums, stadiums, and sports halls (such as New York's Madison Square Garden, built in 1879) were emerging in large numbers. German turners moved into open spaces, and the *Wandervögel* (migratory bird) movement made hiking into the obsession that it remains in Germany today; British horse racing and tennis were welcomed as "grass sports"; the nudist movement took off. This green wave was arrested in the 1920s with a return to concrete stadiums and indoor gymnasiums. Artificial grass (AstroTurf) was invented in 1964 by scientists working for Monsanto, the multinational chemical corporation most vilified by environmentalists. Historically, the European traditions oscillated between considering indoor sports and outdoor sports more "healthy." By contrast, the Indian and Chinese traditions have consistently preferred outdoor spaces because of the perceived connection between body and environment. What Henning Eichberg called the "enclosure of the body" by Western sport is an expression of a more comprehensive change in the configuration of the body and its daily life.[63] In the West this configuration was increasingly organized by the "performance principle": indoor spaces removed the negative effect of inclement weather on sports performances, and artificial surfaces enabled better performances. Moreover, the artificial "exploitation" of space reflected the increasing intervention of the state in the spatial disciplining of social life.

The counterculture movement of the 1960s in North America and Europe, which sought to reclaim a holistic vision of humankind, health, and the environment, led not only to the rise of alternative medicine but also to an environmentalist critique of sport. The environmental movement started to pose serious obstacles for the Olympic Games. Denver was awarded the rights to host the 1972 Winter Games, but protests by environmentalists against new facilities in the Rocky Mountains and a worsening economic situation resulted in Denver's withdrawal, and the Games were transferred to Innsbruck, Austria. The Munich 1972 Olympics were billed as the "green Olympics," but the fact that the landscape and plantings surrounding the main stadium were completely artificial helped to kick off the ecological critique of sport in West Germany. Eichberg, perhaps the only anthropologist to delve into "sport ecology," was among a group of German scholars who were spurred to a radical criticism of sport by those Olympic Games.

In 1981, Japanese environmentalists' opposition was one reason that Nagoya's bid for the 1988 Summer Games was defeated by Seoul, and in 1994, Vancouver withdrew its bid for the Winter Games due to similar pressure. As a result, the International Olympic Committee (IOC) began to take a proactive stance on environmental issues. In 1999 it developed Agenda 21 for Sport and the Environment, and "environment" was named the "third pillar" of Olympism after "sport" and "culture and education." Environmental protection and improvement were included in the evaluation of Olympic bid cities, and environmental NGOs such as Greenpeace and the Worldwide Fund for Nature began to work with organizing committees instead of against them. While sport mega-events provided a platform for increasing public awareness and publicizing the causes of environmental organizations, the overall trend was in the direction of a continued separation of body from environment through ever more high-tech equipment and facilities.

SPORTS MEDICINE AND DOPING

Experimentation with performance-enhancing substances is as old as sport. A Chinese bamboo slip manuscript dating from 165 BCE states that the herb *Aconitum* (wolfsbane) is good for "hardening the body and doubling strength [which] for days makes a person become excellent at racing."[64] Even Galen dabbled in sports medicine, creating the "Olympic victor's dark ointment," an eye salve used to treat boxers with injuries to the skin around the eyes; the British Museum tested his formula and found it an effective means of delivering morphine for transdermal pain relief.[65] The St. Louis 1904 Olympics were an occasion for experimentation with medicaments on the Olympic athletes. Thomas Hicks, the winner of the marathon, did not ingest strychnine (a poison), as is commonly stated, but rather strychnine sulfate, a stimulant. Any advantage he received was no doubt canceled out by his being denied water in the belief that hydration would hinder his performance, although he was sponged with hot water from a car radiator.[66]

It was not until the 1960s that doping received systematic attention from scientists, spurred by the heightened importance attached to international sport in general and the Olympic Games in particular amid the political tension of the Cold War. The East German government initiated a secret doping system in the 1960s that has been well documented since the fall of the Berlin Wall. It involved a cadre of scientists who experimented on athletes, including minors, with little concern for their health and psychological well-being, and often without their knowledge. The focus on the horrors of East German doping has hindered exploration of the ways in which doping developed in parallel with globalization as a whole during and after the Cold War. It was and is a global system that is integrally connected with transnational medical science. Susan Brownell, who competed in track and field in the 1970s and 1980s, remembers well reading about the death in 1985 of a fellow competitor in the heptathlon, the West German Birgit Dressel, from what appeared to be too many steroids and painkillers in her body. Many of Brownell's fellow competitors were coached by Chuck Debus, who was later banned for life by the US Track and Field Federation for, among other things, giving anabolic steroids to female athletes, including a minor, who were told they were vitamins. By the Rio de Janeiro 2016 Olympics, the World Anti-Doping Agency (WADA) was finally cracking down in a way intended to contain doping practices rather than whitewash them, including threatening to kick Russia out of the Olympic Games altogether after revelations that centrally organized doping had been revived leading up to the Sochi 2014 Winter Olympics. In the end, the entire Russian track-and-field team was excluded along with athletes in other sports who had histories of positive tests. It was the first time the IOC had taken such firm steps.

WADA's ominously named Anti-Doping Code, which subjects elite athletes to extremely invasive and stringent regimes of control, is steeped in underexamined assumptions about race, gender, sexuality, and class. It is, as Kathryn Henne has pointed out, based on a Western conception of "fair play" that is underpinned by Western ideological claims about what is "pure" and "natural."[67] It leaves many questions unanswered. One of these questions, which has received little attention despite its ubiquity in many parts of the world, is the question of what constitutes performance enhancement. Throughout Africa (and many other parts of the world), the main concern is not doping as WADA officials understand it but witchcraft and magical paraphernalia. In both wrestling in urban Senegal and soccer in Cameroon, for example, the consumption of Western-style pharmaceuticals is considerably less worrisome than the amulets, potions, prayers, and other substances and practices that athletes use openly (in wrestling in Senegal) and in secret (in soccer in Cameroon), and that, everyone is convinced, provide an unfair advantage to athletes who use them. Senegalese wrestlers accuse each other of using magic to become impervious to blows or make themselves momentarily disappear, and soccer players in Cameroon believe firmly that "medicine," "juju," or "jars," as magical substances are locally called, confer extraordinary physical powers onto those who use them (although they also do so at their peril as the use of these substances can backfire).[68] Steeped in post-Cartesian assumptions about the separation of the mind from the body and the power of science as an explanation of everything, WADA and other sport regulating agencies can only express their dismay. "We received a lot of examples, going from things that we know but also going into absolutely unknown things for me. If I don't know the names, how can I know what they contain," stated Michel D'Hooghe, chairman in 2010 of the Medical Committee for the Fédération internationale de football association. "This is certainly a challenge for WADA.... If we don't have control over these specific traditional medicines, then we can't say we have control over all the medication in football."[69]

Generally speaking, scholars recognized that the doping problem would be impossible to eliminate because it was much bigger than sport: for the past one hundred years, high-performance sport has been "a gigantic biological experiment carried out on the human organism," reflecting science's inherently amoral nature, capitalism's obsession with quantified performance, and competitive rivalries generated by the world system of nation-states.[70] In the realm of sport it is therefore possible to detect two simultaneous but contradictory trends. On the one hand, sport contributed to the attempt to recuperate the holistic body-self with an emphasis on diet, lifestyle, and harmony with the environment, a movement that was a backlash against the limitations of biomedicine, with its focus on drugs and surgery. On the other hand, in the quest for better performances, sports medicine was a leader in the treating of the alienated body of the athlete as an inanimate tool.

A GLIMPSE OF THE FUTURE THROUGH SPORTS MEDICINE

As disturbing as the Cold War legacy of the ingestion and injection of substances might be, in the second decade of the twenty-first century it was becoming clear that the future held increasingly various technologies bringing along increasingly complicated ethical dilemmas. Wheelchair athletes had long ago exceeded the records of track and road runners, but the clear separation between human and machine had allowed their segregation into Paralympic sports overseen by the International Paralympic Committee rather than the IOC. The Paralympic Games remained a separate event, albeit one of increasing prestige and social acceptance. However, when the South African 400-meter runner Oscar Pistorius reached top world levels running on two carbon-fiber prosthetic legs, the International Association of Athletics Federations quickly commissioned a study that seemed intended from the outset to exclude him from competitions with able-bodied athletes. Although Pistorius had been born with a defect that necessitated the amputation of both feet, the leaders of international sport, acquainted with the lengths to which athletes and trainers will go, understood that he was opening the door for desperate athletes to undergo amputations in order to gain an advantage through prostheses that performed better than human legs.

Pistorius challenged the decision that his Flex-Foot Cheetahs gave him an unfair advantage, and the case went to the Court of Arbitration for Sport. The first ruling was reversed based on a second study, although the study's findings were mixed. It concluded that he was "physiologically similar but mechanically dissimilar" to a runner with intact legs: his body used oxygen the same way natural-legged sprinters do (this was an open question because, lacking lower legs, he had less blood in his body and a modified circulatory system), but his body moved differently. The average elite male sprinter moves his leg from back to front in 0.37 second, but Pistorius's foot strikes were as quick as 0.28 second, largely because his prostheses were lighter than a human leg. This finding did not result in the conclusion that he gained an unfair advantage because, as it turned out, the biomechanics of running were still poorly understood even after a century of research. The scientists themselves could not agree whether it was an advantage for a runner's foot to stay on the ground for a longer or shorter time.[71] Pistorius was cleared to compete in the London 2012 Olympics, where he made it as far as the semifinals of the 400-meter race.

Genomic engineering is a futuristic technology that (as far as we know) has yet to be perfected for the use of sports, although WADA tried to get ahead of it as early as 2004 by adding gene doping to its Prohibited List, defined as the "non-therapeutic use of genes, genetic elements and/or cells that have the capacity to enhance athletic performance."[72] In 2011 an international team of researchers set off alarms when they published the results of a genetic alteration that produced "super mice" that were two to three times more muscular than normal mice, were more aggressive, and had better endurance.[73] Sport has become a leading edge of the permeation of new technologies into the human body, with associated social and ethical dilemmas. The question is whether we are heading toward "transhuman athletes" who have exceeded the bounds of normal human capabilities—and, if we are, should we try to stop it or go with the flow? Sport philosopher Andy Miah's position is that the question itself is faulty as posed, because it assumes a standardized level of species-typical ability and "natural" (nonenhanced) health and performance, both of which are impossible to establish.[74] Philosophers and sports administrators concerned with "ethics" will no doubt be debating these questions for years to come, but the area awaits research by sport anthropologists who can approach the dilemma as a question of actual practices and social negotiations rather than universal philosophical truths.

CONFIGURATIONS OF SPORT, MEDICINE, AND ENVIRONMENT

The body does not stop at the surface of the skin but reaches into the space surrounding it in ways that vary across time and across cultures.[75] As this chapter has shown, sport and exercise are enmeshed in larger cultural imaginaries about the structure of the cosmos, in particular the relationship of humans to the natural environment—many non-Western traditions define "health" as the product of a harmonious relationship between the two. In the late nineteenth century, mainstream Western biomedicine largely severed that link, although alternative voices have constantly contested that separation up to the present.

Sport industries are rapidly growing and truly global, which makes sport an excellent lens for inquiry into the contemporary bodily conditions of globalization and modernity, a realm that will become increasingly important as climate change and environmental degradation have an ever-greater impact on public health. Clearly there is much that anthropologists could say about sport, health, and the environment. However, sport anthropology does not have the size and influence of medical anthropology or environmental anthropology. As a critical mass of scholars emerges, sport anthropology will be better positioned to engage with the scholarship on health and the environment.

Perhaps if there were a greater interchange of ideas between sport anthropologists, medical anthropologists, and environmental anthropologists, all subfields might have a greater theoretical impact on the discipline, and perhaps even a greater impact on public opinion. The way to meet in the middle is to situate both sports and medicine within a holistic account of the culture of the body, which includes local definitions of the healthy and diseased body as well as its relationship to the natural environment and the larger cosmos.

FOUR

Sport, Social Class, Race, and Ethnicity

FEW ASPECTS OF EVERYDAY SOCIAL life foreground social class, ethnicity, and race more dramatically than sport, precisely because the workings of social hierarchies in society at large, which are normally so complex and often hidden from view, are so prominent in sport. However, the ways in which difference and inequality emerge in sport can be complicated and often deceptively opaque, intersecting with other kinds of social difference, including nationality, migrant status, and of course gender (discussed in chapter 5). Here we will show that ethnographic studies of sport are particularly suited to illuminate the complexity and positionality that characterize class, ethnicity, and race.

SPORT, SOCIAL DISTINCTION, AND HABITUS

Like other forms of leisure, consumption, and popular culture, sport presents a paradox: people engage in it, as either athlete or spectator, with the conviction that they are simply following their own personal inclinations, while in fact their choices are shaped by their position in the social structure, such as their class affiliation. This entanglement of social class with sport was theorized most imaginatively in the 1980s and 1990s by Pierre Bourdieu, the celebrated French sociologist who exerted considerable influence on anthropology, particularly in North America.

Bourdieu's theory is usually referred to as "practice theory" because it emphasizes how everyday practices, which are shaped by the objective conditions of daily life, inculcate a system of enduring dispositions, a habitual way of being, into the body; it is the "history incarnate in the body."[1] Bourdieu called these dispositions, which determine how people move, stand, sit, and interact with others and with the contexts in which they find themselves, *habitus*. Habitus is the product of both the structural conditions in which people find themselves, including their class position, and of their agency, in that it is manifested in bodily action. Habitus is what mediates between the individual's subjectivity and the objectivity of structures.

A vivid illustration of how this process works was provided by Greg Downey's work on Brazilian capoeira.[2] Capoeira combines dance, ritual, music, and martial arts and is generally performed by two partners inside a *roda,* or "ring" of fellow *capoeiristas,* who engage each other in continuous movement to the accompaniment of traditional instruments and call-and-response songs. An important part of the dance/sport is the legendary and politically charged history that traces its roots to African slaves and links it with resistance—although, like so many "traditional" sports, it was systematized and internationalized in the course of the twentieth century. Downey had a unique perspective on the techniques of the body involved in the sport since he studied it for a decade with a famous group in Salvador, the Brazilian city considered to have preserved the most authentic African cultural heritage. The learning of a new movement style could cause practitioners to become aware of their former, previously unconscious movement styles, some of which may have been shaped by the expectations of their gender, class, race, and so on. This could have the effect of reshaping their perception of social relationships and, in essence, remaking the way they perceived and interacted with the world around them. While Downey validated Bourdieu's theory of habitus, he also criticized Bourdieu for overemphasizing the cognitive facet of habitus and largely ignoring its neurobiological substrate of motor learning, emotions, and self-control.

Before Bourdieu, social scientific approaches to sport and related activities attributed the preference for different kinds of sporting activities by different groups in society to personal choices, without offering a theory about how such "taste" is socially constructed. In contrast, Bourdieu set the terms of debate by insisting that people's choices of sporting activities (as with many other kinds of activities, such as listening to music), either as practitioners or spectators, are profoundly informed by their class positions. As discussed below, in 1895 the international governance of rugby split into a professional (rugby league) and an amateur (rugby union) federation, with rugby union remaining a last bastion of amateurism until it finally allowed professionals in 1995. In contemporary urban France and England until recently, rugby union was distinctly associated with the middle classes, while soccer was generally practiced and watched by the working classes, even though the two sports require roughly comparable equipment and services and thus presuppose very similar kinds of economic investments (this is evidently in the process of changing in some contexts, as discussed below). Demonstrating the intersection of social class with other forms of social inequality, other factors traversed these class associations, such as region (in France, rugby is traditionally associated with the southwest), race and ethnicity (in Britain, amateur rugby is largely a white sport), and gender (male rugby players may be popular heroes, while female players are denigrated for violating norms of femininity).

But while the majority of fans and players may be of working-class backgrounds, the owners of professional teams and the leadership of powerful clubs tend to be wealthy and powerful elites. For example, the West Ham United soccer club, which is renowned for the loyalty of its quintessentially working-class East London followers, was founded in 1900 in an attempt to dissipate worker unrest and was owned by the local Cearns family dynasty from 1900 to 2006.[3]

The social-class "value" of particular sports is displayed and reproduced in social institutions like schools and clubs, in the configuration of corporate investments, in the activity choices that people make, and in myriad other ways. For example, social and cultural norms can develop in a sporting context, and so those who attend specific sports events or practice particular sports feel at home in each other's presence precisely because they share the same social position, while those who occupy different social positions feel or are made to feel excluded. In a sense, the reproduction of the social-class value of sport takes on a Weberian quality, in that class affiliation is a matter of class situation.[4] For Max Weber, social-class affiliation was fluid, and the boundaries of a class were best identified by determining the lines that the members of a class could not easily cross due to limits on social mobility. Members of a class do not automatically develop a "class consciousness," as Karl Marx posited; rather, people in the same social class act in the same fashion in a given situation because others will hold them in esteem for making the right lifestyle decisions. In these terms, when working-class people gravitate toward soccer in Britain, they contribute to the constitution of a working class.

Sport tends to exaggerate class differences by including some groups and excluding others and, working in tandem with other markers of social class, it transforms them into inequalities. As Bourdieu understood it, the social-class value of a particular sport is created in contrast with other sports; for example, tennis is viewed as a bourgeois sport in many parts of the world in contrast to other sports that do not have this connotation, and this evaluation correlates with the social position of people who typically play tennis—they constitute a bourgeoisie in contrast to members of other social classes. In Bourdieu's emphasis on the formation of such "distinctions," one can see the influence of French structuralism as it was originally conceptualized by Claude Lévi-Strauss, who posited that belief systems are organized into structures of binary oppositions that reinforce each other.[5] An example of such oppositions, elaborated below, is the historical association of soccer in Europe with violent, unrestrained, working-class masculinity, in opposition to refined, controlled, middle-class masculinity (with its closer link with femininity and the family).

Bourdieu went beyond Lévi-Strauss in the landmark work *Distinction: A Social Critique of the Judgement of Taste,* in which he combined a structuralist analysis of symbolic structures with a Marxist-inspired analysis of social class.[6] The book included a treatment of sport that was elaborated in other articles published before and after the book, most notably "Sport and Social Class" and "Program for a Sociology of Sport."[7] Bourdieu originally prepared the paper for the historic International Conference on the Olympics and Cultural Exchange held in association with the Seoul 1998 Olympics, which we describe in the introduction.[8] In all these works, Bourdieu demonstrated the systematic patterning of "taste" and its association with more classic determinants of class as it was traditionally conceived, such as income, capital, profession, and educational achievements. Sport choices are aesthetic choices similar to choices in music, food, art, and interior decoration: they constitute what Bourdieu termed "symbolic capital" that can be "converted" into other forms of capital, particularly social and material capital.

For example, in Buenos Aires, Argentina, rugby's Anglophile origins gave the sport strong elitist associations that contrast with the working-class associations of soccer, the sport of the masses—even though it had similar Anglophile origins.[9] The sport is played primarily in private clubs located in exclusive neighborhoods, whose members include current players, their fathers, and grandfathers, who are often former players, as well as women relatives, who play field hockey when they are young. Members frequent the clubs with their families from early childhood, forming tightly knit cohorts of age-mates who spend considerable time together throughout their lives, most notably in rugby training while they are in the prime of their early twenties. Most rugby players are poised to take over family corporations or professional practices after their university studies. They frequently find their spouses among fellow players' female relatives, who are likely to be field hockey-playing members of the club, and they nurture social ties with other members with whom they will later form professional networks of mutual support that will last a lifetime.

Argentine rugby clubs are thus prime sites for the production of elite privilege and its reproduction over lifetimes and generations. They illustrate sport as symbolic capital that can be converted into other forms of capital, including social and affinal ties, and professional networks. Particular moral values attributed to the sport are also said to characterize their position in the social hierarchy. This morality showcases fair play, loyalty to the immediate group, and respect for tradition, all deemed to be the sport's "true values." The genealogy of these values harks back to the ideology of gentlemanly behavior of English Victorian elites. This morality animates nonsporting activities that club members organize, including religious "missions" to disadvantaged neighborhoods, where members visit the sick, feed and clothe the poor, and organize games and artistic activities for children of indigent families. Participants in these "solidarity activities" view them as the enactment of a moral stance concerned with the disadvantaged Other and not with material gain—although, from an anthropological perspective, they serve to maintain the same social hierarchies that are enacted through sport. Paying attention to social dynamics that parallel sport, rather than simply focusing on sport itself, demonstrates that ethnography can shed light on the relationship between sport and the social and ideological contexts in which it operates.

Participants rationalize the socially laden value of sport not in terms of social class but in terms of personal choices. Working-class people in Argentina avoid rugby events because of the pretentiousness and exclusivity they associate with them, and their own boisterousness is not particularly welcomed by the upper-middle-class people who attend games. In contrast, traditionally middle-class British people until recently did not attend soccer matches because they disliked the swearing, drunkenness, and disorderliness of soccer stadiums, which frequently exploded into soccer hooliganism. The spectacular demonstrations of working-class masculine power, capacity for violence, and taste for revelry and excess that characterized soccer hooliganism were perhaps the most class- and gender-marked of sport-related phenomena in the past half century.[10] The middle-class explanation of the dislike of soccer as a matter of "taste" is an example of what Bourdieu called "misrecognition," namely the denial that actions are politically and economically motivated despite their clear association with political and economic interests.

Misrecognition is also at the root of the commonly held view that the characteristics of sport in general or specific sports in particular are inscribed onto the bodies and dispositions of members of particular social classes, being part and parcel of habitus. Thus, in France at the time Bourdieu was writing on the topic, sports like boxing, soccer, and rugby expressed an instrumental relation to the body among the working classes in which energy, pain, and even danger played an important role. Rugby had "affinities with the most typically popular dispositions, the cult of manliness and the taste for a fight, toughness in 'contact' and resistance to tiredness and pain, and [a] sense of solidarity . . . and revelry."[11] In contrast, sports that are largely practiced by members of the middle classes (e.g., walking, jogging, gym training) treat the body as an end in itself and generate a "body-for-others." In China during the Maoist period, peasant women were viewed as particularly suited to become professional athletes because agrarian work and social oppression had prepared them for the hard physical work, obedience to authority, and "bitterness" of sport training.[12] Similar views about rural black Cubans informed the national elite sports programs in revolutionary Cuba, reinforcing racial inscriptions etched onto Cuban athletes, as we discuss later in this chapter.

Of course, certain sports require capital and time that only members of privileged classes can afford. Such is the case of sports like polo, hang gliding, and alpine skiing, all of which assume, as they are practiced today in complex societies, access to expensive equipment and services (e.g., travel, facilities, personnel). Thus the correlation between sport and social class can appear straightforward in terms of the material resources that members of different social classes can access. However, material power may explain why only some social classes practice certain sports, but it does not completely explain why certain sports attract the interest of members of particular social classes. Stock car racing is a pastime one associates with the working classes of the American South, despite the fact that racing cars involves vast amounts of money and other material resources (perhaps most dramatically expressed in the winner's wastage of champagne at the end of the race), to which most fans do not have access.[13] One can also argue that the materiality of the practice of certain sports is the result, rather than the precondition, of their class affiliation. When Niko Besnier lived in Switzerland as a child in the early 1960s, skiing was a threadbare affair that involved regular warm clothing, wooden skis that most people could afford, and affordable lift passes up the slopes, which were located just a few kilometers from home. It was only when the sport gained popularity among middle and upper-middle classes in industrial countries in the post–World War II boom years that it began to "require" expensive equipment, specialized clothing, and onerous travel. These are the "hidden entry requirements . . . that keep these sports closed to the working class . . . and which maintain them . . . among the surest indicators of bourgeois pedigree."[14]

One important aspect of the entanglement of sport with social hierarchies is that a specific sport may have radically divergent class values across different societies. For example, while soccer in Europe and South America is largely associated with the working classes and with masculinity, in North America, where interest in the sport is relatively new, it has strong stereotypical associations with white middle-class privilege, in addition to having been popular among Hispanics for a long time. It is also prominently a women's sport; when the United States won the 2015 FIFA Women's World Cup, it had more registered female soccer players than the rest of the world combined.[15] The stereotype of the "soccer mom" in US society, who ferries her brood of soccer-playing children in an oversize SUV, has come to embody the intense commitment of middle-class North American parents to youth sport in particular, and to their children's futures in general.[16]

In some societies, social class may be largely irrelevant to the meaning of particular sports. Such is the case of Pacific Island societies like Fiji, Tonga, and Samoa, where rugby union is a national passion shared by virtually everyone and does not index class identification, in sharp contrast to rugby in Britain and North America. In China it is generally believed that *all* sports are identified with the working class due to the traditional bias against manual labor and esteem for education, expressed in the proverb "Those who work with their brains rule; those who work with their brawn are ruled."[17] However, the wealthy cosmopolitan elite that began to emerge as a social class in the new millennium increasingly subscribed to the international class symbolism of sports such as tennis, golf, and Formula One racing, utilizing these sports to mark their elite and cosmopolitan class membership.

The class associations of a sport may change over time. The building of all-seater soccer stadiums in England in the 1990s attracted more affluent fans and family groups, who had previously been intimidated by the working-class fans in the standing sections.[18] In South Asia a contact sport called *kabaddi* was for a long time associated with the rural lower classes and castes until it emerged in the late twentieth century as a national symbol in India and Bangladesh and as a symbol of ethnic distinction among overseas Indians, sparking considerable interest and a sudden influx of large sums of money into the sport in the homeland.[19]

Rugby in France has followed a complex geographic and social trajectory. Originally introduced from Britain by Pierre de Coubertin after the French defeat in the Franco-Prussian War of 1870–71, ostensibly to boost the morale of the dispirited Parisian bourgeoisie, the sport eventually "migrated" to the southwest of the country and for a long time remained associated with that region and with its dominant characteristics (republicanism, anticlericalism, socialism). Since the 1990s the sport has undergone major transformations: heavily mediatized by television channels that found its broadcasting rights more affordable than those of soccer, it also gained corporate sponsors whose models replaced the traditional management structure based on local sponsorship. These new developments increased the appeal of the sport to the middle class, women, and families throughout the country, who gravitated toward it in order to distance themselves from soccer.[20]

Where rugby is an elite sport, its practitioners and aficionados tend to foreground the qualities that elites identify with, such as fair play, generosity (of a certain kind), honesty, and studied disinterest. In Japan rugby is associated primarily with elite universities (particularly Meiji, Waseda, and Keio Universities, three private elite universities in Greater Tokyo founded during the Meiji Restoration of 1868–1912) and secondarily with large corporations that own teams in order to maximize their public visibility. Aficionados and practitioners of the sport see it as embodying specifically Japanese ideals, such as obedience, humility, and respect, which are also deeply conservative, belonging to the gerontocratic and class order, and which together define the "spirit" *(tamashii)* of the sport.[21] As these many examples illustrate, the system of class distinction in sports may not be as watertight as Bourdieu makes it out to be. The class value of sports changes over time; middle-class people are known to engage in "slumming" by participating in working-class sporting activities (e.g., the recent craze for mixed martial arts among London City bankers and lawyers);[22] and the new rich in rapidly developing economies may rapidly remake the traditional symbolism.

In addition, the relationship of sport and social class may be mediated by other kinds of social hierarchies. For example, in US high schools sports such as American football, baseball, and basketball occupy a very prominent place in the life of the institution (much more so than in secondary schools in other countries), as evidenced by the fact that football teams often come to represent metonymically the entire high school. But not everyone plays, watches, or is interested in sports, and thus sports become a definer of different categories of students. In the midwestern high school where linguistic anthropologist Penny Eckert conducted fieldwork in the early 1980s, "jocks" were students whose lives revolved around sport; they displayed a squeaky-clean lifestyle, believed firmly in the school's institutional values, and were viewed as popular and attractive. They could be boys or girls, although the latter had to work harder to achieve popularity, by associating themselves with male jocks, for instance. "Burnouts," in contrast, had no interest in sports and other school-related institutions, were generally rebellious, and were often suspected of taking drugs.[23] While these categories (variations of which are found in many high schools in the country to this day) do not constitute social classes, and they were understood locally as matters of "personality," they mirror social hierarchies: jocks were likely to have middle-class parents and to become middle-class adults (were it just for the fact that they acquired social capital through their acceptance of the institution), while burnouts were generally from working-class families and were heading for a working-class future. Thus sport was pivotal in defining the jock–burnout hierarchy, which in turn was instrumental to the class hierarchies that characterize the broader society. And, incidentally, Eckert's ethnography underlined the little-remarked fact that, far from "empowering" people, sport and all its associations can in fact be deeply alienating for some.

In industrial societies of the Global North, the structure and nature of social class itself have undergone massive changes since Bourdieu developed his analysis of class and sport on the basis of the structure of French society in the 1970s. In many societies of the developing world, class affiliation is crucially dependent on the extent of one's cosmopolitan resources, and the sports one practices both reflect and create this cosmopolitanism. Bourdieu's model of society as a closed system cannot account for this. In Tonga, for example, middle-class people have adopted fitness regimes imported from New Zealand and other places, and they are seen jogging and exercising before dawn, conscious of the fact that bodies exposed in plain sight during daylight hours would be frowned upon by their compatriots. These new practices are also associated with new middle-class ways of seeing the body and a redefinition of the fat body as a "medical problem."[24]

Such rapid transformations of the relationship between class and sports do not invalidate Bourdieu's basic analysis of sport as one component of a class habitus that operates in relation to other components, all of which work together to reinforce the position of a given class in the socioeconomic hierarchy. What is needed, however, is a more flexible model of how the relationship between social class and sport articulates with other dimensions of social difference and inequality.

ELITE SPORT PROFESSIONALIZATION AND SOCIAL CLASS

Professionalization is the transformation of a sport from an amateur activity played by athletes who are officially unremunerated (but who often receive compensations unofficially) into a professional activity in which athletes are salaried. Needless to say, nonprofessional athletes who devote considerable time to an amateur sport must have a way to support themselves and their families, whether from their own or their family's private wealth, school or college scholarships, sponsors, or other means.

Rugby has been the object of acrid debate over professionalization on two occasions in its history, separated by exactly one century. In 1895 conflict arose between players and managers of the sport in the South and North of England. The practitioners of the sport in the South were predominantly privileged gentlemen while practitioners in the industrial North were largely workers who had to give up work time if they wanted to play seriously. The northerners insisted that they had to be compensated for the time off needed for practices and games, while the southerners wanted rugby to remain untainted by material concerns. The conflict was eventually resolved by splitting the sport into two different codes, namely rugby union, which has thirteen-a-side, and rugby league, which has fifteen-a-side. They share many features but also possess interesting class differences.[25] In Britain at least, rugby union has remained a solidly middle- and upper-middle-class sport through its associations with universities, elite clubs, and well-off players; rugby league immediately professionalized after the fission, was long largely confined to the industrial North of England, and has maintained its working-class associations wherever it is played.

One hundred years after the fission of the two codes, rugby union had become a very different sport. It had global reach, involved large amounts of money, was the object of serious commercial interests (e.g., sponsorships, television rights, club ownerships), and was the focus of international mega-events, such as the Rugby World Cup, organized every four years since 1987 by the sport's international governing body, the International Rugby Board (IRB, renamed World Rugby in 2014). But players still could not officially receive a salary and were increasingly unhappy about a situation that had reached a high level of hypocrisy, as top-level clubs found all sorts of roundabout ways of remunerating players. The 1995 World Cup was hosted by the new South Africa, marking its reentry into international sport after the end of apartheid; Nelson Mandela would make it famous by donning the jersey of the Springboks, the national rugby union team, to present the trophy to the captain of the winning South African team, a gesture of enormous symbolic significance given rugby's long-standing association with apartheid. In the months leading to the game, players around the world threatened to go on strike if the IRB did not professionalize the sport. Fearing the cancellation of a World Cup that had particular symbolic significance, not to mention the jettisoning of the enormous commercial interests involved, IRB officials gave in, rugby union was professionalized, and players were finally officially recognized as the professionals that they had long since become.

The IRB's decision had to be implemented by the national unions of each of its member countries, which numbered sixty-seven in 1995. In countries where rugby union continued to have strong elitist overtones, the process was not without conflict. Japanese opponents of professionalization argued that it would damage the "spirit" *(tamashii)* that the sport is supposed to embody and the conservative ideals referred to earlier.[26] Professionalization radically transformed the organization of corporate rugby. Corporations could now hire athletes whose sole occupation was playing rugby, in contrast to pre-1995 days, when athletes worked as full-time corporate employees and trained in their spare time. Instead of lifetime employment, corporations began offering athletes short-term contracts, particularly as Japan went into protracted recession. Clubs could now drop players much more easily, and athletes became much more mobile as their futures became considerably more uncertain.

The Irish Rugby Football Union was the last major European rugby union to turn professional. It did not do so until 2000 after Ulster Rugby, one of the four regional clubs on the island, won the European Cup with a team of amateurs and semiprofessionals against wholly professional clubs from elsewhere in Europe. Professionalism first cut a swath through the ranks of local administrators and coaches as they were replaced by foreign administrators and coaches with university degrees in coaching and sports administration and globally recognized professional qualifications. Local athletes also felt the bite of professionalism as they began to lose their places in Ulster Rugby squads and development programs to professionals imported from South Africa, New Zealand, and Argentina.[27] "Local lads" were displaced by foreign talent, much to the displeasure of Ulster Rugby's core supporters. All told, the professionalization of rugby union transformed local sport into a global competitive field by detrimentally affecting local athletes' working conditions in the sport while also providing additional opportunities previously unavailable to athletes, a topic we take up in chapter 8.

ETHNICITY IN AND THROUGH SPORT

Sport can be deeply embroiled in the politics of ethnic identification in societies where ethnicity holds an important place. Here we understand ethnicity as a form of identification based on an ideology of a common history and common social and cultural practices, such as language, religion, and history. An ethnic group is always defined in reference to a larger context, particularly the state, as well as in reference to other ethnic groups that compete with it for resources or recognition, or that are at least politically relevant to it. Ethnicity differs from the nation in that an ethnic group does not have political sovereignty, although ethnic identification is the basis of claims to political autonomy among some ethnic groups around the world, such as the Kurds and the Uighurs. Ethnicity may or may not overlap with identification in terms of race, which is an ideology of sameness and difference based on putative physiological characteristics. Ethnic identity is as much the product of feelings of commonality within the group as it is the elaboration of difference between the group and other groups, as Norwegian anthropologist Fredrik Barth argued in his classic work on the subject.[28] Ethnic identity constantly needs to be negotiated and affirmed in opposition to other ethnic groups, which may be facilitated by sports, since people can identify as members of a particular ethnic group through the sport they play or do not play, the way they play sport, and the particular role they adopt in sport.

The most straightforward examples of the role that ethnicity plays in sport are ethnic groups that claim ownership of a sport in which few outsiders take part (either because they are not interested or because they are not allowed to do so). Such sports thus serve as cultural and social markers to distinguish ethnic groups from others. These are commonly called folk sports (putting aside the potentially pejorative connotation of the term *folk*), which have been variously presented as evidence of the ingenuity and exoticism of those who practice it, as the focus of ethnic and cultural pride, or as contexts for affirmation of intragroup solidarity. High-jumping among the Tutsi of Rwanda *(gisimbuka urukiramende)*, which we mentioned in chapter 3, was a spectacular competition in which men jumped to reputedly extreme heights. It captured the imagination of generations of Western commentators and generated considerable debate about the alleged physiological capacities of different races, with the Tutsi being equated unproblematically with all "Africans."[29] The Waiwai on the Guyana-Brazil border practice a particular kind of archery competition in which winning is secondary to the framing of the masculine body as a hunter.[30] Mongolian wrestling thrives in China, where most ethnic sports are declining as part of the social changes accompanying rapid economic development. It unites the Mongol ethnic group across Siberia, the Republic of Mongolia, and Inner Mongolia (a province of China).[31] Some sports are widely regarded as national sports in the location where they originated but become ethnic sports when they are practiced in migrant communities that have moved elsewhere; such is the case of sumo, which is widely regarded as a uniquely Japanese sport (despite the increasing presence of non-Japanese participants in the last few decades); when ethnic Japanese people practice it in other locations, it is regarded as an ethnic sport. Marvin Opler's account of sumo in a World War II Japanese American internment camp in California is one of the first accounts of sporting practices published in an anthropology journal.[32] Opler was particularly sensitive to the generational tensions between first-generation migrants and their offspring, which played out as conflicts about the proper protocol in the practice of the sport.

Sports can acquire significant political meaning when ethnic groups characterize themselves as "indigenous," that is, as having a particularly strong attachment to a territory owing to their lengthier history of settlement than other groups that also claim it as home. Indigeneity is associated in particular with settler colonialism, in which a settler group has colonized a territory and subsequently become the dominant majority, marginalizing the original inhabitants (e.g., the United States, Canada, South Africa, Australia, New Zealand, Israel). In Hawai'i, where native Hawaiians are now a largely impoverished indigenous minority, surfing, which was practiced in precontact days, had a complex history of successive disappearance and revival, appropriation and reappropriation: it survived proscription by Calvinist missionaries in the nineteenth century to eventually become an international sport, one of the most exalted symbols of the culture of leisure. Its establishment on different shores around the world rode the tide of US imperialism, while back in its birthplace it remained a focus of political struggles over indigenous rights.[33]

In another settler-colonial society, namely Aotearoa New Zealand, the indigenous population, the Māori, have made rugby their particular trademark. Not only do many Māori men excel at the sport, but also many Māori people see the sport as a way to reclaim a *mana,* or spiritual power, which has been seriously compromised by a century and a half of colonization by white settlers. But this project is fragile: not only are some Māori highly critical of the limited sociopolitical significance of rugby excellence, but also it is confined to the boundaries of the New Zealand nation-state. This means that when Māori rugby players manage to obtain contracts in countries where the sport is not particularly prized, they become ordinary talented sportsmen, devoid of the patina of indigeneity and potentially encumbered by the stigma of race.[34]

In yet another settler-colonial society, namely Australia, the Sydney 2000 Olympics were hailed as the "reconciliation games" because they were supposed to mark the moment when Aboriginal Australians and Torres Strait Islanders, the country's indigenous peoples, began to achieve parity and respect in Australian society and leave behind their great suffering in the course of the European settlement of the country. Cathy Freeman, an Aboriginal Australian, lit the Olympic flame in the opening ceremony and later won the 400-meter race, becoming a national hero. The opening ceremony featured Aboriginal themes in five of seven segments. However, Aboriginal protests leading up to the games gained international attention, and many pointed out that the inspiring public performances contrasted with the reality of social inequality between Aboriginal and white Australians, which had hardly changed over the decades.[35]

Whenever ethnicity is invoked, nationalism (which we discuss at length in chapter 7) usually hovers uneasily in the background, and the often-tense relationship between ethnicity and nationalism is played out through sport. In Australia, for example, the national sports are widely recognized as cricket, rugby union, rugby league, and "Aussie rules" football, depending on the region and social class, but ethnic minorities in this multiethnic nation identify with other sports. Such is the case of Greek and Macedonian Australians, descendants of migrants who moved to Australia when the government favored migration from European countries during the post–World War II years. Greeks and Macedonians brought with them a passion for soccer, which to this day helps them retain an identity distinct from the Anglo majority.[36] The ethnic clubs in which soccer is played are deeply embroiled in old animosities carried over from the old countries. Soccer matches are often ways for members of the ethnic groups to act out political conflicts. For the Australian state interested in a "unified" nation, this divisiveness constitutes a major problem. In the 1990s national bodies responsible for regulating the sport encouraged clubs to change their names to ethnically neutral-sounding ones and attempted to ban from soccer matches ethnonationalist symbols such as flags. Initially, clubs strongly opposed the pressure, but they eventually relented, and soccer became an "Australian game."

Yet despite efforts to downplay ethnic identification and unify the nation, Australia has emerged as a cultural hybrid composed of ethnic groups that maintain their distinct identities even as they also emphasize their integration into the nation. So when clubs yielded to the pressure of changing their names to neutral terms, fans continued to refer to them by their old ethnic names. At games, some fans shout, "Go, Lakers!" while others chant, "Hellas! Hellas!" (the Greek name for Greece). Soccer thus expresses competing ways of imagining a diverse and complex nation and the place of ethnicity in this nation, while simultaneously defining "what it means to be Greek, Macedonian, and Australian in the global world of the late twentieth century."[37]

In many nation-states around the world, no ethnic group forms a clear "minority" that is numerically, economically, and politically inferior to a "majority," but different ethnic groups vie for power with one another on the national level, and sport can be a microcosm of these struggles. Cricket in Trinidad and Tobago is particularly compelling because it had been the focus of one of the foundational texts in postcolonial theory, C. L. R. James's *Beyond a Boundary*, which we discussed in chapter 2.[38] In James's time, Trinidad and Tobago was a British colony under the control of a small group of sugarcane and cocoa plantation owners and other colonial figures, while the bulk of the population, descendants of slaves forcibly brought in from Africa and of indentured laborers brought in from India, worked for the white elites. As James argued, cricket was where Afro- and Indo-Trinidadians beat their colonial masters at their own game, and the sport was a major channel of anticolonial resistance.

After the country's independence from the United Kingdom in 1962, the numerically equal Afro-Trinidadian and Indo-Trinidadian populations began competing for political control of the country, as the collapse of the plantation economy marginalized the white and Creole elites and the country became the richest in the region thanks to significant oil reserves.[39] No longer the anticolonial sport of yesteryear, cricket became a field of competition between the two ethnic groups (which refer to themselves and to each other as "races"): today the majority of club managers and owners are Indo-Trinidadians, but they feel that Afro-Trinidadians actively exclude them from playing the game, while Afro-Trinidadians complain about being excluded from managerial positions. Here, there is no obvious master to fight, as was the case in the colonial period; rather, the situation is one of competing paradigms of mutual marginalization and of competing claims for belonging, in a country where everyone descends from immigrants.

In some situations, sport itself serves as the trigger for the "rediscovery" of ethnicity and its recuperation as a significant aspect of people's self-understanding. In Dakar, Senegal's capital, ethnic identification has somewhat waned as people from different ethnic groups have mixed and increasingly speak the dominant language of the country, Wolof; in fact, urban Senegalese find any mention of ethnic differences distasteful because they believe that ethnicity endangers national unity, as it has done in neighboring countries with often terrible consequences. The social category that has replaced ethnic identification is religious affiliation linked to the distinction between urbanites, stereotyped as cosmopolitan and savvy, and rural dwellers, considered to be unsophisticated country bumpkins. However, the most popular and commercially viable sport in the country, wrestling with punches (*laamb ji* in Wolof), is suffused with "traditional" practices that people associate with the countryside, particularly the use of magic (amulets, potions, Islamic prayers, animal sacrifices, etc.), which is believed to have considerable effects on the outcome of wrestling bouts (see chapter 3). These practices, for which wrestlers contract the services of specialists or *marabouts,* often at considerable expense, are explicitly oriented toward the countryside, where "tradition" is supposed to have survived and where particular magical practices are associated with specific ethnic groups. In recent years, however, wrestlers have been "rediscovering" their ethnic identity (or making it up when in doubt) in order to underline or strengthen their identities as wrestlers. Therein lies a paradox: as urban Senegal is becoming increasingly cosmopolitan and embedded in a globalized world, and wrestling is increasingly commercialized, ethnicity is gaining new visibility through the sport.[40]

Sport may serve ethnic minorities as a political tool for recognition, but sport may also work in a different way when it helps to "make majorities" at the expense of minority groups that the majority is anxious to marginalize.[41] As we briefly mentioned in chapter 2, rugby is the national sport in Fiji, an island nation of close to nine hundred thousand inhabitants in the southwest Pacific. Virtually everyone is a fan. The country specifically excels in rugby sevens, a version of the game played by seven participants per side in a blisteringly fast fourteen minutes. Fijian nationals' interest in the sport verges on an obsession: life stops when important international tournaments are broadcast on television, the game is played daily on every patch of grass available, images of rugby players are displayed prominently everywhere, and professional rugby players are regarded as national heroes.[42]

Almost all male indigenous Fijians play rugby from very early childhood. They see the sport as embodying the central values that they associate with their ethnicity, referred to as *i-Taukei*—namely a deep sense of hierarchy, a strong sociocentric orientation (to the team, the extended family, the village, and the country), and a devotion to Christianity in its various denominations. All games are preceded and followed by prayer huddles, and a biblical verse is emblazoned on the national team's jerseys. Many *i-Taukei* men display a powerful muscularity and large body size that is viewed as particularly well suited to the sport—and is frequently racialized in global rugby, where aggressive offensive moves have become increasingly more common than avoidance.

When rugby sevens was added to the list of Olympic sports for the Rio 2016 Olympic Games, it suddenly gave Fiji a visibility it never had before: only two athletes from Fiji had previously met the qualifying standards for an Olympic sport since the country began participating in the games in 1956. The men's rugby final pitted Fiji against Great Britain, the country's former colonial master, from which it gained independence in 1970.

On the evening of August 11, 2016, Fiji won its first-ever Olympic medal—a gold medal in men's rugby sevens (figure 8). Two of us, Niko Besnier and Susan Brownell, were present in the stands. The atmosphere in the stadium was electric. Many in the audience were rooting for the Fijian team, including some Irish and Argentine fans who were cheering against Great Britain, reflecting long-standing historical tensions. The crowd was festive and lighthearted, and the beer was flowing freely. Like all rugby sevens matches, the game was fast, dynamic, and unpredictable. The match showcased Fijian rugby at its very best: its seven players moved in perfect coordination, the ball seeming to float as it was passed from player to player. The final score was 43–7.

FIGURE 8. A member of Fiji's rugby sevens national team fends off a British defender at Fiji's extraordinary first Olympic gold medal (Rio de Janeiro, August 2016/Niko Besnier).

At the medal ceremony, where International Olympic Committee member Princess Anne Windsor was awarding the gold medals, team members followed the traditional Fijian approach to interacting with a high-ranking person. Each player knelt in front of the princess as she awarded him a gold medal—after which he clapped three times using the hollowed palms of his hands, a gesture called *cobo*. The players' display of respect warmed viewers' hearts, and media coverage of the game and its award ceremony went viral.

The country was united by the team's astonishing victory: the rugby sevens team members, already adulated in Fiji, returned home as heroes, and the government declared a national holiday on August 22 in their honor. Many in Fiji saw the victory as evidence that God was, after all, on Fiji's side, after the devastation of parts of the country in February of that year by tropical cyclone Winston, the second-most powerful cyclone ever recorded in world history. Around the world, rugby audiences responded with wild appreciation to Fijian rugby players' performances of indigeneity, such as the respectful *cobo* at the Olympic medal ceremony and the dramatic *bole* (war dance) they performed before the game, as they generally do.

What few realized is that these performances only represent part of Fiji's population. Fiji is a multicultural society. Indigenous Fijians account for 57 percent of the population; a large proportion of the rest of the population are descendants of immigrants from India who arrived as indentured laborers or free migrants during the late nineteenth and early twentieth centuries, when the islands were a British colony.[43] Interethnic relations in Fiji have been tense in recent history, prompting many Indo-Fijians to emigrate, causing their population to drop to 38 percent.

Indo-Fijians are excluded from rugby in many ways. Very few play it, and indigenous Fijians explain this by saying that their generally slighter physique is unsuitable for the roughness of the sport. When Indo-Fijian young men try to play rugby, they are generally jeered at. Their own families discourage them from playing, saying that it will expose them to physical harm at the hands of the much larger and rougher indigenous Fijians, who might take pleasure in intimidating the Indo-Fijians (whose dominance in the business sector many indigenous Fijians resent). Indo-Fijian parents discourage their sons from playing rugby, arguing that they need them as healthy heirs to the family's business.

Everyone in Fiji—women and men, indigenous Fijians and Indo-Fijians— is brought together by a passion for rugby. But some are relegated to being spectators. Women are largely expected to support their rugby-playing male relatives by cooking meals for teams and washing their muddy clothes after games. Indo-Fijians are typically enthusiastic supporters of the sport, but then again not being so would risk endangering the perception of their allegiance to the country and its political majority.

The men's Olympic win was rightly celebrated; they scored an amazing victory for the sport and for a small country like Fiji. But, as is true of many highly publicized sporting events, behind it lay a complex reality to which most of the world's fans remained oblivious.

ETHNIC GAMES

A different type of ethnic expression in sport is seen in sports events that celebrate ethnic identity, which have typically been organized from the top down by socialist states, and from the bottom up in liberal democracies. The Soviet Union was the first country to promote ethnic games as part of a state policy toward minority ethnicities. Drawing from the German folklore tradition, Soviet ethnologists classified groups into officially recognized minority nationalities, utilizing ethnic games and sports along with weightier categories such as language and religious practice. The Tashkent Games of 1920, also called the First Central Asian Games, were designed to draw the mainly Turkic peoples of what were then independent republics into the Soviet order, at a time when the Soviet state had very little real power on its Central Asian frontiers. The USSR also included demonstrations of folk games and dancing in the opening ceremonies of conventional sporting events, including the First Workers' Spartakiad of 1928.

In a similar vein, the People's Republic of China organized ethnic minorities into fifty-five officially recognized "minority nationalities" that were regulated by the central government. Since 1953 the National Games of Ethnic Minorities have been a major showcase of China's ethnic policy. The events feature sporting activities drawn from the "traditional sports" of the minority populations, such as Mongolian wrestling, Korean swinging, Tibetan archery, dragon-boat racing, top spinning, and shuttlecock kicking. In the reform era (1978 to present) ethnic difference and exoticism have been increasingly reified through tourism and commodification. When Susan Brownell attended the twelfth installment of the Ethnic Games in 2007, she found that the Games had fallen into disrepair because the national attention was focused instead on the upcoming Beijing Olympics, and most of the participants in the sports were Han students from sports institutes recently recruited to learn the "ethnic" sports just for the event. When she asked the Han graduate student who was her chaperone to the opening ceremonies why the dancers in ethnic costume were mostly Han, the student replied that the level of the ethnic minorities was not high enough for national television.[44] Comparable events elsewhere, such as the Arctic Winter Games, which have been held in Canada since 1970, and the North American Indigenous Games, held since 1990, possibly have a less reifying effect in that they feature both "traditional" and Olympic sports played by athletes who actually identify as indigenous minorities.[45]

SPORT AND RACE

As we explained in chapter 3, the pseudoscience of race has long played a central but rather sordid role in the history of modern sport, and some forms of anthropology have been complicit in this role. To this day, pundits continue to attempt to explain why members of certain racial groups are overrepresented in certain sports, particularly at the elite level, by speculating that racial groups are characterized by genetically determined physiological attributes (e.g., muscle structure, height, coordination) that allegedly better prepare them to excel in certain sports. But these arguments always run into counterfactual and logical conundrums. "To argue . . . that a specific athlete is 'naturally' endowed is trivial. To argue that a group is 'naturally' endowed, with any degree of rigor, simply requires a lot of well-controlled data. . . . And if those data are impossible to collect, that means that the question itself was not framed scientifically in the first place."[46] Any attempt to define race and distinguish among racial groups using biological arguments is bound to fail because, however one defines a racial group, there will always be more variation within it than between it and other groups. In addition, physical traits, be they phylogenetic or physiological, are inherited independently of one another, making it impossible to define a race by predicting the occurrence of one trait (say, skin pigmentation or the color of the eyes) in terms of the occurrence of another trait (say, the distribution of muscles).[47] Race, however, is of deep historical, social, and political significance, because as a cultural construction it has been and continues to be employed to justify profoundly significant social inequality, from slavery to discrimination.

The labor market is one location where racialized politics permeate sports. This is true of professional baseball in the Caribbean countries where the sport is played. American and Japanese professional baseball organizations that develop talented youth in the Dominican Republic separate young Latino men from their Anglo and Asian bosses and proceed to evaluate them in terms of the alleged biological traits of "disposition" and projected athletic ability. These labels affect their potential earnings and even determine whether they will continue as employees in these organizations. Being labeled "headstrong" or "head cases" is based on supposed racial attributes not applied to white American prospects.[48] Professional baseball organizations' ongoing search for talent in the Caribbean is part of a broader "progressive ethnocentrism" that permeates not just professional baseball but echoes colonial and neocolonial constructions of colonizing and colonized bodies.[49]

Some have argued that the dominance of traditionally oppressed groups in sport (or at least certain sports) is evidence that sport has become an even field in which meritocratic principles prevail, contributing to the gradual "de-racialization" of society.[50] This argument quickly falls apart when one steps off the playing field or race track and considers sport as a hierarchical structure that continues to be regulated, owned, managed, and coached by (male) members of dominant racial groups and social classes. This situation is not unique to professional sport but permeates sport at all levels.

In many communities in the United States, high school sports play a significant role in the race relations that permeate all social institutions, including the local youth sports infrastructures. In the small town of Tama in Iowa, in America's "heartland," inhabited by whites and Mesqwaki Indians, whites imagined the "Indian" youth in the course of the twentieth century as "natural" athletes who had physical skills linked to "nature," like swimming and running, images that find their roots in American frontier mythology.[51] Any Mesqwaki youth playing a "white sport" such as football or basketball was celebrated as a "super Indian" who sought to assimilate into white ways of life by leaving the Mesqwaki settlement, "escaping poverty," and adopting the outward trappings and signs of the "civilized" world. When Mesqwaki athletes did not make this transition, despite their acclaimed athletic success, they were branded as "hell-raising Indians" who lacked the discipline to make something of themselves. These stereotypes were emblematic of the power relations in which local white leaders actively worked to keep most Mesqwaki youth off the local high school squads. One coach's attempts to recruit and maintain Mesqwaki youth on his teams led to direct conflict with the local Booster Club, an organization of white business leaders, and he was eventually fired. Five other high school coaches shared similar experiences with the Booster Club or other prominent citizens but would not provide the ethnographer, Doug Foley, with details for fear of angering those individuals.

The high school coach's precarious political position is not unique to Tama, Iowa. In a high school in a Texas town where Foley also conducted research, the football coach faced comparable challenges from Anglos and Latinos, whose mutual misrecognition structured the composition of the local football team.[52] Every coach lived under enormous pressure from parents and children of both groups to guide the team to victory, and this pressure was so intense that many coaches did not stay long in the town. The racial tensions affected more than the head coach. The athletes themselves were acutely aware of the effect of the local racial politics in what was supposed to be a haven beyond the realm of politics, namely sport. Authoritarian practices, racist comments, and marginalization within a squad fueled an underlying suspicion that rich whites rigged the local sports scene in favor of their kids, leading many nonwhite youth to simply walk away after concluding that one could be technically, but not socially, good enough to play.

Athletes may socialize and all pull together as a "team," yet they also organize themselves into specific groups that often mirror racial politics in the broader social context. Oaxacan migrants in Los Angeles and Asian Americans in Atlanta both take part in basketball leagues that cater to their specific racialized identities. In Mexico, Oaxacans play basketball to forge a transnational sense of identity that cuts across the US-Mexico border and maintains transnational connections for young migrants.[53] Similarly, South Asian Americans play pickup basketball among themselves in Atlanta and also form "South Asian–only" clubs to play in the amateur community leagues in Atlanta.[54] The "Atlanta Outkasts" faced particularly strident forms of racism associated with life in the American South, where their very presence disrupts the black-white racial binary. In Tennessee, Lao immigrants assiduously avoid sport because the discourse of "playing" carries negative connotations supposedly attached to African Americans and Native Americans.[55] These various examples demonstrate that sport often does not lead to racial integration but rather serves to maintain social difference.

Sports in which participants are both social elites *and* a dominant racial group have frequently been particularly reluctant to open up to other races. When it emerged as an international sport in the late nineteenth century, figure skating was controlled by social elites in western Europe and North America for whom the exclusive clubs served as social clubs that revolved around ice dancing. In the United States the centers for the sport were in Boston, New York, and Philadelphia. A skater had to be a club member in order to take part in the club-organized tests and competitions, a structure that was used to keep minorities out of the sport.[56] Mabel Fairbanks played a key role in changing this.[57] She was born in the Florida Everglades, the child of an African American father and a mother who was part Seminole Indian and part English. She moved to New York at a young age, where she fell in love with the figure skating that she observed in Central Park. African Americans were usually prohibited from entering the rinks, but she managed to get onto the ice through persistence, and after she began to master tricks, she was enough of a novelty that she attracted gawkers and was tolerated by the rink management. She gained the sympathy of two top international coaches, who gave her occasional lessons and encouraged her to mount her own ice shows, which she performed before black and mixed audiences on her own six-by-six-foot portable skating rink.

In 1946 a member of the African American community in Los Angeles brought her to the West Coast "in the hope of obtaining the help in furthering her career which the prejudices in the East had denied her."[58] But in Los Angeles, she fared only slightly better: she was signed up to tour with ice shows outside the United States only in Cuba, Mexico, and the West Indies, where it was judged that mixed audiences would welcome a black performer.[59]

In the late 1940s, Catherine Machado, who was Hispanic, was accepted into the Los Angeles Figure Skating Club. In 1956, after placing third in senior ladies for the second year in a row, she became the first Hispanic to represent the United States in the Olympic Winter Games.[60] However, until the 1960s there had never been a black member of the US Figure Skating Association. Fairbanks took up coaching with the goal of helping minority skaters to achieve that which had been denied to her. She began coaching a talented African American, Richard Ewell, in 1963. In 1964 the Civil Rights Act outlawed discrimination on the basis of race. In 1965, Fairbanks, who had attended law school for some years, finally succeeded after two decades of trying: Ewell was admitted into the All Year Figure Skating Club, and in the same week another student, Atoy Wilson, was admitted into the Los Angeles Figure Skating Club. This paved the way for Wilson to win the novice men's championship in 1966.[61] In 1969, after much behind-the-scenes politicking and several failures, he became the first African American to pass the eighth (most difficult) figure test.[62] He became the first black principal in a major ice show in 1972.

With her red hair and a different color of skates for each day of the week, Fairbanks became one of the most influential developmental coaches in Los Angeles. Whenever talented minority skaters emerged anywhere in California, their coaches would take them to Fairbanks for lessons and confidence building. She mentored Tai Babilonia, Debi Thomas, Tiffany Chin, and Kristi Yamaguchi, among many others. Babilonia, who was of mixed African American, Indian, and Filipino descent, became the first African American national champion at the senior (top) level when she won the pairs championship with her partner, Randy Gardner, in 1976. They won five consecutive national pairs championships and in 1979 became the first American pair to win the World Championship, also a first for a skater of African descent. They became the heartbreak kids of the Lake Placid 1980 Olympics when they had to withdraw from the competition due to Gardner's groin injury. Debi Thomas was the first African American singles national champion at the senior level (1987) and continued on to win the World Championships in the same year and a silver Olympic medal behind the legendary Katarina Witt in 1988. Yamaguchi won Olympic gold in 1992.

However, Fairbanks never received official credit. When her skaters began to compete at higher levels, parents were advised that a respected white coach should be seen standing with their child at the boards. John Nicks took over. When he retired in 2013 at the age of eighty-four, he was a renowned coach who had helped make Southern California into a world epicenter for figure skating. However, it was Mabel Fairbanks who had laid the foundation for the emergence of Southern California's success, since many of the biggest stars from the 1990s onward were minorities, including the biggest star of them all, nine-time US champion and three-time Olympic medalist Michelle Kwan. When Mabel Fairbanks was inducted into the US Figure Skating Hall of Fame, those who knew her marveled at the fact that she had never seemed bitter, yet an oral history on file with the LA84 Foundation does hint at the anger and frustration she must have held inside.[63]

By 2017 an "Asian invasion" had changed the face of this once exclusive and lily-white sport, both internationally and in the United States. Midori Ito's win for Japan in 1989 marked the start of a period when eighteen of twenty-eight world champions in ladies' singles were Japanese, Chinese, Korean, or Americans of Japanese or Chinese descent (1989–2016). At ice rinks around the United States, increasing numbers of young skaters were brought in for lessons by parents who had emigrated from mainland China.[64] At the 2017 US Figure Skating Championships, the ladies' champion was seventeen-year-old Karen Chen, the men's champion was seventeen-year-old Nathan Chen (no relation), and the men's silver medalist was sixteen-year-old Vincent Zhou; all three were children of mainland Chinese immigrants. Smashing negative stereotypes about Asian athleticism, Nathan Chen accomplished a previously unimaginable feat when he became the first man to land five quadruple jumps in one skating program. The rise of Korean, Japanese, and Chinese American skaters had several sources. Ice skating has a centuries-old history in northeast Asia, where the winters are cold enough to freeze lakes and ponds, so many of the immigrants had learned to skate back home and taught their children to skate. Skating appealed to many of these parents more than the more conventional American youth sports (such as soccer, football, baseball, softball) because they were reluctant to allow their children to take part in sports perceived as violent and dangerous. The celebrity skating stars in China, Japan, and Korea provided role models. Finally, since figure skating is a sport in which athletes must start training at a young age to have any hope of reaching world levels, the strict parental authority that is the East Asian family ideal was often key to their children's success.

FIGURE 9. Angelina Huang, the 2017 US novice ladies' figure skating champion (Kevin Phelan/KrPhotogs Photography).

THE "BLACK ATHLETE"

Racism is alive and well in the sports world. Throughout the world, fans continue to harass racially and ethnically marked players, as in the bananas thrown at black players on European soccer pitches. Public statements are periodically heard coming from the mouths of men in charge of the sport industries bemoaning that "there are too many blacks" in sport.[65] Pundits continue to explain the dearth of black managers in sports in which black athletes dominate by invoking unexamined doubts about black people's capacity to lead, coach, or manage.[66]

But racism in sport also operates in subtle forms. In the United States, African American athletes are overrepresented in many sports, such as track and field and basketball, and baseball diamonds are crowded with players with Hispanic names (who actually constitute a racial rainbow in and of themselves), while many other sports (swimming, golf, skiing) continue to be almost exclusively white, making exceptions like Tiger Woods in golf so noticeable and, ultimately, so deeply problematic for mainstream society.[67] This polarization fuels the racial mythology in which supposed biological traits explain the athletic and leadership capabilities of particular kinds of human beings. Some have argued that, far from helping African Americans in the United States, sport in fact aggravates racism by perpetuating long-discredited theories about their physical superiority and intellectual deficiency. While this stereotype combines positive and negative evaluations, it always ends up denigrating its targets.[68]

Sport simultaneously serves to dramatize and accentuate the very conditions of racial subordination that race itself inscribes onto racialized bodies. The persistent icon of the "black athlete," embodied by historical and contemporary figures like Jack Johnson, Jesse Owens, Muhammad Ali, Pelé, Tiger Woods, Venus and Serena Williams, and Usain Bolt, demonstrates the pervasive power of social facts despite scientific evidence to the contrary. The black athlete is now a global racial projection that, on the one hand, serves as an idealized type defining the very boundaries of blackness itself while simultaneously highlighting the black athlete's exceptionality as a human body.[69] Black athletes in particular, and nonwhite athletes more broadly, tend to run the gamut from the "not quite human" to the sometimes human and even the "superhuman," but almost never as normally or ordinarily human. The black athlete remains an ideological projection legitimized by "commonsense" racial science that "proves" his or her physical superiority.[70] Somewhat predictably, this common sense operates even in societies that have also been victimized by it. For example, in Bengal, where people were stereotyped as effete weaklings during the long history of British colonialism, professional clubs actively recruit Nigerian soccer players because they believe black bodies to be "naturally" bigger and better built than the "feeble" Bengalis, naturalizing the inequitable political economy that maintains Nigerian players in conditions of abject poverty.[71]

In Cuba racial politics remain central in everyday life even though the revolution denied race as an object of sociopolitical concern.[72] Nowhere are these politics more evident than in baseball, where racialized understandings about athletic bodies play a prominent role.[73] Throughout the seasons Thomas Carter spent in the stands of the Estadio Latinoamericano, Cuba's national stadium, baseball fans commonly expressed racialized attitudes that cut across class distinctions, irrespective of the speaker's own racial identity. On the streets, in the bars, arenas, and homes of the city's residents, biological differences between the races are common explanations for why so many of Cuba's national champions and international athletes come from the Oriente, the eastern half of the country. Cubans widely believe that the government's Ministry of Sport has scientific evidence that proves the physiological superiority of black athletes.

When urban, "civilized," presumed white athletes, who may not "naturally" be stronger, defeat the more "natural" black athletes from the Oriente, people assume that they do so thanks to their superior *disciplina*—a complex, multiladen term that refers to discipline, training, and civilization.[74] According to this logic, it is civilization that makes the athlete, and the very structure of Cuba's sports programs helps to reinforce this logic. Despite major investment by the Cuban government in sport-related facilities during the first three decades of the revolution, youths already identified as talented in the specialized educational sports schools in each province are brought to Havana for further "development."[75] The combination of the material, geographic realities of Cuba's sports facilities, the *disciplina* of athletic training, and the unequivocal results of sports competition all become "scientific proof" of racial difference as well as the biologically based superiority/inferiority of any such category. Such "evidence" demonstrates the pervasive reality of race and how racial classifications generate differences that obscure power relations by providing allegedly biological explanations for Cuba's social hierarchies.

The overrepresentation of black athletes among Cuba's elite sports programs is not the result of the biological superiority of that population over Cubans of European descent. Rather, in Cuba as elsewhere, it is shaped by structural dynamics that include the labor market that gives preferential treatment to some but not to others, the distribution of wealth and income that favors some over others, and educational institutions that channel some children into academic tracks and encourage others to focus on sport.

While much of the attention on race and sport focuses on a presumed black-white binary, race is in fact much more complex than this binary. In the United States, the black-white binary of the racial order obscures a multiracial reality. The fixation on the black athlete creates all sorts of conundrums for athletes who are neither black nor white. For South Asian American basketball players, "it is simultaneously insufficient and critical to identity formation for South Asian Americans [who] do not transcend the black-white binary but rather directly involve and reconfigure this normative racial logic."[76] The presence of racialized Others outside the black-white binary extends well beyond the borders of the United States. Throughout the world, Latino, Asian, and indigenous (Australian and American) athletes are marginalized to varying degrees because they do not readily fit the black-white racial binary that has now become hegemonic in sport around the world.

It is clear from the anthropological work on race that attention to local racial hierarchies is crucial for understanding the lives of those enmeshed in these myriad power relations. Local social categories are more prevalent and prominent than any broad, supposedly universal means of racially categorizing people.[77] Yet racial categories and identities are never entirely the product of structural power relations. Individuals assert their own subjectivities, racial and otherwise, yet any such subject position never entirely belongs to the individuals who identify with it. Subjectivities are the result not only of personal goals, disciplinary discourses, and institutional, familial, and national locations but also of crucial entanglements with the personal, institutional, and discursive structures of others and, above all, with their fantasies of otherness.[78] Otherness is visibly expressed in the public spectacles of sport, making sport a resilient site for the power and desire that are served by marking Others as different.

SPORT AS MAKER AND BREAKER OF SOCIAL HIERARCHIES

When people are faced with few options in life, sport is often promoted as a good way to "become somebody" and potentially claim recognition or even earn a living. Talented nonwhite, ethnic, and working-class youth are supposed to find social mobility through sport. Yet the politics that permeate school and community sports programs create and reinforce racial borders that many youth simply refuse to cross. Local social institutions led by prominent local citizens, and often former high school athletes themselves, reinforce racial categories.

The various examples that we have discussed in this chapter illustrate that sport both reflects and creates inequalities based on social class, ethnicity, and race. In other words, sport and social hierarchies are in a mutually constitutive relationship. What is particularly interesting about the role of sport in creating and reflecting social hierarchies is that sport continues to be largely associated with play, pleasure, and leisure. This tension between sport as pleasure and sport as serious life lends particular poignancy to the role sport plays in dividing and ranking social groups. At the same time, no social structure is immune from challenge, and sport is no exception. Athletic excellence has the potential to cut across established structures of inequality, bestowing recognition upon members of oppressed, invisible, or marginalized groups. But the effectiveness of such challenges in changing the status quo is subject to debate, leading some to argue that, far from disrupting structures of oppression and domination, excellence in sport in fact aggravates these structures. Whatever the case may be, sport emerges as a particularly rich field in which to observe and analyze fundamental processes in the constitution of social inequality.

FIVE

Sport and Sex, Gender, and Sexuality

IT IS CUSTOMARY TO BEGIN introductory discussions of sex and gender with the statement that, as social scientists use the term, *sex* refers to the genetically determined reproductive anatomy fixed at birth, defining female and male categories. *Gender,* meanwhile, refers to the symbols, behaviors, roles, and statuses that are associated with anatomical sex, that are learned and culturally variable, and that define women and men. Several scholars, such as psychiatrist Robert Stoller and psychologist John Money, claimed to be the first to theorize the distinction, which gained particular traction in the 1960s in Europe and North America in the context of second-wave feminism. However, in anthropology the idea goes all the way back to Margaret Mead's *Sex and Temperament in Three Primitive Societies* (1934), a classic work, although not without problems in the details, on the divergent ways in which women and men conduct themselves (in her words, their "temperament") in three societies of what is today Papua New Guinea.[1] Perhaps the major contribution of anthropologists to this discussion was to point out that gender norms can differ radically across the world's societies, while women and men are biologically constituted in the same way everywhere.[2] *Sexuality* refers to the preferences that individuals express in their erotic desires and practices. With the rise of Western biomedical science, sexuality came to be considered a fixed biological drive, classified by laws and diagnostic handbooks as either normal (heterosexual) or deviant (homosexual). Starting in the 1970s this account changed radically among social scientists and humanists under the influence of Michel Foucault's work, which demonstrated that sexuality has a history, that its form and meaning changed over time, and that it has been shaped (often coercively) by society.[3] However, a split remains between those who subscribe to this view and others who still seek to ground sexuality in a fixed biology.

In the 1990s historian Thomas Laqueur overturned the tried-and-true distinction between biological sex and culturally constructed gender.[4] His analysis of the history of anatomical sex in the Western tradition demonstrated that sex is as culturally constructed as gender because the body itself does not clearly mark distinctions such as male/female, man/woman, and father/mother. Rather, imaginative humans read these distinctions into the body, and so it is impossible to demarcate where sex ends and gender begins. Laqueur drew evidence from the history of anatomical knowledge, including the genre of anatomical illustration that arose in the Renaissance after the invention of mass-printed books. Anatomists who dissected a corpse were confronted by an amorphous mass of tissue and organs, and from Galen (discussed in chapter 3) to the Enlightenment, they believed that both men and women had penises and testes, with women's organs being men's organs "turned outside in"; Laqueur called this understanding the "one-sex model." People did perceive differences between men and women, which they attributed to different degrees of perfection, but they believed that both sexes shared the same essential physiology, vital fluids, and organs. This view differed from the view that arose after the discovery of chromosomes and hormones, which were interpreted to mean that the two sexes were fundamentally different all the way down to the cellular level. In the "one-sex model," the male body was usually taken as the norm, and the female body was a lesser version of it. Bodies were capable of changing sex suddenly, and the line between male and female was not absolute. It was only in the course of the development of modern science during the eighteenth and nineteenth centuries that the sexual biologies of women and men would come to be understood as fundamentally different, with sexuality rooted in biology and gender rooted in society and culture. Laqueur could not have guessed how well his theory would be illustrated by the debates about sex testing in sport that raged two decades after his book was published, when new technologies opened up bodies in different ways, only to find that their sex was just as amorphous as anatomists had found it to be over the course of history.

Because sports entail public displays of bodies and movements that may either conform with or violate gender norms, they always have gendered meanings, and in the West they have played an important role in propping up the distinction between sex and gender. The distinction between the sexes was an integral part of the emergence of "modern" Western sport that we have analyzed in previous chapters, and this distinction was bound up with the history of biomedicine since the authority of biological science was

deployed to defend it. Sport's relation to sex and gender may have been con-
figured differently outside the West, but due to Europeans' and North
Americans' domination of global sports organizations and economic structures, many sports are grounded in Western cultures and, further, the entire
international sports system is inevitably shaped by the fact that the lion's
share of the global sports economy is marketed as a masculine spectacle. This
has had the effect of pressing people to conform with the Western sex-gender
paradigm, muffling expressions of alternative sexes, genders, and sexualities,
most clearly evident in the way that the regulations for sex testing in sport
have forced sportspeople and fans worldwide to adopt the Western biomedical understanding of sex difference.

Contrary to its intent, the science of sex testing that developed in the late
twentieth and early twenty-first centuries demonstrated that there is no single biological marker of sex that can straightforwardly categorize all humans
as male or female; rather, there are many markers, none of which is found in
all people labeled either male or female.[5] Sex, then, can be considered a statistical average or combined effect of a variety of factors that change over time,
that mutually influence each other in a complex feedback loop, and that
respond to environment and lifestyle.

For over two hundred years, biomedical research was predicated on the
assumption that sex was straightforwardly grounded in biological facts fixed
at birth. As a result, today we have a limited understanding of the biology of
sex. The lack of well-designed research on healthy bodies in motion discussed
in chapter 3 is even more true when matters of sex and sport are involved.

SEX TESTING AND THE COLD WAR

In the early years of international sport, when women were largely excluded,
sex was not an issue. From the second to the fourth modern Olympic Games,
women were allowed to take part in elite sports such as golf, tennis, archery,
and figure skating, but the image of the skirt-clad gentlewoman taking part
in these competitions did nothing to incite suspicions about males masquerading as females. It was not until the political tensions of the Cold War that
international sports authorities became interested in developing unassailable
methods for distinguishing men from women. As a result, sex testing emerged
right after World War II, so it is easy to simplistically conclude that the tensions of the Cold War provoked a paranoia that political rivals would cheat

by passing off men as women.[6] A small but widely publicized number of cases of female athletes who transitioned and became men after retirement created a perception that there was a problem to be controlled.[7] However, the concern was so overblown, given the rarity of such cases, that it is more likely that sport tapped into a broader phenomenon driven by the anxieties around sex and gender that invariably accompany war and militarization.[8] The postwar transition resulted in a clampdown on the women who had become liberated while their men were absent, so it is no coincidence that the first sex verification was instituted in the year after World War II, because it was only then that being both virile and a woman was defined as "cheating."[9]

Track and field was and still is the sport in which sex is viewed as most problematic. Dora Ratjen, the German who had placed fourth in the women's high jump in the 1936 "Hitler" Olympics and won the gold medal with a world record in the 1938 European Championships, had a male anatomy. Dora became Heinrich at his own request, and since he refused interviews until he died in 2008, details of his story have remained shrouded in mystery. Conspiracy theories have maintained that he was a man whom the Nazis pressured to impersonate a woman in order to win medals, or that the Nazis were looking for a way to replace Jewish high jumper Gretel Bergmann on the German Olympic team. In 1939, Ratjen was arrested for "fraud" on the basis of masquerading as a woman and was eventually acquitted. Police files made available in 2009 indicated that he was born with a misshapen penis; after initial confusion, the midwife had declared him a girl at birth; his parents, simple farmers, had registered him as such and never openly questioned it; and he had expressed relief to the police when he was exposed. There was no evidence that the Reich Ministry for Sport knew about Ratjen's sexual ambiguity before the police investigation in 1939.[10]

As international sports resumed after the war, the International Association of Athletic Federations (IAAF), the world's governing body for track and field, began requiring in 1946 that women bring a medical certificate from their doctors attesting to their sex. The International Olympic Committee (IOC) followed with a similar ruling at the first postwar Olympics in London in 1948.

Before a world championship in track and field was established, the USA-USSR dual meet initiated in 1958 attracted huge public and government attention. However, in 1958, the sport hardly existed for women in the United States, so the Soviet insistence on calculating a total score (the United States insisted on separate men's and women's scores) meant that the United States lost the first seven installments of the meet, as the American women were generally weak and were largely propped up by the famed African American women from the Tigerbelle program at Tennessee State University. The pressure to match the Soviet athletes slowly provoked a modicum of support for women's track and field in the United States.[11]

The postwar world order was changing rapidly. China became a nuclear power in 1964, the year Tokyo hosted the Olympic Games, the first to be hosted outside the cultural West. That year, the United States managed to defeat the Soviet Union for the first time in the track-and-field dual meet, 187–156 (the American men won 139–97; the women lost 48–59). The United States began systematic bombing of Vietnam in 1965, prompting the Soviets to withdraw from the USA-USSR dual meet in protest from 1966 to 1968.[12]

Political tensions were expressed in a gender idiom: Western commentators dismissed the achievements of Eastern Bloc women by denigrating them as unfeminine—or even as transvestite cheaters—as a way of dismissing the political challenge posed by socialism's agenda to achieve gender equality in sport (and in work) at a time when Western women were oppressed by the postwar cult of domesticity. In Europe and North America in the early 1960s, the second-wave women's movement began to push back against this oppression, and more events for women were added into the Olympic Games. When men's and women's volleyball were included in 1964, women had their first Olympic team sport (Japan won the women's gold, the USSR the men's).

Representing the Soviet Union in the 1960 and 1964 Olympic Games, Irina and Tamara Press won a total of one silver and five gold medals between them, Tamara in shot put and discus, Irina in 80-meter hurdles and pentathlon. In 1965, as a guest at the US indoor championships, Tamara demolished her American competitors in the shot put, giving rise to the enduring trope of the "Russian female shot-putter" in American popular culture. As discussed below, one of us, Susan Brownell, competed in the heptathlon, in which one of the events was the shotput, in the late 1970s and 1980s, and so she was well acquainted with the jokes.

The Ratjen incident incited surprisingly little international attention at the time of his outing. It is telling that in 1966 the media, particularly *Time* magazine in the United States, conjured up a much-distorted version of Ratjen's case along with several other past examples of women who had transitioned into men after retirement, so as to fuel suspicions about the Press sisters' sex.[13] A decade before the Press sisters, another Soviet athlete, Aleksandra Chudina, had delighted in crossing gender lines rather flamboyantly: she was six foot

FIGURE 10. Tamara Press, representing the USSR, in the Women's Discus Throw Final, Tokyo 1964 Olympic Games (© 1964 Comité international olympique).

two (1.88m), drank, chain-smoked, played cards with the men, and had affairs with female athletes.[14] She competed at top levels in field hockey, volleyball, and track and field, winning silver medals in the long jump and javelin and bronze in the high jump at the 1952 Olympics. These being the Soviet Union's first Olympics, she became hugely popular in her homeland. She retired several years before sex testing was initiated and was largely forgotten by Western sport historians.

In interviews in 2015, Nina Ponomareva and Galina Zybina, shot and discus throwers on the Soviet national team, recalled that in the 1950s and 1960s the presence of "men" on the women's team was an open secret, and that the minister of sport and national team coach supported these athletes because they were under pressure to win medals. At the 1958 Soviet national championships, Zybina and another shot-putter refused to stand on the same award podium as Tamara Press, and they were punished as a result and their wages withheld. Zybina recalled that the team doctor had whispered to her, "Galina, fight until the end. I studied the documents, three years ago, the Press sisters had surgery."[15]

So it was in 1966, just as the course of history was drawing together sport with nationalism and gender, that international sports organizations took sex testing out of the hands of women and their local physicians and required them to parade in the nude before a panel of female physicians, and at some events to undergo a gynecological examination. Shortly afterward, Tamara and Irina Press, along with two other Soviets and several athletes in other Eastern Bloc countries, announced their retirement, and the timing has been taken as evidence that they could not have passed the visual examination.[16] No further evidence has ever emerged, and apparently no scholar has followed up—even though the Press sisters both had long and distinguished careers as administrators in the Soviet and Russian sports systems, apparently as women. Irina died in 2004, and Tamara was evidently still alive in 2016. Decades later, at least three fellow competitors stated that Tamara was a "hermaphrodite," while Irina seems largely to have been guilty by association.[17] Today, along with Dora Ratjen, they appear on a list of (at the time) infamous transgender sportspeople on websites that advocate for the transgender movement.

The fact that politically powerful Eastern Bloc men supported the presence of (alleged) intersex or transgender individuals in sport and that it was not a secret inside the USSR would suggest that cultural attitudes about such matters in the Eastern Bloc were not as rigid as in western Europe and North America, at least for sports celebrities. Given the opprobrium heaped upon anyone in American sport whose gender and sexuality did not conform to rigid norms then and for the next two decades, and the slowness with which women's sports gained government support even though the losses to the Soviets and East Germans were considered embarrassing, it is hard to imagine that the men who controlled the American sports world would have accepted an intersex or transgender athlete no matter how many medals she or he could win. This is illustrated by the types of athletes who were held up for national adulation. In the United States, particularly before the federal Title IX of the Educational Amendments of 1972 opened up opportunities in sports to women, figure skaters and tennis players were the only female athletes hailed as heroes in the popular media. Tennis player Billie Jean King and figure skater Peggy Fleming were the most famous. The rigidity of norms of gender and sexuality meant that King's lesbianism became public knowledge, against her will, only when a former lover filed a lawsuit against her in 1981. Fleming's rise coincided with the arrival of a new era in sports television, illustrated by ABC's *Wide World of Sports* launch in 1961 with figure skating as one of its marquee sports.[18] At the Grenoble 1968 Olympics, Fleming won the gold medal, sporting a chartreuse dress sewn by her mother and a beehive of hair piled atop her head, the epitome of US femininity at the time. She signed a half-million-dollar contract for five television specials, which were surprisingly popular and propelled her toward becoming one of the best-known American athletes of any gender during the last half century.[19]

Demonstrating a faith in the physical superiority of men—even equivocal ones—over women, people widely believed that the records held by the suspected intersex or transgender athletes were unbeatable. There were calls to delete Tamara Press's records from the record book, but women's sport was developing rapidly, and most of the records fell quickly. "Most surprising," according to the West German magazine *Der Spiegel,* was that two years after Press set the discus world record, West German Liesel Westermann surpassed it by a meter and a half.[20] A big source of the surprise: Press had not only stood 6 feet tall (1.84m) and weighed 216 pounds (98 kilos), while Westermann stood 5 feet 7¾ inches (1.72m) and weighed 161 pounds (73 kilos), but Press also did not smoke, drink, or flirt, while Westermann smoked, had a liking for champagne, and had a beau who followed her on sports trips.

SEX TESTING AND THE INTERSEX

After sports governing bodies introduced visual examinations of their naked bodies, athletes complained that these were extremely humiliating, so the following year the IOC, without much examination of any scientific evidence, adopted the "chromosome test" that remained in use until 1991.[21] This test involved a cheek swab to test cells for presence of the Barr body, which indicates the presence of at least two X chromosomes. This test was predicated on three assumptions: that every cell contains the same genetic material; that all "women" have two X chromosomes; and that all "men" have only one X chromosome and therefore will have no Barr bodies. None of these assumptions is correct. At the time, scientists already knew that the Barr body test did not correlate with physiological and anatomical sex and that there were chromosomal combinations that would not be identified by the test, in particular Klinefelter's syndrome (47,XXY).

There are at least six biological markers of sex: chromosomes, gonads, hormones, secondary sex characteristics, and external and internal genitalia. Sexual development can vary at any point, and so any one of these markers may combine with another marker that is typically associated with the opposite sex.[22] There are more than fifteen diagnoses to explain "non-dimorphic sexual development" and multiple "conditions" that fall under the category "intersex" (and new ones periodically come to light).[23] There is no reliable estimate of the proportion and distribution of intersex persons in human populations. One comprehensive review of data from international studies estimated that all variations account for 1.7 percent of live births, and that 1.62 percent of the population undergoes genital surgery. However, only a few of the studies surveyed in this review concerned populations outside Europe and North and South America.[24] Yet anthropologists have documented the particularly high incidence of certain intersex conditions in countries like Papua New Guinea and the Dominican Republic. The dearth of research on non-Western populations has led to comments by medical officials over the years describing intersexes outside the West as unknown territory and a challenge to testing.

For female athletes who did not know that they had chromosomal anomalies until genetic screening, the result was devastating: it ended their athletic careers and ruined their personal lives. In the late 1980s, Brownell was aware of an age-group middle-distance champion in China who fell under suspicion when she did not develop breasts at puberty. After testing showed that she was intersex, she was sent back to her rural village, crushing her hopes of using sports for social mobility and perhaps her chances of a good marriage, which was particularly important for rural women. In 1985, Spanish hurdler María José Martínez Patiño failed the test and refused to retire with an "injury" as instructed. She had complete androgen insensitivity syndrome (CAIS), with XY chromosomes, internal testes, and testosterone levels in the typical range for males. Based on her chromosomes, gonads, and hormones, she was deemed male, but she had external female anatomy and had never suspected that she was anything other than a woman. Twenty years later, after she had written a PhD dissertation on the difficulties faced by women in sport, become a professor of political science, and emerged as a staunch critic of sex testing, she recalled,

> I was expelled from our athletes' residence, my sports scholarship was revoked, and my running times were erased from my country's athletics records. I felt ashamed and embarrassed. I lost friends, my fiancé, hope, and energy. But I knew that I was a woman, and that my genetic difference gave me no unfair physical advantage. I could hardly pretend to be a man; I have breasts and a vagina. I never cheated.[25]

She fought a three-year court battle, arguing that her condition did not give her an unfair advantage. She won and was reinstated.

In 1988 the IAAF dropped the sex test in favor of a visual "health check" of both women and men by team doctors, and in 1992 it dropped all tests because, as the antidoping effort had ramped up, every top athlete would have been observed urinating into a cup, and it was presumed that genitalia could be checked at that point.[26] In many sports, Lycra had also made the shape of the rest of the body transparent. A reserve clause allowed the IAAF medical manager to initiate a confidential "gender verification" by a medical panel if he had "reasonable grounds." Demonstrating the newfound understanding of the complexity of sex, the expert panel required one gynecologist, one genetic expert, and one endocrinologist, and it could include additional specialists.

Despite growing opposition from geneticists, athletes, feminists, and even politicians, the IOC refused to eliminate sex testing from the Olympic Games. At the Barcelona 1922 Olympics, it experimented with a new cheek-swab test that looked for the presence of a gene (DYZ1) usually found on the Y chromosome. If a test came back positive, a second test was conducted to look for the presence of the sex-determining region of the Y chromosome, or SRY, a DNA-binding protein that initiates the formation of the testes and was thus believed to be key in determining male sex. In the preliminary trial of males and females from the general population, the DYZ1 test had sorted males and females with 100 percent accuracy. However, much to the surprise of the scientists, among the 2,406 females tested in Barcelona, eleven women showed the presence of DYZ1, but only five were confirmed by the SRY test. A physical examination of those five women seemingly resulted in their being allowed to compete. The scientists who conducted the "experiment" (as they described it) could not explain the results. They hypothesized that parts of the Y chromosome had translocated to the X chromosome. The overall conclusion was that the test was flawed.[27]

At the Atlanta 1996 Olympic Games, 3,387 female athletes were tested for the presence of SRY, with another gene (galactose-1-phosphate uridyltransferase) used as a control. Eight women had positive results on both tests: of those, seven had androgen insensitivity and one had 5-alpha steroid reductase deficiency. All had XY chromosomes. All but two of the women (both androgen insensitive) were evidently aware of their conditions, because they had already undergone gonadectomies to remove their internal testes. All were given sex verification certificates and allowed to compete. The doctors in charge continued, however, to puzzle over the "apparently high frequency of Y chromosome material in elite-class, female athletes."[28]

In the Olympic Games, in the quarter century from 1972 to 1996, 11,373 athletes had undergone testing, of whom twenty-seven (0.24 percent) had turned up positive results.[29] In the face of the imperfect science, the minute percentage of positive tests, and the fact that no male masquerading as a female was ever unmasked, the IOC's insistence on maintaining sex testing for so many years confounded critics. Part of the reason was that from 1967 to 2002, the testing was under the charge of Prince Alexandre de Mérode, chairman of the IOC Medical Commission, a Belgian aristocrat who had no medical training and whose policy decisions were often based on moral and ethical arguments rather than on scientific arguments. Historical hindsight has been unkind to him on many counts, including his refusal to acknowledge and respond to the growing problem of doping.[30] The many publications of the man who finally replaced him, Arne Ljungqvist, hint at years of tension with Mérode.[31]

In 1999, on the eve of the Sydney Olympics, the IOC announced the elimination of all sex testing. In its place, it initiated a "gender verification" policy similar to that of the IAAF, in which any female athlete might be challenged. In 2009, eighteen-year-old Caster Semenya from South Africa won the 800-meter race at the 2009 World Championships, and a challenge was filed. During the eleven-month investigation the IAAF banned her from competitions, finally clearing her for competition and allowing her victory to stand, but not without seriously delaying her athletic career. The investigation was botched from beginning to end. The press violated her right to confidentiality, and commentators humiliated her and ridiculed her appearance. Leaked reports said that the test results indicated an intersex condition: she had no uterus or ovaries and had undescended testes producing androgens at three times the typical level for females. Her case and the outcry against the violations of her privacy led to heated debates and a revision of both the IAAF and IOC policies.[32] She went on to win the silver medal in the 2012 Olympics and gold in the 2016 Olympics (discussed below).

The Semenya case and others like it (e.g., those of Indian track-and-field athletes Pinki Pramanik, Santhi Soundarajan, and Dutee Chand) highlighted the fact that the sex of athletes of poor and rural backgrounds in the Global South was considerably more likely to come to the attention of sports authorities than that of athletes from the Global North. Whereas some tried to explain this by claiming that athletes who grew up in the developing world were less likely to have access to regular medical care and that their intersex conditions were likely to remain undetected, others compared the scrutiny of athletes from the Global South today with that of the "femininity" of athletes of the Eastern Bloc during the Cold War. Medical scrutiny is thus not random; it follows geopolitical relations, reflecting the anxieties that bodies from non-Western societies arouse in the Western centers of world political power.[33]

Scholars writing about sex verification have tended to criticize it as a top-down effort by largely western European men imposing hegemonic gender norms upon female bodies. While they are certainly correct, it is also important to remember that there was strong bottom-up pressure from women who perceived it as unfair to have to compete against athletes whom they considered "men," and these women were sometimes punished for protesting. This is particularly true of an era when there was almost no public knowledge about intersex categories. On the one hand, one can empathize with athletes who spend years in training and find themselves faced with what they think, whether rightly or wrongly, is the unfair advantage of other competitors. Even now, when athletes may acquire a better understanding of intersex, the nature of fellow athletes' protests has not changed radically compared to previous decades. On the other hand, many aspects of people's physiologies confer physical advantage, often more clearly than intersex conditions. US swimmer Michael Phelps, winner of twenty-eight Olympic medals from 2004 to 2016, was once tested for a rare condition, Marfan syndrome, which results in unusually long limbs and superior flexibility, characteristics that would give him an undeniable advantage in the swimming pool. Doctors concluded he did not have the condition.[34] But if he did, should it be considered unfair? In this vein, a South African writer's essay after Semenya's gold medal in Rio argued that those who felt Semenya's medical condition gave her an unfair advantage were ignoring the much more significant advantages held by athletes from large, wealthy countries over athletes from small countries with inferior training conditions and facilities.[35]

TESTOSTERONE DREAMS

The new policies of the IAAF and IOC abandoned the fraught phrase "gender verification" and attempted to narrow down the question to one and only one quantifiable phenomenon: hyperandrogenism. The key assumption was that masculinizing hormones (androgens) confer a competitive advantage in sports. An athlete would be allowed to compete in the women's division if she was (1) legally recognized as a female in her nation and (2) had a testosterone level below the "male range." If she had testosterone within the male range but had androgen insensitivity (like Martínez Patiño), she would be allowed to compete. The rest would be allowed to compete only if they agreed to medical intervention (typically, pharmaceutical intervention and/or gonadectomy).[36]

Both male and female bodies produce a variety of androgens that interact with each other and with tissues in complex ways. In practical terms, the new IAAF and IOC policies focused on testosterone, the androgen produced in the largest amount; women typically produce about one-tenth the level of males. The policy assumed that there is a measurable "male range" and set its lower limit slightly higher than the range given as "normal" in the most authoritative endocrinology compendium. However, it is known that roughly 5 percent of the population does not fall into the "normal" male and female ranges. Moreover, testosterone levels vary from one moment to the next. They have been shown, for example, to rise after athletic victories.

The more serious obstacle was the dearth of studies of the hormonal profiles of elite athletes. A 2014 study of 693 elite athletes that tried to fill this lacuna confused the picture even more: it found significant overlap between the serum testosterone levels of elite male and female athletes in a variety of sports, with 16.5 percent of the men falling within the female range and 13.7 percent of the women falling within the male range. Furthermore, hormone levels varied greatly by sport, raising the possibility that testosterone levels adapt to the type of training specific to different sports.[37] The scientists concluded that the IOC and IAAF policies were untenable and open to legal challenge. Their findings were presented to the IAAF/IOC Expert Working Group on sex verification "rather sadly, to no effect."[38]

Even before this study, scholars had questioned the single-minded focus on testosterone as "the master molecule of athleticism."[39] What was it about testosterone that resulted in its being attributed such extraordinary power? The hormone was first isolated from bull testicles to create the anabolic steroids in 1935, during the rise of fascist ideologies of masculinity. In an ironic full circle of history, the discovery was made by the Swiss Jewish scientist Ernst Laqueur, great uncle of Thomas Laqueur, whose rethinking of the cultural construction of sex we described earlier.[40] Anecdotal accounts indicate that testosterone derivatives were given to the Nazi Gestapo and troops, and records from Adolf Hitler's personal physician suggest that he was injected with them to improve his sexual potency.[41] It was hailed as an elixir of youthful life force with sensationalistic claims of sexual rejuvenation, renewed energy, and a more productive society.[42]

After the use of animal testicular extracts became popular at the end of the nineteenth century, the consumption of sex hormones permeated everyday life, and a vast global market arose to serve it.[43] In the twenty-first century, the use of testosterone and anabolic steroids is rampant among bodybuilders, police officers, male HIV patients, and athletes. In the United States, testosterone, which is commonly dispensed by general practitioners, is rare among commonly abused drugs in that it has a generally positive image. Its association with masculine potency means that it is inevitably viewed through the lens of gender and sexuality in which male sexual potency is valued.

Two of the most systematic and persistent scholars criticizing the science of testosterone-based sex tests are anthropologist and bioethicist Katrina Karkazis and biologist and gender studies scholar Rebecca Jordan-Young. Clearly, anthropology's disciplinary embrace of humans as both biological and cultural beings makes it suitable for intervening in this issue. Karkazis and Jordan-Young have critiqued the assumption that androgenic hormones are the primary components of biological athletic advantage, pointing out the many gaps in the science of testosterone:

- Nearly all research on testosterone and athletics has been conducted on men.
- Most research focuses on nonhealthy nonathletes with testosterone disorders.
- Clinical studies show that testosterone helps increase muscle size, strength, and endurance, *but* there is no evidence showing that successful athletes have higher testosterone levels than less successful athletes.
- Testosterone is just one element in a complex neuroendocrine feedback system, which is just as likely to be affected by as to affect athletic performance.
- Women with congenitally high testosterone (congenital adrenal hyperplasia, or CAH) are often short, obese, and have life-threatening illnesses.
- Conversely, several top athletes have been women with CAIS, meaning that testosterone has no effect on their tissues.[44]

They ask, does endogenous testosterone actually confer athletic advantage in a predictable way? If there *is* advantage from naturally occurring variation in testosterone, is that advantage *unfair?* After all, it occurs *naturally,* in the same way that unusual lung capacity, particularly long limbs, and robust muscularity do.

They conclude that the problem of male impostors does not exist and that athletes should have the right of choosing their gender expression. Of course, this is not feasible, because most nations do not offer citizens the right to self-define their gender. There are many ways to divide up sports in the interest of fair competition, and sex segregation is not the best way in all cases. Sex segregation should be one way to ensure fairness, not the ultimate goal.[45]

In 2015, in judging an appeal by the Indian sprinter Dutee Chand, who had been found to have testosterone levels exceeding the allowed "female range," the Court of Arbitration for Sport threw out the limits on the testosterone levels of female athletes, stating that the IAAF had failed to show that higher testosterone levels provide women with a significant advantage in sports.[46] This meant that intersexes no longer had to take measures to reduce their testosterone levels. Semenya had not matched her 2009 best time until she finally set a personal best in winning the gold medal in the Rio 2016 Olympics. Ironically, her South African national record of 1:55.28 was still one second short of the longest-standing world record in track and field, the 1:54.28 that Czechoslovakian Jarmila Kratochvílová set in 1983. That record is widely believed to have been enabled by anabolic steroids.

SEX SEGREGATION: A FAILURE OF IMAGINATION

Karkazis and Jordan-Young were the latest in a long line of scholars whose research questioned the segregation of women and men in sport. Is this segregation instituted with the intent of protecting fairness for women, as it has often been stated, or is it designed to ideologically maintain the borders between the genders? It is significant to remember that in all these years there has never been a sex test conducted on "men." The assumption has always been that it is the sex of "women" that is problematic, and that it must be confined within certain norms that are based on the assumption that women are biologically inferior to men in sports.

There are mixed-sex sports in the Olympic Games: all three equestrian disciplines (dressage, three-day eventing, stadium jumping), sailing, and mixed doubles in badminton, ice dance, and pairs figure skating. There are many more commonly contested options for mixed-sex sports that are not included in the Olympic Games, such as mixed doubles in tennis and table tennis, mixed-sex running and swimming relays, and mixed-sex volleyball.

Shooting at the Olympic Games was originally open to women, though only a few were selected for national teams. In 1976, American Margaret Thompson Murdock won the Olympic silver medal in 50-meter rifle-three positions. The contest with her American male teammate was so close that it required a recheck. When it was announced three hours later that he was the winner, she believed that she had been placed in second due to her gender; her gold-medal-winning teammate asked her to join him on the top step of the medal podium.[47] In 1984 a separate event was created for women in that event, even while other shooting events were still mixed. In the 1992 Olympics, Zhang Shan from China won the gold medal in skeet shooting, a mixed-sex event. Months before those Olympics, the world governing body for shooting (Union internationale de tir, or International Shooting Union) had decided to ban women from trap and skeet shooting at the following Olympics and to create separate male and female categories in a new event, double trapshooting. The female president of the Canadian International Trapshooters Association, Susan Nattrass, protested the decision to no avail.[48] As a result, at the 1996 Olympics, only men were allowed to contest skeet and trap shooting, and both men and women competed in double trap shooting. And so Zhang did not have the opportunity to repeat her gold medal, and the women had been reduced from two mixed events to one women's event. Not until the 2000 Olympics did women finally have their own skeet and trap shooting events.

Even mixed-sex sports are suffused with conservative gender norms. After African American figure skater Debi Thomas wore a unitard (a one-piece tight-fitting garment with long legs) in the Calgary 1988 Olympics, the International Skating Union implemented a ruling that "ladies" must wear skirts and men must wear full-length trousers and may *not* wear tights.[49] The skirt requirement was rescinded for singles in 2004 but remains in effect for female ice dancers, presumably because it is considered more important in that discipline to exhibit male-female difference.[50] Heterosexual female skating fans still recall with nostalgia the shape-revealing tights worn by Alexander Zhulin, silver medalist in ice dance in the 1992 Olympics, before the crackdown.

In 2011 the IAAF decided to recognize women's world records only in women-only running races, prompting the *New York Times* to dryly observe, "Now added to the list of banned performance-enhancing substances for female distance runners: men."[51] The reasoning was that running with men who were, in essence, acting as "pacers" gave women in mixed races an advantage—this even though men's races commonly use male pacers and their records are still recognized. As a result, there are now two world records in every recognized road running distance from the 10k to the marathon because the pre-2011 times have not yet been surpassed; one record is marked with "mx" for "mixed" and the other with "wo" for "women." The two marathon world records are held by the same person, Paula Radcliffe (mx = 2:15:25, wo = 2:17.42).

Each of these examples raises questions about what underlies sex segregation in sport. Is it really necessary for the purposes of fair play that men and women look different from each other, with women revealing their legs and buttocks while men conceal theirs? Why is it necessary to create separate divisions for women in sports in which they can beat men? Why are so few mixed-sex sports contested at the international level and in the Olympics when there are many more possibilities?

For many years, supported by some scientific evidence, critical thinkers have proposed that lean body mass alone explains the differences in the performances of men and women in sports in which there is a difference; if sports were segregated into weight divisions, women and men might be able to compete against each other on a level playing field.[52] Why have no sports organizers experimented with this idea? It is possible to imagine a sports world in which the major division is not that between males and females, but the sex-gender system that regulates and organizes sport suffers from a failure of imagination.

SPORT AS A "MALE PRESERVE" IN WESTERN EUROPE AND NORTH AMERICA

While women have made great strides in claiming the right to sport in many societies, sport in Western societies continues to be a gendered field jealously guarded by men. The reasons must be sought in the history of sport in western Europe and North America, where much of this gendering originated, to be exported to other parts of the world. As described in previous chapters, from the mid-nineteenth century onward, in both Britain and continental Europe, sport became an important component of the education of middle- and upper-middle-class men. Its advocates promoted it as a way of training men for capitalism, colonialism, and militarism. They incorporated the ideal of fit male bodies inspired by reinterpretations of ancient Greek ideals into the emerging ideologies of nationalism, bolstered by religion in the form of muscular Christianity. Women were more or less excluded from the emerging international sports system; their main contribution to the new sports clubs—voluntary associations—that were popping up worldwide was to organize social activities. In Brazil the state went as far as legally prohibiting women from playing soccer in 1941, arguing that "women will not be allowed to practice sports incompatible with the conditions of their nature," which it understood as being primarily designed to bear children for the nation. The edict was repealed only in 1979.[53]

In continental Europe, the turner movement, which advocated gymnastics and other physical activities for nationalistic ideals, was more accommodating to women than the British-American sport movement. Among other reasons, turner sports were located in clubs anchored in communities rather than elite schools and universities. In addition, women could be given their own specific brand of gymnastics that emphasized grace, and they took part in elite sports like archery, croquet, golf, and tennis. But track and field, which both the British-American and the continental sport movements practiced, remained closed to women until the organization of successful "Women's Olympics" and International Women's Games challenged this exclusion in the 1920s. The threat posed by the success of these events forced the IOC to incorporate a few women's events in the 1928 Olympics.

Pierre de Coubertin, the founder of the modern Olympic Games, was opposed to the participation of women, feeling that their role should be as spectators to the valor of the men. Like other classically educated elite men, he believed this to have been true in ancient Greece because the late-nineteenth and early twentieth-century classical scholarship that supported the Olympic revival conveniently omitted that women had participated in games to honor Zeus's wife, Hera (see chapter 1). In 1935, the same year that testosterone was synthesized, Coubertin stated, "The true Olympic hero is, in my view, the adult male individual."[54]

And so it was from the mid-nineteenth to early twentieth century that sport became, according to sport sociologist Eric Dunning, a "male preserve" that reinforced gender differences.[55] In that period the public display of physical violence had become less acceptable for middle-class and elite men with the expansion of white-collar occupations, where strength and aggression were counterproductive. Urbanization and industrialization drew men

FIGURE 11. The Fijianas, Fiji's national women's rugby sevens team, compete for the first time in the Olympic Games (Rio de Janeiro, August 2016/Niko Besnier).

more closely into the family, which was increasingly a nuclear rather than an extended unit, but men feared that this close association with women and the domestic realm would "feminize" them. However, the arena of "combat" sports (which represent a make-believe fight between individuals or teams) allowed men to express ritualized and controlled physical violence in a socially acceptable way. Men were hostile when women attempted to invade this realm, too. Still today, the exclusion of women from a particular sport is often more a result of cultural definitions of a sport as "masculine" and less a result of women's physiological inability to compete, and yet these stereotypes have had a powerful impact on women's efforts to gain recognition in sports, no matter how skilled they can be.

Such seems to be the case of bullfighting in Spain, often described as the epitome of Mediterranean machismo, a spectacle that has even been analyzed as an erotic performance whereby the bullfighter seeks to dominate the bull and appropriates its hypermasculinity by killing it—an analysis to which early anthropologists of Spanish culture actively contributed. In fact, there is a long, if somewhat uneven, history of women participating in the sport over the last three centuries, even though the Spanish state periodically passed, and later repealed, laws forbidding female bullfighters. Yet many commentators, including anthropologists, have relegated women's participation to a marginal position by denigrating it, ridiculing it, or simply not mentioning it. Bullfighting being an already highly competitive profession, many male bullfighters see women bullfighters as unwelcome rivals. Yet at other times in the history of the sport, women bullfighters have gained considerable popularity.[56]

The fact that many sports operate in a near-exclusive masculine domain does not preclude the participants from gendering them in more subtle ways than meets the eye. Olympic weightlifting in the republic of Georgia, for example, is a profoundly masculine sport—the presence of a woman makes athletes, coaches, and other participants deeply uncomfortable. Yet everyone involved knows that women practice the sport and excel at it. Coaches find women's technique graceful, controlled, and superior to men's, and exhort their male athletes to combine "male" brute force with "female" grace and skill, bestowing to a sport largely controlled by men in this setting an ambivalent gender.[57]

NON-WESTERN CONFIGURATIONS: NO CLEAR "MALE PRESERVE"

The Western construction of sport as a male preserve was the product of a specific history and cultural context that was reinforced by biomedicine, but there are other possible configurations of gender and sport. In some cases, the Western culture of sport contributed to the reshaping of non-Western cultures that did not originally display a strict male-female division. Sumo wrestling in Japan was originally practiced by both women and men until women's participation was outlawed in 1925, as fascism in Japan was refashioning gender roles, inspired in part by Japan's close association with the Prussian military tradition. To practice the sport today, the athlete must belong to an all-male "stable" *(heya),* where he lives and trains, and where social life is strictly hierarchical yet characterized by strong bonds of sociality between members. In Japan the sport is widely defined as a bastion of mas-

FIGURE 12. Turkish oil wrestling at the Kırkpınar festival (Edirne, Turkey, July 2012/Armin Zink).

culinity, a den of corruption, and a national symbol, although newcomers from other countries, such as Mongolia, have begun to disrupt these values since the end of the twentieth century.[58]

Another fascinating example is Turkish oil wrestling, which is also practiced in various forms in other areas of West Asia and the Balkans. In rural Turkey it is widely considered the national sport. Wrestlers wear only three-quarter-length leather trousers and anoint their bodies with a generous coating of olive oil that renders their bodies very slippery, so that a wrestler's only possible holds require him to reach into his opponent's trousers, although he is theoretically not allowed to grab his opponent's genitals or anus. Women are of course excluded from participating in this very homoerotic sport, in which participants nevertheless deny vigorously any undertone of sexuality. It is all about power between men, in which women are almost entirely incidental: it is about male honor and chivalry, but also about losing face, about guile and deceit, and about the tension between morality, purity, and physical strength. It thus exposes the dominant patriarchal order as potentially fragile and inconsistent.[59]

Western gender concepts accompanied the importation of Western sports into China, where understandings of sex and gender in the first place were not built upon Western biomedicine but upon the Chinese medical and religious traditions. Chinese medicine assumes that the difference between male and female bodies is a difference of degree rather than kind (Laqueur's "one-sex" model). Because the theory underlying traditional martial arts is that *qi* is the source of strength, in theory both men and women could be equally strong fighters—and because the cultivation of *qi* requires years of practice and sage-like wisdom, the most accomplished fighter could be a withered elderly man with a white beard.

Thus, in Chinese literature, there was an ancient tradition of women warriors. As early as the first century CE, the origin of the art of sword fighting was attributed to the legendary Woman of Yue.[60] Hua Mulan was another popular heroine. She took the place of her ailing father during compulsory military conscription and rose to lead men into battle. The woman warrior provided an archetype for twentieth-century understandings of China's star female athletes. They were likened to Mulan and described with classical phrases like "headdress heroines." In the 1990s the world record-setting distance runners were known as the Ma family army *(Ma jia jun)*, a wordplay on the title of the sixteenth-century Ming dynasty novel *Yang family generals (Yang jia jun)*, which features a matriarch and her daughters-in-law who take up arms to avenge their male kin.[61]

When Susan Brownell arrived in China in 1985, she brought with her assumptions about the relationship between gender and sport based on her own experiences as a member of the "Title IX generation," the first cohort of women in the United States to have the opportunity to participate in high school sports and gain full athletic scholarships to universities. She was surprised to find that the hostility that men regularly expressed toward female athletes in the United States did not seem to exist in China, and that there were no jokes about female shot-putters. She located this difference not only in the different medical tradition but also in differences between Chinese and European and American history. Unlike industrializing Europe, early twentieth-century China was a hierarchical agrarian society in which over 80 percent of the population were peasants. Elites set themselves apart by their ability to avoid hard labor and order others to do it in their place. The emperor and his imperial court oversaw a well-developed bureaucracy staffed by scholar-officials chosen through a national-examination system. Because written examinations were the main path to social mobility, a respect for education permeated the culture. In the late nineteenth and early twentieth centuries, Westerners indoctrinated into muscular Christianity who visited China were horrified to find that the masculine ideal was a slim, slope-shouldered bookworm who wore thick, black-rimmed glasses. Needless to say, physical education did not occupy an important place in the education of elite males; on the contrary, when first exposed to it, elite men considered it a form of manual labor and an insult to their status. In this context, sport did not become a "male preserve" in China as it had in the West.[62] Women were primarily prevented from participation in sports because the vast majority of them were hobbled by bound feet; in addition, elite women were not permitted to leave the courtyards of their homes and associate with men.

After the founding of the People's Republic of China in 1949, Communist ideology adopted the combination of sport masculinity and nationalism that had been promoted by the North American YMCA. A system of sports boarding schools was established in 1955 and is still the core of the national sports system. It gave equal support to men and women athletes. If one takes Title IX as the affirmation of the US government's commitment to gender equity in sport, then China's preceded it by over two decades.

The Communists eliminated horse racing and equestrian sports, the sports most identified with upper-class privilege; they were the only sports on the Olympic program that did not exist within the Chinese state sports system (they were reinstated in 2008).[63] In the popular mind, sports kept their association with lower-class manual labor. People commonly cited the proverb "Esteem literacy and despise martiality" *(Zhong wen qing wu)* to explain the low status of sport, referring to a tradition in which scholars were admired above generals. Since sports were identified with lower-class manual labor, elite men were not threatened when women entered that realm. There was popular resistance to women in sports, but it did not come from elite men protecting their "last bastion." Rather, parents were concerned that hard exercise might affect women's fertility, which was very important for their marriage prospects and continuation of the patrilineal lineage (even though from 1978 to 2015 most were limited to only one child).

However, these fears were overcome by the prospect of a better life. Then as now, the vast majority of athletes ended up in sports boarding schools because their parents expected that it would be a path to upward social mobility, and the majority came from worker and peasant families. Having particularly limited paths to mobility, female peasants were the main talent pool for sports regarded as particularly "bitter," such as race walking, long-distance running, weightlifting, and judo.

In 1980s and 1990s China, "masculinity" and "femininity" were not as important as social status in choosing a mate. It was generally considered best if husband and wife were of similar social status, but hypergamy was also a strongly held ideal, especially for women. Top female athletes aspired to marry men with advanced degrees from distinguished universities. Moreover, marriage and producing a child were nearly universal, so the general assumption was that everyone was heterosexual. While people were becoming aware that homosexuality existed in the West, most stated unequivocally that it did not exist in China. Brownell once had an experience in the dormitories at the Shanghai Institute of Physical Education that contrasted with the homophobia that she had learned to expect in the United States. During the rest hour, a javelin thrower and a shot-putter lay on top of the other in their underwear, stroking each other and whispering in each other's ears. Their three other roommates ignored them. Brownell later asked one of the roommates what kind of relationship the two girls had. "They are good friends," she replied. Unwilling to drop it at that, Brownell commented that in America, when two women lie together like that, people sometimes think they are homosexuals. The teammate replied, "We don't have homosexuals in China." It would take several more decades before a gay identity coalesced in urban China, and in the absence of a politicized gay identity, people engaged in a wide range of same-sex physical contact without having to question their sexual orientation. However, the parental and social pressure to marry and reproduce remained so heavy that around 2013 it came to public attention that large numbers of gays and lesbians were arranging "cooperative" or "fake" marriages in order to maintain appearances, either with a heterosexual partner or between a lesbian woman and gay man.

Chinese gender changed rapidly during the era of economic reform initiated in 1978 as an increasing proportion of the economy became market based. Men's professional basketball and soccer leagues were created in the mid-1990s, but women's professional leagues in volleyball and soccer were never financially viable and required government subsidy—even though China was a world leader in those sports. Still, for another decade, corporate sponsors did not seem to care much whether women were "feminine" or attractive but only whether they could beat the rest of the world at their sport. However, women's beauty was gaining importance in society at large, and something of a turning point was reached when the diver Guo Jingjing, winner of double gold medals at the 2004 and 2008 Olympics, became the female athlete most sought after by corporate sponsors—including

McDonald's. Chinese people considered her beautiful, and after the 2004 Olympics she began dating Kenneth Fok, scion of one of the wealthiest and most powerful lineages in Hong Kong, whom she married in 2012. Some people heard the echoes of history, recalling the beautiful 1930s swimming star Yang Xiuqiong, who was forced by a Sichuan warlord to become one of his eighteen concubines.[64]

THE GENDERED BODY: BODYBUILDING AND FITNESS

Bodybuilding is a sport with particularly strong associations with gender and sexuality. Alan Klein summed up his ethnography of bodybuilders at "Olympic Gym" on the West Coast of the United States in the early 1980s with these words: "Musclemongering is, at its very root, a male issue; a primary, albeit perhaps atavistic signifier of male status."[65] Olympic Gym's bodybuilders were overwhelmingly working-class men whose identities revolved around gender separation based on sexual dimorphism, an extreme view of masculinity aimed above all at proving that they were not women—that is, were not weak, dependent, and emotional—and not gay either. Their definition of masculinity was a definition by negation.[66] There were women who worked out at Olympic Gym, but the men did not wholeheartedly accept them. When a television crew came in to film the first women in the gym, one of the men bellowed at them, "Hey, they already got doctors, lawyers, cops, and now bodybuilders. Next thing you know they'll wanna be queer!"[67]

As Klein put it, "Society's institutions line up in service of genderizing biological males and females."[68] However, this gendering may take different forms in different gender cultures. In China after the Communists came to power, bodybuilding was banned as a kind of bourgeois narcissism. This referred only to men's bodybuilding, since women's bodybuilding did not exist. The ban was rescinded after China opened up to the outside world, but the reaction to women's bodybuilding revealed different gendered power structures from those discussed by Klein for the United States. In China the fault line took a Confucian path and ran between high-status senior men on the one side and subordinate junior men and women on the other. The meanings of the bodies of Klein's bodybuilders were not framed by a hierarchical senior-junior relationship. In 1985, China joined the International Federation of Bodybuilders, paving the way for the participation of Chinese athletes in international competitions. This posed a problem: international rules required women to wear bikinis, but controls on obscenity and pornography were very strict at the time, and opponents of women's bodybuilding felt it was "obscene."

Bikinis were considered a sign of Westernization, since Chinese women did not wear bikinis on beaches, whereas Western women had, by that time, been wearing bikinis for twenty years. Opponents felt that the baring of the female body might incite social disorder and have a "bad social influence." Upon closer analysis, it was evident that a large part of the fear of social disorder originated from a traditional hierarchy in which senior men decided what was appropriate for women and junior men; the sexuality of junior men was considered threatening to social order, so women had to be prevented from stimulating it. State leaders were not inclined to take the risk because bodybuilding was not an Olympic sport, so no gold medals could be gained. Finally, the leadership of the ministry of sports prevailed, but competitions with bikinis could be held only in sports venues controlled by them and not on theater stages controlled by the Ministry of Culture—which opposed them. The sports leaders argued that bikinis represented an attack on "feudalist thinking" and a move toward internationalism, and that they allowed individual expression through the "pursuit of beauty."[69]

Confucian gender ideals played out in a different way in Japanese fitness clubs in the 1990s.[70] Aerobic dancing was marked as a foreign form of exercise, and as a new technology of self-regulation, aerobics was used by young Japanese women to transform what it meant to be a "proper" or "good" Japanese woman and by extension a good "productive" citizen. It was their choice to go to these new gyms for aerobics classes. By going to aerobics classes, they were working on themselves, on their body shape, and on their physical fitness. Although they were influenced by images of slender, blonde Western models, their concept of the ideal body was not Western; the single most important measure of beauty was the shape and thinness of their legs. Women did not want to gain too much muscular bulk or do intense cardiovascular workouts. They viewed male bodybuilders as narcissistic and potentially gay. As in China, the bodies of these women also acquired meaning from a hierarchical family system in which women were expected to marry, have children, and subordinate their own needs: thus, the women should not lose so much weight that they stopped menstruating (amenorrhea), and being too skinny was a sign of selfishness.

While the fit, bare body was clearly fraught with issues of gender and power in these American, Chinese, and Japanese examples, the specific details combined into very different configurations in each cultural context.

Since the Victorian era, sports have often reinforced heteronormativity—a sex-gender system in which men and women are divided into male and female genders, marriage is only between "opposite" sexes, and "compulsory heterosexuality" enforces this structure. Thus, it is considered "normal" for biological sex, sexuality, gender identity, and gender roles to be in alignment, while any deviation from this alignment is "abnormal." Heteronormativity is often associated with homophobia—fear of and prejudice toward homosexuality. Whether recreational or professional, sports have traditionally been hostile to lesbian and gay participants.[71] The scandal that erupted at the Rio 2016 Olympics around gay and lesbian athletes demonstrated that homophobia was alive and well in sport: at the beginning of the Games, a reporter with the US news website the *Daily Beast* took it upon himself to arrange fictive dates with Olympians through a popular same-sex dating website and entrapped several dozen athletes, publishing their names on the news website, thoughtlessly unconcerned about the consequences that the act may have had for the careers and lives of athletes, particularly those from countries where homosexuality is illegal and potentially severely punished.[72]

The reasons that sport should be so homophobic are complex, but they are grounded in the emergence and promotion of sport in single-sex institutions like British public schools and the YMCA, as we discussed in chapter 2. In fact, the YMCA heritage of men loving men has left a legacy to this day. In the United States, the "cruising" scene intensified during World War I because of the YMCA's collaboration with the army and navy, and the YMCA became known in the United States and throughout the world as a meeting place for men attracted to other men. In 1978 this well-known secret was immortalized by the hit song "YMCA" by the Village People, a group that came together in the gay scene of New York's Greenwich Village and whose members assumed personae inspired by the hypermasculine "clone" stereotypes of the time. Today the energetic song and its accompanying dance, which mobilize all the camp potential of its disco origins, are still popular entertainment at many sports events, with many in the audience unaware of its origins. The long life of the YMCA cruising tradition demonstrates the lack of understanding of male relationships and sexuality by the leaders who tried to control it, failing to understand that it provided an acceptable social alternative in which emotional needs could be met, and it provided meaning to the yearnings of gay and bisexual men who, particularly before the 1960s, did not have the vocabulary to articulate it themselves.[73]

In addition, gender anxieties tended to crystallize in sport because it is a field of practice that places extreme value on the perfectibility of the body according to specific norms and then displays that body in public performances, making nonconforming bodies and persons deeply problematic. The pioneer sexologists like the Austro-German psychiatrist Richard von Krafft-Ebing (1840–1902), the British physician Havelock Ellis (1859–1939), and the British poet and classical historian John Addington Symonds (1840–93) all attempted to explain same-sex desire by appealing to the concept of "sexual inversion," which referred to a mismatch between a person's physiological sex and his or her gender identity (i.e., mannish women, effeminate men). It was used to explain homosexuality.[74] What is interesting is that only the persons who displayed deviant gendering needed to be "explained"—the scholars imagined the sexual partners of inverts as normatively gendered individuals who did not qualify as inverts because their partners "resembled" the opposite gender, toward which their sexual response was heterosexual. In sexual intercourse, it was believed that the invert adopted the role of the opposite gender; for example, a male-bodied invert adopted the "passive" role supposedly associated with females, while his male partner adopted the "active" role supposedly associated with males, thus playing a role congruent with his or her normative gender. In fact, early sexologists' theories were shaped by the way in which gender and sexuality were organized in their times.

In the decades following World War II, a considerable amount of research in psychology and psychiatry, particularly in the United States, was devoted to the "problem" of gender-nonconforming children and to curing boys by encouraging them to play sports and, conversely, by coaxing girls away from sports.[75] Sport thus emerged as a mechanism for the control of gender conformity. While in practice modern sexuality has become somewhat divorced from this heteronormative gender order, the specter of this order continues to loom large in stereotypes, which often depict gay men as feminine and therefore allegedly unskilled at and uninterested in sport, and lesbians as masculine and therefore too interested in sport.

Homophobia in sport is also fueled by the homosociality that is central to many sports, particularly team sports. Scantily clad bodies of the same sex come into close physical contact on wrestling mats, in rugby scrums, in changing rooms, and in displays of victorious exuberance. This contact could be easily redefined as erotic.[76] In the late 1970s folklorist Alan Dundes's cleverly titled article "Into the End Zone for a Touchdown" sparked considerable controversy with its psychoanalytic analysis of American football, which even earned him death threats. His homoerotic reading cataloged a preponderance of sexual metaphors: the ritualized patting of rear ends, the tight uniforms that exaggerate crotches and buttocks, and the three-point stance in which a player bends down in front of another player as if offering him his bottom.[77] Without necessarily subscribing to the simplistic psychoanalytic premises on which his analysis is based, one must nevertheless acknowledge that the boundary between heterosexuality and homosexuality in human life is opaque, and that few contexts showcase the entanglement of the two more dramatically than sport.[78]

Homophobia is particularly rampant in elite sports, as evidenced by the fact that in the course of history very few high-ranking athletes have publicly "come out." Those who have, have often been outed against their will, like tennis player Billie Jean King, or have done so at the end of their career, like Welsh rugby player Gareth Thomas. Biographies of lesbian or gay athletes report that their commercial sponsorship contracts often evaporated after they made their sexuality public; such is the case of Greg Louganis, who came out as both gay and HIV positive and eventually had to face bankruptcy as a result of the combination of his dwindling income, financial mismanagement, and exploitation by others.[79] Australian rugby league player Ian Roberts was the target of particularly aggressive tackles after his coming out.[80] Still others found it increasingly difficult to obtain professional contracts, as illustrated by the unfortunate story of Justin Fashanu, a British soccer player of Nigerian and Guyanese origin, who, after unwisely declaring his homosexuality to a tabloid newspaper in 1990, was shunned from top-level soccer (and by his family), traveled around the world playing for lackluster teams (including Wellington, New Zealand, where Niko Besnier met him), and eventually committed suicide in 1998 after facing allegations of sexual assault. The level of homophobia in some sports is greater than in others, and it is tied to the gender stereotypes associated with them and probably to other factors, such as the material interests involved (and thus the possibility that these interests are compromised by an association with homosexuality). Boxing and American football operate in particularly homophobic environments; men's soccer is also deeply heteronormative, but women's rugby has traditionally been a meeting place for lesbians, at least in the United States. Even where there is less hostility, gay and lesbian athletes are tolerated only if they keep quiet about their sexuality and do not challenge the rampant homophobia.[81]

It is ironic that the surveillance of elite athletes' sexual desires toward the goal of enforcing heterosexuality (homosexuality is, after all, legally allowed in all Western countries) has occurred at the same time that truly illegal sexual misbehaviors have been left unchecked until scandals erupt. The image of the womanizing male sports star who preys on adulating female fans is all too common throughout the sports world. The emergence of Pentecostalism and other forms of religious fundamentalism have disrupted this image in some parts of the world (chapter 6), but these come with their own forms of patriarchalism and sexual domination. In past decades, US university athletic programs have been rocked by numerous scandals regarding cover-ups of the sexual misconduct of male athletes and coaches—starting with the 2008 revelation of at least fifteen years of sexual abuse and assault of underprivileged youths by an assistant football coach at Penn State, which resulted in the firing of the legendary football coach Joe Paterno, the university president, and the athletic director. In 2015 a Duke University male basketball player's multiple sexual assaults against female students were ignored by the university, and at the University of Missouri-Columbia official inaction following a swimmer's complaint that an athlete on the university football team had raped her contributed to her suicide.[82] In 2016 a scandal raged in the United Kingdom regarding allegations of sexual abuse of underage players by scouts and other officials in soccer clubs, with clubs offering bribes to players not to speak out.[83] Even when minors are not involved, stories abound about coaches taking sexual advantage of the power they hold over athletes over long periods. These forms of condoned sexual violence stand in stark contrast to the homophobia rampant in the sports world, bearing witness to the hypocrisy of dominant moral standards.

The institutionalization of homophobia in the Olympic Games motivated US decathlon Olympian Tom Waddell and others to found the Gay Games in the early 1980s. The event was first held in San Francisco in 1982 and has been held ever since in an uninterrupted four-year cycle in various cities in North America, western Europe, and Australia. Waddell had originally planned to call the event Gay Olympics until the organization was sued by the IOC and the US Olympic Committee shortly before the 1982 games to prevent it from using the trademarked word *Olympics,* even though they had granted permission to use the term to some other groups, such as the Special Olympics.[84] The Gay Games showcase a range of sports similar to Olympic Games and are accompanied by cultural and social events oriented to gays and lesbians. However, they have been criticized for being just as captive to the market and complicit with capitalism as the Olympics, catering principally to young wealthy gay men from the urban Global North while subtly discriminating on the basis of race, gender, and class.[85]

SEX AND GENDER IN SPORT AS IDEOLOGICAL CONSTRUCTS

Rather than pinpointing the biological basis of sex, the new science of sex testing unwittingly demonstrated that the insistence on separating men and women is grounded in ideology rather than science. The many examples discussed in this chapter reveal how arbitrary this ideology was and how unstable was its presumed biological foundation. There was no foolproof test for separating "men" from "women," nor was there scientific evidence that testosterone conferred an advantage in sports. This meant that there was no good scientific explanation for the differences in sports performances between men and women except, perhaps, weight and height differences. There are some sports in which women can compete with men, but they are forced to compete with women anyway. The sexual orientations of athletes are probably representative of the general population, but this has yet to be acknowledged: male athletes are subjected to intense homophobia, and a wall of public denial still surrounds gay athletes, while female athletes in traditionally "male" sports are believed to be lesbians whether they are or not. Homophobia and transphobia, its transgender-focused counterpart, are primarily symptoms of anxiety about gender, which is particularly acute in the realm of sport.[86]

All these examples strengthen the central argument in the anthropology of gender: male and female are sociocultural constructs forming a cherished binary opposition that must be maintained and defended against threats.[87] Clearly, in the eyes of many sports officials (who have almost all been male), the hierarchical distinction between male and female must be maintained, even if it is at great cost to living human beings. And in this, sports merely reflect the sex-gender system of the society at large.

SIX

Sport, Cultural Performance, and Mega-events

ONE OF ANTHROPOLOGY'S UNIQUE contributions to the study of sport is its ability to explain sport's seemingly "irrational" aspects—that is, its symbolic and emotional power. While many pundits have observed that sport is like a religion, no other discipline offers the theoretical tools to take this observation beyond its superficial interpretation to unpack the precise relationships among sport, ritual, and religion. As we discussed in chapter 1, the idea that sports evolved over time from religious to secular events has had a long life in the discipline of history, but without a robust theory of either ritual or religion, that discipline has been unable to generate a deeper understanding of the observation. Anthropology has its own distinct tradition of the study of cultural performances that dates back more than a century and is anchored in studies of rituals.

In the last two decades, scholarly interest has burgeoned in the world's two biggest sports events, the Olympic Games and the FIFA World Cup in soccer. Although most scholarship has emanated from disciplines other than anthropology, some of the major theorists build their analyses on a foundation borrowed from anthropological theories of ritual. One limitation of this scholarship is that it has been much more theoretical than empirical. Mega-events tend to invite quantitative analyses that count the huge number of participants and audience members, as well as the expenditures and revenues, but it is challenging to figure out research methods that produce qualitative insights into the experiences of all those involved, be they athletes, spectators, volunteers, employees, shopkeepers, sex workers, executives, dignitaries, or citizens whose lives are disrupted. Even more challenging is establishing the entry point for ethnographic research, which at first glance may seem so limited in its scope as to be incapable of providing insights into the totality of such huge events. Perhaps for these reasons, anthropologists have been slow to take on the challenge of studying either sports as a global system or the mega-events that sit at the pinnacle of the system. Yet anthropologists have no reason to be intimidated: the ethnographic method can be used to great effect.

THE PERFORMATIVE TURN

The concepts of *cultural performance* and *performance genre* were put forward by anthropologist Milton Singer, who conducted fieldwork in India in the 1950s. He argued that public events such as weddings, temple festivals, and music, dance, and drama performances could serve as basic units for the study of a culture, a point that Clifford Geertz also makes, without citing Singer, in "Notes on the Balinese Cockfight" (discussed in chapter 1).[1] Geertz's interpretation of the cockfight as "a story the Balinese tell themselves about themselves" has influenced many approaches to cultural performances. These insights, along with those of Victor Turner, opened up new opportunities for applying interpretive and symbolic approaches as cultural performances were recognized as temporally condensed moments when participants consciously represented and evaluated values, roles, and societal institutions.

Here, we should observe that there is another brand of performance theory associated with the philosopher Judith Butler, but this theory has little connection with the anthropological tradition discussed in this chapter.[2] Butler used "performativity" to analyze, most prominently, speech acts, day-to-day behavior, and gender presentation—not collective performances. While individual and collective performativity are related, the two kinds of performance theory focus on different categories of human experience. Some ethnographies combine the two approaches, particularly those that examine the culturally specific ways in which spectators contribute to soccer matches or baseball games in Mexico, England, Japan, or Cuba. In each instance, specific "genres" are generated in which embodied values are performed that contribute to the overall performance of that sport spectacle.[3]

A series of symposia funded by the Wenner-Gren Foundation for Anthropological Research probed the potential of interpretive and symbolic approaches to cultural performances. Max Gluckman, Sally Falk Moore, and Victor Turner organized the first in 1974 under the title "Secular Rituals

Considered: Prolegomena toward a Theory of Ritual, Ceremony and Formality," which included many luminaries of the time, such as Erving Goffman, Jack Goody, and Terence Turner. The challenge of the conference was to break through the traditional assumption that rituals must be connected with religious or magical procedures, that is, with the realm of supernatural powers. The recognition that some rituals are not fundamentally religious was a bold assertion at the time. The introduction of the book that was based on the symposium asserted that if the supernatural element is stripped away from it, secular ritual would be a "vast subject."[4] As inclusive as they thought secular ritual might be, however, this group of theorists stopped short of including sport in their lists of forms of secular ritual.

As an aside, it is interesting that, in creating the modern Olympic Games, Pierre de Coubertin aspired to create a secular religion out of sport, which he called *religio athletae*.[5] He had no doubt encountered the concept of secular ritual during his Jesuit education, since the Jesuits had invented the concept in the seventeenth century to describe the non-Christian, Confucian rituals they witnessed in China.

Max Gluckman, the founder of the Department of Social Anthropology at the University of Manchester and the major figure in what came to be known as the Manchester school, had already taken up the topic of sport in his invited address at a large international conference, "Sport in the Modern World: Chances and Problems," organized in conjunction with the Munich 1972 Olympic Games. Gluckman was a fan of the famed Manchester United Football Club and would sometimes take his students to games in order to illustrate his theories; Turner was among them.[6] With Mary Gluckman, he directly took up the question of whether sport should be considered a secular ritual and concluded that it should not.[7] Sports, they acknowledged, are sometimes held in conjunction with rituals; they are governed—like rituals—by formal and conventional rules; and they embody—like rituals—moral principles. But they lack the "confidence in ultimate mystical effect" that characterizes rituals. Broadening the heretofore limited category of ritual to refer to any "collective formality" is not helpful, they argued. It would be Gluckman's last publication; he died shortly after the symposium.

A second Wenner-Gren symposium, titled "Cultural Frames and Reflections: Ritual, Drama and Spectacle," organized by Turner, Barbara Myerhoff, and Barbara Babcock, was held in 1977. It resulted in a book edited by John MacAloon, *Rite, Drama, Festival, Spectacle: Rehearsals toward a Theory of Cultural Performance*.[8] MacAloon's contribution to that book will be discussed further below. The final two symposia were held in 1982 as the outcome of the bond that had developed in the 1977 symposium between Turner and Richard Schechner, whose background was in experimental theater.

Singer and Geertz had asserted that cultural performances were merely a reflection or condensation of the social system. Turner went much further; he argued that the relationship between cultural performances and mundane, everyday sociocultural processes was not just unidirectional; it was reciprocal and reflexive. Cultural performances were a "text in context," a dialectic between dramatic and sociocultural processes in a given place and time. Moreover, cultural performances might be characterized by "anti-structure," meaning that instead of reflecting the status quo they might invert it.[9] Out of these meetings of great minds, three core ideas emerged that have had staying power in subsequent works on sports events and other matters.

The first is the idea that—like rituals—cultural performances typically pass through three phases, an idea that Turner borrowed from Belgian folklorist Arnold van Gennep's work on rites of passage of the early twentieth century: (1) spatial, temporal, and symbolic separation from "normal" social structures; (2) liminality, or a state of being in-between states, and (3) reincorporation into social structure.[10]

The second key idea is that cultural performances highlight qualities of *communitas* and reflexivity. Communitas is a generalized human bond, a sense of communion, which liminal events generate among the participants. Performative reflexivity results from the fact that rituals present the "as if," the "world as we want it to be"; they are "play."[11] They provide an occasion when participants, temporarily freed of normative constraints, may reflect back on the status quo and perhaps question it. They generate a highly contrived and deliberate reflexivity in which a group "bends back upon itself" and "people think about how they think."[12] This means that while rituals generally function to reinforce the existing social structure, they possess revolutionary potential and thus are frequently surrounded by a great deal of social tension and anticipation as the people involved wonder how they are going to turn out. Elites will try to ensure that they do reinforce the status quo, and governments will try to ensure that rituals legitimize their authority rather than challenge it.

The third key idea is that—like rituals—cultural performances "do work," that is, they accomplish social transformations. Although the original theorists of cultural performances did not acknowledge it, we assert that sports events reaffirm core beliefs that people hold about their social worlds, provide some structure for social change, and provide an embodied context that expresses the ways in which those worlds are changing and how those changes should be understood. For example, Heather Levi's ethnography of *lucha libre* (Mexican wrestling) demonstrates the myriad ways in which cultural performances, such as wrestling matches, act as ritualistic events.[13] *Lucha libre* makes sense because it draws on and reproduces a series of broadly intelligible social contradictions shared by its fans, yet it problematizes the model of a universal trajectory toward modernity, the model that other sports often embody. What matters in these performances are the enacted social relations—the affinities, connections, loyalties, and enmities—and not a win-loss record. A championship is not gained through the accumulation of victories but by answering challenges. Victory does not shift a numerical balance sheet, but it can realign relationships. *Lucha libre* provides a kind of commentary on contemporary social issues in its live and mediated performances, commentary that cannot be reduced to its performers or its audience.

The Turnerian approach is best applied to intentionally organized events of limited duration which have an identifiable beginning, middle, and end. However, since the 1980s, scholars have extended the concept of ritual to many kinds of behavior that do not fit these criteria, sometimes regarding much of mundane life as consisting of everyday rituals or ritualized behavior. These efforts are diametrically opposed to how Turner defined ritual, namely as activity that stood apart from the flow of everyday life. Turner was even somewhat dismissive about the potential of *habits* as an object of study, assuming that people try to articulate meaning through rituals and other cultural performances, but not through habitual actions.[14] (His position was thus opposed to Bourdieu's concept of habitus, discussed in chapter 4.) One implication of Turner's perspective for research methodology is that it is very important to study the organization work that precedes the ritual because that is when most of the symbolic meaning is crafted, but this never became the dominant approach in anthropology and ritual studies, in which the focus has been on interpreting the symbols seen in the ritual performance itself. This has been as true of studies of Olympic opening ceremonies as of studies of ritual.[15]

Furthermore, Turner drew a distinction between truly "liminal" phenomena (rituals in premodern and agricultural societies) and "liminoid" phenomena (performance genres such as theatrical plays, sport competitions, and music concerts in industrialized societies). This distinction captured the dichotomy between work and leisure, which is so central to modernity. For him, both the liminal *and* liminoid are present in modern societies, with the liminal being evident in churches, fraternity initiation rites, and Masonic orders, whereas the liminoid is generally expressed in "performative" genres such as literature, theater, and sport. Underpinning Turner's distinction between the liminal and the liminoid is the sacred. The liminoid phenomena Turner identifies are spectacular and often commodified performances, whereas liminal phenomena are not, and possibly cannot be, transformed by capitalism because of their sacred nature.[16] He wrote,

> A soccer game in the huge Maracanã Stadium between the great Rio rivals Flamengo and Fluminense has something of a ritual quality too, with its "*baterias*" of drummers, banners borne aloft when a team scores, fireworks, clouds of powder ejected upwards, club colors, praise songs, corporate groups of supporters each based on traditional *bairro* of the city. . . . But to call *Carnaval* and *Futebol* "ritual" is perhaps to strain unduly the sense of this term.[17]

Turner argued that one feels "moral pressure" to attend religious services, even in contemporary, secularized societies, but one willingly pays to attend sports events. To put it more broadly, social obligation underpins individual participation in liminal activities, whereas a sense of voluntarism (and consumerism) motivates participation in liminoid activities. "One works at the liminal, one plays with the liminoid."[18]

He excluded sport from liminal genres, seeing it as an event that merely confirmed the social order and did not possess liminal qualities; that is, it did not bring about social transformations. Nowhere did Turner argue that liminoid performances transformed their participants once they returned to the structured world of work, food, and sleep. There is no transformative threshold through which individuals pass comparable to that which participants experience in ritual performances. In short, they are not transformed, and for Turner that is the defining characteristic of a ritual: a ritual brings about a social transformation.

Like Gluckman and Turner, Allen Guttmann saw a clear separation between sport and ritual that reflected the difference between tradition and modernity, as we discussed in chapter 1. His "from ritual to record" theory posited a unilinear evolution of "modern" sport out of "traditional" ritual practices. All three theorists wrote during a time when modernization theory had yet to be seriously questioned, so the difference between "tradition" and "modernity" was conceived in black-and-white terms. Guttmann reflected a viewpoint that persists today, to which Gluckman and Turner might have subscribed—that international sport is somehow quintessentially "modern." Anthropologist Henning Eichberg disagreed that the ritual had been stripped away from modern sport and argued that in fact the pursuit of sports records had made sport into a "ritual of the record."[19] Modernization theory was discredited in the 1980s when the rapid economic development of Japan, South Korea, Singapore, and Taiwan contradicted the facile predictions that "traditional" family structures and collectivism prevented modernization. Since that time scholars have discarded Turner's distinction between liminal performance genres in "traditional" societies and liminoid performance genres in "modern" societies and have applied the theory of liminality across all cultures.

The postmodern turn of the 1980s led scholars to question whose interests are served by the symbolism in cultural performances and whether communitas is not an overly optimistic concept that fails to recognize that not every participant and spectator is equally vested in the event. One result of the postmodern turn has been skepticism toward cultural performances, which, borrowing from Marx, one can view as an "opiate of the masses" that elites utilize to dupe subordinate classes into accepting their subordination.[20] In the realm of activism, the Bread Not Circuses Coalition, formed in 1990 to oppose Toronto's bid for the 2008 Olympic Games, has repeatedly raised this criticism. The group's name was inspired by the Roman poet Juvenal's (ca. 100 CE) complaint that government officials of his day were using handouts of grain and costly circus games (*panem et circenses*, "bread and circuses") to buy the votes of poor people. A theoretical split emerged between scholars and pundits who emphasized the capacity of sports events to create a sense of communitas and those who emphasized the ways in which sports events deceive and manipulate the public. MacAloon has pointed out the irony that it is common for cynical academics, who are critical of Olympic Games when they are being organized in their home cities, to get caught up in the celebration once the Games arrive. One such academic living in London wrote a personal account explaining his own hypocrisy after he "became aware that my viewing response to the recent London Olympics seemed somewhat paradoxical":

> I confess that I enjoyed watching the 2012 London Olympic "spectacle," the very spectacle that was the direct result of the excessive expenditure, bogus justifications and dodgy politics that I disparage and have publicly critiqued.[21]

Actually, Turner himself acknowledged the contested nature of rituals and wrote an entire book about the ineffective effort of an Ndembu elder to establish himself as a village headman by organizing a ritual. Rather than legitimizing his authority, the ritual sparked even greater conflict due to his inability to unite fellow villages behind the effort.[22] Thus, as the title of the book indicated, rituals could result in *either* schism *or* continuity by forcing people to take sides. However, subsequent applications of Turnerian theory have emphasized that rituals strengthen solidarity. What remains to be explored is a middle ground that combines both perspectives, acknowledging that rituals and sport mega-events can simultaneously build solidarity among some factions and increase schisms between others. Organizing events is challenging—making all the arrangements, attracting the attendees, and smoothing over conflicts involve complicated political maneuvering and thus are very revealing of social relationships. Anyone who has ever organized a wedding or a funeral can attest to the difficulties involved. Ethnographies that focus on the organizational work leading up to such events have their finger on the pulse of the important social negotiations as they occur, but such studies are rare.

The main reason that Gluckman, Turner, and others believed that sports were not a form of ritual was that they did not believe sport events brought about social transformations. However, organizers of sport mega-events frequently conceive of them as having the capability of bringing about social transformations. Examples of transformations that Olympic Games and Soccer World Cups were intended to bring about have included racial and ethnic reconciliation (Australia and South Africa), urban regeneration (Barcelona and London), and the emergence of the host nation as a superpower (Japan, Korea, China, Brazil). Portions of the audience buy into this viewpoint, while others may not—but is that really so different from small-scale rituals? And so, contra Turner, sport mega-events *are* apparently often believed to do "work," to effect social transformations. Whether they actually succeed is a separate question—and that is a particular challenge of large-scale events.

SPORT AND RELIGION: THE VIEW FROM THE FIELD

Henning Eichberg had gotten us to acknowledge that there is no clear division between sport and ritual, but as yet we have no theory constructed from the opposite assumption: that religion and sport are closely related. Niko Besnier's GLOBALSPORT research team had not originally pinpointed religion as a focus, but the ethnographies conducted by his team members in 2012–17 revealed that religious practice and athletic endeavor are often closely intertwined.[23] The long-term ethnography conducted by the team enabled them to see the relation of sport to religion from the inside out. From that perspective, it was clear that sporting and religious practices were seamlessly connected in the everyday lives of athletes and coaches.

The young men from upper-middle and upper-class families in Buenos Aires who grew up playing rugby in exclusive clubs, among whom Sebastián Fuentes conducted fieldwork, organized spiritual retreats for an institution whose logo was a cross inside a rugby ball. Although authorized by the church, the movement is largely organized by the young men themselves. After the retreat, some continued to meet weekly in a group called a "scrum," after one of the sport's signature formations in which players' bodies are gathered very close together, which symbolizes solidarity. Fuentes related this movement to a shift in Catholicism since the 1980s toward highlighting the individual experience of religion, which has resulted in blurring the line between religion and sport. As some of the young men told him, every baptized person is supposed to "sanctify everyday life." Fuentes observed, "They play Catholicism as if it were the sport they feel passion for. And they pray in rugby as if it were a religion." Some clubs prayed to Our Lady of Rugby and placed outside the door of their club building a statuette brought back from the Our Lady of Rugby chapel in southwest France.

In Fiji, sport and religion are so interconnected that Daniel Guinness coined the term *rugby theology* to capture the collection of ideas and practices that connected godliness, moral discipline, and religiosity with professional success in rugby. Young Fijian men drew strength both from their warrior tradition as indigenous *i-Taukei* and from their religious faith—traditionally Methodist or Catholic, but increasingly Pentecostal. No matter their religious faith, the religious practices of Fijian rugby players shared a concern with controlling destiny—helping athletes to cope with the uncertainty entailed in enduring difficult, unpaid rugby training in the hope that it would lead them to overseas careers. Success was explained by "giving glory to God," and the daily regimens of rugby players-in-training included sermons, prayers, and religious discussions. Players and coaches believed that both physical and spiritual preparation were necessary; being aware of Fiji's limited access to facilities and sport science, they believed that spiritual preparation was the element that would allow them to prevail in the world of rugby.

FIGURE 13. Every soccer game in Buea, Cameroon, begins with a prayer huddle (September 2014/Uroš Kovač).

Similarly, the young male soccer players among whom Uroš Kovač conducted fieldwork in Cameroon, where soccer is by far the most popular sport, hoped to secure professional contracts in wealthier countries where they could earn money for themselves and their kin. Spurred by the economic crisis that had persisted since the late 1980s, a version of Pentecostal Christianity that preached the benefits of acquisition of material wealth had gained a strong foothold (figure 13). Young soccer players frequently consulted the Pentecostal "men of God," self-proclaimed prophets and evangelists. This was a break with customary practice, since soccer had been notorious for its witchcraft: players were alleged to use potions and other magical paraphernalia to score amazing goals, run with exceptional speed, or unfailingly guard the goal.[24] They were also believed to attempt to harm opposing players out of jealousy by causing career-ending injuries. The players who adhered to Pentecostal denominations wanted to both protect themselves from witchcraft and distance themselves from it. They "tapped the power of the Holy Spirit" by anointing their hands and feet with oil and holy water in order to achieve similar goals to those sought through witchcraft—successes on the playing field. Players would also bring their passports to the man of God, who would rub his hands with anointed oil and pray for the passports to be filled with visas enabling them to play overseas.

FIGURE 14. Senegalese wrestling star Modou Lô (left, sitting in the plastic chair) with his *mystique* arsenal (Dakar, July 2015/Mark Hann).

In both Fiji and Cameroon, as elsewhere around the world, including Brazil, Pentecostalism advocates a new kind of masculinity that emphasizes abstinence from alcohol and sex, self-discipline, and individual spirituality—in contrast to traditional forms of masculinity.[25] The global expansion of Pentecostalism has connected with the global sport industries as they expand into previously peripheral pools of "talent." Together, both are shaping young men and their masculinity to fit the individualism and self-discipline demanded by the neoliberal definition of "professionalism" in the sport industries.

As we explained in chapter 3, young Senegalese men who competed in traditional wrestling—the most popular sport in Senegal—employed the services of marabouts whose mix of traditional magic and religion *(mystique)* would ensure their success.[26] The *guerre mystique* (mystical warfare) starts as soon as the combat is scheduled, and wrestlers spend large sums of money on an arsenal of prayers, amulets, potions, and animal sacrifices to mobilize *djinn* (supernatural spirits) against the opponent (figure 14). During the contest, each side's marabouts crouched in their chambers, uttering prayers and incantations counted on prayer beads. Rumors even circulated about wrestlers desecrating the graves of their opponents' ancestors, animals being buried alive, and even human sacrifices. While some of these practices were largely tolerated in traditional wrestling, in 2013 the Senegalese Soccer Federation banned all maraboutic practices from stadiums, giving the reason that "soccer should not become wrestling." However, on local teams soccer players consulted marabouts and wore *gris gris* (charms) underneath their shin pads, hid magical objects in the goals, and solicited prayers to help them score.

Taken together, this research shows how local magical practices, *and* practices linked with world religions, *and* the ideology of scientific professionalism were *all* ways of dealing with the uncertainty of the game and influencing fate toward the goals of securing professional contracts and national acclaim, constructing a respectable masculine subject, and assuring an athlete's social position among his kin and community. Practices intended to control luck and destiny and to create masculine men are inherent in many sports—some of these practices may be called religious and others not.

Conflicts between different sets of practices were just disagreements about their efficacy. The 2006 Fijian national team coach felt that players sometimes "hide behind God," that is, use religion to avoid training hard. The coach in a Senegalese soccer academy told his pupils that only hard work and dedication—not the services of a marabout—would lead to success in soccer; the Muslim players were also forbidden to fast for Ramadan (but they sabotaged this by pretending to drink and spitting the water out when the coach turned his back). It might be tempting to describe these as conflicts between tradition and modernity, superstition and science, or religion and secularism. However, that was not the core difference to the players and coaches, who were just concerned about which practices would secure success on the sports field.

The category of "religion" may not turn out to be particularly helpful here: from the etic (outsider) point of view, it assumes a clear line between certain kinds of practices that did not exist to the practitioners; from the emic (insider) point of view, "religion" per se was not a meaningful category for the athletes, whose worldview was composed of more concrete concepts such as faith, juju, the will of God, or the power of the Holy Spirit. "Religion" is a social science category that imposes upon the everyday practices of the athletes a distinction that is not clearly marked by them. These athletes engaged in a continuum of practices to ensure success in sports and life: sports training prepared the body, magical practices influenced luck and fate, spiritual practices tapped into a higher power—and those who had access to sport psychologists also utilized them to prepare their minds.

These careful ethnographies demonstrated that it is not worth asking the question, is sport a form of religion? Posed this way, the question should be discarded along with its associated dichotomies: the secular and the sacred, scientific rationality and magical thinking, and so on. These categories are the product of a specific Western history in which science and religion became opposed, along with a whole string of associated oppositions that underlay modernization theory, such as the modern versus the traditional, and rationality versus superstition.

It was this fundamental dichotomy that made George Gmelch's famous essay "Baseball Magic" so popular.[27] In this brief article, Gmelch described the multitude of practices that minor-league baseball players employed to bring success, such as tugging on their caps, touching their uniform letters or medallions, crossing themselves, tapping or bouncing the bat on the plate, or swinging the weighted warm-up bat a prescribed number of times. He called these practices "rituals" or "magic" and likened them to the Trobriand Islanders' fishing magic, which Bronislaw Malinowski classically analyzed.[28] Like Trobriand magic, baseball magic assuaged anxiety in the face of uncertainty. The essay has amused generations of students in Introduction to Anthropology classes by asserting that, in a thoroughly "modern" sport like baseball in the United States, the players were actually engaging in magical practices similar to "traditional" peoples.

Ultimately, the interesting question is not whether sport fits into a universal category of religion but rather which notions *do* have meaning for the practitioners and why sport of all things is seen to embody that meaning. The old dichotomies that underlay modernization theory would be best discarded.

RAMIFIED PERFORMANCE THEORY

While Gluckman and Turner had concluded that sports are *not* rituals, MacAloon's theory of ramified performance genres offered an explanation of what sports actually *are*. For MacAloon, the starting point for any study of public events should be an analysis of the native categories that are used to classify them. "Metagenres" or "megagenres" frame events with a set of rules and expectations.[29] Olympic Games are a "ramified performance type" composed of concentric frames with the "games" at their center—the sports. Games have fixed and public rules that separate them from everyday life, they are "fun," and they are rich in symbolism. In turn, they are framed by the "rituals" that surround them—opening and closing ceremonies, medal ceremonies, and so on. Rituals invoke sacred forces and effect social and spiritual

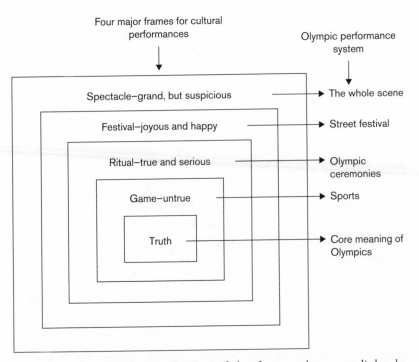

Four major frames for cultural performances

Olympic performance system

Spectacle–grand, but suspicious ———————▶ The whole scene

Festival–joyous and happy ———————▶ Street festival

Ritual–true and serious ———————▶ Olympic ceremonies

Game–untrue ———————▶ Sports

Truth ———————▶ Core meaning of Olympics

FIGURE 15. Diagram of John MacAloon's ramified performance theory as applied to the Olympic performance system (designed by Susan Brownell, partly based on the diagram in John J. MacAloon, "Olympic Games and the Theory of Spectacle in Modern Societies," in *Rite, Drama, Festival, Spectacle: Rehearsals Toward a Theory of Cultural Performance*, ed. John J. MacAloon [Philadelphia: Institute for the Study of Human Issues, 1984], 258).

transformations. These rituals are in turn embraced by the "street festival" taking place outside the arenas, which is unscripted and, above all, joyous. All these nested events add up to the most encompassing frame, the "spectacle."[30] Spectacles are characterized by grandeur bordering on excess and are primarily visual, watched by "spectators."[31] The relationship between the types is as important as the individual frames. MacAloon's neatly ordered system of nested frames reflected Coubertin's effort to create a "whole system" united by a single principle, which he sometimes called "eurhythmy."[32] The theory can be diagrammed as shown in figure 15.

In addition to his theoretical contribution, MacAloon was a strong advocate of ethnography as a research method for researching Olympic Games. In a barbed comment aimed at the tendency of scholars to write about Olympic Games based on watching television and reading the popular media, he offered this definition of ethnography: "minimally, the resolve to try not to write professionally about peoples and events that could have been but were not seen, discussed, and lived with face to face."[33] He posed ethnography against the fetishization of theory in the academy, seeing it as a way for scholars to discover and, as much as possible, experience for themselves the concrete and particular social relations that go into making the Olympic Games.

While John MacAloon led a team research project on the Los Angeles 1984 Olympics, and he and Kang Shin-pyo followed the Seoul 1988 torch relay across Korea for three weeks, the first published attempt at a comprehensive ethnography of the Olympic Games was by a research team that studied the Lillehammer 1994 Winter Olympics, led by Arne Martin Klausen of the University of Oslo. The book was framed by the concept of "secular ritual" and the ritual theories outlined above.[34] However, MacAloon's call for more ethnography of Olympic Games has largely been unheeded because few anthropologists have turned their attention to them, and they have largely been studied by sociologists, historians, and sport studies scholars. There is a dearth of ethnographies of mega-events of all stripes, including World Expos and FIFA World Cups. The books by Susan Brownell on the Beijing 2008 Olympics and by John Horne and Wolfram Manzenreiter on the 2002 World Cup in Japan are exceptions, but, although based on ethnography, both of those were actually published before the events in order to provide background for understanding them.[35]

MEGA-EVENTS: FROM WORLD'S FAIRS TO OLYMPIC GAMES

Around the world, public events are becoming larger, more numerously attended, and more important. What is driving this trend? On the surface, it appears that governments and businesses are increasingly invested in them because they are considered important in "city branding" and national image promotion. Festivals, in particular, are considered important for cultural heritage preservation and city branding. Since the end of the Cold War, governments have put ever greater investment into public diplomacy (strategic efforts by governments to directly win the support of citizens of another country and bypass traditional diplomacy) and have sought to supplement hard power (military threats and force, economic payments and sanctions) with soft power (attractive values and culture, typically purveyed by nongovernmental institutions), as discussed further in chapter 8.

While large-scale gatherings have convened since ancient times (an estimated forty thousand spectators attended the Olympic Games at their peak in the first centuries CE), "mega-events" are generally understood as a distinctly modern phenomenon. Sports events in general often serve as a focal point of public attention whatever their size. Yet the enormous scale of the biggest international sports events suggests that they are a unique form of event. Sociologist Maurice Roche defined *mega-events* as large-scale cultural and commercial events, including sports events, that have a dramatic character, mass popular appeal, and international significance. For Roche, only Olympic Games, world's fairs, and FIFA World Cups satisfied these requirements.

The Crystal Palace Exhibition in London in 1851 was the first industrial exposition to claim an international rather than national scope. After the first modern Olympic Games in Athens in 1896, the next three Olympic Games were all held in conjunction with major international expositions: the 1900 Paris Exposition, the 1904 Louisiana Purchase Exposition in St. Louis, and the 1908 Franco-British Exposition in London. The second through fourth Olympic Games were, as Coubertin phrased it, the "humiliated vassal" of the world's fairs, which occupied pride of place as the sole mega-event of the times.

World's fairs and Olympic Games played an important role in early forms of globalization from the mid-nineteenth century onward. They formed a global circuit of events through which flowed people, ideas, and capital. They facilitated technology transfer, transmitted modern aesthetics in art and architecture, and provided templates for globalizing cities and improving urban infrastructure. They aided the movement of multinational corporations into new markets by creating global audiences of consumers. Finally, they justified and glorified colonialism and imperialism.[36]

The Olympic Games began to gain international importance at the Stockholm 1912 Olympics, held during a period of escalating nationalist conflicts that would lead to the outbreak of World War I two years later. Governments began interfering in the groupings in the parade of nations and the flags to be raised in case of victory. The Austrian Empire protested the presence of an independent delegation from Bohemia, and the Russian Empire lodged a similar protest about Finland. The International Olympic Committee (IOC) thus took on its role as one of the important arbiters of which peoples may represent themselves as "nations." It took symbolic control by insisting that the head of state could only briefly declare the opening of the games, while in other matters it was the IOC that reigned supreme.

In the next decades, the power of monarchs waned while that of elected heads of state and dictators waxed, and along with it ideologies of modern nationalism. Since 1928, world's fairs have been held under the auspices of the Bureau international des expositions, an intergovernmental organization established by treaty; it now limits the frequency of the biggest fairs, designated World Expos, to once every five years. While their frequency has not decreased, World Expos no longer attract the media attention that they once did or occupy as important a place in the global public imagination. Historians pinpoint Berlin in 1936 as the first Olympics to blossom as a global mega-event and the exposition in New York City in 1939 as the last great fair.[37] What happened to cause this switch?

MacAloon attributed the rise of the Olympic Games to their successful interlocking of various performance genres into one mega-event after a period of experimentation. There had been some failures, in particular the association with world's fairs and the diffuse sports programs that continued over many months. Still, the history of the Olympic Games from 1900 to 1936 is a "story of the simultaneous differentiation, elaboration, and lamination of the performative genres of game, rite, festival and spectacle. . . . The development of this new 'ramified performance system' accounts more than anything else for the fantastic global interest in the Olympics and its emergence, over all rivals, as *the* dramatic celebration of world-historical process."[38]

Anthropologically trained historian Mark Dyreson offered another explanation. He pointed out that television made its Olympic debut in 1936 when the Nazis beamed images to closed-circuit televisions in several cities. The next two Olympic Games were canceled due to the war, but after they resumed in 1948, "television simultaneously strangled the expositions and fertilized the Olympics."[39] Exhibition halls teeming with cutting-edge machines were replaced by stadiums teeming with finely tuned athletic bodies. MacAloon emphasized the Olympic Games' success in creating an event composed of richly layered bodily experiences; Dyreson emphasized nonbodily experiences mediated by television.

Assertions about the historical importance of world's fairs and Olympic Games in globalization beg for a theoretical explanation of why these events could be so important. After all, they were merely public events, seemingly peripheral to more important economic and political realms. Answers to this question have generally drawn on anthropological theories about the important role played by ritual in social life.

Roche presented a detailed case for the social importance of mega-events, describing them as temporal and cultural markers in identity work, used especially by nations to construct the "story of the country," thereby leading to the creation of permanent cultural displays—public museums, department stores, amusement parks. Mega-events contributed to the rise of mass media and communication technologies. Before television, they served as important channels for the exchange of information, values, and technology. They cultivated mass interest in consumer culture, tourism, and sports. As a result, mega-events fostered the formation of an international public culture for the expression of national identities within an international world of nations. Mega-events structure the space and time of modernity, creating a sense of predictability and control over the pace and direction of social change by creating localized difference within the frame of global homogeneity. At the same time, against the grain of the excessively rationalistic world that they helped to bring forth, they promise the occurrence of the extraordinary.[40]

Mega-events are typically organized by a combination of governmental and international nongovernmental organizations. While they appear at intervals on the global calendar as periodic events of limited duration, the gap between the planning of the bid and the execution of the event lasts a decade and overlaps with other bid and preparatory cycles, so that at any moment many mega-events are being planned, developed, staged, and paid for in an unending rhythm. This creates a continuous state of ferment in a number of global cities.[41]

Roche also put forward the concept of the *event ecology* or the *performance complex*. This concept extended the notion of a performance system beyond the scope of a single individual event by linking multiple events. Mega-events sit at the pinnacle of a structure that includes events of decreasingly smaller scope targeting, for example, world regional, national, and local audiences.

Roche's event ecology echoes the model of the *ritual system* developed in ritual theory—although, as discussed earlier, the original theorists of this model did not apply it to sports events. In a ritual system, the center of state power (court or capital) is a "civilizing center" whose power radiates outward through rituals that emulate the spectacular state rituals organized by the central power. One example is the "theater state" in Bali that Geertz famously analyzed, in which spectacular mass ritual performances were so entwined with state power that the ritual was not a device to shore up the state; rather, the state was a device for the enactment of the ritual. Power served pomp rather than vice versa.[42] The *doctrine of the exemplary center* meant that the court provided a paragon of civilized excellence, and the polity was shaped in its image.

Another example is sports in contemporary China, where one might ask whether the Chinese National Sports Games could be considered a "ritual of state." The National Games sit at the pinnacle of a ritual system (or event ecology) intended to harmonize and synchronize the bodies and spirits of the populace. The system of sports games parallels the layers of government, from national games (College, Workers', etc.) to city-level (college, primary, and middle-school championships, etc.), and even to the annual sports meets of primary and middle schools. These events always begin with an opening ceremony complete with a parade of athletes, opening speeches by the relevant stratum of officials, performances by marching bands or flag teams, and an artistic performance. The ceremonies at high-profile international or national events produce a ripple effect throughout the country as lower units imitate the latest trends seen on television. For example, when China participated in the Los Angeles 1984 Olympic Games after a twenty-eight-year absence from the Summer Games, Chinese television viewers were shocked to see a different kind of opening ceremony from the mass calisthenics that were the standard in China. Choreographers immediately began to emulate the "artistic" type of show seen in Los Angeles. At the next National Games three years later, they experimented with martial arts and "ethnic" dancing and drumming—a departure from the Communist revolutionary symbolism of previous games. Martial arts and drumming performances were then incorporated into the city collegiate meet in Beijing, and then into local opening ceremonies around the country, in a trickle-down effect.

In Beijing's Haidian District, Yangfangdian primary school remade its annual sports meet as a "mini–Olympic Games" in 2002, after Beijing won the bid to host the 2008 Olympics. In the school's opening ceremonies, students marched into the stadium representing different countries, wearing the countries' "traditional" dress, shouting the Olympic slogan "One world, one dream" in the national languages, and performing dances associated with the countries. In the 2005 installment, the traditional dress of the "US team" consisted of blue jeans and denim jackets, a bandanna, and a cowboy hat. In the next years, dozens of primary and middle schools in Beijing also turned their annual sports meets into mini–Olympic Games, with opening

FIGURE 16. Mini-Olympics schoolchildren with torch (Deyang, Sichuan, China, July 23, 2008/Susan Brownell).

ceremonies that emulated the Olympic opening ceremonies. After the cata-strophic earthquake in Sichuan Province in May 2008, Susan Brownell accompanied an informal group into the disaster zone led by the physical education teacher who had spearheaded the effort at Yangfangdian school. The team conducted mini–Olympic Games at six schools affected by the earthquake (figure 16). In her role as "international friendly person," Brownell declared the mini–Olympic Games open. The domestic segment of the Olympic torch relay was just then traveling throughout the province, and the children could view it daily on television. They were wildly enthusiastic when the torch entered the stadium in the mini-Olympics, to the point that the torchbearer was mobbed at the first stop and had to be assigned a security team of six male students at the next schools. The torch was an actual Olympic torch adorned with stylized a "lucky clouds" motif, which had been carried by one of the team members when the domestic torch relay went through Inner Mongolia. When asked why they were so enthusiastic, the students said it was because it was a "real" Olympic torch.

The grassroots imitation of the mega-event not only helped generate a sense of national unity by linking local rituals with national rituals, but it also facilitated a sense that China was now taking its place in the world by linking the national system with a global ritual.[43] These examples show how Roche's "event ecology" or Geertz's "ritual system" can work in tandem with the political system.

ENTER TELEVISION

Television has had a transformative effect on the world of sport, particularly since the 1990s. Until the 1980s, television channels in most countries (other than North American countries) were controlled by the state. A turning point occurred in the context of the worldwide turn to neoliberalism—economic policies advocating three principles: (1) the deregulation of markets, (2) privatization, and (3) the withdrawal of the state from the provision of welfare to the citizenry. These policies had roots in economic theories developed between the two world wars by the Vienna school, in particular by the economist Friedrich Hayek, but the fall of the Berlin Wall and end of state-controlled communism in 1989 gave a particularly effective global boost to neoliberal policies. In one country after the other, governments ended their monopoly on television channel ownership, opening up the market for private ownership, which came to play an increasingly important role in sports.[44] The cutthroat competition that ensued among privately owned channels, especially among pay-TV platforms, gave rise to a dramatic increase in the rights fees channels were willing to pay to broadcast major sports events. At the same time, clubs and teams around the world became increasingly corporatized, and there emerged a collusion among three entities: (1) sports clubs (which were concerned with ensuring their economic survival), (2) private television channels (which were eager to fill the airwaves with sports programming that involved relatively little technological investment), and (3) commercial sponsors (which were willing to pay increasingly exorbitant sums for the right to advertise in sports arenas and during television commercial breaks). Within the same economic logic, the salaries and transfer fees of top athletes in the global sports rose astronomically.

Soccer, the most ubiquitous global sport, is a prime example of how television rights in the early 1990s played a crucial role in globalizing and commercializing sport.[45] In 1992, Rupert Murdoch's BSkyB signed exclusive rights with the then newly formed English Premier League for £304 million (renewed in 1996 for £670 million and in 2003 for £1.1 billion).[46] This cemented its control of the market and spearheaded a new era in which the sports governing bodies, teams, and clubs became subservient to the interests of satellite television corporations. Leagues in Italy, Spain, France, and Germany replicated this model, and soon their revenues rose exponentially. Sales of World Cup broadcasting rights rose from $140 million in 1998 to $1.66 billion in 2002, so the Fédération internationale de football association (FIFA), the sport's world governing body, also greatly profited from television rights and transformed itself from a nonprofit body to a multinational organization with increasingly financial goals.[47] The corruption scandals that finally erupted in 2015–16, which we discuss in chapter 8, were precisely the outcome of the paradoxes inherent in a supranational entity with powers and budgets that equal those of a major state being run as a business by a tight-knit group of elderly men. Infusion of television into soccer also led to sponsorship deals, as the multinational companies recognized the huge exposure available to them via sponsoring elite forms of the game.[48]

This inflow of money became essential to sports governing bodies and the corporate sponsors, and television networks began to dictate the organization of sports events. For example, FIFA World Cup finals in Mexico in 1986 and the United States in 1994 saw many matches being played during the hottest time of the day in order to provide prime-time live soccer on European television. During the Beijing 2008 Olympic Games, the authorities implemented stringent measures to limit access along the routes of the cycling road races, the marathon, and the torch relay to approved spectators in order to prevent protesters from disrupting the television broadcast. World heavyweight boxing title fights in London are often staged at midnight in order to suit the North American networks. Television has even triggered changes in the rulebooks of some sports, transforming sports events into television sport.[49] In the digital age, the value of live sports allows television to remain a key player in the media landscape, as sports events capture particular audiences that are valuable to sponsors—largely young men, but Olympic audiences are unique for their large proportion of women viewers. This has deepened even further the interdependence of sponsors, television broadcasters, and sports administrators.

Another key change in the 1990s was that new broadcasting satellites enabled TV coverage to reach even the most remote corners of the world. In sub-Saharan Africa, for example, the number of television sets grew exponentially, and they were no longer confined to urban elites. Transnational television broadcasting blossomed, breaking down governmental media monopolies and boosting the number of entertainment and sports programs at the expense of news and educational programs. Everywhere, satellite television broadcasts of sports events seeped deeply into the everyday lives of ordinary people.

The spread of satellite TV provided a new way in which sports became part of global systems. Television allowed some players, clubs, and competitions to gain followers in distant parts of the world, creating a new global marketplace where local sports teams compete with global clubs. For example, many soccer fans in Africa shifted their attention from soccer stadiums to local bars where television sets showed matches from the English Premier League. The Premier League was already well known on the continent, and it offered fans a chance to view African elite soccer athletes playing in Europe. For many spectators worldwide, European soccer became more attractive than local competitions.[50]

The neoliberal era in sports is defined by the promotion of privatization and free markets, although no sport is entirely subservient to market forces, as sports governing bodies (and nation-states) continue to regulate the commercialization of the sport industries. However, the appeal of mass growth in revenues and fan bases has meant that most sports have significantly restructured since the 1990s to maximize commercial opportunities. The industry is now defined by new sorts of competition—between sports for market share and between clubs for commercial viability. Ultimately, these are competitions for the attention of the public, and consumer demand and corporate investment focus on "the spectacular." In contact sports such as rugby and American football, there is now more high-impact action and more crowd-pleasing and photogenic violent offensive strategies, with now well-documented consequences for the players' health.[51] The entanglement of sport with other forms of entertainment is evident in halftime shows featuring pop superstars and rapid-fire highlight clips in television ads.

EXTREME SPORTS: COUNTERCULTURAL
RESISTANCE AND CAPITALIST CO-OPTATION

Extreme (or "alternative" or "action") sports are one type of sport for which mediatization and commoditization have been most visible. These sports, which emerged in the 1980s, feature high levels of risk. Practitioners pit themselves against the natural or the built environment in ways that most regard as dangerous—tumbling down steep nature paths on bicycles, skiing off mountaintops, climbing cliff walls with little safety equipment, throwing themselves from airplanes, bungee jumping off bridges, or performing acrobatics at high speed in urban environments.[52] Extreme sports tend to attract young men who often define themselves as countercultural and have enough spare time to master skills that demand considerable training.

Practitioners often think of extreme sports as a critical commentary on late-capitalist "risk society," which they fault for its overanxious preoccupation with safety and the control of danger.[53] Instead of avoiding risk, extreme sports enthusiasts embrace it. Extreme sports are also frequently infused with an ideology of a romantic "return to nature," although the considerable amount of equipment, support, travel, and free time that some of these sports require somewhat mitigates these high ideals. They tend to be a nexus for the formation of anarchic subcultures, and they emphasize the rush of the activity, its potentially subversive (sometimes illegal) qualities, and the spectacular.[54]

Precisely because of their spectacular potential, they make good film footage, and this is where the tension arises: extreme sports are practiced as subcultural, defiant, and existentially motivated endeavors, but they also attract the media's taste for stunts such as those that punctuate action films. Extreme sports enthusiasts tend to devote considerable time and other resources to these activities, and the lure of getting remunerated for performing for media is difficult to resist for many, but it risks bringing upon oneself the opprobrium of others who are committed to keeping the sport countercultural and "untainted" by commercial interests.

One example of an extreme sport in which conflicts between "purity" and "selling out" are particularly tense is parkour, also called "free running," a form of acrobatic engagement with the urban environment whose practitioners, or *traceurs,* use walls, public sculptures, tunnels, bridges, and other features to launch fluid and rapid acrobatic moves.[55] The term *parkour* is a jazzed-up version of the French word *parcours,* "obstacle course," bearing witness to the origin of the sport in France in the late 1990s. It is alleged to have been invented by a French former soldier and firefighter and his son with inspiration from elite military training, although it traces its philosophical roots back to an early twentieth-century exercise movement called *hébert-isme*.[56] Its now globalized practice emphasizes individualism, self-reliance, self-improvement, and adaptability, all recognizable features of the neoliberal self—yet *traceurs* also see parkour as a resistant, countercultural practice.

Right from parkour's inception, the sport's particularly photogenic qualities began to attract media attention, and it was soon co-opted by television for commercials and documentaries, and by the film and video game industries. It has now been featured in many big-budget Hollywood productions, the most famous of which probably is the James Bond movie *Casino Royale* (2008), which features a parkour performance as its opening sequence. But many enthusiasts, including the founders of the sport, are strongly opposed to what they see as its co-optation by capitalist interests. The resulting tensions between, on the one hand, proponents of parkour as a morally inflected practice untainted by material concerns and those who favor the mainstreaming and commoditization of the sport in fact echo similar conflicts that have characterized sport throughout its history.

One important development in the direction of turning extreme sports into formalized, competitive, and commercialized events was the creation of the X Games in 1995 by the US sports television network ESPN. The aim was to reach a young "hip" audience that was not watching the network's conventional televised sports. The sports disciplines vary but have included skateboarding, BMX biking, motorcycling, rally car racing, surfing, and video games. They quickly became a hot brand, attracting two hundred thousand spectators and television audiences of several tens of millions, and demonstrating the ability to make sports celebrities overnight. The first Winter X Games followed in 1997 with such events as snowboarding, skiing, and snowmobiling. They expanded into Asia and the Pacific in 1998, with events also held in Europe. The growing popularity of a number of the sports, as well as the popularity of the X Games as a whole with the younger generation, spurred the IOC to incorporate some of the sports into the Olympic program in an attempt to reverse the waning interest in the Olympics among younger viewers. These included mountain biking (1996), snowboarding (1998), and BMX (2000), with the number of subdisciplines increasing over time. The inclusion of snowboarding in the Winter Games, in particular, led to a clash of cultures. The world's best half-pipe snowboarder, Norwegian Terje Haakonsen, boycotted the first Olympic event in order to protest being turned into a "uniform-wearing, flag-bearing, walking logo." Stereotypes were confirmed when Ross Rebagliati, the first Olympic snowboarding gold medalist, tested positive for marijuana. Over time snowboarding grew into one of the most popular Winter Olympic sports. On the surface, these sports appear to have traveled a simple path "from oppositional to co-opted," but actually the path was not simple, as it involved ongoing tensions resulting in compromises on both sides, including on the part of the IOC, which had to make room for the athletes' expressions of hip rebelliousness.[57]

MEDIA EVENTS

The ritual theorists of the 1970s and 1980s did not have much to say about television, so their theories were ill prepared to embrace the television explosion of the 1990s. Direct human bonds (communitas) and multiplex sensory experience were so central to their conception of ritual that they could not conceive that aspects of the theory might apply to rituals experienced in part or in whole through watching television. Communications scholar Eric Rothenbuhler creatively utilized ritual theory to analyze the way in which Americans watched television broadcasts of the Los Angeles 1984 Olympic Games. Based on a survey questionnaire of households about their viewing practices, his research found that people engaged in a ritualized viewing of television that was unlike their regular viewing habits. They watched in celebratory groups that created a "living room festival," or they went to public places.[58] Rothenbuhler's later books combining ritual theory with communications theory have been all but ignored by anthropologists.[59]

In 2006, MacAloon recalled that when he wrote his original essay in the 1980s, he had believed that television could not create festival, but he had since changed his mind—though he still wanted to prioritize direct experience. He was willing to concede that the massive big screens at the "live sites" where fans could gather to watch Olympic Games seemed to facilitate the street festival.[60] On the evening of August 5, 2016, while the opening ceremony of the Rio Olympics was taking place inside Maracanã Stadium, Besnier and Brownell went to Praça Mauá, a square in the city's port area that had been redeveloped for the games. The square, one of the games' three official live sites, featured a stage framed by two giant screens broadcasting the event. It drew a youthful crowd, largely Brazilian, along with small, diverse groups of people from many other countries. Although the mood was festive, the audience was polite and not as rowdy and colorful as the two anthropologists expected. The attention of the viewers was riveted by the bright lights of the big screens broadcasting the opening ceremony; their focus on the screens instead of on each other somewhat diluted the festival atmosphere. Many spectators were sandwiched between two virtual realities—the giant screens and their smartphones, as they were texting friends and taking selfies during the broadcast. MacAloon's reservations seemed to be correct—watching a big television screen is not the same bodily experience as the real thing, though it is still much more festive and creates more collective solidarity than watching a television alone at home.[61]

Media scholars Daniel Dayan and Elihu Katz utilized ritual theory in their conception of the *media event,* a historic occasion that transfixes a nation or the world through the festive viewing of television. They divided media events into the "three Cs"—contests (politics and sports), conquests (epic achievements), and coronations (the rites of passage of global elites). Examples in each category are, respectively, Olympic Games, the Apollo XI moon landing, and Princess Diana and Prince Charles's wedding.[62] Media events attract the largest audiences in the history of the world; they often integrate communities larger than nations. The broadcasting and viewing of media events are very different from routine television and news events. Broadcasts of these events typically interrupt routine programming so that they may be shown live, often with massive hours devoted to the broadcast. The broadcasts are meticulously preplanned, but the events are organized outside the media, typically by public bodies, whether governmental or nongovernmental, or by political parties.

Dayan and Katz's innovation was to highlight the ways in which media events resemble rituals. Television anchors typically present the happenings with reverence and ceremony; journalists suspend their normally critical stance and assume a "priestly" role. There is much ceremony and ritual, and advertising may be temporarily suspended as inappropriate. Because so many people are glued to the television, it becomes almost mandatory to watch; viewing is collective, and the home is a major site for watching. Viewers assume ceremonial roles such as mourner, citizen, juror, or sports fan. The message of media events is of reconciliation, loyalty, and sentiments that support social integration of the highest order. They may be a kind of civil religion, seen in the fact that governments may declare a holiday during this period. While critics tend to view them as political manipulations, this is not accurate because they are organized outside the government and public approval is required for their success; they cannot be imposed on the unwilling. The audience, in a sense, has veto power. Furthermore, some media events possess a liminal (reflexive) function, with all the revolutionary potential that entails.

When Dayan updated their theory before the Beijing 2008 Olympic Games, he was not as optimistic as in the original publication. Since those Olympic Games were highly controlled by the authoritarian Chinese government, they contradicted the assertion that media events are organized outside the government. In their original formulation, Dayan and Katz had referenced Walter Benjamin's notion that the *simulacrum,* the reproduction of an object, is more important than its original, observing that, in the broadcasting of media events, reality is uprooted to become a Hollywood set. The Beijing Games had become even more of a simulacrum made for TV. For Dayan, media events now produce cynical believers; they foster rather than suspend disbelief.[63]

MEGA-EVENTS AND THE TRANSNATIONAL PUBLIC SPHERE

Television coverage of the Olympics and FIFA World Cups in the last decade was estimated to reach between 50 and 70 percent of the world's population. These two mega-events provide ever-increasing numbers of global citizens with a common talking point about political systems, and the Internet is increasingly opening up a space for discussion across national borders—an emergent *transnational public sphere* that helps to form global public opinion. Many theorists have argued that important ritual events, major sporting events, mega-events, or media events create a powerful fantasy of unity that strengthens a sense of shared membership in a single community, a new, unbounded version of what Benedict Anderson labeled an *imagined community.*[64] The resulting sense of community has stimulated transnational alliances between nongovernmental organizations and discussions about issues that are perceived as common challenges to the global community, such as environmentalism—a major theme of the Rio 2016 Olympics. A *public sphere,* as political theorist Jürgen Habermas defined it, is characterized by critical debate about issues of shared concern. Public spheres are realms in which citizens may come together for rational debate, arriving at a more or less consensual public opinion that exerts pressure on leaders, legitimizes policy decisions, and in some cases delegitimizes them.[65]

Envisioning the debates that surround major sports events as a public sphere enables us to understand the paradox about rituals raised earlier in this chapter. Actually, imaginary unity and the heated public debate that often accompany it are two sides of the same process of social integration. When people feel solidarity, it emboldens them to express discontent and demand improvements. The various scholars mentioned previously have all observed this paradox under different labels: ceremonial politics versus parliamentary politics (Dayan and Katz); representative publicness versus deliberative democracy (Habermas); the dialectic between the floating and fixed worlds, the "world as we wish it to be" and the "world as it really is," the sacred and the mundane, community and hierarchy (Turner).

Anderson and Habermas conceived of imagined community and public sphere in the context of a nation-state, but as the world has shrunk, international publics are demanding accountability from governments in ways that transcend national boundaries. In a world governed by nation-states, there are few mechanisms by which citizens of one nation can demand accountability from decision makers located in another nation, but the hosting of sport mega-events has become a platform through which international NGOs are trying to do just that.

In the lead-up to the Beijing Olympic Games, Human Rights Watch, Amnesty International, the Free Tibet groups, and other NGOs attempted to pressure the Chinese government to improve its human rights record.[66] That effort was largely unsuccessful because there was no legal system to enforce it, but more importantly, Chinese leaders and Chinese people were not full participants in the debates, which therefore largely consisted of Westerners talking to each other about problems in China. Four years later, some degree of dialogue between Chinese and Western publics was evident in social media commentary comparing the opening ceremonies of the Beijing and London Olympics as representative of the Chinese and British political systems.[67] There was a surprising level of consensus between the Chinese and Western netizens, with both sides approving the frugality and "humanism" of the London ceremonies. Four years after China's lavish coming-out party, most Chinese bloggers—including, at both extremes, nationalists derogating London and critics derogating the Chinese leadership—criticized the government expenditure in Beijing as excessive. An example was an online comment that in London, "missing was the Chinese-style waste, paying no attention to whether the country's people live or die, nothing but grandeur and splendor—what damn use is that?"[68]

Hosting Olympic Games and other sport mega-events always involves major restructuring of host cities, with the construction of new sports venues and housing complexes, the destruction of sometimes entire neighborhoods to give way to new developments, and the upgrading of cities' infrastructures, such as public transportation networks, waste-management systems, the labor force, and tourist-hosting facilities. The financial, social, and human cost of these transformations invariably raises far-reaching questions, heated political debates, and often angry demonstrations: who benefits from these transformations, what is their impact on the citizenry, and how sustainable are they? Sustainability is always a particularly thorny issue, since it involves gambling on a future that is more often than not completely unpredictable. Thus, in the context of Brazil's ongoing political and economic crisis, the press reported that barely six months after the closing of the Rio Olympics and Paralympics, the city's sports venues were falling apart, and the rebranding of the Olympic Village as a luxury residential complex had failed miserably.[69]

The IOC has enshrined "positive legacy" in its Olympic Charter, and legacy planning has played an increasingly important role in the bidding competitions between host city candidates.[70] But a gulf separates the rhetoric from the reality, and the actual implementation of the high ideals is a complex affair that is far beyond the capacities of an international sports organization.

For example, the London 2012 Olympics, whose legacy planning was far more comprehensive and far reaching than any other Olympic Games to date, involved the ambition to accelerate the regeneration of a vast area in the eastern part of the city. Here, the decline of industry had produced a neglected site where manufacturing businesses still inhabited a polluted, semiderelict landscape that was nevertheless appreciated locally because of the wildlife and natural environments that had over the preceding decades reclaimed the waterway habitats.[71] Amid the postindustrial blight, green spaces prevailed: one area was occupied by urban gardens, which were the inalienable gift, dating back to 1900, of an English philanthropist to the working-class inhabitants of the area to afford them a degree of food self-sufficiency.

The construction of new sports venues, parklands, housing and transport developments, health centers, and business spaces all necessitated the demolition of these pockets of life, raising far-reaching questions about the incommensurability of value, or the fallacy that value can be reduced to a single measure, which has been a particular preoccupation of environmental economists for the last couple of decades.[72] Does offering new swimming pools to children of low-income families make up for the loss of pockets of greenery where unique wildlife once thrived? Is the common good enough justification for the forced commoditization of inalienable allotment land?

The public discussions that surround sport mega-events promote a more sophisticated understanding of different political systems and express the common concerns of citizens about the obligations of governments to their people, how they should spend taxpayer money, and what future orientations they should pursue. In today's increasingly connected world, sport mega-events may be bringing the world's citizens closer to a global consensus on key political issues.

SPORTS AND THE GIFT ECONOMY: BIG EVENTS AND BIG MEN

Since the end of the Cold War, there has been a rising crescendo of voices criticizing the massive expenditures involved in hosting mega-events. The public criticism of the huge economic costs and social trade-offs of mega-events has missed the point that they are not economically rational from the perspective of classical economics.

At the turn of the last century, anthropologists were already arguing against the economists' vision of the profit-seeking *Homo economicus*. For nearly a century, students have read Malinowski's description of the kula exchange in the Trobriand Islands off the coast of Papua New Guinea. There, high-status men devoted considerable time and effort to acquiring from their trading partners on nearby islands ungainly seashell necklaces and armbands. The objects were seldom sold for currency, and most of the armbands were so small that few adults could wear them. As Malinowski wrote, "They are merely possessed for the sake of possession itself, and the ownership of them with the ensuing renown is the main source of their value."[73] Because the kula objects never rested in any one person's hands for long and the relationships between the trading partners were supposed to be lifelong, the kula ring had the effect of tying together thousands of people living on islands scattered over an immense ocean area.

Another century-old insight from anthropology is that humans will go into deep and even ruinous debt to fund rituals and ceremonies. While this may not make sense using the logic of the market economy, it does make sense according to the logic of another kind of economy—the gift economy, in which material goods are exchanged rather than being bought and sold. Not just goods but also labor, services, hospitality, dances, and even rituals and festivals may be exchanged in such a system. Credit is measured by a person's reputation and honor, and the bonds of trust that develop over a long time between givers and receivers strengthen solidarity. When people are involved in a gift economy, they have to give as well as accept gifts. As Marcel Mauss, who first put forward the concept, put it, "To refuse to give, to neglect to invite, as to refuse to take, is equivalent to declaring war; it is to refuse alliance and communion."[74]

Sometimes anthropologists have found that during ceremonial events, goods and wealth were handled in a downright destructive way. For example, Eric Wolf concluded that fiestas in rural Mexican villages involved such great expenditures because they redistributed wealth, helping to balance out inequalities that might incite unrest. "By liquidating the surpluses, it makes all men rich in sacred experience but poor in earthly goods."[75] It often seems that sport mega-events leave the taxpayers who funded the government projects in the same condition. The potlatches of the Tlingit and Haida Indians on the northwest coast of North America sometimes became a competition between rival clans in which a participant might endeavor to demonstrate that he was richest and most madly extravagant by throwing great numbers of objects into the fire to destroy them.[76]

Whether ceremonies funded by village elites even out the difference between the haves and the have-nots is debatable. The appearance of extravagant generosity on the part of elites can be misleading because it can mask economic benefits that increase the gap between the rich and the poor—even while the latter are feeling grateful to the elites who fund exciting events. Likewise, the combination of wealth accumulation and redistribution that accompanies mega-events deserves closer scrutiny.

In sum, it is by now well known that, under certain conditions, humans will exert a great deal of effort and spend considerable sums of money to acquire objects that have only symbolic value, assume ruinous debt to fund a celebration, or throw away vast amounts of wealth to impress a rival. They are caught up in a system of relationships and exchanges that is not market based. Rather, they trade in honor, trust, solidarity, prestige—in other words, in emotions and symbolism, not commodities.

Turner's student G. Whitney Azoy conducted fieldwork in Afghanistan in the 1970s on a sport that vividly demonstrated the workings of a gift economy.[77] Considered the national sport of Afghanistan at the time,

FIGURE 17. Competing for the goat carcass in a *buzkashi* game (Panjshir valley, Afghanistan, February 2011/Peretz Partensky).

buzkashi ("goat dragging" in Farsi) is a competition in which horseback-riding men attempt to carry a goat or calf carcass and place it within a goal. Buzkashi games were commonly held to celebrate the circumcision of a boy and, less commonly, the marriage of a son, the two main male rites of passage in Afghan society. They were typically hosted by a khan, a politically important man with a "name" (i.e., a reputation) and a collection of dependent clients. One of the important ways in which a khan's reputation was created was through acts of generosity, which included hosting feasts such as those that accompanied buzkashi games. The horseback players of the game were mostly clients of the khan who received a salary, although sometimes the khan himself or his sons took part. Like other examples we discussed in chapter 5, buzkashi was deeply embedded in a gendered world of men and their competition for power and influence.

The buzkashi festivals were attended by hundreds or even thousands of neighbors, who were fed and sheltered with elaborate hospitality. To help him carry out the event, the khan relied on his close patrilineal kin, relatives by marriage, friends, dependent clients, and allies. This group had no formal existence outside the organization of the event. On the occasion of the rite of passage of a particularly important family, invitations were issued across northern Afghanistan. Khans stayed with other khans on the way there and preferred to go on horseback. Guests presented a gift, usually cash, upon arrival, striving to present the highest gift for prestige—but not too high. The payments reimbursed part of the expenses involved and were split up as the prizes for the buzkashi.

All the elements found in the buzkashi festivals are found in the Olympics, but on a much grander scale. Global sport has become a vast network with tentacles reaching into the very pinnacles of power in the global political economy. The Rio de Janeiro 2016 Olympics brought together 10,500 athletes from 206 national Olympic committees, and that number was dwarfed by the numbers of officials and coaches, members of the international sports world, journalists, and broadcasters, as well as a half-million foreign visitors. If one believes the media and the publicity, then the most important community whose solidarity was strengthened was the "global community"—that is, over seven billion people, most of whom never have and never will meet face-to-face. Can anthropological theories scale up to such massive numbers?

An unusual feature of Olympic Games and other sport mega-events is that they would not be financially feasible at all if not for the vast number of volunteers, many from other countries, who pay for their own travel and board to take on jobs chaperoning delegations, directing crowds, translating for foreigners, collecting quotes from athletes for the world's journalists, running results, and a host of other tasks. The donation of labor is reminiscent of the support provided by the Afghan khan's network for the buzkashi festival. The Rio 2016 Olympics mobilized forty thousand volunteers. That number was cut back from seventy thousand in the budget cuts accompanying the economic crisis—while the labor may be free, the volunteers are typically fed and supplied uniforms. Is there any other time when thirty thousand laborers willing to work for no wages must be turned away? Many domestic Olympic volunteers are motivated by loyalty to their country. Young people may believe that the experience will look good on their résumés—which is not so different from a young person who hopes that helping out the khan will win the favor of the big man so he can provide them future opportunities.

If not all aspects of sport mega-events follow the logic of the market, then we might ask whether any aspects follow the logic of the gift economy. Hospitality, which Mauss identified as an especially salient aspect of gift economies, is an important aspect of gift economies, particularly when hosting distrustful strangers. As in buzkashi, hospitality is a crucial aspect of sports events. Olympic Games and World Cups themselves are "hosted," meaning that the people who attend are "guests." This is why they always move from one city to the next, like kula valuables. Greece did attempt to make itself the permanent home of the Games after hosting the first modern games in 1896, and there have been discussions of developing a permanent site—which would certainly make more economic sense and avoid the problem of unused, white elephant arenas. However, this idea has never gained serious traction.

Mauss's statement that "to refuse to invite is tantamount to declaring war" may help explain why cities and countries feel compelled to bid for Olympic Games even when they have hostile relationships with half the world (like Moscow during the Cold War) or do not possess the necessary financial and infrastructure resources (like Athens in 2004). During summer Olympic Games and FIFA World Cups, governments, large corporations, billionaires, and celebrities bring in friends, families, leadership teams, potential partners, suppliers, distributors, and outstanding employees for wining, dining, and spectating. As many as two hundred thousand to three hundred thousand such guests may be hosted.

The Chinese leadership saw the 2008 Olympics as China's opportunity to return the hospitality of the other host nations that had previously invited China into their homes. The host-guest relationship, expressed in the Chinese characters *zhu/ke,* is extremely important in Chinese culture and involves elaborate protocol. He Zhenliang, China's senior member of the IOC, spoke passionately on this point to Susan Brownell in the lead-up to Beijing's games. He explained, "When I host a major sport event, I invite you to my home as my guest, and there I put you in the seat of honor, feed you the special foods, and give you the special gifts unique to my hometown. The cultural performances in the Olympic opening ceremonies are like the unique foods that you receive as my guest, which are not available in your own hometown." Like many Chinese people, he felt that the fierce criticism of China's human rights, air pollution, and other issues coming from advocacy groups, international politicians, and the Western media were inappropriate. He said that the West's criticism of China was as if the host invited a guest to his home and the guest responded by criticizing the host before even arriving. What kind of guest would do that?

During World Cups and Olympic Games of the last two decades, countries, corporations, and sports federations have organized massive hospitality programs in "hospitality houses," some of which attract tens of thousands of visitors. These programs started very timidly at the Barcelona 1992 Olympics with a tent set up by the Netherlands, but they grew exponentially up to the Rio Olympics, which set a new record with fifty-four houses scattered throughout the city (including first-ever houses by the US National Basketball Association and the Fédération internationale de volleyball). National hospitality houses are designed as visitor centers for athletes, officials, and VIPs from the country they represent, but most are also open to visitors, who generally pay a nominal fee to enter and can sample the country's cuisine and drinks, visit exhibitions, shop, enjoy concerts, take their kids to play areas, take part in conferences and cultural events, and watch the games on big-screen televisions. Many host parties, particularly if one of the country's athletes happens to win a medal. There is a tacit competition as to which country organizes the most lavish house, provides the best entertainment, and hosts the best party.

Alongside national houses are corporate houses. Some, like the Omega House at the Rio Olympics, are elegant and exclusive invitation-only venues, while others brashly advertise the corporation's product to whoever cares to come in, like the Coca-Cola House, which was adjacent to a store selling Coca-Cola souvenirs. But corporate interests are a visible presence in national houses as well, where corporations based in the relevant country market their products or advertise their activities. In fact, the very first such hospitality house, the Heineken Holland House at the Barcelona 1992 Summer Olympics, was precisely the result of the joint effort by the beer manufacturer and the country's Olympic committee. In 2008 the US Olympic Committee and Anheuser-Busch teamed up to run Bud House, which entertained fifteen thousand invited guests over the two weeks of the games. For Rio they created the largest US house yet, with a footprint of twelve thousand square feet (1,115 m²) and space for six hundred people.

But beyond selling soft drinks, beer, T-shirts, and trinkets, these hugely expensive programs do not have a clear, well-defined purpose, since they do not lead in any substantial way to increased sales of the products and services that sponsors market. When Brownell interviewed staff at the IOC, Anheuser-Busch, and the Beijing Olympic Organizing Committee, they produced noncommittal responses about whether sponsor hospitality programs resulted in long-term business partnerships or financial benefit. In 2008 the multinational mining corporation BHP Billiton, headquartered in Melbourne and with interests all over the world, spent more than $100 million on over one thousand packages worth up to $16,000 apiece to entertain clients, but the chairman did not talk business with the president of Aluminum Corporation of China as they sat next to each other during the opening ceremony because (as he told investors some days later in a conference call) their focus was on "having fun in Beijing."[78] In 2015 the US Securities and Exchange Commission issued an order against BHP Billiton, having judged that BHP's hosting of government officials at the Beijing Olympics constituted bribery to facilitate obtaining mining access rights in Congo, Guinea, Burundi, the Philippines, and other countries. The SEC order assessed the largest-ever civil penalty, $25 million.[79]

Because sport mega-events serve as centers for a chiefdom-like redistributive economy, they make no rational economic sense, as the protests frequently leveled against them attest. But viewed in light of anthropological insights, the widespread enthusiasm for sport mega-events begins to make sense. The theories based on research in small communities *do* scale up—along with the uncertainty that is built into the gift economy. Unlike market exchanges backed by law, these are unquantifiable, unpredictable human emotions. The criticism of mega-events as a misuse of taxpayer money diverts the public debate away from the disconcerting realization that this costly mega-event may not be motivated by measurable and rational impulses in the first place.

MEGA-EVENTS, GLOBALIZATION, AND TRANSNATIONALISM

Mega-events actually comprise multiple forms of cultural performance. The most obvious are the events that happen on the fields of competition. Other cultural performances, most especially for events like the Olympics, are the opening and closing ceremonies, in which the host nation puts on a spectacle that demonstrates the core values and history of that nation. Away from the stadiums, a third form of cultural performance occurs, one that the transnational capitalist class perform among themselves organized around the gift economy.

Mega-events are celebratory performances of capitalist excess in which civic leaders, National Olympic Committee members, national government officials, IOC members, and high-ranking officials of numerous transnational corporations exchange services and other gifts to display their own status and, in some cases, raise the standing of themselves and others. Hosts provide hospitality and tickets to sports events, luxurious accommodation, in-city transport, and other services that demonstrate the wealth of the city and host nation as well as individual leaders' ability to govern. These conspicuous gifts to potential investors and other global figures are provided in the hopes that such lavish local hospitality demonstrates that the hosting officials and leaders are fit for inclusion in the global political and economic elite. In exchange for this lavish hospitality, the providers of these gifts hope and expect that capital investment will then be directed their way. These forms of capital investment are designed to benefit not the population at large of any particular host city or nation but the civic and business leaders who have provided these gifts in the first instance. Such exchanges only really come to light when they become so excessive and conspicuous that they are seen as corruption and bribery, as has happened on occasion.[80]

As in the case of the kula ring and buzkashi, hosting a mega-event plays a role in the "ritual construction of political reality."[81] Governments strive to demonstrate their suitability to act as players in the global capitalist economy. The ability to host mega-events like the Olympics has increasingly become an essential litmus test for cities and nations to strategically claim "world-class" status. Localities intervene to transform, if not control, their own circumstances in the global political economy. These performances are part of the "economy of appearances," the self-conscious cultural performances necessary to attract capitalist investment.[82] These creative processes create the conditions for what Anna Tsing calls "spectacular accumulation" in which "the national specificity of attraction to investments disappears in the excitement of commitments to globalism in the financial world."[83] Thus, capital accumulation in the global economy becomes a spectacle that corporations, governments, and others must perform to demonstrate and assert financial viability and status. It is crucial that hosts' performances validate them as potentially viable sites of exchange within the global capitalist economy. Mega-events become a prerequisite performance that either reconfirms the existing status or affirms the new status of a mega-event's hosts in this global network of capital exchange. For places like Rio, where the 2014 FIFA World Cup and 2016 Summer Olympics were hosted, leaders and other officials had to be *seen* to be dynamic, progressive, and modern—in a word, "global"— before actually economically becoming so.

The theory of cultural performances has provided a rich set of conceptual tools for understanding sports as part of a performance system, but sport also provides a lens through which we can enrich these theories. Viewing sport as a performance system reveals that it includes a variety of interlocking layers of performance genres that may target audiences of different scales (local, national, world regional, global), helping to knit them together into increasingly more encompassing communities. While mega-events await more ethnographic research, there is reason to believe that many elements of the theories originally designed to elucidate rituals and cultural performances in face-to-face communities are relevant to events at a vastly larger scale. While it was originally believed that television weakened the system by eliminating the all-important face-to-face interaction, creative analysis by media studies scholars has suggested that this is not the case, and that people tend to utilize television broadcasts as a tool to create festival rather than being used by them. Sport mega-events bring large groups of people together in collective displays of devotion and celebration, they produce moments of reflexivity, and they provide cultural resources for reflecting upon identity and enacting agency. They facilitate the orientation of nations to international or global society.[84] Just as Singer and Turner argued that cultural performances were central to the agrarian societies of their fieldwork, theorists have argued that sport mega-events and global sport culture are central to late-modern capitalist societies and urban modernity.[85]

SEVEN

Sport, Nation, and Nationalism

WHEN 204 NATIONAL TEAMS marched into the stadium in the opening ceremony of the Beijing 2008 Olympic Games, it marked the moment when the world system of nation-states, which had been expanding across the globe since the late eighteenth century, could be said to have reached its logical culmination. For the first time, every inhabited inch of the planet had been assigned to the jurisdiction of a national Olympic committee. Although some entities with a claim to be considered a "country" for the purpose of the Olympics had lobbied to have their own separate representation, there were no official boycotts or exclusions, with one exception—Brunei, whose sultan was sitting in the VIP seats, had failed to send any athletes due to a domestic political spat, which would have brought the number to 205. The Marshall Islands, Montenegro, and Tuvalu were the last patches of earth to enter the parade. Henceforth, new delegations could be the result only of the splitting up of previously unitary Olympic committee jurisdictions. Having developed alongside modern nationalism for over a century, the Olympic Games had become the major public arena for announcing the existence of a country to a world audience. As John MacAloon put it, "To be a nation recognized by others and realistic to themselves, a people must march in the Olympic Games Opening Ceremonies procession."[1]

Why did the idea of the ancient Olympic Games resonate with farsighted thinkers of the nineteenth century who invented the modern Olympic Games? The answer partly lies in the rise of nation-states. In the classical period the ancient Greek city-states were large and strong enough to be hostile and competitive with one another, and they were frequently at war, but they were so small that none of them alone was ever able to dominate the others to establish an empire and erase their individual identities as city-states. At the end of the nineteenth century, when the world became a smaller place thanks to technological innovations (the steamship, the telegraph, postal service, etc.), western European nation-states emerged in a somewhat similar situation: they were large and strong enough to become hostile and competitive with one another, and while many of them had colonial empires in distant parts of the world, they were unable to permanently conquer and rule their neighbors in western Europe. As in ancient Greece, this produced a situation of constant warfare and sometimes terrible human suffering. And as in ancient Greece, the destructive rivalries between states simultaneously produced a desire to develop mechanisms to overcome them. The modern Olympic Games do not commemorate a supreme God in the way that the ancient games honored Zeus, but they do commemorate the supremacy of the nation-state as the most important political unit in today's world. In some respects, nationalism is the new state religion of the modern era.[2]

NATIONS AND STATES

Nation refers to a group of people who feel they share an identity based on citizenship and a common history, language, and symbols. *Nationalism* is broadly understood as a system of cultural beliefs about this social grouping—the "nation"—and the sense of identity that emerges among those who feel that they belong to it. The nation is a relatively recent form of political organization that emerged in western Europe and its colonies in the late eighteenth century, moved eastward to Greece in the early nineteenth century, and reached China in the Far East in the early twentieth century. The concept of the nation emerged out of European romanticism of the late eighteenth and early nineteenth centuries, particularly German romanticism as epitomized in the philosophy of Johann Gottfried Herder (1744–1803). The romantic notion was that members of nations shared a kind of inborn "primordial sentiment" or "essential character" that made them French, German, or some other identity, and that a nation should be coterminous with the state that governs it. Romantic nationalism assumed that the nation was a "natural" grouping of people who had the right to be represented by a sovereign state, which rose organically out of their midst. Those who advocated it saw the spread of the nation as an indicator of a "civilized" world order in which democratic forms of governance replaced other forms of state formation, such as loosely structured empires, absolute monarchies, and theocracies.

Nations are distinct from "states." The state is a complex form of centralized government running the gamut from agrarian empires such as the Ottoman Empire and Qing dynasty China to industrialized nations such as the contemporary Hellenic Republic of Greece and People's Republic of China. In what could be widely considered a "classic" definition, social theorist Max Weber defined the *modern* state as a continuously operating compulsory political organization that claims a monopoly over the use of legitimate physical force in the enforcement of its order.[3] Whether democratic or violently oppressive, the state is commonly understood as the political management of a delineated geographic space and its inhabitants through the bureaucratic mechanisms of centralized governmental institutions staffed and controlled by a small number of specialists.[4]

The relationship between nation and state was never as simple and happy as the romantic thinkers imagined it to be. In reality, government was often forced from the top down upon peoples who either did not identify with the proclaimed nation or were actively oppressed and excluded from national governments. States must generally engage in intensive efforts to convince their citizens that they do share a national identity—thus, the creation of a national public educational system, which incorporates physical education, is one of the hallmarks of a modern central government. There are nations that do not have their own state, such as Palestine, and sometimes there are states that do not have nations, such as the Tibetan "government in exile" in India. The hyphenated expression *nation-state* captures this tension. We use it to refer to the ideal of a nation and state that are one and the same, but this is only an ideal into which messy realities are slotted. Until the 1980s political thinkers tended to view the nation through rose-colored lenses as a legacy of the romanticism that gave rise to the concept. More recent theorists, notably Benedict Anderson and Eric Hobsbawm, criticized these approaches; we will discuss below how sports fit into their theories.

A major problem with the nation-state ideal is that it portrays all nation-states as somehow equivalent, even though the population of the People's Republic of China (where Susan Brownell conducted fieldwork) is more than one hundred thousand times bigger than that of Tuvalu (where Niko Besnier originally conducted fieldwork), and it is hardly fair that the two must compete against each other in the Olympic Games. When reality does not conform to official rhetoric, the gap may cause conflict in the world of sports. For the first century of its existence, the International Olympic Committee (IOC) decided on its own "sporting geography," as Pierre de Coubertin called it, by allowing countries to participate in the Olympics that were not internationally recognized sovereign states, but were subnational regions, colonies, territories, protectorates, or other anomalous polities—such as Bohemia (a region of the Austro-Hungarian Empire), Malta and Rhodesia (British colonies before their independence), and Saarland (in limbo between France and Germany after World War II). Puerto Rico, Guam, American Samoa, the US Virgin Islands, and the British Virgin Islands, under US and British political jurisdictions, compete as separate "countries," while athletes from other semiautonomous territories with active independence movements, such as French Polynesia and New Caledonia, have to compete under the flag of the colonial metropole (in these cases, France). Palestine, which has been under Israeli military occupation since 1967, has been represented in the summer Olympic Games since 1996. When Susan Brownell and Niko Besnier were watching the broadcast of the opening ceremony of the Rio Olympics on the big-screen television at a live site, the crowd gave one of the most enthusiastic rounds of applause to Palestine's Olympic delegation.

However, in 1996, the IOC revised its charter to state that henceforth the national Olympic committees must represent member states of the United Nations. Existing national Olympic committees were grandfathered into the IOC. The status of today's Greater China in the Olympic Movement illustrates that politics cannot be straitjacketed into the one-size-fits-all model of the nation. Officially, the People's Republic of China claims Hong Kong, Macao (Macau in the local Portuguese), and Taiwan as territories within the boundaries of the sovereign state of the People's Republic. However, Hong Kong and Taiwan select their own national teams and march separately into the Olympic stadium—Hong Kong because it was grandfathered into the IOC when it was returned to China in 1997, and Taiwan because it is in reality governed by an autonomous government, although the "Olympic formula" established in 1979 obligates the Olympic system to follow the "One China Principle" and depict Taiwan as a province of China by calling it Chinese Taipei. Macao did not have a recognized Olympic committee before its return to China in 1999, so there were no grounds for grandfathering it in. Even though China has petitioned the IOC to allow Macao to have its own Olympic team, the IOC has not agreed, and its athletes must beat out Chinese competitors to make the Olympic team. The representation of "China" in international sports has been hotly contested for over sixty years now.

SPORT, GOVERNMENTALITY, BIOPOWER, AND
DISCIPLINE

Wherever they live around the world, people strategically, yet constantly and continuously, reify the state, but they tend to forget how fragmented and inconsistent the state actually is.[5] Paradoxically, in one moment people blame this ill-defined yet vital presence in their lives for their failures as they would a living human being, yet in the next moment they appeal to its impersonal "thingness" as the ultimate guarantor of disinterested authority. That authority is reinforced through cumulative effects of everyday encounters with bureaucratic structures that conjure the effects and conditions of the state's own objectification.[6]

Perhaps the most creative thought about the nature of state power was advanced by Michel Foucault in the 1970s with his concepts of *governmentality* and *biopower*. In his analysis, the focus of state power shifted in the eighteenth century from sovereignty and the control of things (the material economy) to governmentality and the control of the people (the population). The invention of social statistics and the development of demography made it possible for rulers to understand their subjects in new ways. Sexual behavior, reproduction, consumption, and population growth rate were targeted for government intervention. New laws (such as the laws criminalizing homosexuality that replaced the old sodomy laws across Europe and North America starting in the mid-nineteenth century) and institutions (such as hospitals, public schools, military barracks, and prisons) arose to regulate the bodies and minds of the population. Increasingly, governing became a science bolstered by new classes of professionals in law, medicine, and education. The concept of governmentality avoided reducing the state to a limited set of functions and captured Foucault's belief that the state

> does not have this unity, this individuality, this rigorous functionality, nor, to speak frankly, this importance; maybe, after all, the state is no more than a composite reality and a mythicized abstraction, whose importance is a lot more limited than many of us think.[7]

He labeled this version of state power "biopower" or "biopolitics," a politics concerned with governing populations, which operates by controlling bodies through regulatory and disciplinary systems and by increasing its capacities for surveillance in areas such as family, health, sexuality, birth, and death.[8]

Foucault's focus on the body opened up a new way to understand the relationship between sport and the state. It is no coincidence that the discipline of physical education developed along with the rise of modern nation-states and national public school systems. In sports one can often clearly see at work Foucault's "microphysics of power."[9] Sports discipline bodies, shape thoughts, and display the product of this process as an exemplar to an audience. The lives of athletes in China's state-supported sports system in the mid- to late 1980s illustrate Foucault's theory. In this period, when the market reforms had not yet taken firm hold, Chinese society was characterized by an intrusive and authoritarian state, and the lives of athletes revealed with crystal clarity the way in which that state operated. Athletes were tracked at a young age into provincial and municipal sports boarding schools where they lived semimilitarized lives. They were categorized and studied; their movements, diets, and bodily functions were monitored; their day revolved around training, eating, and sleeping, which were strictly scheduled from early morning roll call to evening curfew; males were forbidden to smoke cigarettes and females to wear their hair long and loose, and both were forbidden to date and marry. Regular "thought education" and "political education" were intended to instill good sportsmanship and socialist morality. All these constituted what Foucault called a regime of "discipline" intended to produce docile bodies.

Susan Brownell personally experienced socialist sports discipline when she represented Beijing in the 1986 National College Games and took part in a two-and-a-half-month training camp beforehand. Both athletes and coaches alike took seriously their duty to represent the college students of the capital city, Beijing, which, they believed, should act as a center for the promulgation of "spiritual civilization" (see chapter 6 for a description of sport and the theory of the "civilizing center"). Team members were required to memorize songs and slogans, study a booklet about competition ethics, and listen to lectures about sportsmanship and the spirit of the meet. After morning roll call at the sports field, they practiced marching in preparation for leading the nation's students into the stadium in the opening ceremonies. The performance included goose-stepping and shouting slogans such as "Study diligently!" and "Defend the nation!" alternating with the chorus, "Train the body!" Three decades later, Brownell can still remember the slogans because repeating them in time with body movements turned the body into a mnemonic device for memorizing the slogans, a technique which was that much more effective because individual bodies were also synchronized with the bodies of the group. Having mastered these forms of discipline, the team also served as an exemplar for others, whether fellow teams in the opening ceremonies or the audience watching on national TV. Brownell "fulfilled her duty" by winning a gold medal in the heptathlon, running on two silver-medal relay teams, and being selected as a "spiritual civilization athlete." She summed up the experience by observing that the modernity of these techniques of training the body for the nation consisted in that they were far more continuous, detailed, calculated, and normalizing than the disciplinary regimes of the imperial (pre-1912) era.[10]

NATIONALISM

Nation-states would not exist if they were not legitimized by an accompanying ideology. Generated, at least initially, through positive feelings of association, nationalism can turn into reactionary sentiments toward a perceived Other. This Other generally consists of other nations, that is, people on the other side of a political border. But this Other can also be an internal group, such as a minority ethnicity or race. Thus nationalism can often be expressed either through celebratory shouts of self-recognition and assertion or through the denigration of other groups in an assertion of superiority.

Sport facilitates both self-congratulation and the demonization of others. This was especially the case in international sports contests at the height of the Cold War in the second part of the twentieth century. The "miracle on ice" victory of the US ice hockey team over the hitherto undefeated Soviet team in the Lake Placid 1980 Winter Games, held against the background of growing political tensions between the two countries, epitomized American nationalism, from the chanting of "USA! USA!" by spectators in the crowd to narratives of the American team's plucky underdog fighting spirit in the face of the Soviet juggernaut. At the Melbourne 1956 Olympics, held on the heels of the suppression of the Hungarian revolution by the USSR, Hungary's victory over the Soviet Union in water polo is another famous example. The Hungarian players had seen the gunfire and smoke from their mountain training camp before being evacuated; by the end of their 4–0 victory, the water was pink with blood.[11] In the opening match of the 2002 FIFA World Cup held in Japan and Korea, the Senegalese team's victory over the defending world champions, France, symbolized the Senegalese overthrow of French colonialism. While the French media barely registered the loss, thousands celebrated in the streets of Dakar, as if the national team had won the entire tournament. These victories often become incorporated into

FIGURE 18. A member of the Fiji women's national team celebrates emotionally as her male compatriots win the country's first Olympic gold medal (Rio de Janeiro, August 2016/Susan Brownell).

particular national histories as momentous instances of national victory over an adversary.

As Benedict Anderson, one of the most influential theorists of nationalism, argued, nationalism is a socially and culturally constructed "imagined community."[12] It is "imagined" because in most nations no single person will ever come face-to-face with all other members of the nation. He emphasized the fundamental role played by "print capitalism" (the business of printing and selling newspapers and other print media) in the rise of nationalism starting in the late eighteenth century. By extension, today, electronic mass media are central to the construction of nationalism. Mass media disseminate images that foreground commonality and downplay differences, particularly when the nation is at stake such as in time of war, pulling ever-larger groups of people into the imaginary of a national identity. In today's entertainment industries, the "unholy trinity" of sport, culture, and the media implicates sports in building and maintaining the nation.[13]

The television broadcasts of the Super Bowl of American football are among the most watched in US broadcast history. The winner is anointed as the "world champion" even though only teams from the United States participate—prompting one British blogger to advise, "Dear America: you can't be world champions if no one else takes part."[14] The televised pregame show presents the Super Bowl as a national holiday, celebrating the values, mores, and norms of acceptable "Americanness." In his analysis of the NBC broadcast of the pregame show for the 1986 Super Bowl, Lawrence Wenner, one of the leading scholars of sports and media, found that grand pronouncements by the commentators reinforced the theme expressed in the opening graphic, "SUPER SUNDAY: AN AMERICAN CELEBRATION."[15]

At the same time, nationalism is constantly reinforced by everyday objects and acts that are so commonplace that people barely notice them, but they have a subliminal effect. Sociologist Michael Billig termed this phenomenon "banal nationalism."[16] Flags, images on currency, and the names of sports organizations (e.g., the National Football League and the National Basketball Association [NBA], with no mention of what nation "national" refers to) are examples of such items. Almost every sports event in the United States begins with the singing of the national anthem by spectators facing a national flag, led by either a recording or an invited singer. The flag and anthem are not as ubiquitous in the rest of the world—in fact, although the Western media contain much alarmist reporting about ultranationalism in China, Chinese visitors to the United States hosted by Susan Brownell were typically appalled at what they saw as the raw national fervor displayed even at low-key sports events. Even more appalling to one of her guests was the sight of the normally decorous gymnastics spectators erupting into chants of "USA! USA!" at the 2016 US men's gymnastics Olympic Trials in St. Louis, even though the only competitors were Americans.

For a nation-state to take its place as an equal among the sports powers, it must also possess a national sport history, preferably dating back to antiquity, which then becomes part of the arsenal of symbols that gives legitimacy to the nation and to the state that governs it. Nations that are considered members of "Western civilization" can trace their sporting roots back to the Olympic Games in ancient Greece. A bibliography published in 1984 listed 186 books and articles on the ancient Olympic Games and 1,345 sources on ancient Greek sports in general published in English, French, German, and other languages since 1752.[17] In contrast, although Chinese civilization is just as ancient as Western civilization and its history is just as well documented in surviving annals, the first history of sport in China was not written until 1919, and in 1984 only a few books on Chinese sport history existed.[18]

The writing of national sport histories constitutes one part of the process by which many non-Western nations attempt to write themselves into world history today; therefore it is important that these histories be published in English or another major international language. It is interesting that nations often portrayed in the West as antagonistic to internationalization and interchange with Western ideas may look like newcomers eager to join the game in light of their efforts to promote their national sport histories. For example, a large number of books and articles, and even a museum exhibition at the IOC's Olympic Museum in Lausanne, were produced in association with China's Olympic bids and emergence as a sports power.[19] In 2006 the Iranian Olympic Academy organized the international symposium "The History of Sport in Iranzamin [Greater Iran]," the first-ever attempt by academics to systematically address the topic. The forewords written by S. Mohammad Khatami, the president of Iran who had just left office, and the president of the Iranian Olympic Committee advanced typical nationalist arguments: Iran has a rich ancient civilization that has made great contributions to world culture; sport is one of the most important means of dialogue between civilizations today; although humanistic studies of sport have been neglected, it is now time to develop them to promote Iranian culture to the world and facilitate dialogue with other cultures and civilizations.[20]

Sport has worked well as an instrument of nationalism in many cases in which the hyphenation of the "nation-state" is potentially problematic, such as in authoritarian regimes, and so the state goes to great efforts to appropriate sport to try to garner the support of the nation. In the years of strongman Hosni Mubarak's autocratic regime in Egypt before its spectacular downfall in 2012, the state in general and Mubarak in particular used soccer strategically for this purpose.[21] In contrast to other parts of the world, where team ownership was privatized in accord with the neoliberal trend, in Egypt many of the top teams belonged to the state, and the state invested large amounts of money in infrastructure such as shiny new stadiums (which remained largely empty because people preferred to watch television). Mubarak, a keen soccer fan, would often appear at important games and make frequent phone calls to the national team when they played overseas. After the team's victories in the African Cup of Nations in three consecutive installments in 2006, 2008, and 2010 prompted huge demonstrations of national jubilation, Mubarak held heavily publicized receptions at the national palace for the players, posing as the father of the nation. This is what Achille Mbembe calls "the vulgarization of power," whereby the state "comes down" to the level of the people and attempts to consolidate its legitimacy, particularly when this legitimacy is largely based on oppression and is therefore fragile.[22]

CONTESTING THE NATION

Of course, human beings derive a sense of identity from categories other than the nation to which they belong, and this is perhaps even more true today than it was when Anderson formulated his theory of imagined communities. Anderson admitted this fact in his posthumously published memoir:

> It was not until much later, in fact after I finally retired, that I began to recognize ... that using the nation and nation-states as the basic units of analysis fatally ignored the obvious fact that in reality these units were tied together and crosscut by global political-intellectual currents such as liberalism, fascism, communism and socialism, as well as vast religious networks and economic and technological forces. I had also to take seriously the reality that very few people have ever been solely nationalist. No matter how strong their nationalism, they may also be gripped by Hollywood movies, neoliberalism, a taste for manga, human rights, impending ecological disaster, fashion, science, anarchism, postcoloniality, "democracy," indigenous peoples' movements, chatrooms, astrology, supranational languages like Spanish and Arabic and so on.[23]

Due to these competing loyalties, the nation needs to be constantly reinforced for its members to believe in it, and large-scale sports events clearly serve to buttress the nation, even for the most skeptical. When people imagine themselves as a nation, such as "the United States," they place themselves in opposition to other nations, such as Russia and China, and these oppositions are what give international sports events their spectator appeal. However, the entire fantasy of the "USA" versus, say, "Cuba" is based on an illusory portrait of nations as homologous political units. The United States of America and Cuba are not actually similar and equal political units, but on the baseball diamond, the athletics track, and in the boxing ring, they seem much more equitable in prowess and skill.

Nationhood is often claimed by social groups that could logically constitute limited, sovereign, and imagined communities. Based on the belief that they constitute nations, separatist movements in Catalonia and the Basque Country (Euskadi or Euskal Herria in Basque), Tibet (under Chinese control), and Chechnya (under Russian control) have all sought to secede from the nation-states in which they are embedded. Sports organizations are venues in which separatists can seek official recognition for their nations: the archives of the IOC contain hundreds of letters from different groups requesting recognition and the right to send a team to the Olympics.

Alternative sports events affirm the claims to nationhood of politically unrecognized groups. One such event is organized by the Confederation of Independent Football Associations (ConIFA), "a global umbrella organization for national teams not under the auspices of FIFA—representing nations, minorities, isolated dependencies or cultural regions."[24] Founded in 2013, it is an association of politically eclectic entities that do not have recognition as FIFA members but have nationalist aspirations or are connected to separatist movements. They include teams of Kurds (often said to be the world's biggest stateless people, with an estimated population of thirty-five million that straddles Iraq, Iran, Syria, and Turkey), Tibetans (Tibet is a province of China, but the Dalai Lama, the spiritual leader of Tibetan Buddhism, lives in exile in India, and the team comes from that Tibetan exile community); Uighurs (Muslim inhabitants of the Xinjiang Uygur Autonomous Region in China, where a separatist movement is active but violently repressed by the Chinese government;[25] the ConIFA team was founded by exiles in the United States); northern Cypriots (from the largely unrecognized Turkish-controlled northern area of Cyprus); and Chagos islanders (who were forcibly removed from their Indian Ocean homeland by the British government during the Cold War to make way for a major US military installation, and are now living in poverty in Mauritius and Britain).[26] But the confederation also includes Padania, a separatist far-right movement in northern Italy, and Skezely Land, a Hungarian minority group in Romania with politically extremist elements. The 2016 ConIFA World Cup was held in Sokhumi, Abkhazia, but it drew few spectators, thus remaining a largely symbolic gesture, although one that clearly demonstrated the power of sport in asserting nationalism, even while it expressed disenchantment with the materialism, corruption, and celebrity cult that characterized mainstream world sport.[27]

NATIONALISM, SPORT, AND THE INVENTION OF TRADITION

Philosophers of the romantic era believed that an essential national character was expressed in language, religion, laws, dress, songs, dances, and local customs. This conviction gave birth to the discipline of folklore, the purpose of which was to catalog such practices and supply materials for the construction of modern national identities. Although not as prominent a concern as language and religion, games and sports were among the "customs" that folklorists collected.

According to Michael Herzfeld, in Greece, the interrelation between nationalist ideology and folklore was personified in Nikolaos G. Politis, the founder of the discipline of folklore in the country.[28] What Herzfeld did not remark was that Politis, a professor at the University of Athens, was also member of the competitions committee of the Athens 1896 Olympic Games, architect of the renovation of the Panathenaic Stadium, where the opening and closing ceremonies were held, and author of two chapters in the official Olympic Games report.[29] A subcommittee originally proposed that folk dancing and reenactments of customs should take place between the athletic contests or in the evenings, but this was canceled due to budget cuts and the reluctance of the rural female dancers to perform for a public audience.[30] While Politis was not on the committee that made the proposal, the theory that local customs embodied national character was encapsulated in the committee's belief that the performances would complement the display of the antique glories of Greece (embodied in the revived Olympic Games) with a demonstration of the current conditions of Greeks from the far corners of the world.

The revival of the Olympic Games was in fact part of a general trend in Western countries from 1870 to 1914, when a cluster of new institutions and practices were invented, such as the British Royal Jubilee, French Bastille Day, the Daughters of the American Revolution, May Day, the singing of "The Internationale" (the socialist anthem), the English FA Soccer Cup, the Tour de France, and the institution of flag worship in the United States. British historian Eric Hobsbawm coined the phrase "invention of tradition" to describe this phenomenon.[31] "Invented traditions" are repetitive practices that seek to inculcate certain values and norms and attempt to establish continuity with a historic past, a continuity which is often tenuous. They are governed by overt or tacit rules and are ritualized and symbolic. They include both "traditions" deliberately invented and constructed by a single initiator who can be identified by a historian, as well as those that emerge and become rapidly established in a less traceable manner within a datable period. Ultimately, all traditions are invented, a point that has led to criticism of the utility of the adjective "invented" in Hobsbawm's phrase.

In the sports world, the revival of the modern Olympic Games in 1896 by Coubertin is a prime example of a deliberate invention. As discussed in other chapters, the ceremonies that we now take as "natural" evolved over a period of several decades that saw the creation of the Parade of Athletes and the award ceremonies in 1906 and 1908, and the torch relay in 1936. Although the modern Olympics are often said to continue the tradition of the ancient Olympic Games, in fact nearly twenty-five hundred years stood between them, and the sports disciplines and ceremonies have almost nothing in common. The invention of the modern Olympics is an example of the "use of ancient materials to construct invented traditions of a novel type for quite novel purposes," as Hobsbawm phrased it.[32]

Hobsbawm contrasted invented traditions with conventions and routines that serve practical functions, although he observed that the two may be combined. The helmet traditionally worn in equestrian foxhunting might have a practical effect in case of a fall, but in combination with "hunting pink" (the scarlet jacket worn by men) and other accessories, it composes an invented tradition.[33] The shape of the helmets worn by armies will be changed if another shape can be shown to provide more effective protection, but it required decades to replace the black-velvet-covered riding hat, even when it was known that it did not provide adequate protection in the case of a fall. Safer versions were developed in the 1970s, but for many years afterward they were used for training and not competitions. This illustrates one feature of invented traditions—they can be very difficult to change because of their link to a romantic past.

Hobsbawm felt that the invention of traditions occurs more frequently when rapid social changes destroy the social patterns for which the old traditions were designed and new social patterns take their place. He argued that in the past two hundred years the invented traditions of European nationalism replaced baroque festivals, flags, temples, processions, bell ringing, gun salutes, folk songs, games, dances, and so on. A nation had to have certain paraphernalia: a capital, a flag, an anthem, and military uniforms. Still today, sports events are often surrounded by multiple other performance genres that were originally invented to serve nationalism, such as flag raising, anthem singing, parades, processions, festivals, and inauguration ceremonies. It is instructive to consider that for a national Olympic committee to be recognized by the IOC, it must submit four items for approval: its name, flag, anthem, and bylaws. Those four superficial items are what constitutes a nation in the Olympic system.

Unlike the old religious values and local "superstitions" (which Enlightenment thinkers disapproved of), the new patriotic values tended to be ill defined—but that did not prevent them from being virtually compulsory. In Britain and America standing for the singing of the national anthem or the raising of the flag became compulsory rituals that demonstrate respect for sovereignty. They reflected the entire culture of a nation. However, the new nationalist traditions did not entirely fill the hole left by the decline of the old traditions and customs in the agrarian societies.

Perhaps this explains why sport, one of the most significant new social practices of our period, according to Hobsbawm, has gained so much importance since the late nineteenth century.[34] Sports in general, and particularly soccer in Europe, became a "mass proletarian cult" in the 1870s to 1880s, when it acquired many of its institutional characteristics. As sports were invented and institutionalized on a national and international scale, they provided a new medium for expressions of national identity. International sports contests soon became more important than national ones.

As is the case with other instances of invented traditions, the invention of national sporting traditions can follow complicated trajectories. For example, *muay thai,* or "Thai boxing," is widely presented (by its name alone) as the quintessentially national sport of Thailand. Yet the sport originated in rural northeast Thailand among marginalized Lao minorities of the province of Isaan. There, the sport was an avenue for boys of a very young age from poor families who joined muay thai training camps in hope of gaining recognition and eventually moving to the country's capital, Bangkok.[35] As found in many other contexts (chapter 8), sport came to represent dreams of socioeconomic mobility where rigid social hierarchies offered very few possibilities to rural men of nonmainstream ethnicity. In the rural Thai context, however, muay thai was intertwined with Buddhism in multiple ways: training and matches were accompanied by elaborate religious ritual, and the desire to earn money through the sport was motivated by Buddhist precepts of filial duty to one's parents. Social mobility through boxing paralleled another escape route out of poverty and abjection, namely becoming a Buddhist monk. The two career paths shared many characteristics, such as the emphasis on rigorous training, obedience to authority, and adherence to strict codes of morality, even though boxing showcased violence and worldliness, while the monkhood required asceticism and renunciation.[36]

Beginning in the 1980s, urban middle classes began appropriating the sport. In the process its rules were standardized, its technical range reduced, and its meaning transformed: its religious undertones all but disappeared, and it was transformed into a form of leisure, a far cry from its role as a way out of poverty for rural practitioners. Around the same time, the sport began attracting the attention of global audiences and practitioners, who saw it as another form of martial art, largely devoid of the meanings that rural Thai attached to it. The combination of these dynamics turned the sport into Thailand's national sport: matches are televised daily, numerous magazines and newspapers cover the sport, champions are household names, and it is presented to the rest of the world as embodying the essence of the Thai way of being rooted in a timeless past.[37] Today, it feeds a lucrative business as aficionados around the world flock to training schools in the country's urban centers. The sport's trajectory illustrates that what ends up counting as tradition in the making of a national sport can be the result of complex dynamics of appropriation, transformation, and innovation in which both local and global agents take part.[38]

Why does sport play such an important role in nationalism? Hobsbawm provided a clue when he asked how far invented traditions can be manipulated. In politics there are always obvious attempts to manipulate traditions, but these are frequently met with cynicism. The most successful examples of invented traditions combine invention with spontaneity, planning with organic growth; these are cases in which the practices clearly meet a felt need. The unscripted nature of sport makes it hard to control and plan; sport was one facet of nationalism that escaped the control of those who found it advantageous to manipulate it.

SPORT AS CULTURAL HERITAGE

The folklore approach that links traditional games and national identity continues into the twenty-first century, with traditional sports and games often regarded as "cultural heritage." To preserve what he called *ludodiversity,* namely "the wide diversity in games, sports, physical exercises, dances, and acrobatics," Belgian sport studies scholar Roland Renson (one of the early members of the Association for the Anthropological Study of Play, discussed in chapter 1) created the Sportimonium in Hofstade, near Mechelen, Belgium, a museum that combines Belgian Olympic history with exhibits on folk games.[39] The games can be played on the grounds, and the equipment can be checked out. In 2011 the Sportimonium became the first sports-related institution to be inscribed on the UN Educational, Scientific and Cultural Organization's register of best practices for safeguarding intangible cultural heritage.

A core element of cultural heritage is nostalgia for something that has been lost. This nostalgia is what has been driving American tourists since the late 1990s to attend Cuban national league games in the Estadio Latinoamericano, circumventing US restrictions on travel to Cuba. They seek to see a romanticized, exoticized sport spectacle that they feel holds something that can no longer be found at home, namely athletes who "play for the love of the game" instead of "being driven by the desire of money."[40] Their experience invokes a temporal shift to an imagined past that fails to recognize that Cuba has already changed considerably. It also reinforces the commoditization of the exoticized Other into consumable ethnic commodities, as tourism becomes an increasingly important aspect of the Cuban economy.[41]

Nations construct monumental buildings to impress citizens and commemorate national history. Heritage is made all the more tangible in the construction of national stadiums. Sports stadiums not only impress with their size but also become major tourist attractions. Some are celebrated for their remarkable architecture, others for the memories of what happened on their grounds. The Olympic stadiums in Berlin (1936), Tokyo (1964), Barcelona (1992), and Beijing (2008) are all major tourist sites. Maracanã Stadium in Rio de Janeiro, mainly used for soccer but also the site of both the 2014 World Cup final and the opening and closing ceremonies of the 2016 Olympic Games, is legendary. Other stadiums, like Yankee Stadium in New York City or Old Trafford in Manchester, are landmarks because of the regularity of their clubs' championships. Closely affiliated with specific clubs, these stadiums often are central edifices of the city in which they are located, attracting people from around the world in the same way that medieval cathedrals have been celebrated for their architecture and evocation of emotions.

Hobsbawm's insight that the anxiety around tradition is highest when society changes rapidly also applies to heritage. A striking illustration is the emergence of camel races in the United Arab Emirates.[42] The country is a federation of seven sheikhdoms in the Persian Gulf that gained independence from Britain in 1971 and has been transformed in the space of a few decades from a sleepy backwater of the world into an economic powerhouse based on the country's vast oil reserves, which the country began extracting for export in 1962. In pre-oil days, camel races were held on the occasion of Islamic holidays, the rites of passage of important people, and dignitaries' visits, and they were primarily associated with the nomadic camel herders, or Badu. As the Badu were sedentarized (but remained marginal citizens) and the country became very wealthy, the camel lost it importance.

In the mid-1990s, however, the state built ultramodern and lavish camel-racing tracks, with separate grandstands for the royals, ordinary citizens, and Westerners. Royals owned prize racing camels, which Badu men bred, managed, and trained, while the heavy work in the stables was taken care of by immigrant workers from West and South Asia and East Africa (who are the labor force of the country, outnumbering its citizens by a huge margin, but who do not have civil rights). Camel races are the occasion for recitations in praise of the country's royal leaders, in a poetic style that harks back to ancient times, and the proceedings are all televised—television is essential because the spectators can witness only a fleeting moment in the race along a ten-kilometer track. Both the camel racing and the praise poetry seal the construction of the present as rooted in the past, consolidate the nation as equivalent to the state, and confirm the authority of the rulers. The irony here is that modern camel racing depends crucially on the expertise of the otherwise marginalized Badu and the hard labor of disposable and exploited migrant workers. But then how different is this situation from many sports in the industrial West, where athletes are predominantly members of ethnic and racial minorities that are largely impoverished and disenfranchised?

SPORT AND GENDER IN THE CONSTRUCTION OF THE NATION

Feminists long ago pointed out that notions about gender are integral to identities at whatever level they are conceived and acted out, but it has often been overlooked that gender constitutes a fundamental aspect of national-ism. Indeed, Anderson's original depiction of nationalism as "a deep, hori-zontal comradeship, [a] fraternity that makes it possible, over the past two centuries for so many millions of people, not so much to kill, as willing to die for such limited imaginings" has received considerable criticism from schol-ars attuned to issues of gender.[43] The imbrication of gender and nationalism is particularly evident in the world of sports, one of the prime institutions where nationalism becomes gendered.

These dynamics are front and center in the work of another theorist of nationalism, namely historian George Mosse, who was writing at the same time as Anderson. Mosse grew up during the rise of fascism in Germany, which he fled in 1933, and as both a gay man and a Jew, he was intimately acquainted with the gendered workings of nationalism. In his historical work on the rise of nationalism in nineteenth- and twentieth-century central Europe, he argued that nationalism, modern masculinity, and middle-class respectability evolved in parallel with one another and that German institutions like all-male schools and universities, all-male clubs, and the army were pivotal in cinching the close connection among these three institutions and relegating women to the home, where their role was to give birth to new citizens and nurture them. Industrialization and urbanization had generated fears of "decadence" that would produce weak men, whom Mosse termed "dangerous countertypes," eventually identified by the Nazis as Jews, homosexuals, the Roma (gypsies), the homeless, the criminal, the disabled, and the mentally ill, with well-known catastrophic consequences. World War I had tied nationalism and masculinity closer together than ever before by producing a new "image of man"—a warrior stereotype of masculinity suffused with Christian imagery of discipline, sacrifice, and purification through war, analogous to Christ's sacrifice (themes that are also found in the contemporaneous muscular Christianity in Britain and North America). War and sports were the antidote to degeneration, partly because of the male camaraderie but also because nationalist masculinity was founded on an idealization of an athletic, beautiful, and virile male body; nationalist ideology was constructed by men for men, and women played no role in it other than to act as an Other to masculinity. Mosse argued that the basic shape of European masculinity and its relationship to sport have not changed greatly in the subsequent century. In fact, they have influenced images of masculinity in other societies, where one finds an adulation of athletic masculinity that might not have been there before, along with its contrast with a docile, domestic femininity.[44]

A comparison of the entanglement of nationalism and gender in the West with the Chinese version both highlights the constructed nature of nationalism and illustrates the different configuration of this construction outside the West. As European ideas about nationalism were introduced into China in the late nineteenth century, Chinese intellectuals and statesmen began to contrast the bound-footed and semisecluded Chinese woman with Western women, who were said to be nearly equal to Western men. In reformist thought, the "oppressed Chinese woman" became a symbol of China's backwardness and weakness as a nation. From its beginning, then, Chinese nationalist ideology was intertwined with gender ideology.[45] The dreaded label of the "sick man of East Asia," which patriots (apparently erroneously) said was applied to China by Japan and the West, became a battle cry for reforming the effeminate scholar in his robe and queue and his bound-footed wife.[46]

The feminization of Chinese men and the eroticization of Chinese women were a common tactic in the ideology of Orientalism that postcolonial scholar Edward Said theorized.[47] Orientalism fueled the North American YMCA's work to introduce sport in China, save Chinese women, and support Chinese nationalism, which, conveniently for them, attracted followers to what was their more important cause, namely conversion to Christianity. Thus, physical education and sports became linked with nationalist ideology and gender.

This link had long been cinched when in 1981 the Chinese women's team won the FIVB Volleyball Women's World Cup in Tokyo, sparking a turning point in the revival of national pride and patriotism after the Cultural Revolution (1966–76). Along the way they defeated China's main global rivals, the USSR, the United States, and Japan. Any Chinese person who was of age at the time recalls this event as a turning point in national history. In Beijing people flooded into the streets, setting off firecrackers, some openly weeping. The team went on to win five consecutive world titles, including Olympic gold in 1984, and play the part of China's most visible national heroines for the next decade. By comparison with Western sports heroines, the team's gender and its implication for the women's movement were not emphasized to the degree one might expect. They were Chinese first and women second. One of the hundreds of letters sent to the team by Chinese students studying in West Germany, for example, concluded, "You've told the world, 'These are the Chinese!'"[48]

The official rhetoric emphasized that the team had realized the long-held revolutionary dream of erasing the label of "the sick *man* of East Asia" (*dongya bingfu;* the male bias is present in the original Chinese *fu*). Although the official rhetoric often *said* that the women had erased the label, the sentiments of national inferiority remained, and official party rhetoric continued to repeat the trope. Twenty-seven years later, official rhetoric was still claiming that the Beijing 2008 Olympic Games would *finally* erase the label. Although it did not disappear overnight, it did appear that after those successful games, young people were no longer motivated to righteous patriotic anger by the phrase.

In the years following the women's volleyball victory, Chinese female athletes generally had greater success in international sports than male athletes, so they became the symbolic figureheads in the revival of Chinese nationalism. Chinese people often cited the proverb "The yin waxes and the yang wanes," and wondered, "What's wrong with Chinese men?" Actually, nothing was wrong with the men, but the state-supported sports system, which funded men's and women's sports equally, gave a relative advantage to the women compared to their international competitors, who were generally underfunded and marginalized in most sports. The public debate about the lackluster achievements of Chinese sportsmen revealed a sentiment that the state of affairs was not desirable or even natural—the underlying assumption seemed to be that the men really should be the ones to carry the national banner. As much as people loved the women's volleyball heroines, they would also admit that if the Chinese men's soccer team ever got its act together enough to win a major world title, *then* there would be a celebration like none before.

In the new millennium, as market forces increasingly replaced the state-planned economy, sexualized female bodies were prominent in advertising and popular culture, complementing the emergence of new forms of masculinity tied to the nation. Chinese men began to recover their potency domestically and in the world's political-economic arena, where Chinese leaders began flexing their muscles. International men's soccer had more fans in China than any other sport, with the American NBA running a close second, and female athletes no longer occupied center stage as did the volleyball players in the 1980s. Yao Ming became an NBA star and demonstrated that Chinese men could hold their own with the world's biggest and best athletes; he carried the national flag in the Parade of Athletes in the 2004 and 2008 Olympics, and the next Chinese basketball player to make it in the NBA, Yi Jianlian, was the flag bearer at the 2012 Olympics. Physical height is regarded as an expression of national strength, so it was no surprise that very tall basketball players carried the flag during this period when China replaced Japan as the second-largest economy in the world. As President Xi Jinping began to speak with a more assertive voice in the international arena, he also stated that winning and hosting the FIFA World Cup were official national goals.

Nationalist conflicts in sport can take on the form of different definitions of gender norms. In his ethnography of Los Telecotes de los Dos Laredos (the Owls of the Two Laredos), a professional baseball team that played from 1985 to 1994 in both the United States and Mexico, Alan Klein found that one particularly salient source of tension was the contrasting codes of masculinity that players from both sides of the border abided by.[49] Differing notions of masculinity and nationalism played out in the relations among players and between players and managers. Located in the twin cities of Laredo, in Texas, and Nuevo Laredo, in the state of Tamaulipas, which are separated by the US-Mexico border, "Los Tecos" were the recipients of financial and training expertise from their Major League Baseball affiliate, the Atlanta Braves. The fact that no other Mexican league team received similar benefits reinforced the team's uniqueness, but while press coverage emphasized the fraternal basis of this uniqueness, interpersonal relations between fans, management, and the players were often rife with dislike and nationalistic prejudice, reflecting the tense historical and contemporary relations between the two countries. Mexican players, for example, resented players from the other side of the border (*importados,* "imported"), who were given better salaries, traveled by plane instead of bus, and were allowed to live on the US side. Some US players returned the antipathy by making disparaging remarks about Mexicans and cursing them when they did not understand English.

While there was a tendency for Mexicans to follow stereotypical codes of Mexican machismo in their performance of gender, in many cases this was mitigated by nonstereotypical practices, such as the expression of affection for each other through playful tussling, hugs, and evident emotion, playing with children, and taking part in domestic chores at home. These behaviors contrasted sharply with the stoic, hard, and distanced emotions of the American players, who considered emotional vulnerability a weakness rather than a strength. The players misunderstood and violated each other's cultural norms of masculinity, leading to heated confrontations and resentments. Even though this binational team strove to bring the two different forms of nationalist masculinity together into a coherent whole, the tensions that these efforts generated eventually led to the breakup of the team.[50]

Masculinity and nationalism (or localism) in the professional sports of late capitalism pose contradictions for the century-old formula of nation-masculinity-sport. Local teams are purchased by corporations or owners who have no particular local attachment and are transformed into consumer products marketed transnationally. Their ties to their country or city of origin become only a minor aspect of this consumption.[51] Manchester United, the Chicago Bulls, and the New Zealand All Blacks are perceived to represent particular places, but in reality they are primarily products that can be purchased worldwide in the form of fan club memberships and franchised clothing. Teams symbolize a deeply local masculine identity that continues to be central to their marketing due to fans' identification with local teams, which translates into sales of tickets and licensed products, fan club subscriptions, and above all TV ratings that lead to advertising revenues. Paradoxically, the teams themselves are now staffed by large numbers of transnational migrants (or the offspring of migrants). The migrant team-sport athletes embody the pride of local and national communities that do not necessarily respect them as full members. When a racialized or foreign player misses a goal on the soccer field, the tense politics of autochthony and belonging that dominate the public sphere in countries like France, the United Kingdom, and the Netherlands easily rear their aggressive head. Twentieth-century nationalism is increasingly insufficient to embrace the relationships among transnationalism, localism, masculinity, and belonging in the contemporary world.

MOVING CITIZENSHIP: THE POLITICS OF NATIONAL IDENTIFICATION AMONG ATHLETES

FIFA World Cups, Olympic Games, and other international events are the premier occasions for displaying to a global audience a world order divided into citizens happily loyal to their individual nations.[52] But is the world really so neatly ordered? A look beneath the surface at the athletes who "represent" these nations reveals that nations are not the cleanly divided political units seen in this happy family portrait. Confusing the issue is the difference between citizenship and nationality. Citizenship denotes legal belonging to a particular state, while nationality marks emotional and other ties to a particular nation. Athletes and coaches can and do manipulate the systems of citizenship to their advantage so as to be able to compete at higher levels and to continue their careers in other states when it proves difficult at home. Athletes' exchange of citizenship, called "code-switching" behind the scenes, provides a fascinating glimpse into the changing balances of global power in the twenty-first century.

In the last few years, well-heeled Persian Gulf states have attracted athletes from other countries with a more established sporting tradition by offering them money, training facilities, and the possibility to qualify for the Olympics and other global sports events, in contrast to the extremely competitive field back home. Often, when citizenship is a requirement for competing internationally, these athletes are fast-tracked through naturalization but can retain their original citizenship if their country of origin allows dual citizenship. Under the best of circumstances, the diminutive but oil-rich emirate of Qatar has played only a very modest role in world sports. In recent years, however, the country has acquired considerable visibility in the sports world with its huge investments in sport. Thus, for example, the Qatari national team that reached the finals at the 2015 Men's Handball World Championship (to be defeated by the French team) had only four players on the squad originating from Qatar—the rest were all non-Qatari.[53]

Bahrain gained its first Olympic medal in 2008 when Rashid Ramzi, originally from Morocco, won the men's 1,500-meter race. It was later rescinded because he tested positive for doping, but in 2012 Maryam Yusuf Jamal, originally from Ethiopia, followed with a bronze medal in the women's 1,500 meters. Bahrain sent its largest-ever contingent of thirty athletes to the Rio 2016 Olympics, of whom only four were born in Bahrain. There were sixteen track-and-field athletes born in Ethiopia, Kenya, Nigeria, Jamaica, and Morocco; a Russian weightlifter rounded out the delegation.[54]

Some have contrasted the generous offer of citizenship to athletes with the difficult fate of the numerous migrant workers from South and Southeast Asia who may spend decades in Gulf countries without ever qualifying for citizenship. Other commentators portray the athletes as turncoats who betray their nation of origin and as rapacious individualists who place money over sportsmanship.

These representations touch a sensitive chord in the athletic world: since modern sports were invented in nineteenth-century Europe and North America, they have been buoyed by lofty ideals of fair play, allegiance to country, and material disinterest. The importance given to these values stems from the fact that many sports were originally played by wealthy ruling elites, whose detachment from material concerns was easy and whose attachment to the country they ran was understandable. Despite the momentous transformations that sport has undergone over the decades, these values continue to have an uneasy relationship with the enormous sums of money involved in some sports—as well as the ease with which elite athletes switch clubs, teams, and countries.

However, and not entirely surprisingly, if we turn our attention to the complexities of athletes' transnational mobility, a different and more complex picture emerges. First, it is not just wealthy countries with a limited pool of talent such as Qatar that finance elite athletes to compete under a flag with which they have few or no previous associations. Take the United States: the US Army offers a World Class Athlete Program that recruits "world class" athletes with the goal of seeing them qualify for the upcoming Olympics or Paralympics. The program is not developmental—each sport has clear standards ensuring that athletes are already members of US national teams or are already among the best in the world. Since non-US-born military recruits may apply for US citizenship without satisfying the normal five-year residency rule (a law that came into effect in the aftermath of 9/11), athlete soldiers who are accepted into the program can compete for the United States immediately.[55] The US track-and-field squad in Rio included four Kenyans who benefited from this program. In addition, of the 129 track athletes who competed under the US flag, four came to the United States from African countries to attend high school or college, three were children of Nigerian immigrants, and one had been naturalized in 2004 after winning medals for Kenya in the 2000 and 2004 Games.[56] Qatar's citizenship fast-tracking in sport garners considerably more attention because it stands out against the previous invisibility of the country in world sport (and migrant athletes are much more likely to settle permanently in the United States than in Qatar), but there are many other countries with the same practices.

While we can applaud the way in which sport offers opportunities to athletes seeking to escape poverty and build careers and lives, it is important not to lose sight of the higher-level power struggles that help to open (or close) these doors. Qatar bought athletes to support its larger ambition of increasing its international influence through sports. It hosted the Asian Games and the indoor and outdoor World Track and Field Championships. In 2022 it will be the first Middle Eastern nation to host the FIFA World Cup. Doha put forward an unsuccessful bid for the 2020 Olympic Games in 2012. The bid committee was chaired by Sheikh Tamim bin Hamad Al Thani, who was also the president of the Qatar Olympic Committee and a member of the IOC. At that time he was heir apparent, but he became emir of Qatar in 2013 when his father stepped down and Qatar had its first succession without a coup. Qatar is one of several Middle Eastern countries in which the ruling aristocracy utilize high positions in the sports world to bolster their power and prestige both domestically and abroad. They have also been accused of corruption for using their considerable wealth to buy support. Because the IOC considers widespread sports participation and Olympic success a desirable trait in bidding countries, Qatar is under pressure to develop its sports system—but it has proved faster to buy it.

Kazakhstan has emerged as the most powerful state in central Asia, and it also has Olympic ambitions. It hosted the 2011 Asian Winter Games and bid unsuccessfully for the 2022 Winter Olympics. In the lead-up to the unsuccessful bid, which was decided in 2015, Chinese patriots were angered when two Chinese female weightlifters won gold medals for Kazakhstan in the London Olympics. The Chinese sports officials who had approved their move defended their permission by stating that the athletes had been young, and they had not considered them to be the best prospects. However, in Chinese sports circles there was some suspicion that the officials had been paid off by Kazakhstan, perhaps to help the country win medals that would help its Olympic bid.

Throughout this chapter we have emphasized nationalism's connections to sport, paying particular attention to the ways in which the invented traditions of both sport and nationalism mutually reinforce each other. In the wake of the crisis resulting from the millions of refugees flooding into Europe from North Africa and the Middle East, the Rio 2016 Olympics included the first-ever Refugee Olympic Team of ten athletes competing under the Olympic flag.[57] There had been a long-standing practice of allowing Independent Olympic Athletes to compete when their national Olympic committees were temporarily defunct or banned, but the refugee team was an innovation. While historically significant, in many ways it confirmed the stranglehold that the nation has on how athletes must define themselves.

In sum, the world system of nations is not as neatly ordered as it appears to be in the Olympic Parade of Athletes. Beneath the surface lies a mess of transnational wheeling and dealing by power brokers facilitating moves by athletes seeking to get the most reward for their hard work and talent, both for themselves and for their families and friends.

TRANSNATIONAL SURVEILLANCE AND SECURITY: THE END OF THE NATION-STATE?

Transnationalism refers to the increasing and varied connections between humans across national lines, enabled by new technologies of mobility. One of the foundational anthropological works on the topic, by Swedish anthropologist Ulf Hannerz, began with a sports example: a local entrepreneur in his home village had brought in a star ice hockey player to advance the fortunes of a local team, but the player was soon hired by a Canadian team in the National Hockey League and had not been seen in Sweden since.[58] Transnational linkages are not "international," in that they do not strictly involve states, but include a diverse range of actors such as individuals, groups, movements, and business enterprises.

One particularly significant realm in which new configurations of the nation-state and transnational forces are emerging is the security and surveillance practices that accompany sport mega-events. For Foucault, surveillance played a crucial role in the governmentality associated with nation-states, but sport mega-events have provided a platform on which national, international, and transnational actors collaborate to produce surveillance systems on a scale that Foucault never imagined. Sport mega-events are *theoretically* ideal for terrorist attacks and for the spread of pandemics, although historically they have rarely been targeted by terrorists or spread infectious diseases. Even if the risk is infinitesimal, government officials and event organizers must produce the appearance of concern to cover themselves if the unlikely event occurs. The heavily publicized security measures around Olympic Games are rituals that provide reassurance in the face of unpredictability.

Anthropologist Vida Bajc coined the phrase "security meta-ritual" for such attempts to control uncertainty in potentially catastrophic situations. The concept, which borrows Gregory Bateson's notion of metacommunicative frames (described in chapter 1), refers to the pressure on Olympic organizers to define and regulate certain aspects of social life and certain spaces as "security risks." Practices and spaces so identified are fenced in with protocols, technologies, statistics, and computational modeling in order to minimize uncertainty, with the goal of ensuring that the events unfold in a predictable, linear fashion. Bajc points out that security is organized around data-sharing networks that may be municipal or national, but may also extend beyond the nation. Therefore, the security apparatus sometimes violates the principle of state sovereignty, while in other ways it may reinforce the power of the state. The general trend has been toward the formation of an increasingly global security apparatus.[59]

One can see how fears of pandemics spurred by the Olympics arise.[60] The thought of half a million foreign visitors converging on the epicenter of a little-understood illness is scary. But that vision has to be tempered, because history has shown that the likelihood that the Games will spark a pandemic is minuscule, while the likelihood that a pandemic will come from a completely unanticipated source is very high. A 2009 review of the literature covering infectious diseases at Olympic Games, FIFA World Cups, and

UEFA European Championship soccer tournaments held between 1984 and 2006 documented not a single case of an increase in infectious diseases at major sports events.[61]

Nevertheless, because mega-events offer such good opportunities to improve systems for monitoring disease spread, a far-reaching data-sharing network has been forming around mega-events since 2008. The Beijing Olympics, held five years after the badly mismanaged SARS epidemic, marked the escalation of international involvement in medical surveillance at Olympic Games, which had previously been largely left to local health authorities. The World Health Organization (WHO) sent a team to Beijing and afterward established its Interdepartmental Mass Gatherings Group, which provided impact assessments and expertise to subsequent summer and winter Olympic Games and FIFA World Cups, as well as the Haj to Mecca. The Haj is the world's largest annual mass gathering, dwarfing the Olympic Games with several million pilgrims from some 180 countries over a five-day period, and thus the Saudi Arabian government was a key supporter of the WHO initiatives. WHO also initiated a Mass Gatherings Observer Programme at Olympic Games to bring in and train specialists from countries that were planning to organize major sports events.[62]

The London 2012 Olympics further pushed forward the development of new statistical tracking methods and surveillance structures, and UK experts played key roles in the WHO network. In advance of the Games, a "syndromic surveillance system" conducted daily reviews of reports of infectious diseases coming from across the United Kingdom. The surveillance team discovered that the existing data did not provide daily information from "out of hours" visits to general physicians or from visits to walk-in clinics and emergency rooms (precisely the services that overseas visitors use). This was corrected in the surveillance done during the Games and was subsequently incorporated into the standard surveillance routine. More rapid laboratory diagnostic tests were also implemented. In the end, no major health incidents occurred.[63]

These strengthened collaborations between municipal and national governments, national health organizations (such as the American Centers for Disease Control and Public Health England) and the major international health organization (WHO) have pushed forward the design of more comprehensive surveillance systems that combine new laboratory technologies, information-gathering procedures, and statistical methods. The epidemic of the zika virus that raged in Brazil in the lead-up to the Rio 2016 Olympic

Games raised alarm worldwide about the potential for a pandemic. Actually, the zika epidemic itself might not have been identified but for the improved global surveillance system. Zika is mainly transmitted through mosquito bites, from mother to child, and sometimes through sexual intercourse, and produces fever, a rash, joint pain, and conjunctivitis. However, about 80 percent of infected people had no symptoms at all. Niko Besnier contracted the virus during fieldwork in Tonga in April 2016, but his rash disappeared within forty-eight hours. What caught the eye of the medical experts was a rise, at the end of 2015, in the number of babies in Brazil born with microcephaly (small, malformed heads) and other severe brain defects. It required several more months before the deformities were confirmed as the result of zika infections in pregnant mothers. The worldwide medical surveillance system was on high alert for the Rio Olympics, but there was no evidence that the games facilitated the spread of the virus.

One can also see how fears of violence against Olympic Games keep many experts awake at night—among other reasons, the numbers of heads of state gathered there make the Olympics a security nightmare for any host nation. The Black September massacre of eleven Israeli athletes at the Munich Games in 1972 and the bombing in Centennial Olympic Park in Atlanta in 1996, which killed one person, have actually been the only fatal attacks. Nevertheless, Olympic Games have strengthened global security networks by creating partnerships between domestic and international governments, Interpol, defense contractors, and security experts, and by providing opportunities to test ever more complex surveillance systems. The United States and Israel are two key players that provide training, expertise, and know-how to Olympic hosts. Surprisingly, given the perception in the United States of China's growing military threat, the United States helped to train Chinese antiterrorism squads in preparation for the Beijing 2008 Olympic Games. The Israeli company International Security and Defense Systems managed security for the Rio Olympics.[64]

Some scholars have argued that the urban renewal that accompanies Olympic Games, typically resulting in mass evictions of poor people from areas targeted for improvement, should be seen as a kind of ritual purification. Anthropologist Erika Robb Larkins combined the notion of purification with spectacle theory to analyze the 2011 "pacification" of Rio's largest favela (slum), Rocinha, in the lead-up to the Olympic Games.[65] In a surprise maneuver, dozens of armored tanks "invaded" (the word that favela residents prefer over the official "pacify") the favela, followed by the infamous Special

Forces Unit and supported by helicopters in the air. Ahead of the occupation, the construction of a state-of-the-art sports complex had been intended to win over the hearts and minds of the residents. Within hours, the Brazilian flag was raised along with the black skull-and-dagger banner of the Special Forces Unit. This "spectacular violence" was a performance of state power, legitimized by the argument that it was necessary to make Rio safe for the 2014 World Cup and 2016 Olympic Games. This strange marriage of transnational symbols with the nation-state is made even more interesting by the fact that the favela pacifications were modeled after the "community policing" that Mayor Rudolph Giuliani implemented in New York City in the 1990s, which was ostensibly designed to combat crime but ended up involving widespread police harassment of homeless people, the closure of community service centers, restrictions on street vendors and busking, and the "Disneyfication" of Times Square, known until then for its peep shows, sex workers, and low-rent housing—all perfect examples of ritual purification.[66] (Giuliani was hired as a highly paid security consultant by the State of Rio de Janeiro in the years leading to the Games.)

A particularly dramatic illustration of ritual purification is the moral panic over sex work and human trafficking that accompanies sport mega-events. For example, prior to the 2014 FIFA World Cup in Brazil, police arrested sex workers, closed down establishments, and "cleaned up" neighborhoods known for prostitution, despite the fact that sex work is legal in Brazil.[67] Like the "pacification" of favelas, moral-panic-driven ritual cleansing in Rio did not target all nonnormative sexual expressions: while the police in Rio were harassing sex workers, who are overwhelmingly poor and nonwhite, the city was busy advertising itself as a haven for well-heeled gay and lesbian tourists from overseas, whose pink dollar it was eager to attract.

Since the Athens 2004 Olympics it has become standard for host cities to crack down on sex work and human trafficking leading up to sport mega-events, even though since that time scientific research has yet to generate reliable data proving that they represent a problem. Control efforts are spurred by politicians wanting to ensure that nothing besmirches their city's image, NGOs wanting to promote their agendas, and journalists looking for salacious stories. In fact, sex workers often complain about the lack of work during sport events, when potential clients are too busy watching sport and too tired (or inebriated) to do much else. The ritual cleansing of sexuality is often organized by coalitions of state agencies with transnational evangelical organizations and transnational conservative feminist NGOs (part of the movement that sociologist Elizabeth Bernstein calls "carceral feminism").[68] Although quantitative evidence has proved elusive, volunteer civic groups engaged in combating sex trafficking in the United States are convinced that the Super Bowl is a major hub for sex trafficking based on the activity that they track on the "dark web" (the hard-to-access part of the Internet where illegal activities are conducted). Armed with their qualitative research, volunteers assemble each year at the event to stake out likely street corners and call in suspicious activities. They do not report their activities to journalists because they want to hide their tracking methods from perpetrators.[69]

Hannerz cautions us not to forget the continued importance of the national when we are looking at the transnational.[70] It is clear in these examples that although many of these processes are changing the ways in which sport is organized, practiced, and consumed, elements of nationalism continue to inform these macroscale processes. In the next chapter, we turn to the international, global, and transnational process of world sport.

EIGHT

Sport in the World System

THE LEADING GLOBAL SPORTS organizations, such as the International Olympic Committee (IOC) and the Fédération internationale de football association (FIFA), claim that their sports embody universal values, and they assume that these values can be appreciated by a universal humanity. For example, the Olympic Charter—the IOC's bylaws—makes this point crystal clear in its first Fundamental Principle (emphasis added):

> Olympism is a philosophy of life, exalting and combining in a balanced whole the qualities of body, will and mind. Blending sport with culture and education, Olympism seeks to create a way of life based on the joy of effort, the educational value of good example, social responsibility and respect for *universal fundamental ethical principles.*[1]

For decades, Olympic studies scholars have been researching and debating the "Olympic values" with little attention to the fact that these values emanate from a particular moment in the history of sport and a particular Western worldview. Perhaps more than any other cultural practice, today's sport gives the impression of being part of a shared global "monoculture." But the previous chapters have demonstrated that there is nothing inherently universal about modern sport. If it appears to be universal today, it is a result of the two-hundred-year process of distilling thousands of local games and contests into a global system, a process that started in western Europe at the end of the eighteenth century.

These processes and those that followed them up to this day have had different kinds of engagement with the nation-state and all that it represents. In this chapter, we examine the international, transnational, and global processes that shape the world of sport, knit together national sports systems, and crosscut other forms of identity that are more grounded in local territories and cultures.

KEYWORDS: INTERNATIONALISM, TRANSNATIONALISM, GLOBALIZATION

Located firmly within the purview of nation-states, the internationalism in sport reinforces the contemporary world system of nation-states. This system is sometimes referred to as the "Westphalian system," after the 1648 Peace of Westphalia—the first of many agreements between modern "nations," a category that was just solidifying at the time—which upheld the local authority of territorial states on the basis of principles of national sovereignty, diplomacy, equality, nonintervention, and international laws.[2] Internationalism is founded on the sovereignty of the state and reinforces it. Emerging in the late-nineteenth and early-twentieth century out of the imperial and colonial processes discussed in chapter 2, internationalism in sport was a phenomenon in which governments, workers' organizations, and other nongovernmental actors implemented sport for specific political agendas. Governments in particular increasingly used sport as a diplomatic tool, while nongovernmental actors adopted sport as a mechanism for various agendas.

In contrast, transnationalism connects people, ideas, and symbols across national boundaries in ways that are not dependent on the sovereignty of the state but do not challenge it either.[3] Internationalism differs from transnationalism in that it largely concerns nation-states and their agents, while transnationalism is in the hands of nonstate agents, whose power to undermine the authority of the state is limited but who can nevertheless act across national boundaries, maintaining an involvement in different nation-states at once. The circulation of professional players across national borders is an example of transnational dynamics in sport.

Globalization takes a bird's-eye view that encompasses the vantage points of both internationalism and transnationalism: it occurs in the discrete spaces of state-based territories and in the global system of governance that sometimes bypasses state sovereignty. The globalization of sport was a process that detached sporting practices from specific national territories. Sport exists in a "global space" that transcends national, cultural, and political boundaries. Globalization is broadly defined as an intensified interconnectedness that also compresses and stretches space while accelerating time.[4] It has two distinct but closely connected processes: intensified global connectivity and growing social consciousness of the world as a single place.[5] Through their pageantry, ceremonialism, and marketing of slogans and symbols of unity, sport mega-events such as the FIFA World Cup and the Olympic Games play an important role in enhancing a consciousness of humankind and offering a powerful fantasy of unity—a global "imagined community."[6]

Globalization exists in mutual interdependency with local contexts, since people in specific locales adapt and redefine any global cultural product to suit their needs, beliefs, and priorities, and they do not necessarily do so in a coherent, unified manner. This process has sometimes been referred to by the portmanteau *glocalization,* made up of *local* and *global,* which captures the simultaneous and seemingly contradictory trends of convergence and divergence seen, for example, in the way that Olympic and World Cup host cities display their local identity while making major accommodations to the international practices entailed in hosting the events.[7]

Internationalism, transnationalism, and globalization overlap and inform each other, and they frequently operate simultaneously, yet the underpinning ethos of each makes it apparent that these are distinct processes. The distinction lies in how each shapes basic understandings of the world. Since the bread and butter of anthropological inquiry is to get at the forces that underpin people's everyday lives and their presumptions about the way the world works, exists, and thrives, an important anthropological endeavor is to unpick the intertwined processes that shape sport.

SPORT AND INTERNATIONAL RELATIONS

When it is situated in the arena of international relations, sport can be transformed from an embodied practice oriented to the development of the individual into an attempt to convince groups of people of something that they might otherwise ignore or disagree with. In this process, sport is not practiced for its own intrinsic values but is deployed for its ability to demonstrate and develop values extrinsic to the sport in question.[8] In this vein, sport is harnessed as a tool for diplomacy and for international development.

States have used sport as a means of extending their spheres of influence, maintaining control of conquered territories and populations, and providing a softer diplomatic tool than military intervention, even as sport often accompanied military invasions, sometimes for the simple reason that sports were part of soldiers' practices. The US government deliberately mobilized baseball to increase its influence around the world, as we discussed in chapter 2. American sportsman and businessman Albert Spalding firmly asserted that baseball should "follow the flag."[9] He organized a world baseball tour for the express purpose of asserting an American empire that would demonstrate its superior vigor, vitality, and civilization.[10] The program of President Obama's historic 2016 visit to Cuba—the first by an American president since 1928—included an exhibition baseball game played between the Tampa Rays and the Cuban national team, in which the Obama family and Cuban president Raúl Castro sat side by side.

Almost from the start, the IOC situated itself as a broker between nation-states, using sport as means to bring otherwise intractable opponents together to reach accords. International governing bodies can act as diplomatic channels to facilitate greater interaction and accord between openly and tacitly hostile rivals.[11]

The most memorable example of sports diplomacy was "Ping Pong diplomacy" in the 1970s between China and the United States. After the Communist Party came to power in the People's Republic of China in 1949, its foreign policy did not allow official Chinese participation in any event or organization that recognized the Republic of China, the defeated regime that had fled to Taiwan and claimed, with the support of the United States, to be the legitimate government of all of China. In 1958 the People's Republic withdrew from the IOC (and most other international sports federations) because it refused to expel the Republic of China. Due to a quirk of history, the International Table Tennis Federation was one of only three international sports federations of which the People's Republic was a member, but the Republic of China was not. The reason was that its founder and president, Lord Ivor Montagu, was a member of the British Communist Party with strong sympathies for the People's Republic (he was later revealed to have been a spy during World War II for the Soviet Union, a British ally at the time).[12] As the People's Republic began returning to normalcy after the worst years of the Cultural Revolution (1966–69) had passed, Chairman Mao began making discreet overtures to the United States, which the latter ignored. At the thirty-first World Cup in Table Tennis in Japan in 1971, while the Cultural Revolution was still ongoing, US table tennis player Glenn Cowen "accidentally" boarded the Chinese national team's bus and struck up a conversation with the team captain, Zhuang Zedong. When the bus reached its destination, the two men publicly exchanged gifts in front of a waiting throng of international correspondents. Images of the two smiling men shaking hands and holding their gifts spread around the world, providing visual evidence of the common interests of two seemingly intractably opposed worlds. Cowen and Zhuang came to embody a thawing in international relations between China and the United States.[13]

Subsequently, a US delegation visited China, and the United States reciprocated by inviting a Chinese delegation, paving the way for China's admission to the United Nations in October 1971 following the Republic of China's expulsion from the international body. A series of international table tennis invitationals in Beijing from 1971 to 1973 also served as platforms for the establishment of diplomatic relations with African and Asian countries. President Nixon's historic visit to the People's Republic in 1972 marked the beginning of rapprochement, but it would be eight more years before the establishment of official diplomatic relations between the People's Republic and the United States in 1979, following which the country was finally admitted to the IOC on its own terms.[14]

Ping Pong diplomacy illustrates how sport can act as a catalyst and conduit in international relations between two nation-states: individual athletes from antagonistic countries may form friendships; sports exchanges may pave the way for a diplomatic rapprochement; and shady international power brokers may also use sports behind the scenes, a topic that deserves considerably more research attention than it has garnered to date.

SPORT AS SOFT POWER IN THE
INTERNATIONAL ARENA

For all these reasons and more, sport has gained increasing recognition as way in which a country may strengthen its "soft power," namely its ability to exert political influence in the international arena through noncoercive means, that is, other than military force, economic sanctions, or conditions attached to economic assistance.[15] Most forms of soft power lie outside the control of governments, although they can attempt to guide soft power through domestic policies. These attempts fall under the rubric of "public diplomacy," referring to attempts to reach out directly to the citizenry of another state ("winning hearts and minds") while bypassing its government. US soft power, for example, is produced by the movie, music, and fashion industries, while Japan's lies in the global appeal of manga, anime, and figures like Hello Kitty. Sport can also be a very effective (or, from a different perspective, insidious) form of soft power. The number of worldwide viewers of sports (including Major League Baseball, the National Basketball Association, and the National Football League's Super Bowl) rivals that of viewers who watch American movies (7.3 billion in 2003).[16]

Nowhere in the world is the pursuit of soft power via sports currently more intense than in East Asia. In the mid- to late 1990s, first Japan and then South Korea implemented government policies to promote their national "cultural industries" as a means of increasing their international influence. China then entered the competition in 2007 as President Hu Jintao declared that strengthening China's soft power was an official policy. This was the year before the Beijing Olympics, and there was general agreement both inside and outside China that these Olympic Games were a perfect platform for doing just that.[17] China's success in hosting the most grandiose Olympic Games to date sparked the rivalry with Korea and Japan that resulted in there being three consecutive Olympic Games to be held in East Asia from 2018 to 2022—the Pyeongchang 2018 Winter Olympics, the Tokyo 2020 Summer Olympics, and the Beijing-Zhangjiakou 2022 Winter Olympics.

SPORT FOR DEVELOPMENT AND PEACE

Perhaps the most visible form of public diplomacy is international development assistance (which used to be referred to as "foreign aid"), in the form, for example, of infrastructure (roads, public buildings, water-catchment systems) that proudly display plaques stating "a gift from the government of X." China's "stadium diplomacy" is the most extreme example of this kind in the realm of sports: since 1958, China has built about 140 stadiums in Africa, Asia, Latin America, the Caribbean, and the Pacific Islands, either as outright gifts, partial gifts, or partnerships. Over one hundred of these have been built since 2000; all six African Cup soccer tournaments from 2008 to 2017 were held in Chinese-built stadiums with the exception of the 2013 tournament in South Africa.[18] For over fifty years, international development has provided a remarkably stable framework within which policy makers, officials, and other members of the political and economic elite have understood the relationship between the affluent West and its Others. Anthropologists have criticized the assumptions underlying development programs, arguing that they perpetuate colonial relations, keeping impoverished populations of the world in their exploited conditions.[19] The unequal political and economic relations between what was termed the underdeveloped third world and the developed first world produced a collective guilt over the impoverished lives in the third world, necessitating "aid" as a means for assuaging guilt. Like all gifts, however, international aid incurs a debt, in which the giver tacitly expects something in return, and the act of giving is a form of power. Aid maintains third world nations indebted to the first world and transforms their economies while maintaining the same structural relationships between colonizers and colonized.

In the past two decades, the growing use of sport has been a recent shift in development practice. While the United Nations Educational, Scientific, and Cultural Organization (UNESCO) had recognized sport as a basic human right in 1978, that acknowledgement had not led to any explicit practice on the ground.[20] Similarly, in 1989, the United Nations formally recognized play as one of the rights of every child through Article 31 of the Convention on the Rights of the Child.[21] The idea that sport could be used as a tool in development and peace gained legitimacy within the United Nations in 2001 when UN secretary-general Kofi Annan appointed a Special Adviser to the UN Secretary-General on Sport for Development and Peace and created an interagency task force, which was eventually consolidated in 2008 as the UN Office on Sport for Development and Peace (UNOSDP). One goal for Annan was to update the image of the United Nations, and sport was a good way to do that. Additionally, sport was already being used by quite a few agencies in the areas of development and humanitarian affairs, most prominently UNESCO and the UN Children's Fund, and the UNOSDP could better coordinate their efforts. The programmatic statement that accompanied its founding asserted that sports programs can employ refugees, provide an incentive for children to enroll in school, promote gender equity, reduce child mortality by promoting health messages, improve maternal mortality by involving mothers from socially excluded groups in sporting activities, and, finally, assist global development through the creation of sport and peace networks and conferences.[22]

Today, a large portion of development aid falls into the hands of nongovernmental organizations (NGOs), which have proliferated in the last few decades. NGOs take many forms, ranging from very localized organizations focused on a specific human problem (e.g., domestic violence, microfinance, legal aid) to large-scale, well-funded organizations with operations around the world and

FIGURE 19. Girls from a local orphanage take part in an introductory tennis clinic put on by the Zhongshan City Tennis Team, an example of "sport for development" efforts (Guangdong Province, China, September 2008/Matt Haugen).

diverse portfolios, like Save the Children, Human Rights Watch, and World Vision. In some parts of the world, the power of NGOs has replaced that of the state.[23] Sometimes they in fact reinforce the concept of a state by highlighting the fact that they are not the state while they themselves perform tasks that are traditionally associated with the responsibilities of the state.[24]

While there is no denying that some NGOs have improved people's lives in some contexts, they also raise questions that are often left unaddressed, including the claim that they represent a "global conscience," with all the problems associated with this kind of universalization; the selective way in which they often identify the solution to social problems as a matter of individual "empowerment," neglecting structural conditions; the fact that they sometimes have covert agendas, such as religious or political proselytism; and the fact that they are not accountable to anyone, unlike the state, which is (theoretically) answerable to its citizens.[25]

Over the last couple of decades, sport has become increasingly visible in the panoply of areas where NGOs seek to address social ills, and a new category, "sport for development and peace" (SDP), has emerged. One of the first such efforts was the brainchild of speed skater Olympian Johann Olav Koss, who won one gold medal at the Albertville 1992 Winter Olympics and three at the Lillehammer 1994 Winter Olympics, setting three world records. Before the Lillehammer Games, Koss had traveled to Eritrea under the auspices of the IOC's Olympic Aid Commission, established in 1963 to promote sport in the newly independent former colonies of Africa. He was so moved by the destitution he witnessed that after winning the medal, he donated his earnings to Olympic Aid. The Norwegian media roundly criticized Koss for organizing a drive to provide sports equipment for Eritrean refugee children, the prevailing view being that "Eritrea will be out of food by September, and he's taking sports equipment to hungry children." However, when Eritrean president Isaias Afewerki received Koss, he retorted, "This is the greatest gift we have ever received. This is the first time we've been made to feel like persons and not just things to be kept alive."[26] Koss's action raised the profile of Olympic Aid, and he became its most prominent ambassador. In 2000, Olympic Aid was incorporated in Canada as the nonprofit NGO Right to Play, but Koss's celebrity and charisma ultimately led the organization to outgrow the IOC. They finally parted ways when the IOC excluded Right to Play from the Olympic Village at the Vancouver 2010 Winter Games.

The history of Right to Play illustrates some of the problems associated with SDP in particular and international NGOs in general. Right to Play's China office, established in Beijing in 2007 in the lead-up to the Olympic Games, hired one of Susan Brownell's Chinese graduate students. The office had a very hierarchical structure, with a well-paid male Canadian expatriate at the top, female expatriates below him, and the poorly paid Chinese student at the bottom. Because none of the expatriates spoke Chinese, the student's job was to spend hour after hour translating their materials into Chinese and translating Chinese into English while the boss was often away from the office on visits back to Canada. Right to Play had developed a highly systematized set of games that were copyrighted as intellectual property. This meant that the games could not be freely borrowed by interested Chinese and that, when the foreign employees took the games into poor schools, they were very rigid about conducting them according to the original design and not adapting them to the cultural context. Brownell's student observed some games that made the children uncomfortable because, for example, one child had to stand in the center of a circle of children, which violated the cultural emphasis on humility and collectivity. Right to Play's reputation in Africa is generally positive, but in Beijing they had failed to consider that they were not entering a poor, underdeveloped country, but rather one of the world's fastest-growing economies, with a longer and richer tradition of children's games than the West.

In a different situation, efforts by NGOs in Liberia, a country where a terrible civil war had recently raged, to implement SDP programs had effects that were the opposite of what the NGOs intended.[27] These efforts targeted former child soldiers and other youths, who were commonly characterized as either victims of the conflict or impulsive, violent, and irresponsible revolution seekers, but who found themselves stranded with no clear position in Liberian society. The NGOs saw soccer as a way to provide them with a sense of purpose. In traditional rural contexts in Liberia, the transition to adulthood was marked by initiation rituals, while in modern urban contexts it was defined by marriage and some indication of economic autonomy. Because of the civil war and the precarious political and economic conditions that it had created, many "youth" in their twenties and thirties were unlikely to achieve adult status according to these definitions. However, instead of helping them become full-fledged adult members of society, playing soccer reinforced their marginality by emphasizing their status as aging youth, a category for which there is no place in Liberian society.

In addition to frequently lacking an understanding of local dynamics, NGOs that work in the SDP paradigm tend to narrowly focus on specific social problems without addressing the fact that these are commonly the result of larger structures of inequality. As a result, they often end up aggravating the problems rather than solving them. In addition, because common Western understandings of sport tend to showcase the individual's willpower and moral worth, the ideology underlying SDP programs often reduces solutions to matters of personal self-reliance, responsibility, and "empowerment," in typical neoliberal fashion. Witness, for example, the vision statement of one SDP organization:

> [International Sport Alliance] envisions a world in which once marginalized young people have become *agents of change*. By participating in Sport for Development activities, they have learned to shape their own future, have strengthened their confidence, have become active citizens and have committed themselves to building up their communities. They have moved away from the vicious cycle of poverty, violence and inequality that has kept them and their families on the margin of society.[28]

What this vision statement and others like it leave untouched is the fact that, no matter how much individual responsibility people take for their own lives, poverty, marginalization, oppression, and other factors may present formidable obstacles to the improvement of their life conditions. More often than not, people cannot solve the structural conditions of their lives by simply "moving away" from them.

A closely related NGO-driven effort is the promotion of sport in conflict-ridden areas of the world to promote peace and reconciliation. "Sport for peace" occurs in tandem with "sport for development," as the acronym *SDP* indicates. Sport for peace is driven by the belief that bringing people together in a conflict situation on an even, neutral field encourages them to erase political differences and foreground interpersonal bonds of respect and trust, a process that allegedly replaces structural dynamics with interpersonal ones. An example of an NGO focused on peace building through sport is Football 4 Peace International (F4P), an initiative that brings coaches, community leaders, and volunteers together in divided communities around the world where entrenched hostility is latent and pervasive. In Israel, for example, it organized soccer camps, soccer matches, and workshops that brought together Jewish Israeli and "1948 Palestinian" (Palestinian with Israeli citizenship) children in various parts of the country from 2001 to 2012.[29]

F4P's Israel operations, and those of its successors, were embedded in a context in which soccer is profoundly political. While the Israeli state touts soccer as a means to bring people of different ethnic identities together, and it is one of the few public contexts in which the Jewish majority tolerates Arab citizens of the country to display their skills, the sport is also a realm for expressions of deep and overt racism. Its most dramatic expression is the fans of one of the major teams in the country, Beitar Jerusalem, who regularly chant "death to Arabs" during games.[30] Soccer in Israel is also deeply political in more covert ways, as in the constant discrimination toward Palestinian players and teams and in the neglect of infrastructures in Palestinian-dominated parts of the country. Israel's treatment of "1967 Palestinian" players and teams from the Occupied Territories (the West Bank and Gaza) is even more blatantly oppressive. To cite only two of many examples: on January 31, 2014, Israeli soldiers at a checkpoint in the West Bank deliberately shot promising soccer players Jawhar Nasser Jawhar and Adam Abd al-Raouf Halabiya in the feet, ensuring that these would never play again; and in August 2016, Israel prevented the head of the Palestinian Olympic delegation from leaving the Gaza Strip and stopped the shipment of the athletes' equipment ahead of the Rio Olympic Games, forcing it to purchase new gear in Brazil.[31] These incidents, and many others like them, fueled calls for FIFA to ban Israel, which the Israeli government countered with an aggressive diplomatic campaign targeting one hundred sports ministries and soccer officials around the world to convince them not to support the ban.[32]

F4P's activities are examples of what is commonly called in the region and beyond the "dialogue industry" or "peace industry" in reference to initiatives, NGOs, and events designed to promote "dialogue" between parties in conflict without addressing the dynamics of the context. In this case the context is that 1948 Palestinians are second-class citizens whose basic human rights are constantly violated in the country, and that Israel has maintained an oppressive occupation of the West Bank and Gaza since 1967, a larger political context that no dialogue will ever end. Some argue, instead, that dialogue in fact deflects attention from the source of the problem and thus contributes to it.[33]

SDP initiatives may be well-intentioned efforts fueled by genuine concern for the welfare of their recipients, but they often suffer from the same deficiencies that anthropologists frequently find among well-intentioned interventions by Westerners who are not organically connected to the grassroots society and are thus unable to build sustainable change from the ground up. Furthermore, the sport for development movement tends to be limited by international politics since it tends to be organized or at least shadowed by national governments or by the United Nations, an intergovernmental organization whose membership is composed of nation-states. Unlike the United Nations, the IOC and FIFA are nongovernmental organizations with considerably greater flexibility, but their sports aid programs still have to contend with national governments in the receiving locales.

THE TRANSNATIONAL CIRCULATION OF ATHLETES

Transnationalism refers to a realm that is not as limited by national politics as the international realm; it operates across national boundaries and concerns entities other than governments—in the first place, people, who move across national borders, sometimes against the wishes of governments, but also ideas, money, commodities, images, and technologies.

The most visible form that transnationalism takes in the sports world is the mobility across national boundaries of professional athletes and professional hopefuls. Almost from the foundational historical moment when sports were invented and codified, male athletes began crossing national borders to play sport, or taking sports with them as they moved transnationally for other reasons, often acting as vectors for the early global diffusion of sports. For a long time, however, the circulation of athletes who migrated specifically to pursue a career in sport was confined to movements between neighboring countries, for the simple reason that club officials and other gatekeepers felt most at ease recruiting nonlocal athletes if they came from countries that they regarded as having linguistic, cultural, and religious affinities to their own, or where they had strong personal connections.[34]

In the last decades of the twentieth century, sport mobility took a new turn. World team sports such as soccer, baseball, basketball, and rugby; individual sports such as track and field, gymnastics, and boxing; and many more localized sports like ice hockey and cricket experienced an enormous increase in the transnational mobility of athletes. These new patterns can be attributed to a number of simultaneous factors, including global changes in the political economy of the sports world, which are all manifestations of the turn to neoliberalism: in the 1980s and 1990s the revenues from television rights fees skyrocketed, clubs and teams became corporate entities, and elite athletes' salaries and transfer fees increased vertiginously in the most popular sports. Faced with increased competition and the need to maximize profit, clubs and teams began searching for talent further and further afield, bringing over players from the developing world. These historical junctures led to a remarkable increase in the number of foreign-born or ethnically marked athletes from developing countries who are employed in athletic workplaces in the industrialized world. In western European professional soccer, non-Europeans today constitute more than 50 percent of foreign players. In US Major League Baseball, foreign-born players reached an all-time high percentage of 29.8 on opening day 2017; 235 of the 259 players were from Latin America and the Caribbean.[35] The racially or ethnically marked composition of many prominent sports teams is another symptom of these dramatic changes.[36]

Concomitantly, in many parts of the world, sport was acquiring an unprecedented presence in people's lives. Television, the very medium that triggered sport's transformation into an industry, is also what contributed to giving sport its global visibility and its importance in the everyday lives of people. In rural Fiji, for example, indigenous boys playing informal rugby games on village greens perform "instant replays" in slow motion during their games, in imitation of the international sports television anchors they hear in televised rugby games, evidence of the power that media images exert on their lives.[37] In particular, sport was now no longer just a form of play but also potentially a form of very lucrative labor, as images of sports stardom and sport spectacles now reached even the most remote reaches of the globe.

These changes were taking place amid increasing material uncertainty in many parts of the world, particularly in the Global South. Many people around the world currently live in deteriorating environmental conditions and crumbling economies undermined by neoliberal government policies and austerity regimes imposed by such bodies as the International Monetary Fund (IMF) and the World Bank, and single-commodity economic regimes at the mercy of futures traders in the financial capitals of the world.[38] The economic crisis that gripped industrial nations in 2008 had ripple effects that compounded economic decline. In many places farming, long the most reliable form of labor, lost its prestige and profitability, often as a result of national policies promoting agriculture for export, leaving local farmers vulnerable to financial speculations taking place in faraway cities. At the same time, a number of legal developments eased the transnational mobility of skilled workers, at least in theory. These included in particular the Bosman ruling (1995), a European Court of Justice decision that abolished quotas on foreign players and the requirement that athletes obtain a release from their current employers, even at the end of their contract, before switching to a new employer (which enabled clubs to charge fees), and the Cotonou Agreement (2000, revised in 2010), signed by the European Union and countries in West Africa, the Caribbean, and the Pacific, which guaranteed the right of free movement to non-European workers within the European Economic Area.

Many countries of the Global South have become emigrating societies as people seek to move to wealthy economies in order to survive. Hope for a better life is oriented almost exclusively toward migrating to wealthy labor markets, and the economies of many nation-states have become largely supported by migrants' remittances. On an ideological level, one has to migrate in order to be valued as a member of society, and everything in society is intertwined with migration—the future is elsewhere.[39] Thus the explosion in the transnational mobility of athletes was the result of changes both in the global political economy of the sport industries and in local transformations of material conditions and symbolic aspirations. National dynamics were also at play, as some governments made the migration of professional athletes a matter of national socioeconomic policy.[40]

For young men in many parts of the Global South, fulfilling the dreams of success that sport engendered almost inevitably required migrating to countries of the Global North: Europe for soccer; North America for baseball or basketball; or Europe, Japan, Australia, and New Zealand for the rugby codes (union and league).[41] These dreams coexisted with the reality lived by most migrants who, often undocumented, worked in miserable conditions in the rural and urban regions of industrial countries and juggled time-consuming sports training with economic survival.[42] As a result, the possibility of emigrating to a career in the sport industries in wealthy areas of the world mobilized a huge amount of energy. While in reality only the lucky few gained widespread recognition, the *possibility* of success in professional sports in the Global North haunted the dreams of countless others, eclipsing the minute *probability* of success.

Migrating to a sport career is predominantly a male aspiration, for a number of reasons. Most straightforwardly, the labor market in sport is overwhelmingly male. But there are other reasons, such as the fact that, in many societies, men, rather than women, are expected to support parents and families as early as they can, yet the collapse of economies in most of the Global South left men, particularly young men, very few opportunities for work or employment. Thus getting married, which in many parts of the world is the principal marker of adulthood, became increasingly difficult for destitute young men. Sport migrations became a way to reclaim a masculine adulthood that had become so elusive. Women athletes also migrated to sport careers, although largely in individual sports, with the notable exception of Scandinavian team sports, which provided a labor market to women from eastern Europe and West Africa.[43]

Athletes from the Global South who migrate to the Global North are invariably involved in networks of indebtedness and exchange with relatives and other people back home, as they carry on their shoulders the hopes of many for a better life. In many contexts, extended families put up the money to cover the cost of a young man's passports, visas, and travel to an industrial country so he can try out with a team, and they see these expenses as an investment with returns that the young athlete hopeful is responsible for generating.[44] Niko Besnier came to know well a professional rugby player who came to Japan from Tonga, a Pacific Island country that exports rugby talent, who estimated that seventy people back in his island country were financially dependent on him.[45] Another up-and-coming young rugby player from Fiji on contract with a French professional club in 2015 sent all of his modest salary to his demanding relatives every month, which left him no money for his own sustenance, until the team's French support staff members had to intervene. For migrant athletes from poor countries, sport means salaried work, the fulfillment of obligations to families, and an inflow of wealth into countries with few resources.[46]

Transnational migrant athletes often face formidable obstacles, particularly in the form of laws that criminalize border crossing by people from poverty-stricken countries, an instance of the never-ending conflict between transnationalism and nationalism.[47] Obtaining visas to travel to wealthy countries, even for a brief visit, and persuading border guards to honor these visas constitute enormous challenges for holders of passports issued by countries of the Global South. In Cameroon, for example, passports and visas are the focus of considerable magico-religious activity.[48]

There are other obstacles to success in transnational sport careers. One is the basic need to be noticed as an athlete of professional potential by individuals with decision-making power (recruiters, managers, coaches, agents), what Thomas Carter calls the "production of visibility," without which no mobility takes place.[49] When Daniel Guinness and Niko Besnier were conducting fieldwork in Fiji in 2016, they visited a small village in the hinterland of the main island where young indigenous Fijian men shared in the national dreams of rugby careers overseas, but their village was so remote that they were unable to afford the bus fare into the city to take part in district competitions, and so they did not stand a chance of being noticed, however skilled they might have been.[50] In contrast, the district of Nadrogā had become known as "rugby country" for the number of migrant players it had produced. Because of its dry climate and beautiful beaches, it was also the location of most tourist resorts in the country, which is where rugby recruiters visiting from overseas stay—which provides a more likely explanation for the region's success than local assertions that the region grows its men big and strong (and raises them to be devoted Christians, whose destiny God will look after).

Migrant athletes face other kinds of constraints. In many countries, national sports governing bodies frequently place restrictions on the number of nonlocal players who can be part of the same squad or who can be on the field at any given time. The definition of "nonlocal" differs across contexts: it is frequently a matter of legal citizenship, although in some situations, it is a matter of time spent in the host country. Clubs and individuals find ways of getting around these restrictions: clubs help foreign athletes through naturalization processes, for example, or recruit athletes from countries known to excel in their sport when they are very young, and make them go through development programs so that they count as "local." It also ensures that they

FIGURE 20. Two Cameroonian soccer players in the front of the disused roadside tavern they share as living quarters with fellow migrant soccer players in rural Poland (winter 2015/Paweł Banaś).

are better adapted to the host country, which is convenient for the club but has the potential of alienating the young athlete from his society of origin. These rules and the search for ways around them represent the constant tug-of-war between nationalism and transnationalism.

As a result of these legal and other hurdles, aspiring athletes' transnational journeys can follow extraordinarily unpredictable paths, leading them to locations that they did not know existed and often stranding them in circumstances where they must create a life, sometimes on the margin of legality, in societies that can easily turn hostile toward them. Douglas Thompson told the story of a young soccer player from a West African country who, with two friends, had contracted the services of a sports agent in their country.[51] The agent promised him a trial with a major eastern European team and the possibility of a professional contract, but he had to first go to Croatia's capital, Zagreb, for the trial. In order to obtain a visa, the young man and his friends traveled to the only Croatian consulate in Africa, in Cairo, Egypt. There, they soon ran out of money as they were waiting for the visa to be issued, and they had to move out of the hotel where they had checked in, but fortunately they were put up by other West Africans they had met playing casual soccer in Cairo.

The young man was finally issued an eleven-day tourist visa to Croatia and managed to travel to Zagreb. Not surprisingly, the trial did not result in an offer of a contract, and after his visa expired, he went to Slovenia, reputed to have more lax immigration and asylum laws. There, he claimed political asylum and was detained in an asylum seekers' center, with no prospect of playing soccer or earning a living. Fortunately, the Slovenian government does not detain asylum seekers (as other European governments do) but allows them to leave the center during the day. The young soccer player eventually got married to a Slovenian citizen, which qualified him for a permanent resident permit, and he started playing professionally in a third-league team, hoping to move up to the premier league and perhaps move to a more desirable country—the United Kingdom being the ultimate dream of all West Africans in similar situations.

For this young man and others like him, the love of the game is embroiled with the desire and duty to send remittances to families. However, they are stuck in marginal areas of Europe, playing in lower divisions (if they are lucky), having to work at menial jobs on the side because teams are not wealthy enough to support their players, which takes time away from training and thus lowers their chances of becoming good enough to play for better clubs. Many become accustomed to their fate and make do with the conditions they encounter by marrying locally or taking up entrepreneurial activities predicated on personal networks, such as import-export ventures with their country of origin, as well as employment opportunities that capitalize on their racial exoticism, such as deejaying, playing music, and dancing. But precarity is the dominant characteristic of migrant athletes' life trajectories.[52]

The transnational circulation of athletes involves a host of diverse entrepreneurs who act as brokers between aspiring athletes and clubs across national boundaries. While this cadre of entrepreneurs includes honest individuals, the business also attracts others who engage in shady and exploitative practices. In the Dominican Republic, scouts in search of young baseball talent for export to baseball teams in the United States are called *buscones* (from Spanish *buscar,* "to look for"), a pejorative term that vilifies them as rapacious opportunists, even though they thrive in the country, which Alan Klein calls "a nation of buscones."[53] Working for a percentage of the player's signing bonus if they land a contract, many are involved in not only the athletic development of young players but also their education, health, and well-being, and often the welfare of their families, and some head complex and financially successful operations.

Some commentators have drawn parallels between the transnational circulation of athletes, particularly young ones, and human trafficking. NGOs like Foot Solidaire, based in Paris and headed by a former Cameroonian migrant soccer player, work explicitly within the principles of international declarations like the Palermo protocols to reduce instances in which players, particularly minors, are given false recruitment promises, offered contracts that lack transparency, and kept in situations of dependence (e.g., confiscated passports, salaries withheld, intimidation).[54] It is clear that some athletes have migrated under conditions that resemble human trafficking.[55] But it is also the case that such situations are always more complex than they appear at first glance, as is the case of human trafficking in general.[56] In particular, athletic migrations are commonly embedded in structures of kinship, in which agents are frequently relatives, and family members are fully supportive of the migration of young athletes.[57] The assumption that antitrafficking efforts mean that athletes are "better off at home" is explicitly contradicted by athletes themselves.[58] Based on their ethnographic fieldwork in Senegal and Cameroon, respectively, Mark Hann and Uroš Kovač report that young soccer players dreaming of a career in European clubs were aware of the risks involved and of the low likelihood of landing a contract with a top-ranking club, but they took calculated risks.

Among the most visible manifestations of the transnational nature of contemporary sport are the "baseball plantations" in the Dominican Republic, which Alan Klein's pioneering work documented, and the soccer academies (derogatorily dubbed "football farms") that European clubs and other entities have established in West and southern Africa.[59] Soccer academies come under many guises, from institutions that responsibly nurture their young charges, from which European clubs seek to recruit the most talented at the cheapest moment of their sport careers, to fly-by-night ventures that promise a great deal and deliver little. At worst, they expose young hopefuls to exploitation and lead them away from formal schooling.

As geographer James Esson shows, soccer academies in Ghana emerged at a moment in history when global and local dynamics converged at both material and ideological levels.[60] The socialist idealism in the impetuous years following the country's independence in 1957, under the charismatic leadership of the father of the nation, Kwame Nkrumah, had raised the development of education to the status of national priority. This is no longer the case today: the neoliberal economic policies of structural adjustment imposed by the World Bank and IMF undermined the state and especially the bureaucracy, which was the most important source of employment for graduates. No longer guaranteeing a place in a labor market now saturated with qualified

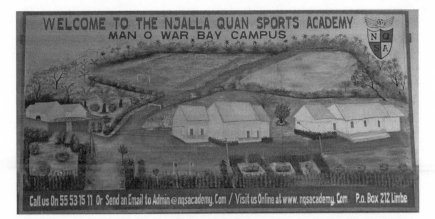

FIGURE 21. Sign at the entrance of the Njalla Quan Sports Academy (Limbe, Cameroon, 2014/Uroš Kovač).

candidates, formal education lost its appeal, especially for boys, who turned in increasing numbers to soccer academies, leaving education to girls and women. Boys today idealize a masculinity characterized by an "X lifestyle" (conspicuous consumption, fame, bad-boy reputation, etc.), an image associated with Ghanaian soccer players who play overseas. The gap between women's and men's priorities is thus progressively widening along with the gendering of life opportunities.

We must therefore understand the remarkable efflorescence of soccer academies within a historical context that includes political-economic changes of various scales, and within a contemporary context that includes the adulation of particular manifestations of masculinity, changing gender relations, and a belief that success necessarily involves migration.

Some commentators have bemoaned the "brawn drain," the depletion of athletic talent from the Global South for the benefit of the Global North, seeing in it a replication of colonial relations of yesteryears in which the colonized world supplied commodities and labor to the colonial powers.[61] Others, however, see athletes' transnational mobility differently. Fiji, for example, is a nation whose visibility in the rugby world dwarfs its relative economic and political insignificance, but whose numerous players have to move overseas in order to pursue international careers because the country is not wealthy and big enough to support a comprehensive rugby structure. Fijian rugby fans do not see this as a problem, as they cheer for whatever overseas team counts Fijian players on its squad. For them, rugby migrants demonstrate to the rest of the world what Fijians are capable of and give the country an international visibility that they cannot hope to achieve through other means. It is as if they have reconfigured their national imagined community to claim a citizenry dispersed around the globe, which is quite distinct from Benedict Anderson's image of the nation as a territorially bounded community.[62]

While the exodus of athletes from the Global South to the Global North has a long history, changes in the world order have created new forms of athletic mobilities in recent decades. For example, cricketers from Britain, Australia, and New Zealand are increasingly spending cricket seasons in India, which has now become the nerve center of the sport, thus reversing the relationship between South and North or, perhaps, calling for a reconsideration of the usefulness of these categories. Along with China's emergence as an economic and sports power, increasing numbers of Chinese coaches and athletes have begun moving out into the world. China dominates table tennis unlike any other country's domination of any sport—its athletes have won thirty-two of thirty-seven gold medals since table tennis became an Olympic sport in 1988, and all the gold medals in 2008, 2012, and 2016. Many players who have no hope of making Chinese national teams are driven to other countries looking for opportunities. Of the 140 singles players who qualified for the Rio Olympics, at least twenty were born in China. Some spent most of their careers in China before moving and were now in their forties or fifties (table tennis athletes can have very long careers). However, a growing trend was for junior athletes to emigrate in their teens seeking a country where the competition was not as fierce. Most of them represented western European nations, where there are professional table tennis leagues, but they also represented the United States, Australia, Singapore, the Ukraine, Turkey, and, of course, Qatar. Two Chinese represented the Republic of Congo, but, interestingly, one of them was born in Brazzaville—reflecting the ever-growing Chinese presence in Africa. Brazil was represented by Gui Lin, who immigrated at the age of twelve to play and was naturalized at eighteen, just in time to represent Brazil at the London Olympics.[63]

While the transnational migration of athletes has some unique characteristics, it also overlaps with other forms of mobility, two of which are the military and the global security industry. Indigenous Fijians, for example, see rugby and armed service, both of which they excel in, as being rooted in the same values: toughness, martial discipline, esprit de corps, and respect for country and church. Both rugby and military service are believed to be anchored in a timeless local history, in which young men were the *bati* (defenders) of the village, in charge of defending it and its chiefly structure. In colonial days, British authorities had constructed indigenous Fijians, like the Nepali Gurkhas, the Punjabi Sikhs, and others, as a "martial race," perfectly suited for recruitment in the armed services; because these groups did not experience colonialism as particularly problematic, they were known for their loyalty to the colonial regimes.[64]

Today, indigenous Fijians enthusiastically join the ranks of the national armed forces, from which many are seconded to UN peacekeeping forces, and the special units that the British military reserves for them.[65] By extension, they also maintain a visible presence in the global private security industry.[66] These employment possibilities are alternatives to rugby careers, but they also involve rugby. Locally, the armed forces (as well as state agencies like the police, the prisons, and the fire brigade) recruit promising athletes who can help their rugby teams win tournaments and the prize money that come with it. When a police officer in Fiji manages to obtain a temporary contract overseas to play rugby, the police force gives him an extended leave, ensuring the continuation of his employment at the end of his contract. It is through these material, political, historical, and ideological dynamics that sport and the military are intertwined as alternative and overlapping transnational careers.

GLOBALIZATION AND SPORT MEGA-EVENTS—THE DECLINE OF THE WEST?

While *globalization* has become an everyday term since the 1990s, its meaning is often left unexamined, largely because it is not easily defined. It is an appealing concept that tends to imply that we are all moving toward becoming one happy "global village," but relying on this observation to define globalization is teleological. In particular, the generality of the concept obscures the local realities of capitalist production and consumption.[67] The "global market" is still largely dominated by the developed West, although that becomes harder and harder to trace as transnational concentrations of financial and political power have become increasingly opaque—as became dramatically clear during the 2008 global financial crisis.

Sport certainly presents advantages for the project of globalization: it is a cultural practice conducted according to standardized rules with an apparent ready-made audience that supposedly renders borders superfluous. While firmly grounded in the recognition and affirmation of the nation-state, the Olympic

Games, the FIFA World Cup, and comparable sport spectacles frequently disregard, transcend, and downplay the traditional power of the nation-state. One example is the "citizenship hopping" that we discussed in chapter 7, whereby some athletes opt for affiliation with countries like Qatar and the United States, which will provide them with the training facilities, material support, and ability to qualify for the national team in contrast to their countries of origin, where such opportunities are absent or are highly competitive.

Sport mega-events and the organizations that sponsor them are global phenomena in other ways.[68] International sports organizations are, technically speaking, nongovernmental and nonprofit, but the IOC and FIFA, among others, require governments to set aside their laws, reserve the right to conduct negotiations directly with host cities, and can demand of national leaders allegiance to the Olympic Charter, thus undermining the very sovereignty of the state.[69] Customs duties are set aside for media, sports teams, and other entities that bring in large amounts of equipment, and extrajudicial courts are set up during the period of the competition to rapidly control violations of intellectual property such as counterfeit souvenirs and ambush marketing. These organizations also control enormous budgets; FIFA's budget is considerably larger than that of many sovereign states. They also possess enormous constituencies: FIFA's "big count" of soccer participation worldwide indicates that about one out of every twenty-five people on the planet plays soccer.[70] In the last two decades, rapid growth has been funded by alliances with multinational corporations and television broadcasters, as well as new infusions of Asian, Russian, and Brazilian wealth, which have created flows of capital that know no national boundaries.

One important question is whether the global political economy in which global sport is embedded has eroded the economic and political domination of the West. This question becomes pertinent when we observe that, in the 120 years from 1896 to 2016, forty-five of fifty-one Winter and Summer Olympics had rotated among Europe, North and Central America, and Australia. Five of the six Winter and Summer Games held outside the cultural West were in East Asia, culminating in China's first Olympics in 2008. Contrasting sharply with the dominance of Western countries in the previous century, in 2016, South America hosted its first Olympics in Rio de Janeiro, and from then through 2022, all Olympic Games will be in East Asia (Pyeongchang, Tokyo, and Beijing-Zhangjiakou). The FIFA Soccer World Cup also exited the West from 2010 to 2022. South Africa's 2010 World Cup was the first mega-event on the African continent. Brazil hosted in 2014, to

FIGURE 22. Coca-Cola ad and boy, Beijing Olympics (August 15, 2008/Susan Brownell).

be followed by Russia in 2018 and Qatar in 2022. The center of gravity thus shifted away from the traditional Western stronghold with respect to the *hosting* of sport mega-events. But does this show that the Western preeminence in the world is in decline?

Actually, now and for the foreseeable future, the West will still dominate the Olympic economy, fueling the greatest part of the skyrocketing revenues with television broadcasting rights fees and global sponsorships. From the 2006–8 cycle (Torino/Beijing) to the 2014–16 cycle (Sochi/Rio), television revenues increased by 60 percent to US$4.1 billion, and global sponsorships increased by 15 percent to US$1 billion—in the midst of a global financial crisis. The US television network NBC paid $2 billion for the rights to the 2010–12 Olympic cycle, more than half of the total revenues of $3.91 billion. Combined with the fees paid by Europe, Canada, Australia, and New Zealand, the West's total contribution came to $3.13 billion, while Asian networks paid only a total of $575 million.[71] Continuing the West's domination of global Olympic sponsorships, in 2017, eight of thirteen global sponsors were Western (six American, two European), and the remaining five were Asian (three Japanese, one Korean, one Chinese).[72]

The 2002 FIFA World Cup finals were the first finals to be held in Asia and the first to be cohosted by two countries, South Korea and Japan. They thus offered an interesting window into the ever-increasing integration of East Asia into the originally Western-dominated global system.[73] The unprecedented, and often contentious, hosting by two countries brought to global attention Japan's and South Korea's vibrant soccer cultures, which had flourished for decades but were overshadowed by the much more visible soccer cultures of Europe and Latin America. East Asian soccer's peripheral position was due not only to a backlash against Western imperialism but also to strong states that refused to bow to the Western-based economic interests that dominate soccer. For example, legal restrictions on tobacco advertising in China had pushed the tobacco giant Philip Morris out of the Chinese national soccer league in 1999. The complexities of the relationship between Japan and South Korea—political, economic, cultural, historical—revealed the difficult accommodations that had to be made in the organization of the mega-event. A knowledgeable insider told Susan Brownell that these difficulties resulted in a decision by FIFA to never again award the games to two countries at once, although this has never been officially stated. Neither did these games launch repeat efforts to host the games in Asia, as was expected (and as happened with the Olympic Games). One conclusion is that the 2002 FIFA World Cup demonstrated that East Asia still operates on the margins of the global soccer system—evidence that globalization is never as easy and thoroughgoing as it appears at first glance.

THE NATION-STATE VERSUS TRANSNATIONALISM

With around one hundred heads of state attending the opening ceremonies of recent Olympic Games, they have become the world's largest diplomatic gatherings—exceeding any meeting of the United Nations, the G-20, and any international government mobilization other than for war. Of the ninety thousand seats available in an Olympic stadium, some thirty thousand are reserved for special guests. But government leaders and their entourages are not the only ones benefiting from these privileges; leaders of the corporate world such as Bill Gates receive personal invitations from the IOC and also attend with a large retinue. In fact, more CEOs may have attended the Beijing Olympic Games than attend the Davos World Economic Forum, although exact numbers are unknown since, unlike politicians, CEOs are not obligated to publicize their itineraries.[74] These VIP guest lists clearly demonstrate that the stakeholders in mega-events are not limited to the nation-state and its representatives. While commentators have argued that mega-events create a powerful fantasy of a panhuman community, closer analysis reveals that global elites may form more of a face-to-face community than meets the eye. Investigation into *who* attends mega-events and *why* reveals that leaders of the global political and economic system *do* convene regularly in one place.

Sport mega-events and their organizers provide abundant evidence of the tug-of-war between a globalized political economy and the rule of national law. As we discussed in chapter 6, the US Securities and Exchange Commission's investigation into the VIP hospitality program of BHP Billiton, an Australia-based mining firm, at the Beijing Olympics concluded that the programs amounted to the bribery of government officials from the Global South, and the SEC imposed a huge fine on the corporation. But another interpretation of this investigation attributes it to the US government's attempt to secure access to minerals and stave off competition from Australia and China for the control of mines.

In May 2015, US and Swiss authorities swooped into the annual FIFA congress and took seven officials into custody, launching an ongoing investigation into racketeering and conspiracy in international soccer.[75] The scandal revealed endemic corruption without oversight from any national authority and raised suspicions that FIFA had allowed Russia and Qatar to buy influence and win World Cup bids. Journalists, academics, and NGOs had criticized FIFA's corruption for years, but it was untouchable, and governments were afraid to take on the organization in countries where soccer was a national passion. Although the IOC had implemented reforms in 2000 to curb corruption in the Olympic bid process after weathering its own scandal, it was still depicted as a coterie of self-aggrandizing individuals whose greed had led to ever-larger Olympic Games, leaving bills that taxpayers, where they could express their opinion, found outrageous. In the case of both scandals, it was the US government that launched the investigations and pressured them to reform, leading some commentators to observe that only the US government was big enough to take on FIFA and the IOC.

THE ANTHROPOLOGY OF SPORT'S CONTRIBUTION TO UNDERSTANDING TRANSNATIONALISM AND GLOBALIZATION

The growth of the global sports system—including the mega-events that punctuate its calendar, the migration networks that supply its athletes and coaches, and the corporations and private owners that fund its commercialization—is an effect of the increasing integration of a global political economy that has little regard for national boundaries. Neither does it have much regard for the laws and regulations of national entities. An important anthropological contribution is to point out that this economy is not entirely market driven, and there are areas in which the principles of a gift economy prevail, whether in the kinship obligations that drive athletes to migrate to wealthier countries or in the networking that politicians, CEOs, and celebrities do at sports events. At the same time, this global political economy can come into conflict with national forces that attempt to control it and redefine its workings as corruption, racketeering, and bribery, recognizable categories that can be punished under national laws. FIFA's and the IOC's troubles are not the result of the actions of a few corrupt individuals, as FIFA's president Sepp Blatter maintained before his spectacular downfall.[76] Rather, they are manifestations of a bigger phenomenon, namely globalization as a whole.

Epilogue

SPORT FOR ANTHROPOLOGY

LET US START BY ZOOMING OUT to look at sport from the lofty point of view of the pinnacle of the global economy. It is the Rio de Janeiro 2016 Olympic Games. In the newly renovated Mauá Pier area, crowds stand in long lines, even in the rain, for the chance to enter the Coca-Cola House in a repurposed warehouse. There, they can plunge into the multisensory experience of being immersed in a room of Coca-Cola, simulated with dark colors, warm lights, and five hundred acrylic globes suggestive of glowing bubbles. If they do not want to wait in line, there is no waiting at the Coca-Cola Store next door, where they can buy T-shirts, pins, and other souvenirs bearing both the Coca-Cola and Olympic logos. Coca-Cola, the oldest Olympic sponsor, with a continuous history going back to 1928, is a leader in the organization of VIP hospitality programs at the Games, with its own in-house team in contrast to other corporations that outsource hospitality services.

What is at stake in these extravagant displays of global capital is reminiscent of the potlatches that were staged by American Indians of the Northwest coast at the turn of the twentieth century, as we discussed in chapter 6: displays of wealth and lavish hospitality that are equally grounded in a precapitalist economic logic even as they employ the tools and ideologies of global capitalism.

Let us now zoom in to the ground level of world sport. Thirty-year-old Isireli Temo was one of the several hundred indigenous Fijian men who have been playing in rugby teams in France since the late 1990s. His wife and two small children have remained in Fiji. Niko Besnier had briefly met Temo during fieldwork with Fijian players and families in southwest France in the first half of 2016 after a friendly match against retired members of the French national team. Unlike the French team, who were set to party well into the night, the

Fijian men and their families had retired to the campsite where they were staying, where the men gathered around a bowl of kava (a slightly narcotic drink made from the roots of the kava plant, which plays a central role in Fijian life). Starting with the ceremonialism associated with kava drinking, with one of the elder members of the community presiding as nominal chief, the men went on to discuss the problems that they faced: accidents, injuries, work visas, short-term contracts, alcohol abuse, the postcareer void, cultural misunderstandings, agents who skimmed their income but were nowhere to be found when problems arose, and the unreasonable expectations of relatives back home. For Temo and many others, these issues were compounded by feelings of loneliness and isolation in a country whose language they barely spoke. He played in the small town of Tarbes, whose rugby team was in the third division. His income was probably modest, making it difficult for him to send remittances, and injury and illness had recently prevented him from playing.

On November 8, 2016, shortly after returning to France from an annual leave to visit his family back in Fiji, Temo hanged himself.[1]

We juxtapose these two vignettes to highlight three points. The first point is that concepts that are familiar to anthropologists (the gift, the potlatch, labor migrations, kinship, gender, ritual, nationalism, consumption, capital, precarity) shed light on sport in all its manifestations, big and small, festive and tragic, global and personal—explaining practices that often make little sense to other observers. In chapters 6 and 8 in particular, we demonstrated that, while they are often criticized for the huge expenditures involved, sport mega-events are motivated by other concerns, including the management of host-guest relations and aspects of gift economies that are fundamental aspects of social life in all societies. We also saw that the transnational migration of athletes, while enabled by the growing corporatization of world sports, generates for the people involved expectations and dreams that may easily end in disappointment and suffering.

The second point is that extravagant displays of wealth at Olympic Games and the self-inflicted untimely death of a young Fijian in France, while seemingly entirely disconnected from one another, are in fact the product of the same system: the corporate capital that suffuses hospitality houses is the same as the capital that has raised the stakes in world sports and created the conditions under which Isireli Temo left his island home to work in a country that, a couple of decades ago, barely figured in the social world of most Fijians. The gift, as Marcel Mauss described it in the early 1920s, can forge bonds of sociality and humanity just as easily as it can become tyrannical.

The third point is that sport, and everything that revolves around it, presents unique social, cultural, and political configurations. Sport as an object of inquiry provides a particularly productive lens through which to accomplish one of the most pressing tasks in contemporary anthropology, namely to explain how the everyday experiences of ordinary (and sometimes extraordinary) people in local settings shape—and are shaped by—large-scale social processes at the level of the national, the regional, the panregional, and the global. In other words, it helps us bring together two seemingly divergent approaches in contemporary anthropology, namely the ethnography of the concrete and of the local, and the anthropology of transnational flows, of the global political economy, and of unanchored social and cultural forms.

We have not aimed to write this book solely about the place of sport in society and culture, that is, an inquiry into how anthropological concepts and methods can be applied to the topic of sport. This prosaic task has been attempted repeatedly, with uneven results; we call it prosaic because ultimately it is of interest only to a small number of social scientists. Rather, this is a book about sport *for* anthropology, by which we mean that it is concerned with what broad questions we can ask through the lens of sport. What does sport tell us about the constitution of society, culture, and politics, and how can sport help us better understand the social and economic relations, political processes, and symbolic systems in which it is embedded? This question is particularly pertinent because, over the past three decades, topics such as the body, nationalism, modernity, globalization, transnationalism, the state, citizenship, gender, and sexuality have played a central role in anthropological theory. They also happen to be fundamental aspects of sport and thus place it at the core of the discipline's contemporary concerns.

The distinction between applying anthropological concepts to the study of sport and seeking to understand anthropology's objects through the lens of sport highlights what is distinctive about anthropology as a contemporary discipline: engagement with the subject that seeks to understand it from different angles, informed by the constant suspicion that what first meets the eye is often oversimplified and that the story one tells about a particular event or practice is often only one story among many.

As a form of human activity that is at once deeply personal and profoundly social, sport offers a particularly attractive forum for an exploration of the way in which the body's movements, its capacities, and its configuration are shaped by and in turn shape the social, cultural, and historical contexts of our world. Sport today is the focus of enormous attention across the planet, mobilizing profound emotions, vast quantities of money, deep-seated anxieties, and entire life projects for billions of people.

More than any other form of human activity, sport embodies some of the fundamental questions that anthropology poses: the articulation of personal projects with structural possibilities and constraints; the body as a fulcrum between the local and the global; the relationship between practice and performance; the persistence of inequalities on a theoretically level playing field; and the future of the nation-state in a neoliberal world order.

The anthropology of sport is just now coming into its own as a subfield of the discipline. This brief survey of the grand sweep of human history has shown that sport has been central to social life across the ages and around the world. Modern sport is not just a product of the modern era; it helped to create it. We hope that this book provides a snapshot of the fascinating ethnographic evidence and creative theoretical insights that sport contributes toward a better understanding of the challenging world in which we live.

NOTES

INTRODUCTION

1. Émile Durkheim, *The Elementary Forms of Religious Life,* ed. Mark S. Cladis, trans. Carol Cosman (Oxford: Oxford University Press, 2008; first published 1912), 284. Durkheim applied the term to religion, but elsewhere in his writings he noted a parallel between religion and play, both of which share a ritualized structure, as we will explain further in chapter 1.

2. "In early use the sense of 'sport' as a diversion or amusement is paramount; by the 18th and 19th centuries the term was often used with reference to hunting, shooting, and fishing.... The consolidation of organized sport (particularly football, rugby, cricket, and athletics) in the 19th cent. reinforced the notion of sport as physical competition." *OED Online,* s.v. "sport," accessed November 28, 2016, http://www.oed.com/view/Entry/187476?rskey=HaVaIa&result=1&isAdvanced=false. The word derived from the Anglo-Norman *disport,* "diversion from serious duties; relaxation, recreation; entertainment, amusement."

3. Richard Mandell, "The Invention of the Sports Record," *Stadion* 2, no. 2 (1976): 250.

4. George P. Mentore, *Of Passionate Curves and Desirable Cadences: Themes on Waiwai Social Being* (Lincoln: University of Nebraska Press, 2005), 211–18.

5. Kenneth E. Read, *The High Valley: An Autobiographical Account of Two Years Spent in the Central Highlands of New Guinea* (New York: Scribner, 1965), 150–51. Claude Lévi-Strauss used this example to distinguish a ritual—an activity in which the goal is to bring participants together—from a game, although he mistakenly identified the sport in question as soccer in *La pensée sauvage* (Paris: Plon, 1962), 44.

6. James Clifford and George E. Marcus, eds., *Writing Culture: The Poetics and Politics of Ethnography* (Berkeley: University of California Press, 1986); George Marcus and Michael M. K. Fisher, eds. *Anthropology as Cultural Critique* (Chicago: University of Chicago Press, 1986).

7. George E. Marcus, "Ethnography in/of the World System: The Emergence of Multi-sited Ethnography," *Annual Review of Anthropology* 24 (1995): 95–117; Bonnie Nardi, "Virtuality," *Annual Review of Anthropology* 44 (2015): 15–31.

8. Nina Glick Schiller, "Explanatory Frameworks in Transnational Migration Studies: The Missing Multi-scalar Global Perspective," *Ethnic and Racial Studies* 38, no. 13 (2015): 2275–82, 2276.

9. Michel Foucault, "Governmentality," in *The Foucault Effect: Studies in Governmentality,* ed. Graham Burchell, Colin Gordon, and Peter Miller (Chicago: University of Chicago Press, 1991; ch. first published 1978), 87–104; Foucault, *The History of Sexuality,* vol. 1, *An Introduction,* trans. Robert J. Hurley (New York: Vintage, 1978; first published 1976).

10. E. R. Leach, *Rethinking Anthropology* (London: Athlone, 1961), 2.

11. Clifford Geertz, "Deep Play: Notes on the Balinese Cockfight," *Dædalus* 101, no. 1 (1972): 1–37; Jerry Leach, dir., *Trobriand Cricket: An Ingenious Response to Colonialism,* prod. Gary Kildea and Jerry Leach (Port Moresby: Papua New Guinea Office of Information, 1976).

12. Kang Shin-pyo, John MacAloon, and Roberto DaMatta, eds., *The Olympics and Cultural Exchange: The Papers of the First International Conference on the Olympics and East/West and South/North Cultural Exchange in the World System* (Seoul: Hanyang University Press, 1988).

13. Arjun Appadurai, "Playing with Modernity: The Decolonization of Indian Cricket," in *Consuming Modernity: Public Culture in a South Asian World,* ed. Carol A. Breckenridge (Minneapolis: University of Minnesota Press, 1995), 23–48; Pierre Bourdieu, "Program for a Sociology of Sport," *Sociology of Sport Journal* 5, no. 2 (1988), 153–61; Ulf Hannerz, "Cosmopolitans and Locals in World Culture," *Theory, Culture & Society* 7, no. 2 (1990): 237–51.

14. http://www.sapiens.org/. Launched by the Wenner-Gren Foundation for Anthropological Research in January 2016.

CHAPTER ONE. SPORT, ANTHROPOLOGY, AND HISTORY

1. Susan Brownell, "Introduction: Bodies before Boas, Sport before the Laughter Left," in *The 1904 Anthropology Days and Olympic Games,* ed. Susan Brownell (Lincoln: University of Nebraska Press, 2008), 1–58; Brownell, *Beijing's Games: What the Olympics Mean to China* (Lanham, MD: Rowman & Littlefield, 2008), 19–47.

2. Otto Schantz, "Französische Festkultur als Wegbereiter der Modernen Olympischen Spiele" [French festival culture as precursor of the modern Olympic Games], in "Studien zur Geschichte der Olympischen Spiele," ed. Manfred Lämmer, special issue, *Stadion* 21–22 (1998): 64–85.

3. Yves-Pierre Boulongne, "The Presidencies of Demetrius Vikelas (1894–1896) and Pierre de Coubertin (1896–1925)," in *The International Olympic Committee, One Hundred Years: The Idea, the Presidents, the Achievements,* ed. Raymond Gafner (Lausanne, Switzerland: International Olympic Committee, 1994), 15–207.

4. Jacob Burckhardt, *The Greeks and Greek Civilization,* trans. Sheila Stern (New York: St. Martin's Press, 1998; first published 1898–1902), 160–213; Victor Ehrenberg, *Ost und West: Studien zur geschichtlichen Problematik der Antike* [East and west: Studies on a historical problematic of antiquity] (Brünn [Brno], Czechoslovakia: Rudolf M. Rohrer, 1935), 93–94.

5. Eric Wolf, *Europe and the People Without History* (Berkeley: University of California Press, 1982).

6. Ibid., 385.

7. Heather L. Reid, "Afterword: Olympic Philosophy between East and West," in *From Athens to Beijing: West Meets East in the Olympic Games,* ed. Susan Brownell, vol. 1, *Sport, the Body and Humanism in Ancient Greece and China* (New York: Greekworks, 2013), 199–222.

8. Donald G. Kyle, *Sport and Spectacle in the Ancient World* (Malden, MA: Blackwell, 2007), 21.

9. "Olympic Movement" is the official label for the Olympic Games and the global structure of institutions that supports them. We use it here in that sense. The IOC is a "social movement NGO" that claims to head a social movement oriented around world peace and the betterment of society through sport.

10. Ian Hodder, *Entangled: An Archaeology of the Relationships between Humans and Things* (Chichester, UK: John Wiley, 2012); Lambros Malafouris, *How Things Shape the Mind: A Theory of Material Engagement* (Cambridge, MA: MIT Press, 2013).

11. Zinon Papakonstantinou, "Epilogue: Fresh Perspectives on Ancient Sport," *International Journal of the History of Sport* 26, no. 2 (2009): 365–67.

12. Stephen G. Miller, "The Organization and Functioning of the Olympic Games," in *Sport and Festival in the Ancient Greek World,* ed. David J. Phillips and David Pritchard (Swansea, UK: Classical Press of Wales, 2003), 1–40.

13. See the website of the Nemean Games, http://nemeangames.org/.

14. Nigel B. Crowther, *Sport in Ancient Times* (Oklahoma City: University of Oklahoma Press, 2010).

15. Ibid.; see also Roger G. Kennedy, *Hidden Cities: The Discovery and Loss of Ancient North American Civilization* (New York: Penguin, 1994).

16. Such as Thomas F. Scanlon, *Eros and Greek Athletics* (Oxford: Oxford University Press, 2002); Michael B. Poliakoff, *Combat Sports in the Ancient World: Competition, Violence, and Culture* (New Haven, CT: Yale University Press, 1987).

17. Johan Huizinga, *Homo Ludens: A Study of the Play Element in Culture* (Boston: Beacon, 1950; first published 1938), 55.

18. Ingomar Weiler, "*'Aien Aristeuein'*: Ideologische Bemerkungen zu einem vielzitierten Homerwort" ["Aien Airsteuein": Ideological observations about a much-cited word in Homer], *Stadion* 1, no. 2 (1975): 199–227.

19. Henning Eichberg, "Olympic Anthropology Days and the Progress of Exclusion: Toward an Anthropology of Democracy," in Brownell, *1904 Anthropology Days,* 350.

20. Henning Eichberg, *Body Cultures: Essays by Henning Eichberg,* ed. John Bale and Chris Philo (London: Routledge, 1998).

21. Adam Bluford, *E Pluribus Barnum: The Great Showman and the Making of U.S. Popular Culture* (Minneapolis: University of Minnesota Press, 1991), 75–180.

22. Burton Benedict, *The Anthropology of World's Fairs: San Francisco's Panama Pacific International Exposition of 1915* (Berkeley, CA: Lowie Museum of Anthropology, 1983).

23. Linda Peavy and Ursula Smith, *Full-Court Quest: The Girls from Fort Shaw Indian School, Basketball Champions of the World* (Norman: University of Oklahoma Press, 2008).

24. Carol Spidel, *Dancing at Halftime: Sports and the Controversy over American Indian Mascots* (New York: New York University Press, 2000).

25. Stewart Culin, *Korean Games with Notes on the Corresponding Games of China and Japan* (Philadelphia: University of Pennsylvania Press, 1895), https://archive.org/details/koreangameswith01culigoog; *Games of the North American Indians* (Mineola, NY: Dover, 2012; first published 1907), https://archive.org/details/gamesofnorthamer00culirich.

26. Stewart Culin, "The Value of Games in Ethnology," *Proceedings of the American Association for the Advancement of Science* (March 1895): 355–58, 356.

27. Erik Larson, *The Devil in the White City: Murder, Magic, and Madness at the Fair That Changed America* (New York: Crown, 2003), 311.

28. McGee preferred to be known by his two initials with no periods.

29. Nancy J. Parezo, "'Special Olympics': Testing Racial Strength and Endurance at the 1904 Louisiana Purchase Exposition," in Brownell, *1904 Anthropology Days*, 87–111.

30. Vernon L. Scarborough and David E. Wilson, eds., *The Mesoamerican Ballgame* (Tucson: University of Arizona Press, 1993); E. Michael Whittington, ed., *The Sport of Life and Death: The Mesoamerican Ballgame* (New York: Thames and Hudson, 2001).

31. Warren D. Hill and John E. Clark, "Sports, Gambling, and Government: America's First Social Compact?" *American Anthropologist* 103, no. 2 (2001): 331–45.

32. Michael E. Whalen and Paul E. Minnis, "Ball Courts and Political Centralization in the Casas Grandes Region," *American Antiquity* 61, no. 4 (1996): 732–46.

33. Timothy R. Pauketat, "America's First Pastime," *Archaeology* 62, no. 5 (2009): 20–25.

34. Nancy Marie White and Richard A. Weinstein, "The Mexican Connection and the Far West of the U.S. Southeast," *American Antiquity* 73, no. 2 (2008): 227–77.

35. Examples of sport histories that follow a modernization narrative are William J. Baker, *Sports in the Western World* (Urbana: University of Illinois Press, 1982); E. Norman Gardiner, *Athletics of the Ancient World* (Mineola, NY: Dover, 2003; first published 1930); Allen Guttmann, *Sports: The First Five Millennia* (Amherst: University of Massachusetts Press, 2004).

36. Wendy Raschke, ed., *The Archaeology of the Olympics: Olympics and Other Festivals in Antiquity* (Madison: University of Wisconsin Press, 1988).

37. Alison Futrell, *Blood in the Arena: The Spectacle of Roman Power* (Austin: University of Texas Press, 2001); Stephen G. Miller, *Arete: Greek Sports from Ancient*

Sources, 3rd ed. (Berkeley: University of California Press, 2012); Michael Scott, *Delphi and Olympia: The Spatial Politics of Panhellenism in the Archaic and Classical Periods* (Cambridge: Cambridge University Press, 2014); Katherine Welch, *The Roman Amphitheater: From Its Origins to the Colosseum* (Cambridge: Cambridge University Press, 2009); Panos Valavanis, *Games and Sanctuaries in Ancient Greece: Olympia, Delphi, Isthmia, Nemea, Athens,* trans. David Hardy (Los Angeles: J. Paul Getty Museum, 2004; first published 2004).

38. Kyle, *Sport and Spectacle in the Ancient World,* 5.

39. Pierre de Coubertin, *Olympism: Selected Writings* (Lausanne, Switzerland: International Olympic Committee, 2000), 512.

40. Kyle, *Sport and Spectacle in the Ancient World,* 21.

41. David C. Young, *The Olympic Myth of Greek Amateur Athletics* (Chicago: Ares, 1984); Angeli Bernardini, "Aspects ludiques, rituels et sportifs de la course féminine dans la Grèce antique" [Ludic, ritual, and sportive aspects of female racing in ancient Greece], *Stadion* 12–13 (1986–87): 17–26.

42. Kyle, *Sport and Spectacle in the Ancient World,* 251–339.

43. Ibid., 280–85, 296–99, 312–19.

44. Ibid., 389–89.

45. Ibid., 302–10.

46. Ibid., 284.

47. John A. Byers, *Built for Speed* (Cambridge, MA: Harvard University Press, 2003), 100–103; Jane M. Packard, "Wolf Behavior: Reproductive, Social, Intelligent," in *Wolves: Behavior, Ecology, and Conservation,* ed. L. David Mech and Luigi Boitani (Chicago: University of Chicago Press, 2007), 35–58, 49–50; John C. Fentress, Jenny Ryon, Peter J. MacLeod, and G. Zvika Havkin, "A Multidimensional Approach to Agonistic Behavior in Wolves," in *Man and Wolf: Advances, Issues, and Problems in Captive Wolf Research,* ed. H. Frank (Dordrecht, Netherlands: Dr W. Junk, 1987), 253–74.

48. Raymond Firth, "A Dart Match in Tikopia," *Oceania* 1, no. 1 (1930): 64–96, 95–96.

49. Huizinga, *Homo Ludens,* 211.

50. Roger Caillois, *Man, Play, and Games,* trans. Meyer Barash (New York: Free Press of Glencoe, 1961; first published 1958).

51. Ibid., 18.

52. Huizinga, *Homo Ludens,* 61.

53. Caillois, *Man, Play, and Games,* 10–11.

54. Gregory Bateson, "A Theory of Play and Fantasy," in *Steps to an Ecology of Mind: Collected Essays in Anthropology, Psychiatry, Evolution, and Epistemology* (Chicago: University of Chicago Press, 1972; ch. first published 1955), 177–96, 179.

55. Ibid., 185.

56. Ibid., 188.

57. Among the *Proceedings of the Annual Meeting of the Association for the Study of Play,* we highlight vol. 1, David F. Lancy and B. Allan Tindall, eds., *The Anthropological Study of Play: Problems and Prospects* (West Point, NY: Leisure Press,

1976); and vol. 10, Bernard Mergen, ed., *Cultural Dimensions of Play, Games, and Sport* (Champaign, IL: Human Kinetics, 1986). From the *Play and Culture* series, we highlight vol. 1, Margaret Carlisle Duncan, Garry Chick, and Alan Aycock, eds., *Diversions and Divergences in Fields of Play* (Greenwich, CT: Ablex, 1998); and vol. 12, Lynn Cohen and Sandra Waite-Stupiansky, eds., *Play: A Polyphony of Research, Theories, and Issues* (Lanham, MD: University Press of America, 2012).

58. Helen B. Schwartzman, "The Anthropological Study of Children's Play," *Annual Review of Anthropology* 5 (1976): 289–328, 291.

59. Edward Norbeck, "The Anthropological Study of Play," *Rice University Studies* 60, no. 3 (1975): 1–8.

60. Brian Sutton-Smith, *The Ambiguity of Play* (Cambridge, MA: Harvard University Press, 1997).

61. Chris Rojek, *Leisure and Culture* (New York: St. Martin's Press, 2000).

62. Huizinga, *Homo Ludens,* 197.

63. Tom Boellstorff, *Coming of Age in Second Life: An Anthropologist Explores the Virtually Human* (Princeton, NJ: Princeton University Press, 2008); Bonnie Nardi, *My Life as a Night Elf Priest: An Anthropological Account of World of Warcraft* (Ann Arbor: University of Michigan Press, 2010).

64. Allen Guttmann, *From Ritual to Record: The Nature of Modern Sports* (New York: Columbia University Press, 1978).

65. Allen Guttmann, "The Development of Modern Sports," in *Handbook of Sports Studies,* ed. Jay Coakley and Eric Dunning (London: Sage, 2000), 248–59, 256.

66. In the afterword of the 2004 edition of the book, Guttmann comments that in the 1970s, he had found East European Marxist analyses of sport available when he wrote the first edition "almost childish in their reductionism." *From Ritual to Record,* rev. ed. (New York: Columbia University Press, 2004), 168. He did, however, take seriously subsequently published works by Marxist sociologists like Richard Gruneau's *Class, Sports, and Social Development* (Amherst: University of Massachusetts Press, 1983) and John Hargreaves's *Sport, Power, and Culture* (Cambridge: Polity, 1986), although he did not necessarily agree with them. See also Susan Brownell, "The Problems with Ritual and Modernization Theory, and Why We Need Marx: A Commentary on *From Ritual to Record,*" *Sport History Review* 32, no. 2 (2001): 28–41.

67. Wolfgang Behringer, "Arena and Pall Mall: Sport in the Early Modern Period," *German History* 27, no. 3 (2009): 331–57; John Marshall Carter and Arnd Kruger, eds., *Ritual and Record: Sports Records and Quantification in Pre-modern Societies* (Westport, CT: Greenwood, 1990).

68. Mihaly Csikszentmihalyi, *Beyond Boredom and Anxiety: Experiencing Flow in Work and Play* (San Francisco: Jossey-Bass, 1975).

69. Victor Turner, *The Ritual Process: Structure and Anti-structure* (Chicago: University of Chicago Press, 1979).

70. Victor Turner, *The Anthropology of Performance* (New York: PAJ, 1988), 25.

71. Clifford Geertz, "Deep Play: Notes on the Balinese Cockfight," *Dædalus* 101,

no. 1 (1972): 1–37, reprinted in *The Interpretation of Cultures: Selected Essays* (New York: Basic Books, 1973).

72. Ibid., 15.

73. William Roseberry, "Balinese Cockfights and the Seduction of Anthropology," *Social Research* 49, no. 4 (1982): 1013–28.

74. Alan M. Klein, *Sugarball: The American Game, the Dominican Dream* (New Haven, CT: Yale University Press, 1991); Klein, *Little Big Men: Bodybuilding Subculture and Gender Construction* (Albany: State University of New York Press, 1993); Klein, *Baseball on the Border: A Tale of Two Laredos* (Princeton, NJ: Princeton University Press, 1997).

75. Alan M. Klein, *Growing the Game: The Globalization of Major League Baseball* (New Haven, CT: Yale University Press, 2006); Klein, *American Sport: An Anthropological Perspective* (New York: Routledge, 2008); Klein, *Dominican Baseball: New Pride, Old Prejudice* (Philadelphia: Temple University Press, 2014).

76. Throughout this book, we employ the US English term *soccer* to refer to association football.

CHAPTER TWO. SPORT, COLONIALISM, AND IMPERIALISM

1. Michael Dietler, *Archaeologies of Colonialism: Consumption, Entanglement, and Violence in Ancient Mediterranean France* (Berkeley: University of California Press, 2010), 18; Carole McGranahan, "Imperial but Not Colonial: Archival Truths, British India, and the Case of the 'Naughty' Tibetans," *Comparative Studies in Society and History* 59, no. 1 (2017): 68–95.

2. Frantz Fanon, *The Wretched of the Earth,* trans. Richard Philcox (New York: Grove Press, 1968; first published 1961); Edward Said, *Orientalism* (London: Penguin, 2003; first published 1978); Gayatri Spivak, *A Critique of Postcolonial Reason* (Cambridge, MA: Harvard University Press, 1999); Homi K. Bhabha, *The Location of Culture* (London: Routledge, 1994).

3. Nicholas Dirks, "Introduction: Colonialism and Culture," in *Colonialism and Culture,* ed. Nicholas B. Dirks (Ann Arbor: University of Michigan Press, 1993), 1–25, 3.

4. Talal Asad, ed., *Anthropology and the Colonial Encounter* (New York: Ithaca Press, 1973); Mona Etienne and Eleanor Leacock, eds., *Women and Colonization: Anthropological Perspectives* (New York: Praeger, 1980); Johannes Fabian, *Time and the Other: How Anthropology Makes Its Object* (New York: Columbia University Press, 1983).

5. C. L. R. James, *Beyond a Boundary* (Durham, NC: Duke University Press, 2013; first published 1963).

6. For example, Richard Cashman, *Patrons, Players and the Crowd: The Phenomenon of Indian Cricket* (New Delhi: Oriental Longman, 1980); J. A. Mangan, *The Games Ethic and Imperialism: Aspects of the Diffusion of an Ideal* (London:

Frank Cass, 1986); Brian Stoddart, "Sport, Cultural Imperialism, and Colonial Response in the British Empire," *Comparative Studies in Society and History* 30, no. 4 (1988): 649–73.

7. Partha Chatterjee, *Nationalist Thought and the Colonial World* (Minneapolis: University of Minnesota Press, 1986); Benedict Anderson, *Imagined Communities: Reflections on the Origin and Spread of Nationalism* (London: Verso, 2016; first published 1983).

8. Maarten van Bottenburg, *Global Games* (Urbana: University of Illinois Press, 2001), 4.

9. John Boli, "Contemporary Developments in World Culture," *International Journal of Comparative Sociology* 46, nos. 5–6 (2005): 383–404, 387; John Hoberman, "Toward a Theory of Olympic Internationalism," *Journal of Sport History* 22, no. 1 (1995): 1–37.

10. IAAF was originally an acronym for International Amateur Athletics Federation, but today it stands for International Association of Athletics Federations.

11. Barbara Keys, *Globalizing Sport: National Rivalry and International Community in the 1930s* (Cambridge, MA: Harvard University Press, 2006), 45.

12. David Rovell, "NFL League Office Relinquishing Tax-Exempt Status," ESPN, April 28, 2015, accessed November 6, 2016, http://www.espn.com/nfl/story/_/id/12780874/nfl-league-office-gives-tax-exempt-status.

13. Amy Burchfield, "International Sports Law," Hauser Global Law School Program, May–June 2014, accessed December 5, 2016, http://www.nyulawglobal.org/globalex/International_Sports_Law1.html.

14. James A. R. Nafziger, *International Sports Law,* 2nd ed. (Ardsley, NY: Transnational Publishers, 2004), 4–7.

15. John J. MacAloon, ed., *Muscular Christianity in Colonial and Post-colonial Worlds* (London: Routledge, 2007).

16. Mangan, *Games Ethic and Imperialism,* among many others.

17. Ann L. Stoler, *Race and the Education of Desire: Foucault's "History of Sexuality" and the Colonial Order of Things* (Durham, NC: Duke University Press, 1995); Alan M. Klein, "Sport and Colonialism in Latin America and the Caribbean," *Studies in Latin American Popular Culture* 10 (1991): 257–72; Robert Morrell, "Forging a Ruling Race: Rugby and White Masculinity in Colonial Natal, c1870–1910," in *Making Men: Rugby and Masculine Identity,* ed. John Nauright and Timothy Chandler (London: Frank Cass, 1996), 91–120.

18. James, *Beyond a Boundary;* Ossie Stuart, "Players, Workers, Protesters: Social Change and Soccer in Colonial Zimbabwe," in *Sport, Identity and Ethnicity,* ed. John MacClancy (Oxford: Berg, 1996), 167–80.

19. Henning Eichberg, "Olympic Sport: Neo-colonialism and Alternatives," in *Body Cultures: Essays on Sport, Space and Identity,* ed. John Bale and Chris Philo (London: Routledge, 1998), 100–110.

20. Andreas Niehaus, "'If You Want to Cry, Cry on the Green Mats of Kôdôkan': Expressions of Japanese Cultural and National Identity in the Movement to Include Judo into the Olympic," *International Journal of the History of Sport* 23,

no. 7 (2006): 1173–92. Here, however, we should acknowledge that the kayak boat that features in Olympic kayak racing originated among the Inuit, Yup'ik, and Aleut, Arctic peoples of North America and Greenland.

21. Allen Guttmann, *Games and Empires: Modern Sports and Cultural Imperialism* (New York: Columbia University Press, 1994), 5.

22. For cricket, see ibid., 16–18, 32; soccer, 44–45, 58; baseball, 73, 76, 80, 84; basketball, 101, 105, 106.

23. Antonio Gramsci, *Selections from the Prison Notebooks,* ed. and trans. Quintin Hoare and Geoffrey Nowell Smith (New York: International Publishers, 1971).

24. Guttmann, *Games and Empires,* 6, 178–79.

25. Pierre Lanfranchi and Matthew Taylor, *Moving with the Ball: The Migration of Professional Footballers* (Oxford: Berg, 2001).

26. John MacAloon, "Humanism as Political Necessity? Reflections on the Pathos of Anthropological Science in Pluricultural Contexts," in *The Conditions of Reciprocal Understanding,* ed. James Fernandez and Milton Singer (Chicago: International House, 1995), 206–35, 234; MacAloon, "Interval Training," in *Choreographing History,* ed. Susan L. Foster (Bloomington: Indiana University Press, 1995), 32–53, 34.

27. Lu Yuanzhen, "Hope Lies in the Revival of Eastern Sport Culture," *Olympic Studies Reader,* ed. Hai Ren, Lamartine DaCosta, and Ana Miragaya, trans. Susan Brownell (Beijing: Beijing Sport University Press, 2010), 82; Susan Brownell, "Multiculturalism in the Olympic Movement," in ibid., 72–74.

28. Joseph S. Alter, *The Wrestler's Body: Ideology and Identity in Northern India* (Berkeley: University of California Press, 1992); Mike Cronin, *Sport and Nationalism in Ireland: Gaelic Games, Soccer and Irish Identity since 1884* (Dublin: Four Courts Press, 1999).

29. William W. Kelly, "Is Baseball a Global Sport? America's 'National Pastime' as Global Field and International Sport," *Global Networks* 7, no. 2 (2007): 187–201.

30. Thomas Hylland Eriksen, "Steps to an Ecology of Transnational Sports," *Global Networks* 7, no. 2 (2007): 132–65.

31. Roberto DaMatta, *Universo do futebol* [Soccer universe] (Rio de Janeiro: Edições Pinakotheke, 1982); Roger Kittleson, *The Country of Football: Soccer and the Making of Modern Brazil* (Berkeley: University of California Press, 2014).

32. Eduardo Archetti, *Masculinities: Football, Polo and the Tango in Argentina* (Oxford: Berg, 1999), 83–87.

33. Jeremy Schaap, *Triumph: The Untold Story of Jesse Owens and Hitler's Olympics* (Boston: Houghton Mifflin, 2007); William A. Baker, *Jesse Owens: An American Life,* rev. ed. (Urbana: University of Illinois Press, 2006; first published 1986).

34. Letter from Franklin Brown to Baillet de Latour, August 12, 1926, in Dikaia Chatziefstathiou, *The Diffusion of Olympic Sport through Regional Games: A Comparison of Pre and Post Second War Contexts* (Lausanne, Switzerland: Postgraduate Grant Programme, IOC Olympic Studies Centre, 2008), 32, accessed June 24, 2017, https://library.olympic.org/Default/doc/SYRACUSE/46479/the-diffusion-of-olympic-sport-through-regional-games-a-comparison-of-pre-and-post-second-war-contex.

35. Chatziefstathiou, *Diffusion of Olympic Sport,* 36–41.

36. Terence Ranger, "Pugilism and Pathology: African Boxing and the Black Urban Experience in Southern Rhodesia," in *Sport in Africa: Essays in Social History,* ed. William J. Baker and James A. Mangan (New York: Holmes and Meier, 1987), 196–213.

37. Guttmann, *Games and Empires,* 67–69.

38. Mangan, *Games Ethic and Imperialism,* 43.

39. Adam Reed, "Contested Images and Common Strategies: Early Colonial Sexual Politics in the Massim," in *Sites of Desire, Economies of Pleasure: Sexualities in Asia and the Pacific,* ed. Lenore Manderson and Margaret Jolly (Chicago: University of Chicago Press), 48–72, 64.

40. Cecil Headlam, *Ten Thousand Miles through India & Burma: An Account of the Oxford University Authentics' Cricket Tour* (London: Dent, 1903), 168–69.

41. Derek Birley, *The Willow Wand: Some Cricket Myths Explored* (London: Queen Anne Press, 1979), 13.

42. Brian Stoddart and A. P. Keith Sandiford, eds., *The Imperial Game: Cricket, Culture and Society* (Manchester: Manchester University Press, 1998).

43. Ashis Nandy, *The Tao of Cricket: On Games of Destiny and the Destiny of Games* (New Delhi: Oxford University Press, 2001); Keith A. P. Sandiford, introduction to Stoddart and Sandiford, *Imperial Game,* 1–8, 1.

44. Hilary Beckles and Brian Stoddart, eds., *Liberation Cricket: West Indies Cricket Culture* (Manchester: Manchester University Press, 1995); James, *Beyond a Boundary.*

45. Leach, *Trobriand Cricket.*

46. Annette B. Weiner, "Epistemology and Ethnographic Reality: A Trobriand Island Case Study," *American Anthropologist* 80, no. 3 (1978): 752–57; Robert J. Foster, "From Trobriand Cricket to Rugby Nation: The Mission of Sport in Papua New Guinea," *International Journal of the History of Sport* 23, no. 5 (2006): 739–58.

47. Richard D. E. Burton, "Cricket, Carnival, and Street Culture in the Caribbean," *International Journal of the History of Sport* 2, no. 2 (1985): 179–97, 179.

48. Kevin A. Yelvington, "Cricket, Colonialism, and the Culture of Caribbean Politics," in *The Social Role of Sport in Caribbean Societies,* ed. Michael A. Malec (Amsterdam: Gordon and Breach, 1995), 13–52, 17.

49. Maurice St. Pierre, "West Indian Cricket as Cultural Resistance," in *The Social Role of Sport in Caribbean Societies,* ed. Michael A. Malec (Amsterdam: Gordon and Breach, 1995), 53–84.

50. Yelvington, "Cricket, Colonialism, and Culture," 21–23.

51. Cashman, *Patrons, Players and the Crowd,* 118.

52. Ibid., 128.

53. Nandy, *Tao of Cricket,* 1.

54. Arjun Appadurai, "Playing with Modernity: The Decolonization of Indian Cricket," in *Consuming Modernity: Public Culture in a South Asian World,* ed. Carol Breckenridge (Minneapolis: University of Minnesota Press, 1995), 23–48; Omar Noman, *Pride and Passion: An Exhilarating Half Century of Cricket in Paki-*

stan (London: Oxford University Press, 1999); Beckles and Stoddard, *Liberation Cricket;* Burton, "Cricket, Carnival, and Street Culture."

55. Sayuri Guthrie Shimizu, *Transpacific Field of Dreams: How Baseball Linked the United States and Japan in Peace and War* (Chapel Hill: North Carolina University Press, 2012), 33–39.

56. Joseph R. Svinth, "Fulfilling His Duty as a Member: Jigoro Kano and the Japanese Bid for the 1940 Olympics," *Journal of Combative Sport,* May 2004, accessed March 31, 2017, http://ejmas.com/jcs/2004jcs/jcsart_svinth_0504.htm.

57. Niehaus, "'If You Want to Cry.'"

58. C. H. Robertson, "A Plan for Promoting Missionary Activity among Association Boys," *Annual Reports of the Foreign Secretaries of the International Committee, October 1, 1909 to September 30, 1910* (New York: International Committee, YMCA, 1910), 19.

59. Antonio Sotomayor, *The Sovereign Colony: Olympic Sport, National Identity, and International Politics in Puerto Rico* (Lincoln: University of Nebraska Press, 2016).

60. James M. Sullivan to William Jennings Bryan, November 1, 1913, file 837.00/962, Department of State Decimal File, Internal Affairs of the Dominican Republic, 1910–1929, General Records of the Department of State.

61. "Public" is the label applied to the elite British private boarding schools such as Harrow, Eton, and Rugby. Eric Dunning, "Sport as a Male Preserve: Notes on the Social Sources of Masculine Identity and Its Transformations," *Quest for Excitement: Sport and Leisure in the Civilizing Process,* ed. Norbert Elias and Eric Dunning (Oxford: Basil Blackwell, 1986), 267–83.

62. Donald E. Hall, ed., *Muscular Christianity: Embodying the Victorian Age* (Cambridge: Cambridge University Press, 1994); John J. MacAloon, "Introduction: Muscular Christianity in Colonial and Postcolonial Worlds," *International Journal of the History of Sport* 23, no. 5 (2006): 687–700.

63. Jeffrey Richards, "'Passing the Love of Women': Manly Love and Victorian Society," *Manliness and Morality: Middle-Class Masculinity in Britain and America, 1800–1940,* ed. J. A. Mangan and James Walvin (New York: St. Martin's Press, 1987), 92–122, 93–100; Allen Guttmann, *The Erotic in Sports* (New York: Columbia University Press, 1996). Nineteenth-century women in Europe and North America also nurtured deep emotional bonds that overshadowed the love between women and men, as Carroll Smith-Rosenberg memorably demonstrated in "The Female World of Love and Ritual: Relations between Women in Nineteenth-Century America," *Signs* 1, no. 1 (1975): 1–29.

64. Richards, "'Passing the Love of Women,'" 107–8.

65. John Donald Gustav-Wrathall, *Take the Young Stranger by the Hand: Same-Sex Relations and the YMCA* (Chicago: University of Chicago Press, 1998).

66. Richards, "'Passing the Love of Women,'" 6.

67. Thomas M. Wilson and Hastings Donnan, *The Anthropology of Ireland* (Oxford: Berg, 2006), 98–102.

68. David Hassan, "Sport, Identity, and Irish Nationalism in Northern Ireland," in *Sport and the Irish: Histories, Identities, Issues,* ed. Alan Bairner (Dublin: University College Dublin Press, 2005), 123–39, 127–29.

69. Cronin, *Sport and Nationalism in Ireland.*

70. Alan Bairner, "Still Taking Sides: Sport, Leisure and Identity," in *Northern Ireland after the Troubles: A Society in Transition,* ed. Colin Coulter and Michael Murray (Manchester: Manchester University Press, 2008), 215–31.

71. David Leeson, "Death in the Afternoon: The Croke Park Massacre, 21 November 1920," *Canadian Journal of History/Annales canadiennes d'histoire* 38, no. 1 (2003): 43–67.

72. Following Greece's hosting of the first modern Olympic Games in 1896, the Intermediate (or Intercalary) Olympic Games were planned for the second year of each four-year Olympiad. However, the 1906 installment was the only one that was held due to Greece's economic and political instability.

73. Michael Herzfeld, "Hellenism and Occidentalism: The Permutations of Performance in Greek Bourgeois Identity," in *Occidentalism: Images of the West,* ed. James G. Carrier (Oxford: Clarendon, 1995), 218–33, 218.

74. Christina Koulouri, "Athleticism and Antiquity: Symbols and Revivals in Nineteenth-Century Greece," *International Journal of the History of Sport* 15, no. 3 (1998): 142–49, 144.

75. Konstantinos Georgiadis, *Olympic Revival: The Revival of the Olympic Games in Modern Times,* trans. Richard Witt (Athens: Ekdotike Athenon, 2003), 123–24.

76. Michel Foucault, *The History of Sexuality,* vol. 1, *An Introduction,* trans. Robert Hurley (New York: Pantheon, 1978; first published 1976), 95.

77. James C. Scott, *Weapons of the Weak: Everyday Forms of Peasant Resistance* (New Haven, CT: Yale University Press, 1985).

78. Jean-Marc Ran Oppenheim, "The Gezira Sporting Club of Cairo," *Peace Review* 11, no. 4 (1999): 551–56.

79. Fanon, *Wretched of the Earth;* for a discussion of "New Whites," see, for example, Peter Geschiere, *Village Communities and the State: Changing Relations among the Maka of South-Eastern Cameroon since the Colonial Conquest* (London: Kegan Paul, 1982), 321.

80. Manuel Schotté, *La construction du "talent": Sociologie de la domination des coureurs marocains* [Constructing "talent": A sociological analysis of the subordination of Moroccan runners] (Paris: Raisons d'Agir, 2012).

81. Trevor Lawson Richards, *Dancing on Our Bones: New Zealand, South Africa, Rugby and Racism* (Wellington, New Zealand: Bridget Williams, 1999).

82. Daniel Guinness and Niko Besnier, "Nation, Nationalism, and Sport: Fijian Rugby in the Local-Global Nexus," *Anthropological Quarterly* 89, no. 4 (2016): 1109–42; Yoko Kanemasu and Gyozo Molnar, "Problematizing the Dominant: The Emergence of Alternative Cultural Voices in Fiji Rugby," *Asia Pacific Journal of Sport and Social Issues* 2, no. 1 (2013): 14–30; Geir Henning Presterudstuen, "The Mimicry of Men: Rugby and Masculinities in Post-colonial Fiji," *Global Studies* 3, no. 2 (2010): 237–48.

83. Teresia K. Teaiwa, "Articulated Cultures: Militarism and Masculinities in Fiji during the Mid-1990s," *Fijian Studies* 3, no.2 (2005): 201–22; Teresia K. Teaiwa, "On Women and 'Indians': The Politics of Inclusion and Exclusion in Militarized Fiji," in *Security Disarmed: Gender, Race, and Militarization,* ed. Barbara Sutton, Sandra Morgen, and John Novkov (New Brunswick, NJ: Rutgers University Press, 2008), 111–35.

84. Athens hosted the 1896 and 2004 Olympics and the 1906 Intercalary Olympics. The Intercalary Olympics were officially recognized by the IOC at the time, but recognition was later withdrawn, a sore point with Greeks even to this day.

CHAPTER THREE. SPORT, HEALTH, AND THE ENVIRONMENT

1. Dona Lee Davis, Anita Maurstad, and Sarah Dean, "My Horse Is My Therapist: The Medicalization of Pleasure among Women Equestrians," *Medical Anthropology Quarterly* 29, no. 3 (2015): 298–315.

2. Norman A. Scotch, "Medical Anthropology," *Biennial Review of Anthropology* 3 (1963): 30–68, 39.

3. Horacio Fabrega Jr., "Medical Anthropology," *Biennial Review of Anthropology* 7 (1971): 167–229, 167.

4. Anthony C. Colson and Karen E. Selby, "Medical Anthropology," *Annual Review of Anthropology* 3 (1974): 245–62, 246.

5. See the discussion of the disjuncture between critical medical anthropology and critical studies of ritual performance in William S. Sax, "Healing Rituals: A Critical Performative Approach," *Anthropology & Medicine* 11, no. 3 (2004): 300–302. A good example of the ritual approach is Edith Turner, *The Hands Feel It: Healing and Spirit Presence among a Northern Alaskan People* (DeKalb: Northern Illinois University Press, 1996).

6. Francesca Bray, "Comments," *Current Anthropology* 40, no. S1 (1999): S58–S59.

7. Translation modified from Plato, *Giorgias* 464b, in *The Dialogues of Plato Translated into English with Analyses and Introductions by B. Jowett,* 3rd ed., vol. 2 (Oxford: Oxford University Press, 1892), accessed July 2, 2017, http://classics.mit.edu/Plato/gorgias.html. *Gymnastikos* was translated as "gymnastic" in the original, but "exercise" is a better translation in today's English.

8. *Hippocrates: With an English Translation,* trans. W. H. S. Jones (London: William Heinemann, 1953), 23.

9. Lesley Dean-Jones, "Too Much of a Good Thing: The Health of Olympic Athletes in Ancient Greece," in *From Athens to Beijing: West Meets East in the Olympic Games,* vol. 1, *Sport, the Body, and Humanism in Ancient Greece and China,* ed. Susan Brownell (New York: Greekworks, 2013), 49–65, 56.

10. Thomas F. Scanlon, *Eros and Greek Athletics* (New York: Oxford University Press, 2002), 121–38. For the praise of the Spartan woman Lampito, see Aristophanes, *Lysistrata* 79–83, trans. Jack Lindsay (Project Gutenberg, 2008; first

published 1925), accessed July 2, 2017, https://www.gutenberg.org/files/7700/7700-h /7700-h.htm.

11. Dean-Jones, "Too Much of a Good Thing," 59.

12. Ibid., 52–53.

13. Hippocrates, *Aphorisms* I3, quoted in Dean-Jones, "Too Much of a Good Thing," 50.

14. Jack W. Berryman, "Exercise and the Medical Tradition from Hippocrates through Antebellum America: A Review Essay," in *Sport and Exercise Science: Essays in the History of Sports Medicine,* ed. Jack W. Berryman and Roberta J. Park (Urbana: University of Illinois Press, 1992), 1–56, 4–5, 15; Galen, *Ars Medica* xxiii, K, I, p. 367, quoted in Plinio Prioreschi, *A History of Medicine,* vol. 5, *Medieval Medicine* (Omaha, NE: Horatius, 2003), 598–99.

15. Jack W. Berryman, "Motion and Rest: Galen on Exercise and Health," *Lancet* 380, no. 9838 (2012): 210–11.

16. George M. Foster, "On the Origin of Humoral Medicine in Latin America," *Medical Anthropology Quarterly* 1, no. 4 (1987): 355–93; Millie Gimmel, "Reading Medicine in the Codex de la Cruz Badiano," *Journal of the History of Ideas* 69, no. 2 (2008): 169–92; Bernard R. Ortiz de Montellano, *Aztec Medicine, Health, and Nutrition* (New Brunswick, NJ: Rutgers University Press, 1990), 202–35.

17. Montellano, *Aztec Medicine, Health, and Nutrition,* 55–58.

18. Ibid., 218.

19. S. Jeffrey K. Wilkerson, "And Then They Were Sacrificed: The Ritual Ballgame of Northeastern Mesoamerica through Time and Space," *The Mesoamerican Ballgame,* ed. Vernon L. Scarborough and David R. Wilcox (Tucson: University of Arizona Press, 1991), 45–71.

20. Dennis Tedlock, *Popol Vuh: The Definitive Edition of the Mayan Book of the Dawn of Life and the Glories of Gods and Kings* (New York: Simon & Schuster, 1985), 105–60.

21. Michel Foucault, *The Birth of the Clinic: An Archaeology of Medical Perception,* trans. A. M. Sheridan (London: Routledge, 1973; first published 1963), 245.

22. Angelo Albrizio, "Biometry and Anthropometry: From Galton to Constitutional Medicine," *Journal of Anthropological Sciences* 85 (2007): 101–23.

23. Ann L. Stoler, "Making Empire Respectable: The Politics of Race and Sexual Morality in 20th-Century Colonial Cultures," *American Ethnologist* 16, no. 4 (1989): 634–60.

24. Philipp Franz von Siebold, *Nippon: Archiv zur Beschreibung von Japan* [Nippon: Archives for the description of Japan], 2nd ed. (Würzburg: Leo Woerl, 1897; first published 1832), accessed June 15, 2016, https://babel.hathitrust.org/cgi/pt?id= hvd.32044107252926;view=1up;seq=343; Herbert Plutschow, *Philipp Franz von Siebold and the Opening of Japan* (Folkestone, UK: Global Oriental, 2007), viii.

25. Ann Fienup-Riordan, *Yup'ik Elders at the Ethnologisches Museum Berlin* (Seattle: University of Washington Press, 2005), 4–5, 27.

26. Larry L. Mai, Marcus Young Owl, and M. Patricia Kersting, *Cambridge Dictionary of Human Biology and Evolution* (Cambridge: Cambridge University Press, 2005), s.v. "Virchow, Rudolf Ludwig Karl (1821–94)."

27. Paul Farmer, *Infections and Inequalities: The Modern Plagues* (Berkeley: University of California Press, 1999).

28. Roy Porter, *The Greatest Benefit to Mankind: A Medical History of Humanity* (New York: W. W. Norton, 1997), 330–33; Daniel Pridan, "Rudolf Virchow and Social Medicine in Historical Perspective," *Medical History* 8, no. 3 (1964): 274–78.

29. Benoît Massin, "From Virchow to Fischer: Physical Anthropology and 'Modern Race Theories' in Wilhelmine Germany," in *Volksgeist as Method and Ethic: Essays on Boasian Ethnography and the German Anthropological Tradition*, ed. George W. Stocking (Madison: University of Wisconsin Press, 1998), 79–154; Andrew Zimmerman, *Anthropology and Antihumanism in Imperial Germany* (Chicago: University of Chicago Press, 2001), 135–47.

30. Roberta J. Park, "The *Research Quarterly* and Its Antecedents," *Research Quarterly of Exercise and Sport Science* 51 (1980): 1–22.

31. Michel Foucault, *Power/Knowledge: Selected Interviews and Other Writings, 1972–1977*, ed. Colin Gordon, trans. Colin Gordon, Leo Marshall, John Mepham, and Kate Soper (New York: Pantheon, 1980).

32. John Bale, "From the Anthropology Days to the Anthropological Olympics," in *The 1904 Anthropology Days and Olympic Games: Sport, Race, and American Imperialism*, ed. Susan Brownell (Lincoln: University of Nebraska Press, 2008), 324–42, 330.

33. Berryman, "Exercise and the Medical Tradition, " 35–47.

34. Berryman, "Motion and Rest," 211.

35. Alain Corbain, *The Lure of the Sea: The Discovery of the Seaside, 1750–1840*, trans. J. Phelps (London: Penguin, 1994; first published 1988).

36. Ernst Jokl, *Medical Sociology and Cultural Anthropology of Sport and Physical Education* (Springfield, IL: Charles C. Thomas, 1964), 44–45, table 2.

37. Venerando Correnti and Bruno Zauli, *Olimpionici 1960* [1960 Olympians] (Rome: Marves, 1964).

38. Alfonso L. de Garay, Louis Levine, and J. E. Lindsay Carter, *Genetic and Anthropological Studies of Olympic Athletes* (New York: Academic Press, 1974), xv.

39. Phenylthiocarbamide (PTC) tastes very bitter to some people and is tasteless to others, based on genetic makeup.

40. H. Evans Robson, review of *Genetic and Anthropological Studies of Olympic Athletes*, by Alfonso L. de Garay, Louis Levine, and J. E. Lindsay Carter, *British Journal of Sports Medicine* 11, no. 3 (1977): 147–48.

41. John Hoberman, *Darwin's Athletes: How Sport Has Damaged Black America and Preserved the Myth of Race* (New York: Mariner, 1987).

42. Ibid., 105.

43. Ted Kaptchuk and Michael Croucher, *The Healing Arts: Exploring the Medical Ways of the World* (New York: Summit Books, 1987), 136–50.

44. Joseph S. Alter, "Heaps of Health, Metaphysical Fitness: Ayurveda and the Ontology of Good Health in Medical Anthropology," *Current Anthropology* 40, no. S1 (1999): S43–S58.

45. Joseph S. Alter, "Reply," *Current Anthropology* 40, no. S1 (1999): S45–S62.

46. Ibid., S45–S51.

47. Joseph Alter, *Gandhi's Body: Sex, Diet, and the Politics of Nationalism* (Philadelphia: University of Pennsylvania Press, 2000), 72.

48. Alter, "Reply," S54–S55.

49. Alter, *Gandhi's Body*, 64.

50. Ibid., 65–68.

51. Ibid., 10–13, 112.

52. For example, Paul Hedges, "Yoga and Violence: International Yoga Day and Indian Religious Politics," *RSIS Commentary*, no. 154 (July 20, 2015), S. Rajaratnam School of International Studies, Singapore, accessed January 31, 2017, https://www.rsis.edu.sg/wp-content/uploads/2015/07/CO15154.pdf.

53. Alter, *Gandhi's Body*, 56.

54. Vivienne Lo, "Imagining Practice: Sense and Sensuality in Early Chinese Medical Illustration," in *The Warp and the Weft: Graphics and Text in the Production of Technical Knowledge in China,* ed. Francesca Bray, Vera Dorofeeva-Lichtmann, and Georges Métailié (Leiden: Brill, 2007), 379–424.

55. Ren Hai, "Animal Imitation: A Comparison of Chinese and Greek Sports in Ancient Times," in Brownell, *From Athens to Beijing,* 35–48; Vivienne Lo, "Training the Senses through Animating the Body in Ancient China," in Brownell, *From Athens to Be ijing,* 67–86.

56. Judith Farquhar's work illustrates this point from multiple angles; see Judith Farquhar, *Knowing Practice: The Clinical Encounter of Chinese Medicine* (Boulder, CO: Westview, 1994); Judith Farquhar and Qicheng Zhang, *Ten Thousand Things: Nurturing Life in Contemporary Beijing* (New York: Zone, 2012).

57. Nancy Chen, *Breathing Spaces: Qigong, Psychiatry, and Healing in China* (New York: Columbia University Press, 2003).

58. Susan Brownell, "Wushu and the Olympic Games: 'Combination of East and West' or Clash of Body Cultures?," in *Perfect Bodies: Sports, Medicine and Immortality,* ed. Vivienne Lo (London: British Museum, 2012), 61–72; David Palmer, *Qigong Fever: Body, Science, and Utopia in China* (New York: Columbia University Press, 2007).

59. Farquhar and Zhang, *Ten Thousand Things*.

60. Jack W. Berryman, "Exercise Is Medicine: A Historical Perspective," *Current Sports Medicine Reports* 9, no. 4 (2010): 195–201.

61. Michael Pratt, Jacqueline N. Epping, and William H. Dietz, "Putting Physical Activity into Public Health: A Historical Perspective from the CDC," *Preventive Medicine* 49, no. 4 (2009): 301–2.

62. Susan Greenhalgh, "Weighty Subjects: The Biopolitics of the U.S. War on Fat," *American Ethnologist* 39, no. 3 (2012): 471–87, 474.

63. Henning Eichberg, "The Enclosure of the Body: The Historical Relativity of 'Health', 'Nature' and the Environment of Sport," in *Body Cultures: Essays on Sport, Space and Identity,* ed. John Bale and Chris Philo (London: Routledge, 1998), 47–66.

64. Vivienne Lo, introduction to *Perfect Bodies: Sports, Medicine and Immortality,* ed. Vivienne Lo (London: British Museum, 2012), 15.

65. Adrian Harrison, Judith Swaddling, and Caroline Cartwright, "Olympic Victor's Dark Ointment," in Lo, *Perfect Bodies,* 71–80.

66. Nancy Parezo, "A 'Special Olympics': Testing Racial Strength and Endurance at the 1904 Louisiana Purchase Exposition," in Brownell, *1904 Anthropology Days,* 59–126, 82.

67. Kathryn Henne, *Testing for Athletic Citizenship: Regulating Doping and Sex in Sport* (New Brunswick, NJ: Rutgers University Press, 2015); Henne, "The 'Science' of Fair Play in Sport: Gender and the Politics of Testing," *Signs* 39, no. 3 (2014): 787-812, 790–91.

68. Mark Hann, "Between Magic and Medicine: Testing for Controlled Substances in Senegalese Wrestling," GLOBALSPORT website, November 3, 2016, accessed November 3, 2016, http://global-sport.eu/between-magic-and-medicine-testing-for-controlled-substances-in-senegalese-wrestling; Uroš Kovač, " 'Juju' and 'Jars': How African Athletes Challenge Western Notions of Doping," *The Conversation,* October 28, 2016, accessed October 28, 2016, https://theconversation.com/juju-and-jars-how-african-athletes-challenge-western-notions-of-doping-67567.

69. Rob Harris, "AP Interview: FIFA Concern over African Stimulants," *USA Today,* February 21, 2010, accessed November 30, 2016, http://usatoday30.usatoday.com/sports/soccer/2010-02-21-1447701226_x.htm.

70. The quotation is by a prominent sports physician, translated from German into English by John Hoberman, the most radical anglophone critic of high-level sport: John Hoberman, *Mortal Engines: The Science of Performance and the Dehumanization of Sport* (New York: Free Press, 1992), 4–5.

71. Rose Eveleth, "Should Oscar Pistorius's Prosthetic Legs Disqualify Him from the Olympics? Scientists Debate Whether Prosthetic Legs Give Pistorius an Unfair Advantage in the 400-Meter Race," *Scientific American,* July 24, 2012, accessed June 14, 2016, https://www.scientificamerican.com/article/scientists-debate-oscar-pistorius-prosthetic-legs-disqualify-him-olympics/.

72. World Anti-Doping Agency, "The Prohibited List 2004," accessed July 2, 2017, https://www.wada-ama.org/sites/default/files/resources/files/WADA_Prohibited_List_2004_EN.pdf.

73. Hiroyasu Yamamoto, "NCoR1 Is a Conserved Physiological Modulator of Muscle Mass and Oxidative Function," *Cell* 147, no. 4 (2011): 827–39, accessed June 14, 2016, www.cell.com/abstract/S0092-8674%2811%2901223-2.

74. Andy Miah, "Towards the Transhuman Athlete: Therapy, Non-therapy, and Enhancement," *Sport in Society* 13, no. 2 (2010): 221–33.

75. Eichberg, "Enclosure of the Body," 60.

CHAPTER FOUR. SPORT, SOCIAL CLASS, RACE, AND ETHNICITY

1. Pierre Bourdieu, *In Other Words: Essays for a Reflexive Sociology*, translated by Loïc J.D. Wacquant and Matthew Lawson (Stanford, CA: Stanford University Press, 1990; first published 1982 and 1987).

2. Greg Downey, *Learning Capoeira: Lessons in Cunning from an Afro-Brazilian Art* (Oxford: Oxford University Press, 2005); Downey, " 'Practice without Theory': A Neuroanthropological Perspective on Embodied Learning," *Journal of the Royal Anthropological Institute* 16, no. S1 (2010): S22–S40.

3. Charles Korr, *West Ham United: The Making of a Football Club* (London: Duckworth, 1986), 1–9.

4. Max Weber, "Class, Status, and Party," in *From Max Weber: Essays in Sociology,* ed. and trans. Hans Gerth and C. Wright Mills (New York: Oxford University Press, 1946; first published 1904), 253–64.

5. See, among his many works, *The Savage Mind,* trans. Julian Pitt-Rivers and Ernest Gellner (Chicago: University of Chicago Press, 1966; first published 1962).

6. Pierre Bourdieu, *Distinction: A Social Critique of the Judgement of Taste,* trans. Richard Nice (Cambridge: Harvard University Press, 1984); the first French edition is *La distinction: Critique sociale du jugement* (Paris: Éditions de Minuit, 1979).

7. "Sport and Social Class," *Social Science Information* 17, no. 6 (1978): 819–40; "Program for a Sociology of Sport" was originally a chapter in *Choses dites* (Paris: Éditions de Minuit, 1987), later translated into English as "Program for a Sociology of Sport," *Sociology of Sport Journal* 5, no. 2 (1988): 153–61.

8. Pierre Bourdieu, "A Program for the Comparative Sociology of Sport," in *The Olympics and Cultural Exchange: The Papers of the First International Conference on the Olympics and East/West and South/North Cultural Exchange in the World System,* ed. Kang Shin-pyo, John MacAloon, and Roberto DaMatta (Seoul: Hanyang University Press, 1988), 67–83.

9. Sebastián Fuentes, "La formación de los cuerpos jóvenes y su diversidad: Un estudio sobre la producción social de los cuerpos masculinos y distinguidos en el rugby de Buenos Aires" [The training of young bodies and its diversity: A study of the social production of male bodies of distinction in Buenos Aires rugby], *Revista latinoamericana de estudios sobre cuerpos, emociones y sociedad* 7, no. 14 (2015): 66–82; "La formación moral de los jóvenes de elite en circuitos de educación privada en Buenos Aires" [The moral training of elite youth in private education circuits in Buenos Aires], *Pro-Posições* 26, no. 2 (2015): 75–98; Daniel Guinness and Sebastián Fuentes, "Argentine Rugby Gets Professional," *Anthropology News* 57, nos. 7–8 (2015): 14–15.

10. Gary Armstrong, *Football Hooligans: Knowing the Score* (Oxford: Berg, 1998); Bill Buford, *Among the Thugs* (New York: Vintage, 1993); Garry Robson, *"No One Likes Us, We Don't Care": The Myth and Reality of Millwall Fandom* (Oxford: Berg, 2000).

11. Bourdieu, *Distinction,* 213.

12. Susan Brownell, *Training the Body for China: Sports in the Moral Order of the People's Republic* (Chicago: University of Chicago Press, 1995), 28.

13. Josh Newman and Michael Giardina, *Sport, Spectacle, and NASCAR Nation: Consumption and the Cultural Politics of Neoliberalism* (New York: Palgrave Macmillan, 2011).

14. Bourdieu, *Distinction,* 217.

15. Benjamin Morris, "Why Is the U.S. So Good at Women's Soccer?" *FiveThirtyEight,* June 30, 2015, accessed October 26, 2016, http://fivethirtyeight.com/datalab/why-is-the-u-s-so-good-at-womens-soccer/.

16. Lisa Swanson, "Complicating the 'Soccer Mom': The Cultural Politics of Forming Class-Based Identity, Distinction, and Necessity," *Research Quarterly for Exercise and Sport* 80, no. 2 (2009): 345–54. On North American middle-class children's sport in general, see Noel Dyck, *Fields of Play: An Ethnography of Children's Sport* (Toronto: University of Toronto Press, 2012).

17. Brownell, *Training the Body for China,* 180–209.

18. Anthony King, "The Lads: Masculinity and the New Consumption of Football," *Sociology* 31, no. 2 (May 1997): 329–46.

19. Joseph S. Alter, "Kabaddi, a National Sport of India: The Internationalization of Nationalism and the Foreignness of Indianness," in *Games, Sports and Cultures,* ed. Noel Dyck (Oxford: Berg, 2000), 81–115.

20. Philip Dine, *French Rugby Football* (Oxford: Berg, 2001); Sébastien Darbon, *Une brève histoire du rugby* [A brief history of rugby] (Paris: L'œil Neuf, 2007); Anne Saouter, *"Être rugby": Jeux du masculin et du féminin* ["To be rugby": Playing with masculinity and femininity] (Paris: Éditions de la Maison des sciences de l'homme, 2000).

21. Niko Besnier, "The Athlete's Body and the Global Condition: Tongan Rugby Players in Japan," *American Ethnologist* 39, no. 3 (2012): 491–510.

22. Zoe Wood, "Where City Suits Strip Off for Some Very Brutal Business: Cage Fighting Lets the Wheelers and Dealers—including Women—Swap the Square Mile for the Violence of the Octagon," *Guardian* (London), September 26, 2009, accessed March 29, 2017, https://www.theguardian.com/business/2009/sep/27/cage-boxing-city-square-mile-sport.

23. Penny Eckert, *Jocks and Burnouts: Social Categories and Identity in the High School* (New York: Teachers College Press, 1989).

24. Niko Besnier, *On the Edge of the Global: Modern Anxieties in a Pacific Island Nation* (Stanford, CA: Stanford University Press, 2011), 186–91.

25. Eric Dunning and Kenneth Sheard, "The Bifurcation of Rugby Union and Rugby League: A Case Study of Organizational Conflict and Change," *International Review of Sport Sociology* 2, no. 11 (1976): 31–68; Tony Collins, *Rugby's Great Split: Class, Culture, and the Origins of Rugby League Football* (London: Frank Cass, 1998).

26. Besnier, "Athlete's Body and Global Condition," 499.

27. Thomas F. Carter, Hastings Donnan, and Huon Wardle, *Global Migrants: The Impact of Migrants Working in Sport in Northern Ireland* (Belfast: Sports Council for Northern Ireland, 2003).

28. Fredrik Barth, introduction to *Ethnic Groups and Boundaries: The Social Organization of Cultural Difference,* ed. Fredrik Barth (Oslo: Universitetsforlaget, 1969), 9–38.

29. John Bale, *Imagined Olympians: Body Culture and Colonial Representation in Rwanda* (Minneapolis: University of Minneapolis Press, 2002).

30. George Mentore, *Of Passionate Curves and Desirable Cadences: Themes on Waiwai Social Being* (Lincoln: University of Nebraska Press, 2005), 211–18.

31. Stefan Krist, "Wrestling Magic: National Wrestling in Buryatia, Mongolia and Tuva in the Past and Today," *International Journal of the History of Sport* 31, no. 4 (2014): 423–44.

32. Marvin Opler, "A 'Sumo' Tournament at Tule Lake Center," *American Anthropologist* 47, no. 1 (1945): 134–39.

33. Scott Laderman, *Empire in Waves: A Political History of Surfing* (Berkeley: University of California Press, 2014); Isaiah H. Walker, "Hui Nalu, Beachboys, and the Surfing Boarder-lands of Hawai'i," *Contemporary Pacific* 20, no. 1 (2008): 89–113.

34. Domenica Gisella Calabrò, "Once Were Warriors, Now Are Rugby Players? Control and Agency in the Historical Trajectory of the Māori Formulations of Masculinity in Rugby," *Asia Pacific Journal of Anthropology* 17, nos. 3–4 (2016): 231–49.

35. David Rowe, "The Bid, the Lead-up, the Event and the Legacy: Global Cultural Politics and Hosting the Olympics," *British Journal of Sociology* 63, no. 2 (2012): 293–301.

36. Loring Danforth, "Is the 'World Game' an 'Ethnic Game' or an 'Aussie Game'? Narrating the Nation in Australian Soccer," *American Ethnologist* 28, no. 2 (2001): 363–87.

37. Ibid., 381.

38. C. L. R. James, *Beyond a Boundary* (Durham, NC: Duke University Press, 2013; first published 1963).

39. Adnan Hossain, "Race, Body and Competing Marginality in Postcolonial Cricket in Trinidad," paper presented at the biannual conference of the European Association of Social Anthropologists, University of Milan-Bicocca, July 22, 2016.

40. Mark Hann, "*Xam Sa Kossan,* 'Know Your Heritage': Senegalese Wrestling and the 'Rediscovery' of Ethnicity," GLOBALSPORT website, September 19, 2016, accessed September 19, 2016, http://global-sport.eu/xam-sa-cossan-know-your-heritage-senegalese-wrestling-and-the-rediscovery-of-ethnicity.

41. We borrow the expression "making majorities" from Dru C. Gladney, ed., *Making Majorities: Constituting the Nation in Japan, Korea, China, Malaysia, Fiji, Turkey, and the United States* (Stanford, CA: Stanford University Press, 1998).

42. Niko Besnier, "Pacific Island Rugby: Histories, Mobilities, Comparisons," *Asia Pacific Journal of Sport and Social Science* 3, no. 3 (2014): 268–76; Daniel Guinness and Niko Besnier, "Nation, Nationalism, and Sport: Fijian Rugby in a Local-Global Nexus," *Anthropological Quarterly* 89, no. 4 (2016): 1109–42.

43. There are other minor ethnicities in Fiji, including "Europeans" and "part Europeans," Rotumans (from the small island of Rotuma in the north of the country), Polynesians and Melanesians from neighboring island groups, and Chinese.

Rotumans, Polynesians, and part Europeans do play rugby, particularly if they identify with the *i-Taukei* majority in lifestyle and values.

44. Susan Brownell, "The Beijing Olympics as a Turning Point? China's First Olympics in East Asian Perspective," in *The Olympics in East Asia: The Crucible of Localism, Nationalism, Regionalism, and Globalism,* ed. William W. Kelly and Susan Brownell (New Haven, CT: Yale Council on East Asian Studies, 2011), 185–203, 186.

45. Victoria Paraschak and W. J. Morgan, "Variations in Race Relations: Sporting Events for Native Peoples in Canada," *Sociology of Sport Journal* 14, no. 1 (1997): 1–21.

46. Jonathan Marks, "The Growth of Scientific Standards from Anthropology Days to Present Days," in Brownell, *1904 Anthropology Days,* 383–96, 395.

47. American Anthropological Association, "Statement on Race," May 17, 1998, accessed September 1, 2016, http://www.americananthro.org/ConnectWithAAA/Content.aspx?ItemNumber=2583.

48. Alan M. Klein, "Headcase, Headstrong, and Head-of-the-Class: Resocialization and Labelling in Dominican Baseball," in *The Social Roles of Sport in the Caribbean,* ed. Michael Malec (Amsterdam: Gordon and Breach, 1995), 125–54.

49. Alan Klein, "Progressive Ethnocentrism: Ideology and Understanding in Dominican Baseball," *Journal of Sport and Social Issues* 32, no. 2 (2008): 121–35.

50. Lincoln Allison, "Biology, Ideology, and Sport," in *Taking Sport Seriously,* ed. Lincoln Allison (Aachen, Germany: Meyer & Meyer, 2010), 135–54.

51. Douglas E. Foley, *The Heartland Chronicles* (Philadelphia: University of Pennsylvania Press, 1995).

52. Douglas E. Foley, *Learning Capitalist Culture: Deep in the Heart of Tejas,* 2nd ed. (Philadelphia: University of Pennsylvania Press, 2010; first published 1995).

53. Bernardo Ramirez Rios, "Culture, Migration, and Sport: A Bi-national Investigation of Southern Mexican Migrant Communities in Oaxaca, Mexico and Los Angeles, California," PhD diss., Department of Anthropology, Ohio State University, 2012.

54. Stanley Thangaraj, *Desi Hoop Dreams: Pickup Basketball and the Making of Asian American Masculinity* (New York: New York University Press, 2015).

55. Kendall Blanchard, "Sport, Leisure, and Identity: Reinventing Lao Culture in Middle Tennessee," *Play & Culture* 4, no. 2 (1991): 169–84.

56. For a fuller account, see Susan Brownell, "The History of Figure Skating in Southern California," in *Sport in Los Angeles,* ed. Wayne Wilson (Fayetteville: University of Arkansas Press, 2017), 135-72.

57. "Mabel Fairbanks Oral History," interview by Sharon Donnan, January 7, 1999, transcript, archives of the LA84 Foundation, Los Angeles.

58. *Los Angeles Sentinel,* "Skater's Skill Breaks Racial 'Ice' at Rink," February 7, 1946.

59. Chico C. Norwood, "Creator of Champions," *Los Angeles Sentinel,* July 24, 1980; Stan Chambers, *KTLA's News at 10: Sixty Years with Stan Chambers* (Lake Forest, CA: Behler, 2008).

60. *Skating,* "Ice Breakers," March 2005, 9.

61. Figure skating competitions are divided into levels determined by a national testing system. The top level is Senior, followed by Junior, and then Novice.

62. Ronald A. Scheurer, "Breaking the Ice: The Mabel Fairbanks Story," *American Visions,* December 1997–January 1998, 12–14.

63. "Mabel Fairbanks Oral History."

64. Susan Brownell has observed this transition as a participant, club officer, and competition organizer in the sport since 1992.

65. The quote, one of many possible illustrations from many different countries and sports, is by Arrigo Sacchi, former coach of the Italian national soccer team. Predictably, it was preceded by "I'm certainly not racist . . . but." *Guardian* (London), "Arrigo Sacchi: 'I'm Not Racist . . . but There Are Too Many Blacks in Youth Teams,'" February 17, 2015, accessed August 31, 2016, https://www.theguardian .com/football/2015/feb/17/arrigo-sacchi-no-racist-too-many-blacks-youth-teams.

66. Ellis Cashmore and Jamie Cleland, "Why Aren't There More Black Football Managers?" *Ethnic and Racial Studies* 34, no. 9 (2011): 1594–607.

67. Orin Starn, *The Passion of Tiger Woods: An Anthropologist Reports on Golf, Race, and Celebrity* (Durham, NC: Duke University Press, 2011).

68. John Hoberman, *Darwin's Athletes: How Sport Has Damaged Black America and Preserved the Myth of Race* (New York: Mariner, 1997).

69. Ben Carrington, *Race, Sport, and Politics: The Sporting Black Diaspora* (London: Sage, 2010), 2–3.

70. Brett St. Louis, "Sport and Common-Sense Racial Science," *Leisure Studies* 23, no. 1 (2004): 31–46.

71. Projit Bihari Mukharji, "'Feeble Bengalis' and 'Big Africans': African Players in Bengali Club Football," *Soccer & Society* 9, no. 2 (2008): 273–85; Paul Dimeo, "Colonial Bodies, Colonial Sport: 'Martial' Punjabis, 'Effeminate' Bengalis and the Development of Indian Football," *International Journal of the History of Sport* 19, no. 1 (2002): 72–90.

72. Fernando Ortiz, *El pueblo cubano* [The Cubans] (La Habana: Editorial de Ciencias Sociales, 1997); Stephan Palmié, *Wizards and Scientists: Explorations in Afro-Cuban Modernity and Tradition* (Durham, NC: Duke University Press, 2002); Pedro Pérez Sarduy and Jean Stubbs, *Afrocuba: An Anthology of Cuban Writing on Race, Politics, and Culture* (Melbourne: Ocean, 1993); Jafari S. Allen, *¡Venceremos? The Erotics of Black Self-Making in Cuba* (Durham, NC: Duke University Press, 2011); Kaifa L. Roland, *Cuban Color in Tourism and La Lucha: An Ethnography of Racial Meanings* (New York: Oxford University Press, 2011).

73. Thomas F. Carter, "Baseball Arguments: *Aficionismo* and Masculinity at the Core of Cubanidad," *International Journal of the History of Sport* 18, no. 3 (2011): 117–38, 129–34; Thomas F. Carter, *The Quality of Home Runs: The Passion, Politics, and Language of Cuban Baseball* (Durham, NC: Duke University Press, 2008), 141–45.

74. Carter, *Quality of Home Runs,* 132–33.

75. Instituto Nacional de Deportes Educación Física y Recreación, *Atlas de la cultura física y el deporte: Cuba* [Atlas of physical culture and sport: Cuba] (Havana:

Instituto Cubano de Geodesia y Cartografía, Instituto Nacional de Deportes Educación Física y Recreación, Instituto de Geografía de la A.C.C., 1991).

76. Stanley Thangaraj, "Playing through Differences: Black-White Racial Logic and Interrogating South Asian American Identity," *Ethnic and Racial Studies* 35, no. 6 (2012): 988–1006, 989.

77. Stephen Gregory, *The Devil behind the Mirror: Globalization and Politics in the Dominican Republic* (Berkeley: University of California Press, 2007); Brackette Williams, *Stains on My Name, War in My Veins: Guyana and the Politics of Cultural Struggle* (Durham, NC: Duke University Press, 1991).

78. Ann Laura Stoler, *Race and the Education of Desire: Foucault's "History of Sexuality" and the Colonial Order of Things* (Durham, NC: Duke University Press, 1996).

CHAPTER FIVE. SPORT AND SEX, GENDER, AND SEXUALITY

1. Margaret Mead, *Sex and Temperament in Three Primitive Societies* (New York: W. Morrow, 1935).

2. See the review of sex and gender in anthropology by Susan Brownell and Niko Besnier, "Gender," in *Handbook of Sociocultural Anthropology,* ed. James G. Carrier and Deborah B. Gewertz (New York: Bloomsbury, 2013), 239–58.

3. Michel Foucault, *The History of Sexuality,* vol. 1, *An Introduction,* trans. Robert Hurley (New York: Vintage, 1978; first published 1976).

4. Thomas Laqueur, *Making Sex: Body and Gender from the Greeks to Freud* (Cambridge, MA: Harvard University Press, 1990).

5. Katrina Karkazis, Rebecca Jordan-Young, Georgiann Davis, and Silvia Camporesi, "Out of Bounds? A Critique of the New Policies on Hyperandrogenism in Elite Female Athletes," *American Journal of Bioethics,* 12, no. 7 (2012): 3–16; Rebecca Jordan-Young and Katrina Karkazis, "Some of Their Parts," *Anthropology News* 53, no. 6 (2012): S12–S14.

6. Lindsay Parks Pieper, *Sex Testing: Gender Policing in Women's Sports* (Urbana: University of Illinois Press, 2016).

7. Vanessa Heggie, "Testing Sex and Gender in Sports: Reinventing, Reimagining and Reconstructing Histories," *Endeavour* 34, no. 4 (2010): 158–63; Laura Wackwitz, "Verifying the Myth: Olympic Sex Testing and the Category 'Woman,'" *Women's Studies International Forum* 26, no. 6 (2003): 553–60; Joanne Meyerowitz, *How Sex Changed: A History of Transsexuality in the United States* (Cambridge, MA: Harvard University Press, 2002).

8. Cynthia Enloe, *Bananas, Beaches and Bases: Making Feminist Sense of International Politics,* 2nd ed. (Berkeley: University of California Press, 2014; first published 1989).

9. The final phrase is from Heggie, "Testing Sex and Gender," 163. She does not feel that the question of when this shift occurred has been answered; following

scholars such as George Mosse, we suspect that the transition occurred in the context of the rigidification of gender norms that accompanied and followed War II. See George Mosse, *Nationalism and Sexuality: Middle-Class Morality and Sexual Norms in Modern Europe* (Madison: University of Wisconsin Press, 1985); Mosse, *The Image of Man: The Creation of Modern Masculinity* (New York: Oxford University Press, 1996); and further discussion in chapter 7.

10. Stefan Berg, "1936 Berlin Olympics: How Dora the Man Competed in the Woman's [*sic*] High Jump," trans. Jan Liebelt, *Der Spiegel,* September 15, 2009, accessed June 19, 2016, www.spiegel.de/international/germany/1936-berlin-olympics-how-dora-the-man-competed-in-the-woman-s-high-jump-a-649104.html.

11. Joseph M. Turrini, " 'It Was Communism versus the Free World': The USA-USSR Dual Track Meet Series and the Development of Track and Field in the United States, 1958–1985," *Journal of Sport History* 28, no. 3 (2001): 427–71.

12. Turrini, "It Was Communism versus the Free World," 434–35, 439–41.

13. *Time,* "Track & Field: Preserving la Difference," September 16, 1966, 74.

14. *Sport Express* (St. Petersburg), "Nina Ponomareva: Chempiunka iz gulaga [Nina Ponomarev: The little champion from the gulag]," interview with Nina Ponomareva, February 6, 2015, accessed June 23, 2016, http://www.sport-express.ru /fridays/reviews/835630/.

15. *Sport Express* (St. Petersburg), "Galina Zybina: Za zhenskuyu sbornuyu SSSR vystavlyali muzhchin. My-to znali [The USSR national team fielded men. We knew that]," interview with Galina Zybina, February 1, 2016, accessed June 23, 2016, http://www.sport-express.ru/chronicle/reviews/953020/; ibid.; Vadim Samokatov, "Olimpiyskie germafrodity—byl' ili skazka [Olympic hermaphrodites—true story or fairy tale]," *Utro,* August 18, 2004, accessed June 23, 2016, www.utro.ru /articles/2004/08/18/341329.shtml.

16. C.L. Cole, "Bounding American Empire: Sport, Sex, and Politics," *Youth Culture and Sport: Identity, Power, and Politics,* ed. Michael D. Giardina and Michele K. Donnelly (New York: Routledge, 2008), 55–68.

17. In addition to Nina Ponomareva and Galina Zybina in the 2015 interviews cited above, in 1980 Olga Fikatova Connolly, a Czechoslovakian gold medalist in the 1956 Olympics who married an American discus thrower and moved to the United States, stated that Tamara was intersex. Neil Amdur, "Women Facing More Than an Athletic Struggle," *New York Times,* December 21, 1980.

18. Kelli Lawrence, *Skating on Air: The Broadcast History of an Olympic Marquee Sport* (Jefferson, NC: McFarland, 2011), 29–33.

19. *Los Angeles Times,* "Peggy Fleming Signs $500,000 Pro Contract," April 4, 1968.

20. *Der Spiegel,* "Eine Viecherei" [A rotten trick], November 13, 1967, accessed June 23, 2016, www.spiegel.de/spiegel/print/d-46209469.html.

21. L.J. Elsas, A. Ljungqvist, M. A. Ferguson-Smith, J. L. Simpson, M. Genel, A. S. Carlson, E. Ferris, et al., "Gender Verification of Female Athletes," *Genetics in Medicine* 2, no. 4 (2000): 249–54.

22. Karkazis et al., "Out of Bounds?," 6.

23. Niko Besnier, "Intersex," in *International Encyclopaedia of Anthropology,* ed. Hilary Callan (Chichester, UK: Wiley-Blackwell, forthcoming).

24. Melanie Blackless, Anthony Charuvastra, Amanda Derryck, Anne Fausto-Sterling, Karl Lauzanne, and Ellen Lee, "How Sexually Dimorphic Are We? Review and Synthesis," *American Journal of Human Biology* 12, no. 2 (2000): 151–66.

25. María José Martínez Patiño, "Personal Account: A Woman Tried and Tested," *Lancet* 366, no. S1 (2005): S38.

26. This was probably overly optimistic, as Susan Brownell can attest. At the 1987 US-Canada heptathlon and decathlon meet, her clueless teenage monitor was too shy to actually observe her urinate into a cup.

27. A. Serrat and A. García de Herreros, "Gender Verification in Sports by PCR Amplification of SRY and DYZ1 Y Chromosome Specific Sequences: Presence of DYZ1 Repeat in Female Athletes,'" *British Journal of Sports Medicine* 30, no. 4 (1996): 310–12.

28. Elsas et al., "Gender Verification of Female Athletes," 252.

29. Ibid., 251–52.

30. Frank Litsky, "Prince Alexandre de Mérode, 68, Head of I.O.C. Antidrug Efforts," obituary, *New York Times,* November 22, 2002, accessed October 24, 2016, http://www.nytimes.com/2002/11/22/sports/prince-alexandre-de-merode-68-head-of-ioc-antidrug-efforts.html.

31. Elsas et al., "Gender Verification of Female Athletes," on which he was a coauthor.

32. IAAF, *IAAF Regulations Governing Eligibility of Females with Hyperandrogenism to Compete in Women's Competition, In force as from 1st May 2011,* accessed June 22, 2016, https://www.iaaf.org/download/download?filename=58438613-aaa7-4bcd-b730-70296abab70c.pdf; IOC Medical and Scientific Department, *IOC Regulations on Female Hyperandrogenism, Games of the XXX Olympiad in London, 2012, June 22, 2012,* accessed November 30, 2016, www.olympic.org/Documents/Commissions_PDFfiles/Medical_commission/2012–06–22-IOC-Regulations-on-Female-Hyperandrogenism-eng.pdf.

33. Rebecca M. Jordan-Young, Peter H. Sönksen, and Katrina Karkazis, "Sex, Health, and Athletes," *BMJ* 2014;348:g2926; Anaïs Bohuon, *Test de féminité dans les compétitions sportives: Une histoire classée X* [Femininity testing in sports competitions: An X-rated story] (Paris: Éditions IXe, 2012); Bohuon, "Gender Verifications in Sport: From an East/West Antagonism to a North/South Antagonism," *International Journal of the History of Sport* 32, no. 7 (2015): 965–79.

34. Michael Phelps, *Beneath the Surface: My Story* (New York: Sports Publishing, 2004).

35. Sisonke Msimang, "Caster Semenya Is the One at a Disadvantage," *Guardian* (London), August 2, 2016, accessed October 31, 2016, www.theguardian.com/world/2016/aug/24/caster-semenya-is-the-one-at-a-disadvantage.

36. IOC, "IOC Addresses Eligibility of Female Athletes with Hyperandrogenism," press release, April 5, 2011, accessed June 21, 2016, https://www.olympic.org/news/ioc-addresses-eligibility-of-female-athletes-with-hyperandrogenism.

37. M.L. Healy, J. Gibney, C. Pentecost, M.J. Wheeler, and P.H. Sonksen, "Endocrine Profiles in 693 Elite Athletes in the Postcompetition Setting," *Clinical Endocrinology* 81, no. 2 (2014): 294–305.

38. Ibid., 294.

39. Rebecca Jordan-Young and Katrina Karkazis, "You Say You're a Woman? That Should Be Enough," *New York Times,* June 17, 2012, accessed June 21, 2016, http://www.nytimes.com/2012/06/18/sports/olympics/olympic-sex-verification-you-say-youre-a-woman-that-should-be-enough.html.

40. Laqueur, *Making Sex,* 15; Daniel M. Rosen, *Dope: A History of Performance Enhancement in Sports from the Nineteenth Century to Today* (Westport, CT: Praeger, 2008), 12.

41. William N. Taylor, *Anabolic Steroids and the Athlete,* 2nd ed. (Jefferson, NC: McFarland, 2002; first published 1982), 181; Henrik Eberle and Hans-Joachim Neumann, *Was Hitler Ill? A Final Diagnosis* (New York: Polity, 2012), 37.

42. John Hoberman, *Testosterone Dreams: Rejuvenation, Aphrodisia, Doping* (Austin: University of Texas Press, 2006), 3.

43. Ibid., 38.

44. Jordan-Young and Karkazis, "You Say You're a Woman?"

45. Ibid.

46. Jeré Longman, "Understanding the Controversy over Caster Semenya," *New York Times,* August 18, 2016, accessed October 31, 2016, http://www.nytimes.com/2016/08/20/sports/caster-semenya-800-meters.html.

47. Ken Corbitt, "No. 5: Murdock Didn't Miss upon Getting her Shot," *Topeka Capital-Journal,* August 26, 2011, accessed June 24, 2016, http://cjonline.com/sports/2011-08-26/murdock-didnt-miss-upon-getting-her-shot#.

48. Mary Jollimore, "Current Olympic Guidelines Mean Women Have No Shot," *Globe and Mail* (Toronto), August 24, 1992.

49. Figure skating is one of two Olympic sports, with tennis, in which the females are officially "ladies" rather than "women."

50. Ellyn Kestnbaum, *Culture on Ice: Figure Skating and Cultural Meaning* (Middletown, CT: Wesleyan University Press, 2003), 41–43; International Skating Union, "Rule 501, Clothing," *Special Regulations and Technical Rules, Single and Pair Skating and Ice Dance (2014),* 74, accessed June 24, 2016, http://static.isu.org/media/166717/2014-special-regulation-sandp-and-ice-dance-and-technical-rules-sandp-and-id_14-09-16.pdf.

51. Jeré Longman and Juliet Macur, "For Women's Road Records, No Men Allowed," *New York Times,* September 21, 2011.

52. Healy et al. found that the women's lean body mass on average was 85 percent of that of the men in the study discussed above, and suggested that this alone, rather than testosterone, might explain differences in their performances. "Endocrine Profiles," 298.

53. Fábio Franzini, "Futebol é 'coisa pra macho'? Pequeno esboço para uma história das mulheres no país do futebol" [Is soccer a men's thing? A brief essay on the history of women in the land of soccer], *Revista brasileira de história* 25, no. 50

(2005): 316–28; Carmen Rial, "Women's Soccer in Brazil," *Revista* 11, no. 3 (2012): 25–28.

54. Pierre de Coubertin, *The Olympic Idea: Discourses and Essays,* trans. John J. Dixon (Stuttgart: Carl-Diem-Institut an der Sporthochschule Köln, 1967), 133.

55. Eric Dunning, "Sport as a Male Preserve: Notes on the Social Sources of Masculine Identity and Its Transformations," in *Quest for Excitement: Sport and Leisure in the Civilizing Process,* ed. Norbert Elias and Eric Dunning (Oxford: Basil Blackwell, 1986), 267–83.

56. Jeremy MacClancy, "Female Bullfighting, Gender Stereotyping and the State," *Sport, Identity and Ethnicity,* ed. Jeremy MacClancy (Oxford: Berg, 1996), 69–85.

57. Perry Sherouse, "Skill and Masculinity in Olympic Weightlifting: Training Cues and Cultivated Craziness in Georgia," *American Ethnologist* 43, no. 1 (2016): 103–15.

58. R. Kenji Tierney, "From Popular Performance to National Sport: The 'Nationalisation' of Sumo," in *This Sporting Life: Sports and Body Culture in Modern Japan,* ed. William W. Kelly and Atsuo Sugimoto (New Haven, CT: Council of East Asian Studies, Yale University, 2007), 67–89; Tierney, "Consuming Sumo Wrestlers: Taste, Commensality, and Authenticity in Japanese Food," *Food, Culture, and Society* 19, no. 4 (2016): 637–53.

59. Martin Stokes, " 'Strong as a Turk': Power, Performance and Representation in Turkish Wrestling," *Sport, Identity and Ethnicity,* ed. Jeremy MacClancy (Oxford: Berg, 1996), 21–42. Turkish police regularly intercept foreign gay tourists who come to watch oil wrestling as a homoerotic performance, in an attempt to prevent a sexual reading of the sport.

60. Mark Edward Lewis, "Swordsmanship and the Socialization of Violence in Early China," in *From Athens to Beijing: West Meets East in the Olympic Games,* ed. Susan Brownell (New York: Greekworks, 2013), 151–72, 162–68.

61. Susan Brownell, *Beijing's Games: What the Olympics Mean to China* (Lanham, MD: Rowman & Littlefield, 2008), 105–80.

62. Susan Brownell, *Training the Body for China: Sport in the Moral Order of the People's Republic* (Chicago: University of Chicago Press), 31–33, 222–36.

63. China was first represented in equestrian sports in the 2008 Olympic Games. Horse racing is enormously important in Hong Kong, where the Hong Kong Jockey Club is a stronghold of elites. It was allowed to set up an equestrian operation in Shenzhen after the 2008 Olympic Games.

64. Yunxiang Gao, *Sporting Gender: Women Athletes and Celebrity-Making during China's National Crisis, 1931–1946* (Vancouver: UBC Press, 2013), 166–207.

65. Alan M. Klein, *Little Big Men: Bodybuilding Subculture and Gender Construction* (Albany: State University of New York Press, 1993), 14.

66. Ibid., 18.

67. Ibid., 161.

68. Ibid., 17.

69. Brownell, *Training the Body for China,* 270–77.

70. Laura Spielvogel, *Working Out in Japan: Shaping the Female Body in Tokyo Fitness Clubs* (Durham, NC: Duke University Press, 2003).

71. Eric Anderson, *In the Game: Gay Athletes and the Cult of Masculinity* (Albany: State University of New York Press, 2005).

72. "Rio 2016: Daily Beast 'Sorry for Outing Gay Athletes,'" BBC News, August 12, 2016, accessed October 31, 2016, www.bbc.com/news/world-37058787.

73. John Donald Gustav-Wrathall, *Take the Young Stranger by the Hand: Same-Sex Relations and the YMCA* (Chicago: University of Chicago Press, 1998), 7, 168–84.

74. Niko Besnier, "Gender and Sexuality: Contested Relations," in Callan, *International Encyclopaedia of Anthropology*; Jeffrey Weeks, *Sexuality and Its Discontents: Meanings, Myths and Modern Sexualities* (London: Routledge, 1985), 61–95.

75. Mary Louise Adams, "No Taste for Rough-and-Tumble Play: Sport Discourses, the *DSM,* and the Regulation of Effeminacy," *GLQ* 19, no. 4 (2013): 515–43.

76. Allen Guttmann, *The Erotic in Sports* (New York: Columbia University Press, 1996).

77. Alan Dundes, "Into the End Zone for a Touchdown: A Psychoanalytic Consideration of American Football," *Western Folklore* 38, no. 2 (1978): 75–88.

78. Eve Kosofsky Sedgwick, *Epistemology of the Closet* (Berkeley: University of California Press, 1990).

79. Greg Louganis, *Breaking the Surface,* with Eric Marcus (New York: Penguin, 1995); Cheryl Furjanic, dir., *Back on Board: Greg Louganis* (Will Sweeney Productions, 2014).

80. Paul Freeman, *Ian Roberts: Finding Out* (Milsons Point, NSW: Random House, 1997).

81. Eric Anderson, "Openly Gay Athletes: Contesting Hegemonic Masculinity in a Homophobic Environment," *Gender and Society* 16, no. 6 (2002): 860–77. Similarly, one elite athlete who came out as transgender reports that the support of his coaches and teammates "did not last beyond the initial publicity." Erica Rand, "Court and Sparkle: Kye Allums, Johnny Weir, and Raced Problems in Gender Authenticity," *GLQ* 19, no. 4 (2013): 435–63, 456.

82. Emma Baccellieri and Nick Martin, "Rasheed Sulaimon at Center of Sexual Assault Allegations prior to Dismissal," *Duke Chronicle,* March 2, 2015, accessed November 30, 2016, http://www.dukechronicle.com/article/2015/03/rasheed-sulaimon-center-sexual-assault-allegations-prior-dismissal; Tom Farrey and Nicole Noren, "Mizzou Did Not Pursue Alleged Assault," ESPN, February 12, 2015, accessed November 30, 2016, http://www.espn.com/espn/otl/story/_/id/10323102/university-missouri-officials-did-not-pursue-rape-case-lines-investigation-finds.

83. Sachin Nakrani and Libby Brooks, "Metropolitan Police to Investigate Sexual Abuse Claims at London Clubs," *Guardian* (London), December 8, 2016,accessed December 8, 2016, https://www.theguardian.com/football/2016/dec/08/metropolitan-police-to-investigate-football-sex-abuse-claims.

84. Caroline Symons, *The Gay Games: A History* (Abingdon, UK: Routledge, 2010), 55–58.

85. Wagner Xavier de Camargo and Carmen Silvia Moraes Rial, "Competições esportivas mundiais LGBT: Guetos sexualizados em escala global?" [World LGBT sport competitions: Sexual ghettos on a global scale?], *Revista estudos feministas* 19, no. 3 (2011): 977–1003; Wagner Xavier de Camargo, "Esporte, cultura e política: A trajetória dos Gay Games nas prácticas esportivas contemporâneas" [Sport, culture, and politics: The trajectory of Gay Games in contemporary sports practices], *Revista USP*, no. 108 (2016): 97–114. These critiques have been leveled against many other aspects of contemporary gay and lesbian life in Western countries by such scholars as Miranda Joseph, *Against the Romance of Community* (Minneapolis: University of Minnesota Press, 2002).

86. There are, however, signs of change; for example, in 2016, gender-neutral athlete Lauren Lubin was the first non-cisgender athlete allowed to compete in the New York City Marathon, and grassroots sports like roller derby are making particularly important headways in breaking down sport's gender conservatism. Jon Shadel, "This Gender Neutral Athlete Wants to End Sex Segregation in Sports," *Vice,* November 11, 2016, accessed April 3, 2017, https://www.vice.com/en_uk /article/this-gender-neutral-athlete-wants-to-end-sex-segregation-in-sports; Alex Hanna, "Roller Derby Doesn't Enforce Gender Separation and Women Still Rule the Sport," *Guardian* (London), August 19, 2015, accessed April 4, 2017, https:// www.theguardian.com/commentisfree/2015/aug/19/roller-derby-gender-separation-women-rule-the-sport.

87. Gayle Rubin, "The Traffic in Women: Notes on the 'Political Economy' of Sex," in *Towards an Anthropology of Women,* ed. Rayna Reiter (New York: Monthly Review Press, 1975), 157–210; Sherry Ortner, "Is Female to Male as Nature Is to Culture?" in *Woman, Culture, and Society,* ed. Michelle Zimbalist Rosaldo and Louise Lamphere (Stanford, CA: Stanford University Press, 1976), 68–87.

CHAPTER SIX. SPORT, CULTURAL PERFORMANCE, AND MEGA-EVENTS

1. Milton Singer, *When a Great Tradition Modernizes: An Anthropological Approach to Indian Civilization* (New York: Praeger, 1972), 71; Clifford Geertz, "Deep Play: Notes on the Balinese Cockfight," *Dædalus* 101, no. 1 (1972): 1–37.

2. Among many works, see Judith Butler, "Performative Acts and Gender Constitution: An Essay in Phenomenology and Feminist Theory," *Theatre Journal* 40, no. 4 (1988): 519–31; *Gender Trouble: Feminism and the Subversion of Identity* (New York: Routledge, 1990) was the launching point for the theory.

3. Roger Magazine, *Golden and Blue Like My Heart: Masculinity, Youth, and Power among Soccer Fans in Mexico City* (Tucson: University of Arizona Press, 2007); Gary Armstrong, *Football Hooligans: Knowing the Score* (Oxford: Berg, 1998); William W. Kelly, "Sense and Sensibility at the Ballpark: What Fans Make of Baseball in Modern Japan," in *Fanning the Flames: Fans and Consumer Culture in Contemporary Japan,* ed. William W. Kelly (Albany: State University of New

York Press, 2004), 79–106; Thomas F. Carter, *The Quality of Home Runs: The Passion, Politics, and Language of Cuban Baseball* (Durham, NC: Duke University Press, 2008), 111–35.

4. Sally F. Moore and Barbara G. Myerhoff, *Secular Ritual* (Amsterdam: Van Gorcum, 1977).

5. Pierre de Coubertin, *Olympism: Selected Writings,* ed. Norbert Müller (Lausanne, Switzerland: International Olympic Committee, 2000), 580.

6. Robert Gordon and Marizanne Grundlingh, "Going for the Reds: Max Gluckman and the Anthropology of Football," in *New Ethnographies of Football in Europe: People, Passions, Politics,* ed. Alexandra Schwell, Nina Szogs, Maglorzata Z. Kowalska, and Michal Buchowki (Basingstoke, UK: Palgrave Macmillan, 2016), 21–36.

7. Mary Gluckman and Max Gluckman, "On Drama, and Games and Athletic Contests," in *Secular Ritual,* ed. Sally F. Moore and Barbara G. Myerhoff (Amsterdam: Van Gorcum, 1977), 227–43, 241–43.

8. Philadelphia: Institute for the Study of Human Issues, 1984.

9. Victor Turner, *The Anthropology of Performance* (New York: PAJ, 1988), 21–22, 29.

10. Arnold van Gennep, *The Rites of Passage,* trans. Monika B. Vizedom and Gabrielle L. Coffee (Chicago: University of Chicago Press, 2011; first published 1909).

11. Turner, *Anthropology of Performance,* 24.

12. Ibid., 25.

13. Heather Levi, *The World of Lucha Libre: Secrets, Revelations, and Mexican National Identity* (Durham, NC: Duke University Press, 2008).

14. Victor W. Turner, personal communication cited in Edward M. Bruner, "Introduction: Experience and Its Expressions," in *The Anthropology of Experience,* ed. Victor W. Turner and Edward M. Bruner (Urbana-Champaign, IL: University of Illinois Press, 1986), 13.

15. For example, two important overviews of ritual studies generally emphasize meaning over the social organization of ritual: Ronald L. Grimes, *Beginnings in Ritual Studies* (Columbia: University of South Carolina Press, 1995); Catherine Bell, *Ritual Theory, Ritual Practice* (New York: Oxford University Press, 1992).

16. Victor Turner, "Liminal to Liminoid in Play, Flow, and Ritual: An Essay in Comparative Symbology," *Rice University Studies* 60, no. 3 (1974): 53–92; *From Ritual to Theatre: The Human Seriousness of Play* (New York: PAJ, 1982); Turner, "Liminality and the Performative Genres," in *Rite, Drama, Festival, Spectacle: Rehearsals toward a Theory of Cultural Performance,* ed. John J. MacAloon (Philadelphia: Institute for the Study of Human Issues, 1984), 19–41; Turner, *Process, Performance, and Pilgrimage: A Study in Comparative Symbology* (New Delhi: Concept, 1979), 51–55.

17. Turner, *Anthropology of Performance,* 49.

18. Turner, *Process, Performance, and Pilgrimage,* 54.

19. Henning Eichberg, "Olympic Anthropology Days and the Progress of Exclusion: Toward an Anthropology of Democracy," in *The 1904 Anthropology Days and*

Olympic Games, ed. Susan Brownell (Lincoln: University of Nebraska Press, 2008), 343–82.

20. There is much academic and public opining on this point. A representative academic work is Helen Jefferson Lenskyj and Varda Burstyn, *Inside the Olympic Industry: Power, Politics, and Activism* (Albany: State University of New York Press, 2000).

21. Richard Pringle, "When the Pleasure Is Political: An Affective Analysis of Viewing the Olympics," in *Sport and the Social Significance of Pleasure*, ed. Richard Pringle, Robert E. Rinehart, and Jayne Caudwell (New York: Routledge, 2015), 116–32, 116.

22. Victor Turner, *Schism and Continuity in an African Society: A Study of Ndembu Village Life* (Manchester: Manchester University Press, 1972).

23. "Sport Careers, Religious Conviction, and Uncertain Futures," panel at the Annual Meeting of the American Anthropological Association, Minneapolis, November 17, 2016.

24. Uroš Kovač, " 'Juju' and 'Jars': How African Athletes Challenge Western Notions of Doping," *The Conversation,* October 28, 2016, accessed October 28, 2016, https://theconversation.com/juju-and-jars-how-african-athletes-challenge-western-notions-of-doping-67567.

25. Carmen Rial, "Banal Religiosity: Brazilian Athletes as New Missionaries of the Neo-Pentecostal Diaspora," *Vibrant* 9, no. 2 (2012): 128–59; Rial, "The 'Devil's Egg': Football Players as New Missionaries of the Diaspora of Brazilian Religions," in *The Diaspora of Brazilian Religions,* ed. Cristina Rocha and Manuel Arturo Vasquez (Leiden: Brill, 2013), 91–115.

26. Mark Hann, "Between Magic and Medicine: Testing for Controlled Substances in Senegalese Wrestling," GLOBALSPORT website, November 3, 2016, accessed November 3, 2016, http://global-sport.eu/between-magic-and-medicine-testing-for-controlled-substances-in-senegalese-wrestling.

27. George Gmelch, "Baseball Magic," *Human Nature* 1, no. 8 (1978): 32–40.

28. *Magic, Science and Religion and Other Essays* (Plano, TX: McCormick Press, 2014; first published 1925).

29. John J. MacAloon, "Olympic Games and the Theory of Spectacle in Modern Societies," in *Rite, Drama, Festival, Spectacle: Rehearsals Toward a Theory of Cultural Performance,* ed. John J. MacAloon (Philadelphia: Institute for the Study of Human Issues, 1984), 241–80, 250.

30. Ibid., 257–59.

31. Ibid., 240–58; MacAloon, *This Great Symbol: Pierre de Coubertin and the Origins of the Modern Olympic Games* (Chicago: University of Chicago Press, 1981), 271.

32. Coubertin, *Olympism,* 451–52.

33. John J. MacAloon, "The Theory of Spectacle: Reviewing Olympic Ethnography," in *National Identity and Global Sports Events: Culture, Politics, and Spectacle in the Olympics and the Football World Cup,* ed. Alan Tomlinson and Christopher Young (Albany: State University of New York Press, 2006), 15–40, 18.

34. Arne Martin Klausen, ed., *Olympic Games as Performance and Public Event: The Case of the XVII Winter Olympic Games in Norway* (Oxford: Berghahn, 1999).

35. Susan Brownell, *Beijing's Games: What the Olympics Mean to China* (Lanham, MD: Rowman & Littlefield, 2008); John Horne and Wolfram Manzenreiter, eds., *Japan, Korea and the 2002 World Cup* (New York: Routledge, 2002).

36. John Rennie Short, *Globalization, Modernity, and the City* (London: Routledge, 2012).

37. Mark Dyreson, "Epilogue: Showcases for Global Aspirations: Meditations on the Histories of Olympic Games and World's Fairs," *The International Journal of the History of Sport* 27, nos. 16–18 (2010): 3039.

38. MacAloon, *This Great Symbol,* 271.

39. Dyreson, "Epilogue: Showcases for Global Aspirations," 3039.

40. Maurice Roche, *Mega-events and Modernity: Olympics and Expos in the Growth of Global Culture* (London: Routledge, 2000), 1–29.

41. David Rowe, "The Bid, the Lead-Up, the Event and the Legacy: Global Cultural Politics and Hosting the Olympics," *British Journal of Sociology* 63, no. 2 (2012): 285–305.

42. Clifford Geertz, *Negara: The Theatre State in Nineteenth-Century Bali* (Princeton, NJ: Princeton University Press, 1980), 2.

43. Susan Brownell, "Qing Dynasty Grand Sacrifice and Communist National Games: Rituals of the Chinese State?," ch. 5 in *Training the Body for China: Sports in the Moral Order of the People's Republic* (Chicago: University of Chicago Press, 1995); Brownell, "Why Were Chinese People So Angry about the Attempts to Seize the Torch in the International Torch Relay?," in *China in 2008: A Year of Great Significance,* ed. Kate Merkel-Hess, Kenneth L. Pomeranz, and Jeffrey N. Wasserstrom (Lanham, MD: Rowman & Littlefield, 2009), 81–87.

44. Raymond Boyle and Richard Haynes, *Power Play: Sport, Media, and Popular Culture* (Edinburgh: Edinburgh University Press, 2009).

45. Peter Alegi, *African Soccerscapes: How a Continent Changed the World's Game* (Athens: Ohio University Press, 2010), 104.

46. Worth in US dollars at the time $520 million, $1.03 billion, and $1.72 billion, respectively.

47. Alegi, *African Soccerscapes,* 105.

48. Alan Law, Jean Harvey, and Stuart Kemp, "The Global Sport Mass Media Oligopoly: The Three Usual Suspects and More," *International Review for the Sociology of Sport* 37, nos. 3–4 (2002): 279–302; John Williams, "The Local and the Global in English Soccer and the Rise of Satellite Television," *Sociology of Sport Journal* 11, no. 4 (1994): 376–97.

49. Steven Barnett, *Games and Sets: The Changing Face of Sport on Television* (London: BFI, 1990); Garry Whannel, *Fields in Vision: Television Sport and Cultural Transformation* (London: Routledge, 1992).

50. Gerard A. Akindes, "Football Bars: Urban Sub-Saharan Africa's Trans-local 'Stadiums,'" *International Journal of the History of Sport* 28, no. 15 (2011): 2176–90; Eriberto P. Lozada Jr., "Cosmopolitanism and Nationalism in Shanghai Sports," *City and Society* 18, no. 2 (2006): 207–31.

51. For example, W. M. Garraway, A. J. Lee, S. J. Hutton, E. B. A. W. Russell, and D. A. D. Macleod, "Impact of Professionalism on Injuries in Rugby Union," *British Journal of Sports Medicine* 34, no. 5 (2011): 348–51. The Hollywood film *Concussion* (Peter Landesman, dir., 2015) is a notably mainstream exposé of a problem that most sports governing bodies would prefer to keep quiet.

52. Patrick Laviolette, *Extreme Landscapes of Leisure: Not a Hap-Hazardous Sport* (Farnham, UK: Ashgate, 2011); "The Neo-flâneur amongst Irresistible Decay," in *Playgrounds and Battlefields: Critical Perspectives on Social Engagement,* ed. Francisco Martínez and Klemen Slabina (Tallinn, Estonia: ACTA Universitatis Tallinnensis), 243–70.

53. Ulrich Beck, *Risk Society: Towards a New Modernity* (Thousand Oaks, CA: Sage, 1992; first published 1986).

54. Francisco Martínez and Patrick Laviolette, "Trespass into the Liminal Urban Exploration in Estonia," *Anthropological Journal of European Cultures* 25, no. 2 (2016): 1–24.

55. Alex Pavlotski, "Visualising Parkour," PhD diss., School of Humanities and Social Sciences, La Trobe University, 2016.

56. Michael Atkinson and Kevin Young, *Deviance and Social Control in Sport* (Champaign, IL: Human Kinetics, 2008), 58–66.

57. Holly Thorpe and Belinda Wheaton, "'Generation X Games,' Action Sports and the Olympic Movement: Understanding the Cultural Politics of Incorporation," *Sociology* 45, no. 5 (2011): 830–47.

58. Eric W. Rothenbuhler, "The Living Room Celebration of the Olympic Games," *Journal of Communication* 38, no. 4 (1988): 61–81; Rothenbuhler, "The Olympics in the American Living Room: Celebration of a Media Event," in *The Olympic Movement and the Mass Media: Past, Present, and Future Issues, International Conference Proceedings,* ed. Roger C. Jackson and Thomas L. McPhail (Calgary: Hurford, 1987), 41–50.

59. Eric W. Rothenbuhler, *Ritual Communication: From Everyday Conversation to Mediated Ceremony* (Thousand Oaks, CA: Sage, 1998); Eric W. Rothenbuhler and Mihai Coman, eds., *Media Anthropology* (Newbury Park, CA: Sage, 2005).

60. John J. MacAloon, "Festival, Ritual, and Television," in Jackson and McPhail, *Olympic Movement and Mass Media,* 21–40.

61. Niko Besnier and Susan Brownell, "Rio's Festival in the Streets: How Does the 21st-Century Technology of Big-Screen TV Square with the Age-Old Human Penchant for Celebrations?" *Sapiens,* August 10, 2016, accessed August 10, 2016, http://www.sapiens.org/culture/rio-2016-olympic-festival/.

62. Daniel Dayan and Elihu Katz, *Media Events: The Live Broadcasting of History* (Cambridge, MA: Harvard University Press, 1992), 1–24.

63. Daniel Dayan, "Beyond Media Events," *Owning the Olympics: Narratives of the New China,* ed. Monroe E. Price and Daniel Dayan (Ann Arbor: University of Michigan Press, 2008), 391–401.

64. Benedict Anderson, *Imagined Communities: Reflections on the Origin and Spread of Nationalism* (London: Verso, 2016; first published 1983).

65. Jürgen Habermas, *The Structural Transformation of the Public Sphere: An Inquiry into a Category of Bourgeois Society,* trans. Thomas Burger (Cambridge, MA: MIT Press, 1989; first published 1962).

66. Susan Brownell, "Human Rights and the Beijing Olympics: Imagined Global Community and the Transnational Public Sphere," *British Journal of Sociology* 63, no. 2 (2012): 306–27.

67. Susan Brownell, "The Olympic Public Sphere: The London and Beijing Opening Ceremonies as Representative of Political Systems," *International Journal of the History of Sport* 30, no. 11 (2013): 1315–27.

68. Comment posted by Post-90 Zhao Xin, July 28, 2012, at 12:40:59, following Yang Ming, "Lundun aoyun kaimushi yinxiang" [Impressions of the London Olympic opening ceremony], July 28, 2012, accessed July 30, 2012, blog.sina.com.cn/s/blog_6f0c6a1f01015sz7.html?tj=1.

69. *Guardian* (London), "Rio Olympic Venues Already Falling into a State of Disrepair," February 10, 2017, accessed February 10, 2017, https://www.theguardian.com/sport/2017/feb/10/rio-olympic-venues-already-falling-into-a-state-of-disrepair.

70. Alan Tomlinson, "Olympic Legacies: Recurrent Rhetoric and Harsh Realities," *Contemporary Social Science* 9, no. 2 (2014): 137–58.

71. Gillian Evans, *London's Olympic Legacy: The Inside Track* (London: Palgrave Macmillan, 2016).

72. Susana Narotzky and Niko Besnier, "Crisis, Value, and Hope: Rethinking the Economy," *Current Anthropology* 55, no. S9 (2014): S4–S16.

73. Bronislaw Malinowski, *Argonauts of the Western Pacific: An Account of Native Enterprise and Adventure in the Archipelagoes of Melanesian New Guinea* (London: Routledge & Kegan Paul, 1922), 89, accessed August 16, 2016, https://archive.org/stream/argonautsofthewe032976mbp/argonautsofthewe032976mbp_djvu.txt.

74. Marcel Mauss, *The Gift,* ed. and trans. Jane I. Guyer (Chicago: University of Chicago Press, 2016; first published 1923–24), 76.

75. Eric R. Wolf, *Sons of the Shaking Earth* (Chicago: University of Chicago Press, 1959), 216.

76. Mauss, *Gift,* 63.

77. G. Whitney Azoy, *Buzkashi: Game and Power in Afghanistan* (Long Grove, IL: Waveland, 2011; first published 1982).

78. John Garnaut, "BHP the Target as Chinese Whispers Turn Into Anger," *Age* (Melbourne), August 28, 2008, accessed March 19, 2017, http://www.theage.com.au/business/bhp-the-target-as-chinese-whispers-turn-into-anger-20080827-443h.html.

79. United States of America Securities and Exchange Commission, release no. 74998, May 20, 2015, administrative proceeding file no. 3-16546 in the Matter of BHP Billiton Ltd. and BHP Plc Respondents, cease-and-desist order, accessed March 19, 2017, https://www.sec.gov/litigation/admin/2015/34-74998.pdf.

80. John J. MacAloon, "Scandal and Governance: Inside and Outside the IOC 2000 Commission," *Sport in Society* 14, no. 3 (2011): 292–308.

81. David I. Kertzer, *Ritual, Politics, and Power* (New Haven, CT: Yale University Press, 1988), 77–101.

82. Anna L. Tsing, "Inside the Economy of Appearances," *Public Culture* 12, no. 1 (2000): 115–44.

83. Ibid., 140.

84. John Horne and Wolfram Manzenreiter, "An Introduction to the Sociology of Mega-events," *Sociological Review* 54, no. S2 (2006): 1–24.

85. Ibid., 17.

CHAPTER SEVEN. SPORT, NATION, AND NATIONALISM

1. John MacAloon, "The Turn of Two Centuries: Sport and the Politics of Intercultural Relations," in *Sport . . . the Third Millennium: Proceedings of the International Symposium, Québec, Canada 21–25 May 1990*, ed. Fernand Landry, Marc Landry, and Magdaleine Yerlès (Sainte-Foy, Québec: Presses de l'Université Laval, 1991), 31–44, 42.

2. Bruce Kapferer, *Legends of People, Myths of State: Violence, Intolerance, and Political Culture in Sri Lanka and Australia* (Washington, DC: Smithsonian Institution Press, 1988); Michael Herzfeld, *The Social Production of Indifference: Exploring the Symbolic Roots of Western Bureaucracy* (Chicago: University of Chicago Press, 1992), 10–47.

3. Max Weber, *Economy and Society: An Outline of Interpretive Sociology* (Berkeley: University of California Press, 1978; first published 1922), 55.

4. Max Weber, "Politics as a Vocation," in *From Max Weber: Essays in Sociology*, ed. and trans. H. H. Gerth and C. Wright Mills (London: Routledge & Kegan Paul, 1948), 77–128, 82–83.

5. Akhil Gupta, "Blurred Boundaries: The Discourse of Corruption, the Culture of Politics, and the Imagined State," *American Ethnologist* 22, no. 2 (1995): 375–402.

6. Eric Wolf, *Pathways of Power: Building an Anthropology of the Modern World* (Berkeley: University of California Press, 2001), 320–34; Partha Chatterjee, *The Nation and Its Fragments: Colonial and Postcolonial Histories* (Princeton, NJ: Princeton University Press, 1993).

7. Michel Foucault, "Governmentality," in *The Foucault Effect: Studies in Governmentality*, ed. Graham Burchell, Colin Gordon, and Peter Miller (Chicago: University of Chicago Press, 1991; ch. first published 1978), 87–104, 103.

8. Ibid.

9. Michel Foucault, *Discipline and Punish: The Birth of the Prison*, trans. Alan Sheridan (New York: Vintage Books, 1997; first published 1995), 26.

10. Susan Brownell, *Training the Body for China: Sports in the Moral Order of the People's Republic* (Chicago: University of Chicago Press, 1995), 155–79, 147–49.

11. There is much lore about the "blood in the water" match. Some say the water was red; some say that was an exaggeration. Susan Brownell knew a spectator who was present and told her that the water was pink.

12. Benedict Anderson, *Imagined Communities: Reflections on the Origin and Spread of Nationalism* (London: Verso, 2016; first published 1983).

13. David R. Rowe, *The Unholy Trinity: Sport, Culture, and the Media* (Buckingham, UK: Open University Press, 1999), 22–24.

14. Steven Wells, "Dear America: You Can't Be World Champions If No One Else Takes Part," *Guardian* (London), September 18, 2008, accessed December 3, 2016, https://www.theguardian.com/sport/blog/2008/nov/18/american-sports-nfl-nba-mlb.

15. Lawrence A. Wenner, "The Superbowl Pregame Show: Cultural Fantasies and Political Subtext," in *Media, Sports, and Society,* ed. Lawrence A. Wenner (Newbury Park, CA: Sage, 1989), 157–79.

16. Michael Billig, *Banal Nationalism* (London: Sage, 1995).

17. Thomas F. Scanlon, *Greek and Roman Athletics: A Bibliography* (Chicago: Ares Publishers, 1984), 55–65. These numbers are based on a count by Susan Brownell.

18. Guo Xifen, *Zhongguo tiyushi* [The history of Chinese sports] (Shanghai: Shangwu Press, 1919). Other sport histories published before 1984 include Gunsun Hoh, *Physical Education in China Physical Education in China* (Shanghai: Commercial Press, 1926) and Xu Yongchang, *Zhongguo gudai tiyu* [Ancient Chinese sports] (Beijing: Beijing Shifan daxue chubanshe, 1983).

19. Susan Brownell provides a fuller argument about sport history and the Western intellectual tradition in *Beijing's Games: What the Olympics Mean to China* (Lanham, MD: Rowman & Littlefield, 2008), 19–47.

20. Hasan Bastani Rad, S. Amir Hosseini, and Haideh Saira, eds., *History of Sport in Iranzamin: The First International Simposium [sic] on History of Sport in Iran (1)* (Tehran: Iranian Olympic and Paralympic National Academy, November 2006), accessed March 1, 2017, www.olympicacademy.ir/olympicacademy_content/media/image/2008/11/1392_orig.pdf.

21. Carl Rommel, "Revolution, Play and Feeling: Assembling Emotionality, National Subjectivity and Football in Cairo, 1990–2013," PhD diss., Department of Anthropology and Sociology, School of Oriental and African Studies, University of London, 2015, 83–87.

22. Ibid., 89; Achille Mbembe, "Provisional Notes on the Postcolony," *Africa* 62, no. 1 (1992): 3–38.

23. Benedict Anderson, *A Life beyond the Boundaries* (London: Verso, 2016), 127–28.

24. ConIFA website, accessed November 30, 2016, www.conifa.org/en/about-us/faq/.

25. Multiple spellings of *Uighur* are in use; we have used the spelling preferred by *Merriam-Webster's Collegiate Dictionary.* The Chinese government prefers *Uygur,* and thus we use that spelling here, in the region's official name.

26. David Vine, *Island of Shame: The Secret History of the U.S. Military Base on Diego Garcia* (Princeton, NJ: Princeton University Press, 2011; first published 2009).

27. María José Riquelme del Valle, "Inside the CONIFA World Cup for Unrecognised States," Al Jazeera, June 6, 2016, accessed November 30, 2016, http://www.aljazeera.com/indepth/features/2016/06/conifa-word-cup-unrecognised-states-160605131006079.html.

28. Michael Herzfeld, *Ours Once More: Folklore, Ideology, and the Making of Modern Greece* (Austin: University of Texas Press, 1982), 97–122.

29. Sp. P. Lambros and N. G. Polites, *The Olympic Games, B.C. 776–A.D. 1896* (Athens: C. Beck; New York: American Olympic Committee, 1896).

30. Konstantinos Georgiadis, *Die ideengeschichtliche Grundlage der Erneuerung der Olympischen Spiele im 19. Jahrhundert in Griechenland und ihre Umsetzung 1896 in Athen* [The intellectual-historical foundations of the revival of the Olympic Games in the nineteenth century in Greece and their 1896 transplantation into Athens] (Kassel, Germany: Agon-Sportverlag, 2000), 70–79; Konstantinos Georgiadis, *Olympic Revival: The Revival of the Olympic Games in Modern Times* (Athens: Ekdotike Athenon, 2003), 77.

31. Eric Hobsbawm, introduction to *The Invention of Tradition,* ed. Eric Hobsbawm and Terence Ranger (Cambridge: Cambridge University Press, 1983), 1–14.

32. Ibid., 6.

33. Ibid., 3-4.

34. Eric Hobsbawm, "Mass-Producing Traditions: Europe, 1870–1914," in Hobsbawm and Ranger, *Invention of Tradition,* 263–308.

35. Stéphane Rennesson, *Les coulisses du muay thai: Anthropologie d'un art martial en Thaïlande* [Muay thai's backstage: ethnography of a martial art in Thailand] (Paris: Les Indes Savantes, 2012); Pattana Kitiarsa, "Of Men and Monks: The Boxing-Buddhism Nexus and the Production of National Manhood in Contemporary Thailand," *New Mandala: New Perspectives on Southeast Asia,* October 2, 2013, accessed January 20, 2017, http://www.newmandala.org/pattana-kitiarsa-on-thai-boxing/.

36. Pattana Kitiarsa, "The Fall of Thai Rocky," *Everyday Life in Southeast Asia,* ed. Kathleen M. Adams and Kathleen A. Gillogy (Bloomington: Indiana University Press, 2011), 195–205.

37. Peter T. Vail, "Modern *Muay Thai* Mythology," *Crosscurrent* 12, no. 2 (1998): 75–95.

38. Many other tangible cultural forms that are today viewed as representing the nation are the product of similar histories. One striking example is Argentine tango, which originated as the pastime of rural underclass Argentinians and was originally looked down upon by the urban elites for its exuberant sexuality and immorality, until Europeans and North Americans in the Roaring Twenties began dancing it, at which point Argentine elites reclaimed it as their national dance. Marta E. Savigliano, *Tango and the Political Economy of Passion* (Boulder, CO: Westview, 1995).

39. Roland Renson, "Safeguarding Ludodiversity: Chances and Challenges in the Promotion and Protection of Traditional Movement Culture," *East Asian Sport Thoughts* 3 (2004): 139–58, 139.

40. Thomas F. Carter, "A Relaxed State of Affairs? On Leisure, Tourism, and Cuban Identity," in *The Discipline of Leisure: Embodying Cultures of "Recreation,"* ed. Simon Coleman and Tamara Kohn (Oxford: Berghahn, 2007), 127–45.

41. Thomas F. Carter, "Of Spectacular Phantasmal Desires: Tourism and the Cuban State's Complicity in Its Commodification of Its Citizens," *Leisure Studies* 27, no. 3 (2008): 241–57.

42. Sulayman Khalaf, "Poetics and Politics of Newly Invented Traditions in the Gulf: Camel Racing in the United Arab Emirates," *Ethnology* 9, no. 3 (2000): 243–61.

43. Anderson, *Imagined Communities*, 7. Works that frame nationalism in a gender context include, among many others, Nira Yuval-Davis, *Gender and Nation* (London: Sage, 1997); Anne McClintock, Aamir Mufti, and Ella Shohat, eds., *Dangerous Liaisons: Gender, Nation, and Postcolonial Perspectives* (Minneapolis: University of Minnesota Press, 1997); Kumari Jayawardena, *Feminism and Nationalism in the Third World* (London: Zed, 1986).

44. This is the case of changing gender expectations of Korean athletes. See Rachael Miyung Joo, *Transnational Sport: Gender, Media, and Global Korea* (Durham, NC: Duke University Press, 2012).

45. Tani E. Barlow, "Theorizing Woman: *Funü, Guojia, Jiating* (Chinese Woman, Chinese State, Chinese Family)," in *Body, Subject and Power in China,* ed. Angela Zito and Tani Barlow (Chicago: University of Chicago Press, 1994), 254, 265.

46. Andrew Morris, *Marrow of the Nation: A History of Sport and Physical Culture in Republican China* (Berkeley: University of California Press, 2004), 26.

47. Edward Said, *Orientalism* (London: Penguin, 2003; first published 1978).

48. Cao Xiangjun, *Tiyu Gailun* [General theory of physical culture] (Beijing: Beijing Institute of Physical Education Press, 1985), 139.

49. Alan M. Klein, *Baseball on the Border: A Tale of Two Laredos* (Princeton, NJ: Princeton University Press, 1997).

50. Ibid., 34–65, 151–69.

51. Toby Miller, Geoffrey Lawrence, Jim McKay, and David Rowe, "Modifying the Sign: Sport and Globalization," *Social Text* 17, no. 3 (1999): 15–33.

52. This section was published in slightly different form in Niko Besnier and Susan Brownell, "Your Olympic Team May Be an Illusion," *Sapiens,* August 4, 2016, accessed August 4, 2016, http://www.sapiens.org/culture/olympics-brawn-drain/.

53. Stefan Nestler, "Qatar: Buying Their Way to Sporting Success," *DW,* February 4, 2015, accessed November 30, 2016, http://www.dw.com/en/qatar-buying-their-way-to-sporting-success/a-18233576.

54. *DT News,* "Record 30 Athletes for 2016," May 12, 2016, accessed November 30, 2016, http://www.newsofbahrain.com/viewNews.php?ppId=20360&TYPE=Posts&pid=&MNU=&SUB=.

55. US Army World Class Athlete Program website, accessed November 30, 2016, http://www.armymwr.com/wcap/default.aspx.

56. Tom Banse, "Run, Soldier, Run! From Kenya, to US, to Rio Olympics," *OPB,* accessed November 30, 2016, http://www.opb.org/news/article/soldiers-kenya-us-rio-olympics/.

57. BBC News, "Rio Olympics 2016: Refugee Olympic Team Competed as 'Equal Human Beings,'" August 21, 2016, accessed November 30, 2016, http://www.bbc.com/sport/olympics/37037273.

58. Ulf Hannerz, *Transnational Connections: Culture, People, Places* (New York: Routledge, 1996), 2–6.

59. Vida Bajc, "Olympic Dilemmas," in *Surveilling and Securing the Olympics: From Tokyo 1964 to London 2012 and Beyond,* ed. Vida Bajc (New York: Palgrave Macmillan, 2016), 387–98.

60. This discussion of medical surveillance at the Olympic Games is drawn from Susan Brownell and Niko Besnier, "Zika at the Rio Games: Pandemic or Panic?," *Sapiens,* August 12, 2016, accessed August 12, 2016, www.sapiens.org/culture/olympics-zika-pandemic/.

61. Andrzej Zieliński, "Evidence for Excessive Incidence of Infectious Diseases at Mass Gatherings with Special Reference to Sporting Events," *Przegląd Epidemiologiczny/Epidemiological Review* 63, no. 3 (2009): 343–51.

62. Or, occasionally, religious events. The Kumbh Mela festival of ritual bathing in India is the world's largest mass gathering: it lasts fifty-five days and rotates between four sacred river sites every three years. An estimated all-time high of 120 million pilgrims visited the 2013 festival in Allahabad, living in a five-acre (two-hectare) temporary settlement of tents made from canvas or corrugated tin. Website of 2013 Kumbh Mela, accessed March 27, 2017, http://kumbhmelaallahabad.gov.in/english/index.html.

63. B. McCloskey, T. Endericks, M. Catchpole, M. Zambon, J. McLauchlin, N. Shetty, R. Manuel, et al., "London 2012 Olympic and Paralympic Games: Public Health Surveillance and Epidemiology," *Lancet* 383, no. 9934 (2014): 2083–89.

64. Embassy of the People's Republic of China in the United States of America, "China's Anti-terrorism Force in Action Ahead of Olympics," June 20, 2008, accessed December 6, 2016, http://www.china-embassy.org/eng/xw/t449403.htm; Yuval Azulai, "Israeli Security Co Ready for Rio Olympics," *Globes,* July 31, 2016, accessed December 7, 2016, http://www.globes.co.il/en/article-israeli-security-co-ready-for-rio-olympics-1001142963.

65. Erika Robb Larkins, "The Spectacle of Security in Olympic Rio," *Anthropology News* 53, no. 6 (2012), accessed June 16, 2017, http://onlinelibrary.wiley.com/doi/10.1111/j.1556-3502.2012.53601.x/full/.

66. Samuel R. Delany, *Times Square Red, Times Square Blue* (New York: New York University Press, 1999).

67. Gregory Mitchell, "Evangelical Ecstasy Meets Feminist Fury: Sex Trafficking, Moral Panics, and Homonationalism during Global Sporting Events," *GLQ* 22, no. 3 (2016): 325–57.

68. Elizabeth Bernstein, "Militarized Humanitarianism Meets Carceral Feminism: The Politics of Sex, Rights, and Freedom in Contemporary Antitrafficking Campaigns," *Signs* 36, no. 1 (2010): 45–72.

69. Based on Susan Brownell's interview with a member of a volunteer search-and-rescue team that provides surveillance at Super Bowls, July 2016.

70. Hannerz, *Transnational Connections,* 6.

1. International Olympic Committee, Olympic Charter, in force from August 2, 2015, p. 13, accessed November 5, 2016, https://stillmed.olympic.org/Documents /olympic_charter_en.pdf.

2. Cathal J. Nolan, *Greenwood Encyclopedia of International Relations* (Santa Barbara, CA: ABC-CLIO, 2002), s.v. "Westphalian System."

3. The foundational text of transnationalism in the context of migrations is Linda Basch, Nina Glick Schiller, and Cristina Szanton Blanc, *Nations Unbound: Transnational Projects, Postcolonial Predicaments and Deterritorialized Nation-States* (Amsterdam: Gordon & Breach, 1994).

4. David Harvey, *The Condition of Postmodernity* (Oxford: Blackwell, 1990); Anthony Giddens, *The Consequences of Modernity* (Cambridge: Polity, 1990); Arjun Appadurai, *Modernity at Large: Cultural Dimensions of Globalization* (Minneapolis: University of Minnesota Press, 1996).

5. Richard Giulianotti and Roland Robertson, "The Globalization of Football: A Study in the Glocalization of the 'Serious Life,'" *British Journal of Sociology* 55, no. 4 (2004): 545–68, 546.

6. The concept of imagined community, discussed extensively in chapter 7, is here given a broader meaning from the one Benedict Anderson intended, since it is extended beyond the bounds of the nation-state, which was Anderson's focus.

7. The term *glocalization* is generally associated with the work of sociologist Roland Robertson. See, for example, "Glocalisation: Time-Space and Homogeneity-Heterogeneity," in *Global Modernities,* ed. Mike Featherstone, Scott Lash, and Roland Robertson (London: Sage, 1995), 25–44.

8. Roger Levermore and Adrian Budd, *Sport and International Relations: An Emerging Relationship* (London: Routledge, 2004).

9. Albert G. Spalding, *America's National Game* (Lincoln: University of Nebraska Press, 1992; first published 1911).

10. Thomas W. Zeiler, *Ambassadors in Pinstripes: The Spalding World Baseball Tour and the Birth of the American Empire* (Lanham, MD: Rowman & Littlefield, 2006).

11. Aaron Beacom, *International Diplomacy and the Olympic Movement: The New Mediators* (Basingstoke, UK: Palgrave Macmillan, 2012).

12. Nicholas Griffin, *Ping-Pong Diplomacy: The Secret History behind the Game That Changed the World* (New York: Scribner, 2014).

13. Thomas F. Carter and John Sugden, "The USA and Sporting Diplomacy: Comparing and Contrasting the Cases of Table Tennis with China and Baseball with Cuba in the 1970s," *International Relations* 26, no. 1 (2012): 101–21, 104.

14. Xu Guoqi, *Olympic Dreams: China and Sports, 1895–2008* (Cambridge, MA: Harvard University Press, 2008), 117–64; Susan Brownell, "'Sport and Politics Don't Mix': China's Relationship with the IOC during the Cold War," in *East Plays West: Essays on Sport and the Cold War,* ed. Stephen Wagg and David Andrews (London: Routledge, 2007), 261–78.

15. The term *soft power* was coined by political scientist Joseph S. Nye Jr., *Bound to Lead: The Changing Nature of American Power* (New York: Basic Books, 1990).

16. Joseph S. Nye Jr., *Soft Power: The Means to Success in World Politics* (New York: Public Affairs, 2004), 47.

17. The Beijing Olympics are discussed in the context of the pursuit of soft power in East Asia in Susan Brownell, "'Brand China' in the Olympic Context: Communications Challenges of China's Soft Power Initiative," *Javnost* 20, no. 4 (2013): 65–82.

18. Hugh Douglass Vondracek, "China's Stadium Diplomacy and Its Determinants: A Typological Analysis of Soft Power," master's thesis, University of Glasgow, 2015, 16–18, accessed March 27, 2017, http://endeavour.gla.ac.uk/58/1/2015Vondrac ekMScdissertation.pdf; Liluntesi, "Feizhou Bei = Zhonguo 'tiyu waijiao' 1.85yi juanjian 3 qiuchang!" [African Cup = Chinese "stadium diplomacy" donates 185 million to build 3 stadiums!], *Wangyi tiyu,* February 8, 2017, accessed March 27, 2017, http://sports.163.com/17/0208/06/CCO13IL400058781.html.

19. Arturo Escobar, *Encountering Development: The Making and Unmaking of the Third World* (Princeton, NJ: Princeton University Press, 1995); James Ferguson, *The Anti-politics Machine: "Development," Depoliticization, and Bureaucratic Power in Lesotho* (Minneapolis: University of Minnesota Press, 1994; first published 1990); David Mosse, "The Anthropology of International Development," *Annual Review of Anthropology* 42 (2013): 227–46; Tanya Murray Li, *The Will to Improve: Governmentality, Development, and the Practice of Politics* (Durham, NC: Duke University Press, 2007).

20. Established in 1978, the charter has been revised, but Article 1 remains the same. UNESCO International Charter of Physical Education and Sport (1991), accessed June 15, 2017, http://unesdoc.unesco.org/images/0023/002354/235409e .pdf.

21. United Nations Convention on the Rights of the Child (1989), accessed March 27, 2017, http://www.unicef.org.uk/Documents/Publication-pdfs/UNCRC_ PRESS200910web.pdf.

22. Sport for Development and Peace International Working Group, *Harnessing the Power of Sport and Peace: Recommendations to Governments* (2008), UN website, accessed March 27, 2017, http://www.un.org/wcm/webdav/site/sport/shared/sport /pdfs/SDP%20IWG/Final%20SDP%20IWG%20Report.pdf. In May 2017, Annan's successor, Antonio Guterres, announced that the United Nations would close UNOSDP because it had established a stronger partnership with the IOC, whose goals would allegedly duplicate those of UNOSDP.

23. David J. Lewis, "NGOs, Donors, and the State in Bangladesh," in "The Role of NGOs: Charity and Empowerment," ed. Jude L. Fernando and Alan W. Heston, special issue, *Annals of the American Academy of Political and Social Sciences* 554, no. 1 (1997): 33–45.

24. Victoria Bernal and Inderpal Grewal, "The NGO Form: Feminist Struggles, States, and Neoliberalism," in *Theorizing NGOs: States, Feminisms, and Neoliberalism,* ed. Victoria Bernal and Inderpal Grewal (Durham, NC: Duke University Press, 2014), 1–18.

25. William F. Fisher, "The Politics and Antipolitics of NGO Practices," *Annual Review of Anthropology* 26 (1997): 439–64.

26. Alexander Wolff, "Still the Boss," *Sports Illustrated*, September 26, 2011, accessed September 30, 2016, http://www.si.com/vault/2011/09/26/106112006/still-the-boss.

27. Holly Collison, *Youth and Sport for Development: The Seduction of Football in Liberia* (Basingstoke, UK: Palgrave Macmillan, 2016).

28. International Sports Alliance website, accessed November 30, 2016, http://www.isa-youth.org/approach/.

29. John Sugden, "Teaching and Playing Sport for Conflict Resolution and Co-existence in Israel," *International Journal of the Sociology of Sport* 41, no. 2 (2006): 221–40; James Wallis and John Lambert, "Reflections from the Field: Challenges in Managing Agendas and Expectations around Football for Peace in Israel," in *Global Sport-for-Development: Critical Perspectives,* ed. Nico Schulenkorf and Daryl Adair (Basingstoke, UK: Palgrave Macmillan, 2013), 99–114; F4P's Israel activities have since been taken over by other SDP NGOs.

30. Tamir Sorek, *Arab Soccer in a Jewish State* (Cambridge: Cambridge University Press, 2007); Hani Zubida, "We Are One! Or Are We? Football Fandom and Ethno-national Identity in Israel," in *New Ethnographies of Football in Europe: People, Passions, Politics,* ed. Alexandra Schwell, Nina Szogs, Małgorzata Z. Kowalska, and Michal Buchowski (Basingstoke, UK: Palgrave Macmillan, 2016), 75–96.

31. Dave Zirin, "After Latest Incident, Israel's Future in FIFA Is Uncertain," *Nation,* March 3, 2014, accessed November 30, 2016, https://www.thenation.com/article/after-latest-incident-israels-future-fifa-uncertain/; Al Jazeera, "Israel Blocks Olympics-Bound Palestinian from Travel," August 2, 2016, accessed August 2, 2016, http://www.aljazeera.com/news/2016/08/israel-blocks-olympics-bound-palestinian-travel-160802202751580.html.

32. Barak Ravid, "Israel Steps Up Diplomatic Action as Fears Grow Over FIFA Suspension," *Haaretz,* May 13, 2015, accessed May 13, 2015, http://www.haaretz.com/israel-news/.premium-1.656254.

33. Faris Giacaman, "Can We Talk? The Middle East 'Peace Industry,'" *Electronic Intifada,* August 20, 2009, accessed August 2, 2016, https://electronicintifada.net/content/can-we-talk-middle-east-peace-industry/8402.

34. Patrick McGovern, "Globalization or Internationalization? Foreign Footballers in the English League, 1946–95," *Sociology* 36, no. 1 (2002), 23–42; Matthew Taylor, "Global Players? Football, Migration and Globalization, c. 1930–2000," *Historical Social Research* 31, no. 1 (2006): 7–30.

35. Major League Baseball, "Opening Day Rosters Feature Record 259 Players Born Outside the U.S.," press release, accessed July 3, 2017, http://m.mlb.com/news/article/222084690/opening-day-rosters-feature-record-259-players-born-outside-the-us/.

36. The ethnic diversity of important teams has become a deeply divisive issue playing into the hands of various political positions; for example, on the politicization of the French national soccer team at various moments in recent history, see

Stéphane Beaud, *Traîtres à la nation? Un autre regard sur la grève des Bleus en Afrique du Sud* [Traitor of the nation? Another look at the French team's strike in South Africa] (Paris: La Découverte, 2011); Paul A. Silverstein, "Sporting Faith: Islam, Soccer, and the French Nation-State," *Social Text* 18, no. 4 (2000): 25–53.

37. Karen J. Brison, "Gendered Modernities among Rural Indigenous Fijians," in *Super Girls, Gangstas, Freeters, and Xenomaniacs: Gender and Modernity in Global Youth Culture*, ed. Susan Dewey and Karen J. Brison (Syracuse, NY: Syracuse University Press, 2012), 85–103, 98–99.

38. James Ferguson, *Expectations of Modernity: Myths and Meanings of Urban Life on the Zambian Copperbelt* (Berkeley: University of California Press, 1999); and many others.

39. See, for example, Niko Besnier, *On the Edge of the Global: Modern Anxieties in a Pacific Island Nation* (Stanford, CA: Stanford University Press, 2011); Charles Piot, *Nostalgia for the Future: West Africa after the Cold War* (Chicago: University of Chicago Press, 2010); Francis Nyamnjoh, "Cameroonian Bushfalling: Negotiation of Identity and Belonging in Fiction and Ethnography," *American Ethnologist* 38, no. 4 (2011): 701–13.

40. Niko Besnier, "The Athlete's Body and the Global Condition: Tongan Rugby Players in Japan," *American Ethnologist* 39, no. 4 (2012): 491–510, 501–2.

41. Thomas F. Carter, *In Foreign Fields: The Politics and Experience of Transnational Sport Migration* (London: Pluto, 2011); Pierre Lanfranchi and Matthew Taylor, *Moving with the Ball: The Migration of Professional Footballers* (Oxford: Berg, 2001). On the Dominican Republic, see Alan M. Klein, *Dominican Baseball: New Pride, Old Prejudice* (Philadelphia: Temple University Press, 2014); Rob Ruck, *The Tropic of Baseball: Baseball in the Dominican Republic* (Lincoln: University of Nebraska Press, 1998; first published 1991). On West Africa, see Paul Darby, "The New Scramble for Africa: African Football Labour Migration to Europe," *European Sports History Review* 32, no. 3 (2000), 217–44; Raffaele Poli, *Les migrations internationales des footballeurs: Trajectoires de joueurs camerounais en Suisse* [Soccer athletes' international migrations: Cameroonian players' trajectories in Switzerland] (Neuchâtel, Switzerland: Éditions CIES, 2004).

42. Manuel Schotté, "La condition athlétique: Ethnographie du quotidien de coureurs professionnels immigrés" [The athletic condition: Ethnography of the everyday life of immigrant professional runners], *Genèses*, no. 71 (2008): 71–105.

43. Sine Agergaard and Nina Clara Tiesler, eds., *Women, Soccer and Transnational Migration* (Abingdon, UK: Routledge, 2014).

44. Uroš Kovač, "Football Dreams, Pentecostalism and Migration in Southwest Cameroon," GLOBALSPORT website, September 7, 2016, accessed September 7, 2016, http://global-sport.eu/football-dreams-pentecostalism-and-migration-in-southwest-cameroon.

45. Besnier, "Athlete's Body and Global Condition."

46. Mike K. Peters, "Being a Good Friend: Practices of Borrowing and Lending among Kenyan Runners in Japan," GLOBALSPORT website, July 30, 2015, accessed July 30, 2015, http://global-sport.eu/practices-of-borrowing-and-lending-money-

among-kenyan-runners-in-japan; Daniel Guinness and Niko Besnier, "Economies of Hope and Rugby Dreams in Rural Fiji," GLOBALSPORT website, April 22, 2016, accessed April 22, 2016, http://global-sport.eu/economies-of-hope-and-rugby-dreams-in-rural-fiji.

47. Niko Besnier, "Qu'est-ce qu'une frontière pour un sportif international?" [What is a border for an international athlete?], in *Dessiner les frontières,* ed. Michelle Auzanneau and Luca Greco (Paris: ENS Éditions, forthcoming).

48. Kovač, "Football Dreams."

49. Carter, *In Foreign Fields,* 124–26.

50. Guinness and Besnier, "Economies of Hope."

51. Douglas Kwaw Koi Thompson, "Success and Failure on the Borga Path: Ghanaian and Nigerian Football Migrants in Eastern and Central Europe," unpublished fieldwork plan, GLOBALSPORT ERC project, University of Amsterdam, 2014; some of the details have been obscured to protect anonymity.

52. Sine Agergaard and Christian Ungruhe, "Ambivalent Precarity: Career Trajectories and Temporalities in Highly Skilled Sports Labor Migration from West Africa to Northern Europe," *Anthropology of Work Review* 37, no. 2 (2016): 67–78; Paweł Banaś, "Playing Football on the Margins: West African Football Players in Poland," GLOBALSPORT website, September 25, 2016, accessed September 25, 2016, http://global-sport.eu/playing-football-on-the-margins-west-african-football-players-in-poland.

53. Klein, *Dominican Baseball,* 69–90.

54. Foot Solidaire website, accessed December 6, 2016, http://www.footsolidaire .org. The Palermo protocols are designed "to Prevent, Suppress and Punish Trafficking in Persons Especially Women and Children, supplementing the United Nations Convention against Transnational Organized Crime," ratified by the UN General Assembly in 2000. Accessed December 6, 2016, http://www.ohchr.org/EN /ProfessionalInterest/Pages/ProtocolTraffickingInPersons.aspx.

55. See Carter, *In Foreign Fields,* 152–79, for a discussion on this topic. Although it is a work of fiction, the French feature film *Mercenaire* (Sasha Wolff, dir., 2016) tells the story of a young Wallis Islander who grows up in New Caledonia playing rugby and is recruited by a devious agent. The agent lies about the young man's weight to a French team manager, who fires him on the spot as the young player arrives in France. He then tries to fend for himself in a fifth-division team in an impoverished provincial town, but the agent violently hounds him to force him to reimburse his expenses. See Niko Besnier, "From the Pacific Islands to France: Migration, Hope and Deceit in the Rugby Industry," *The Conversation,* October 21, 2016, accessed October 21, 2016, https://theconversation.com/from-the-pacific-islands-to-france-migration-hope-and-deceit-in-the-rugby-industry-67343.

56. Elizabeth Bernstein, "Militarized Humanitarianism Meets Carceral Feminism: The Politics of Sex, Rights, and Freedom in Contemporary Antitrafficking Campaigns," *Signs* 36, no. 1 (2010): 45–71.

57. For example, a news documentary that has garnered considerable attention tells the story of underage soccer players from Liberia, Ghana, and Sierra Leone

being sent to play in Laos and kept under miserable conditions; among the interviewees is the mother of one of the "trafficked" boys, who affirms that the boy should stay where he is. Piers Edwards, "Underage African Footballers 'Trafficked' to Laos," *BBC News*, July 21, 2016, accessed December 6, 2016, http://www.bbc.com/news/world-africa-33595804.

58. James Esson, "Better Off at Home? Rethinking Responses to Trafficked West African Footballers in Europe," *Journal of Ethnic and Migration Studies* 41, no. 3 (2014): 512–30.

59. Paul Darby, Gerard Akindes, and Matthew Kirwin, "Football Academies and the Migration of African Football Labor to Europe," *Journal of Sport and Social Issues* 31, no. 2 (2007): 143–61; Klein, *Dominican Baseball.*

60. James Esson, "A Body and a Dream at a Vital Conjuncture: Ghanaian Youth, Uncertainty and the Allure of Football," *Geoforum* 47 (June 2013): 84–92.

61. For example, D. R., "A Looming Brawn Drain," *Economist,* December 18, 2014, accessed November 30, 2016, http://www.economist.com/blogs/gametheory/2014/12/baseball-cuba. The term *brawn drain* was coined by John Bale in *The Brawn Drain: Foreign Student-Athletes in American Universities* (Urbana: University of Illinois Press, 1991).

62. Daniel Guinness and Niko Besnier, "Nation, Nationalism, and Sport: Fijian Rugby in the Local-Global Nexus," *Anthropological Quarterly* 89, no. 4 (2016): 1109–42; Daniel Guinness, "The Battle for Talent? Sport and Contesting Masculinity," GLOBALSPORT website, March 19, 2015, accessed March 19, 2015, http://globalsport.eu/the-battle-for-talent-sport-and-contested-nationality.

63. Tales Azzoni, "Olympic Dream: Move to Brazil Pays Off for Gui," *San Diego Union Tribune*, July 14, 2012, accessed November 30, 2016, http://www.sandiegouniontribune.com/sdut-olympic-dream-move-to-brazil-pays-off-of-gui-2012jul14-story.html.

64. Michael C. Howard, *Fiji: Race and Politics in an Island State* (Vancouver: University of British Columbia Press, 2004), 141–45. More generally, Cynthia Enloe, *Bananas, Beaches and Bases: Making Feminist Sense of International Politics,* 2nd ed. (Berkeley: University of California Press, 2014; first published 1989); Heather Streets, *Martial Races: The Military, Race and Masculinity in British Imperial Culture, 1857–1914* (Manchester: Manchester University Press, 2004).

65. Teresia K. Teaiwa, "Articulated Cultures: Militarism and Masculinities in Fiji during the Mid-1990s," *Fijian Studies* 3, no. 2 (2005): 201–22.

66. Paul Amar, *Global South to the Rescue: Emerging Humanitarian Superpowers and Globalizing Rescue Industries* (Abingdon, UK: Routledge, 2012), 42–44; Yoko Kanemasu and Gyozo Molnar, "Private Military and Security Labour Migration: The Case of Fiji," *International Migration* 55 (2017).

67. James Ferguson, *Global Shadows: Africa in the Neoliberal World Order* (Durham, NC: Duke University Press, 2006); Anna Tsing, *Friction: An Ethnography of Global Connection* (Princeton, NJ: Princeton University Press, 2005).

68. The discussion in the rest of this section is a rewritten version of materials published in Susan Brownell and Niko Besnier, "Sport Mega-events and Global Politi-

cal Economy," *Anthropology News* 57, nos. 7–8 (2016): 16–17; Brownell and Besnier, "Do the Olympics Make Economic Sense?," *Sapiens,* August 16, 2016, accessed August 16, 2016, http://www.sapiens.org/culture/olympics-gift-economy/.

69. Franck Latty, "Les Jeux Olympiques et le droit international: Rendez-vous manqués et rencontres du troisième type" [Olympic Games and international law: Missed appointments and encounters of the third kind], *Annuaire français de relations internationales* 10 (2009): 1–16.

70. John Horne and Wolfram Manzenreiter, "Global Governance in World Sport and the 2002 World Cup Korea/Japan," in *Japan, Korea and the 2002 World Cup,* ed. John Horne and Wolfram Manzenreiter (New York: Routledge, 2002), 1–26. They cite figures from the 2000 Big Count; the most recent one in 2006 revealed similar numbers. FIFA, "FIFA Big Count 2006: 270 million people active in football," May 31, 2007, accessed December 5, 2016, www.fifa.com/media/news/y=2007/m=5/news=fifa-big-count-2006-270-million-people-active-football-529882.html.

71. David Owen, "IOC Broadcasting Revenues Set to Top $4.1 Billion in Sochi-Rio Quadrennium," *Inside the Games,* September 9, 2013, accessed November 30, 2016, http://www.insidethegames.biz/articles/1015932/ioc-broadcasting-revenues-set-to-top-4-1-billion-in-sochi-rio-quadrennium; *Sportcal,* "Olympic Games Set to Break $8bn Revenues Barrier in Four-Year Cycle Ending with London 2012," July 19, 2012, accessed March 27, 2017, http://www.sportcal.com/News/PressReleases/66341; David Owen, "TOP Programme Breaks the $1 Billion Barrier," *Inside the Games,* September 9, 2013, accessed November 30, 2016, http://www.insidethegames.biz/articles/1015935/exclusive-top-programme-breaks-the-1-billion-barrier.

72. "The Olympic Partner Programme," IOC website, accessed August 20, 2017, https://www.olympic.org/sponsors.

73. Horne and Manzenreiter, "Global Governance in World Sport."

74. Mei Fong, "Crowding China's Red Carpet," *Wall Street Journal,* July 16, 2008, accessed November 30, 2016, http://www.wsj.com/articles/SB121615369621055709.

75. US Department of Justice, "Nine FIFA Officials and Five Corporate Executives Indicted for Racketeering Conspiracy and Corruption," May 27, 2015, accessed November 30, 2016, https://www.justice.gov/opa/pr/nine-fifa-officials-and-five-corporate-executives-indicted-racketeering-conspiracy-and.

76. Jeré Longman, "Sepp Blatter Blames U.S. and England for FIFA Arrests," *New York Times,* May 30, 2015, accessed November 30, 2016, http://www.nytimes.com/2015/05/31/sports/soccer/sepp-blatter-blames-us-and-england-for-fifa-arrests.html.

EPILOGUE: SPORT FOR ANTHROPOLOGY

1. Robert Kitson, "Workers' Welfare Becomes First Casualty of Pacific Islands Gold Rush," *Guardian* (London), November 18, 2016, accessed November 25, 2016, https://www.theguardian.com/sport/2016/nov/18/pacific-islands-rugby-union-fiji-samoa-tonga.

SELECTED BIBLIOGRAPHY

For overviews by the authors of the state of the field in sport anthropology and the social history of sport, along with complete bibliographies, please consult these sources:

Besnier, Niko, and Susan Brownell. "Sport, Modernity, and the Body." *Annual Review of Anthropology* 41 (2012): 443–59.

Brownell, Susan. "Sport since 1750." In *The Cambridge History of the World,* edited by Merry Wiesner-Hanks, vol. 7, part 2, *Production, Connection, and Destruction, 1750–Present,* edited by Kenneth Pomeranz and J.R. McNeill, 225–48. Cambridge: Cambridge University Press, 2015.

Carter, Thomas. "On the Need for an Anthropological Approach to Sport." *Identities* 9, no. 3 (2002): 405–22.

The following selected bibliography lists English-language works in anthropology, sociology, and social history published since 2000 to which we make reference in the chapters. Some references are to edited books and journal issues that include works we have cited in the text.

Agergaard, Sine, and Nina Cara Teisler, eds. *Women, Soccer and Transnational Migration.* Abingdon, UK: Routledge, 2014.

Akindes, Gerard A. "Football Bars: Urban Sub-Saharan Africa's Trans-local 'Stadiums.'" *International Journal of the History of Sport* 28, no. 15 (2011): 2176–90.

Alegi, Peter. *African Soccerscapes: How a Continent Changed the World's Game.* Athens: Ohio University Press, 2010.

Allison, Lincoln, ed. *Taking Sport Seriously.* Aachen, Germany: Meyer & Meyer, 2010.

Alter, Joseph S. *Gandhi's Body: Sex, Diet, and the Politics of Nationalism.* Philadelphia: University of Pennsylvania Press, 2000.

Anderson, Eric. *In the Game: Gay Athletes and the Cult of Masculinity.* Albany: State University of New York Press, 2005.

Bajc, Vida, ed. *Surveilling and Securing the Olympics: From Tokyo 1964 to London 2012 and Beyond.* New York: Palgrave Macmillan, 2016.

Beacom, Aaron. *International Diplomacy and the Olympic Movement: The New Mediators.* Basingstoke, UK: Palgrave Macmillan, 2012.

Behringer, Wolfgang. "Arena and Pall Mall: Sport in the Early Modern Period." *German History* 27, no. 3 (2009): 331–57.

Besnier, Niko. "The Athlete's Body and the Global Condition: Tongan Rugby Players in Japan." *American Ethnologist* 39, no. 4 (2012): 491–510.

Boyle, Raymond, and Richard Haynes. *Power Play: Sport, Media, and Popular Culture.* Edinburgh: Edinburgh University Press, 2009.

Brownell, Susan. *Beijing's Games: What the Olympics Mean to China.* Lanham, MD: Rowman & Littlefield, 2008.

———. "'Brand China' in the Olympic Context: Communications Challenges of China's Soft Power Initiative." *Javnost* 20, no. 4 (2013): 65–82.

———, ed. *From Athens to Beijing: West Meets East in the Olympic Games.* Vol. 1, *Sport, the Body, and Humanism in Ancient Greece and China.* New York: Greekworks, 2013.

———. "The Olympic Public Sphere: The London and Beijing Opening Ceremonies as Representative of Political Systems." *International Journal of the History of Sport* 30, no. 11 (2013): 1315–27.

———, ed. *The 1904 Anthropology Days and Olympic Games: Sport, Race, and American Imperialism.* Lincoln: University of Nebraska Press, 2008.

Carrington, Ben. *Race, Sport, and Politics: The Sporting Black Diaspora.* London: Sage, 2010.

Carter, Thomas F. "Baseball Arguments: *Aficionismo* and Masculinity at the Core of Cubanidad." *International Journal of the History of Sport* 18, no. 3 (2001): 117–38.

———. *In Foreign Fields: The Politics and Experience of Transnational Sport Migration.* London: Pluto, 2011.

———. *The Quality of Home Runs: The Passion, Politics, and Language of Cuban Baseball.* Durham, NC: Duke University Press, 2008.

Carter, Thomas F., and John Sugden. "The USA and Sporting Diplomacy: Comparing and Contrasting the Cases of Table Tennis with China and Baseball with Cuba in the 1970s." *International Relations* 26, no. 1 (2012): 101–21.

Chen, Nancy. *Breathing Spaces: Qigong, Psychiatry, and Healing in China.* New York: Columbia University Press, 2003.

Coleman, Simon, and Tamara Kohn, eds. *The Discipline of Leisure: Embodying Cultures of "Recreation."* Oxford: Berghahn, 2007.

Collison, Holly. *Youth and Sport for Development: The Seduction of Football in Liberia.* Basingstoke, UK: Palgrave Macmillan, 2016.

Crowther, Nigel B. *Sport in Ancient Times.* Oklahoma City: University of Oklahoma Press, 2010.

Darby, Paul, Gerard Akindes, and Matthew Kirwin. "Football Academies and the Migration of African Football Labor to Europe." *Journal of Sport and Social Issues* 31, no. 2 (2007): 143–61.

Downey, Greg. *Learning Capoeira: Lessons in Cunning from an Afro-Brazilian Art.* Oxford: Oxford University Press, 2005.

———. "'Practice without Theory': A Neuroanthropological Perspective on Embodied Learning." *Journal of the Royal Anthropological Institute* 16, no. S1 (2010): S22–S40.

Doyle, Jennifer, ed. "The Athletic Issue," special issue, *GLQ* 19, no. 4 (2013).

Dyck, Noel. *Fields of Play: An Ethnography of Children's Sport.* Toronto: University of Toronto Press, 2012.

Eriksen, Thomas Hylland. "Steps to an Ecology of Transnational Sports." *Global Networks* 7, no. 2 (2007): 132–65.

Esson, James. "A Body and a Dream at a Vital Conjuncture: Ghanaian Youth, Uncertainty and the Allure of Football." *Geoforum* 47 (June 2013): 84–92.

———. "Better Off at Home? Rethinking Responses to Trafficked West African Footballers in Europe." *Journal of Ethnic and Migration Studies* 41, no. 3 (2014): 512–30.

Evans, Gillian. *London's Olympic Legacy: The Inside Track.* London: Palgrave Macmillan, 2016.

Farquhar, Judith, and Qicheng Zhang. *Ten Thousand Things: Nurturing Life in Contemporary Beijing.* New York: Zone, 2012.

Foster, Robert J. "From Trobriand Cricket to Rugby Nation: The Mission of Sport in Papua New Guinea." *International Journal of the History of Sport* 23, no. 5 (2006): 739–58.

Gao, Yunxiang. *Sporting Gender: Women Athletes and Celebrity-Making during China's National Crisis, 1931–1946.* Vancouver: University of British Columbia Press, 2013.

Giardina, Michael D., and Michele K. Donnelly, eds. *Youth Culture and Sport: Identity, Power, and Politics.* New York: Routledge, 2008.

Giulianotti, Richard, and Susan Brownell, eds. "Olympic and World Sport: Making Transnational Society?," special issue, *British Journal of Sociology* 63, no. 2 (2012).

Giulianotti, Richard, and Roland Robertson. "The Globalization of Football: A Study in the Glocalization of the 'Serious Life.'" *British Journal of Sociology* 55, no. 4 (2004): 545–68.

Griffin, Nicholas. *Ping-Pong Diplomacy: The Secret History behind the Game that Changed the World.* New York: Scribner, 2014.

Guinness, Daniel, and Niko Besnier. "Nation, Nationalism, and Sport: Fijian Rugby in the Local-Global Nexus." *Anthropological Quarterly* 89, no. 4 (2016): 1109–42.

Guthrie-Shimizu, Sayuri. *Transpacific Field of Dreams: How Baseball Linked the United States and Japan in Peace and War.* Chapel Hill: North Carolina University Press, 2012.

Guttmann, Allen. *Sports: The First Five Millennia.* Amherst: University of Massachusetts Press, 2004.

Heggie, Vanessa. "Testing Sex and Gender in Sports: Reinventing, Reimagining and Reconstructing Histories." *Endeavour* 34, no. 4 (2010): 158–63.

Henne, Kathryn. "The 'Science' of Fair Play in Sport: Gender and the Politics of Testing." *Signs* 39, no. 3 (2014): 787-812.

———. *Testing for Athletic Citizenship: Regulating Doping and Sex in Sport.* New Brunswick, NJ: Rutgers University Press, 2015.

Hoberman, John. *Testosterone Dreams: Rejuvenation, Aphrodisia, Doping.* Austin: University of Texas Press, 2006.

Horne, John, and Wolfram Manzenreiter. "An Introduction to the Sociology of Mega-events." *Sociological Review* 54, no. S2 (2006): S1–S24.

———, eds. *Japan, Korea and the 2002 World Cup.* New York: Routledge, 2002.

Joo, Rachael Miyung. *Transnational Sport: Gender, Media, and Global Korea.* Durham, NC: Duke University Press, 2012.

Karkazis, Katrina, Rebecca Jordan-Young, Georgiann Davis, and Silvia Camporesi. "Out of Bounds? A Critique of the New Policies on Hyperandrogenism in Elite Female Athletes." *American Journal of Bioethics* 12, no. 7 (2012): 3–16.

Kelly, William W., ed. *Fanning the Flames: Fans and Consumer Culture in Contemporary Japan.* Albany: State University of New York Press, 2004.

———. "Is Baseball a Global Sport? America's 'National Pastime' as Global Field and International Sport." *Global Networks* 7, no. 2 (2007): 187–201.

Kelly, William W., and Susan Brownell, eds. *The Olympics in East Asia: The Crucible of Localism, Nationalism, Regionalism, and Globalism.* New Haven, CT: Council on East Asian Studies, Yale University, 2011.

Kelly, William W., and Atsuo Sugimoto, eds. *This Sporting Life: Sports and Body Culture in Modern Japan.* New Haven, CT: Council on East Asian Studies, Yale University, 2007.

Keys, Barbara. *Globalizing Sport: National Rivalry and International Community in the 1930s.* Cambridge, MA: Harvard University Press, 2006.

Kittleson, Roger. *The Country of Football: Soccer and the Making of Modern Brazil.* Berkeley: University of California Press, 2014.

Klein, Alan M. *American Sport: An Anthropological Perspective.* New York: Routledge, 2008.

———. *Dominican Baseball: New Pride, Old Prejudice.* Philadelphia: Temple University Press, 2014.

———. *Growing the Game: The Globalization of Major League Baseball.* New Haven, CT: Yale University Press, 2006.

Krist, Stefan. "Wrestling Magic: National Wrestling in Buryatia, Mongolia and Tuva in the Past and Today." *International Journal of the History of Sport* 31, no. 4 (2014): 423–44.

Kyle, Donald G. *Sport and Spectacle in the Ancient World.* Malden, MA: Blackwell, 2007.

Laderman, Scott. *Empire in Waves: A Political History of Surfing.* Berkeley: University of California Press, 2014.

Laviolette, Patrick. *Extreme Landscapes of Leisure: Not a Hap-Hazardous Sport.* Farnham, UK: Ashgate, 2011.

Lawrence, Kelli. *Skating on Air: The Broadcast History of an Olympic Marquee Sport.* Jefferson, NC: McFarland, 2011.

Levi, Heather. *The World of Lucha Libre: Secrets, Revelations, and Mexican National Identity.* Durham, NC: Duke University Press, 2008.

Lo, Vivienne, ed. *Perfect Bodies: Sports, Medicine and Immortality.* London: British Museum, 2012.

Lozada, Eriberto P., Jr. "Cosmopolitanism and Nationalism in Shanghai Sports." *City and Society* 18, no. 2 (2006): 207–31.

MacAloon, John J., ed. *Muscular Christianity in Colonial and Post-colonial Worlds.* London: Routledge, 2007.

Majumdar, Boria, and Sandra Collins, eds. "Olympism: The Global Vision: From Nationalism to Internationalism," special issue, *International Journal of the History of Sport* 3, no. 7 (2006).

Magazine, Roger. *Golden and Blue like My Heart: Masculinity, Youth, and Power among Soccer Fans in Mexico City.* Tucson: University of Arizona Press, 2007.

Martínez, Francisco, and Patrick Laviolette. "Trespass into the Liminal Urban Exploration in Estonia." *Anthropological Journal of European Cultures* 25, no. 2 (2016): 1–24.

Miah, Andy. "Towards the Transhuman Athlete: Therapy, Non-therapy, and Enhancement." *Sport in Society* 13, no. 2 (2010): 221–33.

Miller, Stephen G. *Arete: Greek Sports from Ancient Sources.* 3rd ed. Berkeley: University of California Press, 2012. First published 2004.

Molnar, Gyozo, and Yoko Kanemasu, eds. "Playing on the Global Periphery: Social Scientific Explorations of Rugby in the Pacific Islands," special issue, *Asia Pacific Journal of Sport and Social Science* 3, no. 3 (2014).

Morris, Andrew. *Marrow of the Nation: A History of Sport and Physical Culture in Republican China.* Berkeley: University of California Press, 2004.

Newman, Josh, and Michael Giardina. *Sport, Spectacle, and NASCAR Nation: Consumption and Cultural Politics of Neoliberalism.* New York: Palgrave Macmillan, 2011.

Palmer, David. *Qigong Fever: Body, Science, and Utopia in China.* New York: Columbia University Press, 2007.

Pauketat, Timothy R. "America's First Pastime." *Archaeology* 62, no. 5 (2009): 20–25.

Peavy, Linda, and Ursula Smith. *Full-Court Quest: The Girls from Fort Shaw Indian School, Basketball Champions of the World.* Norman: University of Oklahoma Press, 2008.

Pieper, Lindsay Parks. *Sex Testing: Gender Policing in Women's Sports.* Urbana: University of Illinois Press, 2016.

Price, Monroe E., and Daniel Dayan, eds. *Owning the Olympics: Narratives of the New China.* Ann Arbor: University of Michigan Press, 2008.

Pringle, Richard, Robert E. Rinehart, and Jayne Caudwell. *Sport and the Social Significance of Pleasure.* New York: Routledge, 2015.

Ren, Hai, Lamartine DaCosta, Ana Miragaya, and Niu Jing, eds. *Olympic Studies Reader.* Vol. 1. Beijing: Beijing Sport University Press, 2010.

Renson, Roland. "Safeguarding Ludodiversity: Chances and Challenges in the Promotion and Protection of Traditional Movement Culture." *East Asian Sport Thoughts* 3 (2004): 139–58.

Rial, Carmen. "Banal Religiosity: Brazilian Athletes as New Missionaries of the Neo-Pentecostal Diaspora." *Vibrant* 9, no. 2 (2012): 128–59.

———. "The 'Devil's Egg': Football Players as New Missionaries of the Diaspora of Brazilian Religions." In *The Diaspora of Brazilian Religions,* edited by Cristina Rocha and Manuel Arturo Vasquez, 91–115. Leiden: Brill, 2013.

Rosen, Daniel M. *Dope: A History of Performance Enhancement in Sports from the Nineteenth Century to Today.* Westport, CT: Praeger, 2008.

Schwell, Alexandra, Nina Szogs, Magłorzata Z. Kowalska, and Michal Buchowki, eds. *New Ethnographies of Football in Europe: People, Passions, Politics.* Basingstoke, UK: Palgrave Macmillan, 2016.

Sherouse, Perry. "Skill and Masculinity in Olympic Weightlifting: Training Cues and Cultivated Craziness in Georgia." *American Ethnologist* 43, no. 1 (2016): 103–15.

Silverstein, Paul A. "Sporting Faith: Islam, Soccer, and the French Nation-State." *Social Text* 18, no. 4 (2000): 25–53.

Sorek, Tamir. *Arab Soccer in a Jewish State.* Cambridge: Cambridge University Press, 2007.

Sotomayor, Antonio. *The Sovereign Colony: Olympic Sport, National Identity, and International Politics in Puerto Rico.* Lincoln: University of Nebraska Press, 2016.

Spielvogel, Laura. *Working Out in Japan: Shaping the Female Body in Tokyo Fitness Clubs.* Durham, NC: Duke University Press, 2003.

Starn, Orin. *The Passion of Tiger Woods: An Anthropologist Reports on Golf, Race, and Celebrity.* Durham, NC: Duke University Press, 2011.

Symons, Caroline. *The Gay Games: A History.* Abingdon, UK: Routledge, 2010.

Thangaraj, Stanley I. *Desi Hoop Dreams: Pickup Basketball and the Making of Asian American Masculinity.* New York: New York University Press, 2015.

Thorpe, Holly, and Belinda Wheaton. "'Generation X Games,' Action Sports and the Olympic Movement: Understanding the Cultural Politics of Incorporation." *Sociology* 45, no. 5 (2011): 830–47.

Tomlinson, Alan. "Olympic Legacies: Recurrent Rhetoric and Harsh Realities." *Contemporary Social Science* 9, no. 2 (2014): 137–58.

Tomlinson, Alan, and Christopher Young, eds. *National Identity and Global Sports Events: Culture, Politics, and Spectacle in the Olympics and the Football World Cup.* Albany: State University of New York Press, 2006.

Uperesa, Fa'anofo Lisaclaire, and Tom Mountjoy, eds. "Global Sport in the Pacific," special issue, *Contemporary Pacific* 26, no. 2 (2014).

Wagg, Stephen, and David Andrews, eds. *East Plays West: Essays on Sport and the Cold War.* London: Routledge, 2007.

Welch, Katherine. *The Roman Amphitheater: From Its Origins to the Colosseum.* Cambridge: Cambridge University Press, 2009.

Xu, Guoqi. *Olympic Dreams: China and Sports, 1895–2008.* Cambridge, MA: Harvard University Press, 2008.

Zeiler, Thomas W. *Ambassadors in Pinstripes: The Spalding World Baseball Tour and the Birth of the American Empire.* Lanham: Rowman & Littlefield, 2006.

Brazil, 4, 51, 98, 109, 144, 248. *See also*
    Olympic Games, 2016 Rio
Brown, Elwood, 58
Buddhism, 59, 88, 208, 211
Buffalo Bill. *See* Cody, William F.
bullfighting, 145–146
Butler, Judith, 159
buzkashi, 189–191

Caillois, Roger, 28–29, 30, 31
camel racing, 213–214
Cameroon, 93–94, 167–169, 243–244,
    246–247
Canada, 50, 63, 109, 116, 236, 252, 283n26
capoeira, 98
Caribbean, 79, 233, 240, 241; baseball, 50,
    59–60, 117; cricket, 40, 50, 55
Cartesian dualism. *See* mind-body dualism
chariot racing, 18, 26–27
China, 1, 16, 86–89, 160, 233, 236–237, 248,
    252; and global politics, 131, 165, 186, 194,
    225, 253; and Olympic Games, 44–45,
    47, 165, 233, 250; gender in, 102, 135, 142,
    147–152, 215–217; National Games of
    Ethnic Minorities of, 116; National
    Games of, 176–178; nationalism in, 198,
    199, 202–203, 205–206, 215–216; Repub-
    lic of China v. People's Republic of
    China, 67, 200; social class in, 102–103;
    women's volleyball team of, 216–217;
    YMCA in, 48–49, 58–59, 216. *See also*
    Asian Americans; Beijing 2008 Olympic
    Games; International Olympic Com-
    mittee, and China; Japan, rivalry with
    China; masculinity, in China; morality,
    in China; medicine, Chinese; opening
    ceremonies, in China; schooling, in
    China; Ping Pong diplomacy; *qi; qigong;*
    soccer, in China; Tibet; Uygurs; women,
    in China; wrestling, Mongolian; wushu
China, Republic of. *See* Taiwan
Christianity, 23, 45, 65, 109, 113, 216;
    Catholicism, 12, 62–63, 166; muscular,
    45, 48–49, 60–62, 82, 144, 148–149,
    215; Pentecostal, 167. *See also* YMCA
chunkey, 22
circus, 17–18; Roman, 23–27, 164
classicism, 12–16, 17

Coca-Cola, 193, 251*fig.*, 255
cockfighting, 4, 7–8, 34–36, 159
Cody, William F., 18
Cold War, 38, 92, 129–133, 138, 172, 188, 192,
    203, 208
colonialism, 12–13, 23, 37–42, 45–55, 109,
    143–144, 173, 200; and decolonization,
    66–68; and development programs,
    233–234; and medicine, 79, 85; and
    neocolonialism, 17; in Africa, 68, 203;
    in Australia, 110; in Fiji, 69–70, 113,
    247–249; in India, 55–56, 123; in
    Ireland, 63–64; in West Indies, 40,
    56–57, 57*fig.*, 111, 117; in New Zealand,
    110. *See also* postcolonial
communitas, 161, 164, 183
Confederation of Independent Football
    Associations (ConIFA), 208
Congo, Republic of, 194, 248
corporate sponsorship, 104, 106, 150–151,
    155, 178–180, 193, 251–252
corruption, 43, 146–147, 179, 195, 208, 221,
    253–254
Cotonou Agreement, 241
Coubertin, Pierre de, 52, 104, 144, 173,
    199–200; and founding of modern
    Olympic Games, 13, 65, 160, 171, 210
Court of Arbitration for Sport (CAS), 44,
    95, 141
cricket, 42, 48, 53–57, 240, 248, 259n2; in
    India, 70; in South Asia, 56–57; in
    Trobriand Islands, 7, 55–56; in West
    Indies, 56–57, 111–112
Crystal Palace Exhibition. *See* world's fairs
Csikszentmihalyi, Mihaly, 34
Cuba, 102, 123–124, 159, 207, 213, 231
Culin, Stewart, 19
curling, 50
Curtius, Ernst, 12–13

dart games, 28
Dayan, Daniel, 184–185, 186
diplomacy, 12, 229, 230–232; public, 172,
    232, 233
disability, 72–73, 94–95
disease, 73, 75–76, 77, 78, 80, 82, 84, 96;
    chronic, 81, 85, 89–90; infectious, 79,
    223–224

distinction. *See* social class
Dominican Republic, 36–37, 117, 245, 246
doping, 92–94, 136, 137
Dundes, Alan, 154–155
Durkheim, Émile, 1, 259n1

East Germany. *See* Germany, East
Eckert, Penny, 105
effeminacy, 24, 154, 216. *See also* masculinity
Egypt, 14, 16, 52, 53, 66–67, 206–207, 244
Eichberg, Henning, 17, 33, 91, 164, 165
environment, 90–92, 94, 96, 185, 187–188
equestrian sports, 18, 141, 149, 210, 285n63
Eritrea, 236
ethnic games, 115–116
ethnicity, 97, 99, 108–116, 125, 203
ethnography, 5–10, 15–16, 97, 101, 166, 257–258; of mega-events, 7, 158–159, 165, 171–172, 196
ethnomedicine, 73
European Union, 241
event ecology, 175–178
evolutionism, 23, 32–33, 46, 71, 81, 82, 163–164
exercise, 6, 37, 71–90, 96, 149, 152, 182, 212, 271n7
extreme sports, 181–183

fair play, 55, 93, 101, 104, 143, 220
Fairbanks, Mabel, 119–121
Falun Gong, 88
Fanon, Frantz, 39–40, 66–67
Far Eastern Championship Games, 52, 58, 70
Fédération internationale de football association (FIFA), 24, 38, 43–44, 68, 208, 226, 239, 253–254. *See also* FIFA World Cup
femininity, 99, 100, 134, 138, 150–151, 215
festival, 147*fig.*, 159, 172, 189, 190–191, 196, 210, 297n62; Olympic, 171, 174, 183–184, 191
FIFA. *See* Fédération internationale de football association
FIFA Soccer World Cup, 5, 7, 38, 158, 172, 173, 192, 203, 221, 223–224; and global politics, 24, 192, 217, 219, 230; and

television, 179, 184; 1986 Mexico, 179; 1994 United States, 179; 2002 Japan and Korea, 203, 252; 2010 South Africa, 250; 2014 Brazil, 195, 226, 250–251; 2015 Women's World Cup, 103; 2018 Russia, 251; 2022 Qatar, 221, 251
field hockey, 41–42, 56, 100–101, 132
figure skating, 119–122, 129, 133–134, 141, 142, 284n49
Fiji, 168. *See also* colonialism, in Fiji; rugby, in Fiji
Firth, Raymond, 28
fitness, 53, 74, 84, 105, 152
Fleming, Peggy, 133–134
flow, 34
folklore, 115, 209, 212
Foot Solidaire, 246
Football 4 Peace International (F4P), 238–239
football, American, 104–105, 118, 154–155, 156, 180; on television, 204–205, 233. *See also* soccer
Foucault, Michel, 33, 40, 66, 78, 81, 127, 223. *See also* biopolitics/biopower
France, 12, 179, 181–182, 200, 203, 219. *See also* rugby, in France

Gaelic sports, 50, 62–64
Gahuku-Gama, 4
Galen of Pergamon, 75–76, 81, 84, 92, 128
gambling, 29, 34–36
Games of the New Emerging Forces (GANEFO), 67
games (non-athletic), 19, 28–32
Gay Games, 156–157. *See also* homosexuality
Geertz, Clifford, 7, 34–36, 159, 161, 175–176, 178
gender, 35–36, 127–129, 143–155, 190, 234, 256, 257; and colonialism, 45, 46, 60, 68; and sport migration, 237; and social class, 98, 99, 101, 157. *See also* effeminacy; nationalism, gender in; sex; sexuality
gene doping, 95
Georgia, Republic of, 146
Germany, 49, 81, 83, 130, 134, 179, 200, 215; and nationalism, 198, 215; and racist

Germany *(continued)*
scholarship, 12–13, 16–17, 79–80, 115;
East, 92, 133. *See also* Olympic Games,
1936 Berlin; turner gymnastics
gift economy, 188–194, 254
Giuliani, Rudolph, 226
gladiators, 24–26
globalization, 36–37, 105, 173–174, 194–195,
229–230, 249–252, 254
Gluckman, Mary, 160
Gluckman, Max, 33, 34, 159–160, 163, 165, 170
Gmelch, George, 170
Goffman, Erving, 34, 160
golf, 44, 48, 123, 129, 144
governmentality, 201, 223
Gramsci, Antonio, 36–37, 49
Greece: ancient, 3, 12–16, 23–24, 144, 198,
205; modern, 64–67, 192, 198, 199, 209.
See also agonal spirit; Olympic Games,
1896 Athens; 1906 Athens, 2004 Athens
Guttmann, Allen, 32, 33, 49–50, 163, 264n66
gymnasium (ancient Greek), 74
gymnastics, 205, 240. *See also* turner
gymnastics

Habermas, Jürgen, 185–186
habitus, 97–106, 162
handball, 220
Hawai'i, 109–110
heptathlon, 131, 203, 283n26
Hinduism, 84–85
Hippocrates, 74–75, 82
Hoberman, John, 83, 275n70
Hobsbawm, Eric, 199, 209–213
hockey. *See* field hockey, ice hockey
homosexuality, 24, 60–62, 127, 150, 153–157,
201, 215
Hong Kong, 151, 200, 285n63
hooliganism, 101
horse racing, 58, 90, 149, 285n63
Huizinga, Johan, 16, 28–29, 30–31
human rights, 88, 186, 192, 207, 234, 239
Human Rights Watch, 186, 235
Hungary, 203
hydrotherapy. *See* naturopathy

IAAF. *See* International Association of
Athletic Federations

ice hockey, 203, 222–223
Igorot, 20fig.
imagined community, 38, 185–186, 204,
230, 248, 298n6
imperialism, 12, 23, 40, 48–50, 64–66, 79,
173, 252; American, 36, 39, 57–60, 110;
British, 39, 53–57, 63–64; cultural, 36, 47
India, 48, 84–85, 111, 115, 137, 141, 159;
colonial 54–55, 123; Tibetan exiles in,
199, 208, traditional medicine in,
74–76, 78, 84. *See also* cricket, in India;
kabbadi; wrestling, Indian; yoga
Indonesia, 35, 67
Intergovernmental Committee for Physical
Education and Sport, 67
International Association of Athletic
Federations (IAAF), 130, 136–139, 141,
142–143, 266n10
International Olympic Committee (IOC),
x, 47–48, 54, 206, 221, 228, 261n9;
271n84; and Africa, 52–53; and aid
programs, 236, 239, 299n22; and China,
58, 67, 200, 231–23; and East Asia,
58–59; and environment, 91; and Gay
Games, 156; and Ireland, 64; and
nationalism, 51–52, 65, 173–174, 199–
200, 208, 210, 231, 250; and sports law,
44–45; and women's sports, 144; and X
Games, 182–183; anti-doping policy of,
93; founding of, 2, 42–43. *See also*
Coubertin, Pierre de; Olympic Charter;
sex, testing; Olympic hospitality
international relations, 230–232
International Rugby Board (IRB). *See*
World Rugby
International Women's Games, 144
internationalism, 152, 229–230
intersex, 133–141; 282n17. *See also* sex testing
IOC. *See* International Olympic
Committee
Iran, 206, 208
Ireland, 10, 41, 50, 51, 59, 62–64, 70, 107–108
Islam, 71, 74, 78, 112, 169, 208, 213
Israel, 14, 109, 200, 225, 238–239, 300n29

James, C.L.R., 40, 111
Japan, ix, 16, 91, 121, 131, 152, 216, 252; economic development, 164–165; rivalry

with China, 216, 217, 231; soft power, 233; YMCA in, 57–59. *See also* baseball, in Japan; FIFA Soccer World Cup, 2002 Japan and Korea; Olympic Games, 1964 Tokyo, 2020 Tokyo; rugby, in Japan; sumo

Jigorō, Kanō, 59

Jordan-Young, Rebecca, 140–141

judo, 4, 47, 59, 149

kabbadi, 47, 103–104

Kang, Shin-pyo, 9, 172

karate, 48

Karkazis, Katrina, 140–141

Katz, Elihu, 184–185, 186

Kazakhstan, 222

Kenya, 53, 220, 221

Killanin, Michael, 64, 67

King, Billie Jean, 133, 155

Klein, Alan, 36–37, 151, 217–218, 245, 246

Koss, Johann Olav, 236

kula, 188, 192, 195

Laqueur, Thomas, 128, 139, 148

Laredo (Texas), 217–218

Larkins, Erika Robb, 225–226

Lévi-Strauss, Claude, 100, 259n5

Liberia, 237

liminality, 34, 38, 161–164, 185

liminoid, 162–164

ludic diffusion, 48

ludodiversity, 212

MacAloon, John, 9, 30, 50, 160, 164, 183–184, 197. *See also* performance, ramified performance theory

Macau, 200

magic, 93, 112, 160, 167–170, 243

Mao Zedong, 231

Māori, 68, 110

marathon, 92, 143, 179, 287n86

martial arts. *See* karate, taekwondo, wushu

Martínez Patiño, María José, 135–136, 139

Marx, Karl, 99, 164

Marxism, 13, 32, 40, 49, 100, 264n66

mascot, 18

masculinity, 4, 24–25, 36, 139, 146, 151, 215; and colonialism, 45; and soccer, 103; and

social class, 100; and sport migration, 168, 218, 219, 247; and YMCA, 61–62, in China, 149–150, 216; in Mexico, 218. *See also* effeminacy; femininity; Christianity, muscular

Mauss, Marcel, 189, 191–192, 256

Mayans. *See* Mesoamerica

McGee, WJ, 19–21

Mead, Margaret, 127

media events, 183–185

medical anthropology, 71–73, 80, 84, 96

medicine: Ayurvedic, 72, 84–85; biomedicine, 37, 71, 72–73, 78–84, 89–90, 96; Chinese, 72, 86–89; Galenic, 75–76; Hippocratic, 74–75; humoral, 71, 74–78, 80, 81–82, 84; Mesoamerican, 76–78; sports, 82–83, 90, 92–95

meditation, 85, 88

mega-event, 7, 9, 27, 38, 91, 165, 172–178, 185–196; ethnography of, 158–159. *See also* FIFA Soccer World Cup; Olympic Games; Roche, Maurice; world's fairs

Mesoamerica, 1–2, 21–23, 76–78

Mexico, 37, 48, 119, 120, 159, 217–218. *See also* FIFA Soccer World Cup, 1986 Mexico; Mesoamerica; Olympic Games, 1968 Mexico City

migration, 38, 110, 241–249, 254, 256

military, 67–68, 146, 182, 201, 221, 231, 248–249; role in dissemination of sport, 54, 59, 60

misrecognition, 101–102

modernity, 23, 31, 45–48, 53, 96, 203, 257; and mega-events, 175, 196. *See also* tradition, and modernity

morality, 101, 137, 147, 154–157, 160, 163, 182, 226–227; in the United Kingdom, 54–55, 61; in China, 88, 202; in Fiji, 166; in Thailand, 211. *See also* fair play

Morocco, 67–68, 220

Mosse, George, 214–215, 281–282n9

Mubarak, Hosni, 206

muscular Christianity. *See* Christianity, muscular

nationalism, 110, 144, 149, 174, 197–200, 203–208, 222, 256–257; banal, 205; gender in, 131–134, 149, 214–219;

nationalism *(continued)*
    invented traditions in, 208–212; tension
    with transnationalism, 227, 243–244.
    See also International Olympic Com-
    mittee, and nationalism
nation-state, 111, 180, 186, 199–200, 203,
    205–207, 258; diplomacy between,
    231–232, formation of, 12, 24, 41, 197–
    198, 202; mega-events and, 249–250,
    253; United Nations and 239; Westphal-
    ian system of, 229. *See also* nationalism,
    security and surveillance
naturopathy, 72, 81–82, 85
Ndembu, 164–165
Nemean Games, 15–16
neoclassicism, 13
neoliberalism, 6–7, 178–180, 182, 206, 207,
    237; and sport migration, 168, 240–241,
    246, 258
New Zealand, 69, 105, 108, 109, 248. *See
    also* rugby, in New Zealand
Nigeria, 123, 155, 220, 221
non-governmental organization (NGO),
    38, 44, 49, 172, 226, 250, 253, 261n9; and
    aid programs, 234–239, 245–246; and
    mega-events, 91, 175, 184, 185, 186, 229
Norbeck, Edward, 30–31

obesity, 90, 140
Olympia, Ancient, 2, 3, 12–13, 14
Olympic Charter, 187, 200, 208, 250
Olympic education, x, 47, 176–178
Olympic Games, 64–66; ancient, 12–16;
    1896 Athens, 65, 173, 209; 1900 Paris,
    173; 1904 St. Louis, 19–21, 51, 63, 82, 92,
    173; 1906 Athens (Intercalary), 43, 64,
    210, 270n72, 271n84; 1908 London, 210;
    1912 Stockholm, 173; 1936 Berlin, 51, 130,
    174, 210, 213; 1952 Helsinki, 82; 1956
    Melbourne, 203; 1960 Rome, 83; 1964
    Tokyo, 67, 131, 132*fig.*, 213; 1968 Greno-
    ble, 133–134; 1968 Mexico City, 83; 1972
    Munich, 91, 160, 225; 1980 Lake Placid,
    120, 203; 1980 Moscow, 192; 1984 Los
    Angeles, 172, 176, 183; 1988 Seoul, 91,
    100, 172; 1992 Albertville, 236; 1992
    Barcelona, 136, 165, 193, 213; 1994 Lille-
    hammer, 172, 236; 1996 Atlanta, 136, 225;
    2000 Sydney, 110, 137; 2004 Athens, 66,
    192, 217, 226; 2008 Beijing, *see* Beijing
    2008 Olympic Games; 2012 London, 95;
    2014 Sochi, 93, 251; 2016 Rio de Janeiro,
    48, 113–116; 2018 PyeongChang, 233,
    250; 2020 Tokyo, 233, 250, 251, 253; 2022
    Beijing-Zhangjiakou, 233, 250; Parade of
    Athletes, 173, 176, 197, 210, 222
Olympic hospitality, 192–195, 253–254
Olympic legacy, 187–188
Olympic Movement, 14, 200, 261n9
opening ceremonies, 110, 162, 183–184, 186,
    200, 252–253; in China, 116, 176–177,
    192, 194, 197, 202–203
Orientalism, 12, 14, 16, 64, 216

Pacific Islands, 9, 50, 103, 233, 242
Palestine, 199, 200, 238, 239
Paralympic Games, 72–73, 94–95
parkour, 181–182
Pentecostalism. *See* Christianity
performance complex. *See* event ecology
performance: genre, 38, 159, 162, 164, 170,
    196, 210; cultural performance, 24, 158,
    159–164, 170–171, 194–196; ramified
    performance theory, 170–172, 174;
    theory, 159
Philippines, 50, 58, 59, 194
physical education, 61, 71, 75, 80–82, 149,
    199, 202, 216
ping pong. *See* table tennis
Ping Pong diplomacy, 231–232
Pistorius, Oscar, 94–95
play, 11, 27–32, 34, 161, 163; among animals,
    27–28, 29–30; deep, 35
Politis, Nikolaos G., 209
polo, 51
postcolonial, 70, 66–67, 69–70; studies,
    39–41, 46, 111, 216
postmodernism, 36–37, 164
potlatch, 189, 255, 256
Press, Irina and Tamara, 131–133
professionalization, 98–99, 106–108,
    168–169
Puerto Rico, 48, 200

Qatar, 220–221, 248, 250. *See also* FIFA
    Soccer World Cup, 2022 Qatar

sport: concept of, 3–5; history of, 9, 16–17, 21–27, 41–70, 205–206. *See also names of individual sports disciplines*
Sportimonium, 212
state, 22–23, 24, 35–36, 44, 91, 178, 206–207, 235; and biopower, 6; and sovereignty, 108, 199–202; 223, 229, 250; city-state, 2, 12, 14, 16, 24, 75, 197–198; theater-state, 175–176. *See also* biopolitics/biopower; governmentality; nation-state
stock car racing, 102
sumo, 109, 146–147
Super Bowl, 204–205, 227, 233, 297n69
surfing, 109–110, 182
swimming, 41, 118, 123, 138, 151, 187–188

table tennis, 231–232, 248. *See also* Ping Pong diplomacy
taekwondo, 47
Taiwan, 50, 67, 164, 200, 231–232. *See also* China
television, 104, 133–134, 174, 178–180, 182, 196, 240, 250; NBC Television, 205, 252. *See also* Beijing 2008 Olympic Games, revenues from television and sponsorship; NBC television; FIFA Soccer World Cup, on television; football, American, on television; media events; X Games
Temo, Isireli, 255–256
tennis, 41, 90, 99–100, 129, 133, 142, 144, 235*fig.*, 284n49. *See also* King, Billie Jean
testosterone, 138–141, 157
Thailand. *See* boxing, Thai
Tibet, 116, 186, 211, 207, 208
Tikopia, 28
Title IX, 133, 148, 149
Tonga, 103, 105, 242
tourism, 81–82, 116, 175, 213, 226, 243
track and field, 3, 43, 67–68, 89, 92–93, 144, 220, 221; USA-USSR meet, 130–131. *See also* sex, testing
tradition, 32–33, 112, 164, 166, 168; and modernity, 7, 8*fig.*, 32–33, 162–163, 169–170; invented, 208–212, 222. *See also* Hobsbawm, Eric; "traditional" sport
"traditional" sport, 7, 33, 116

transgender, 133–134, 157, 286n81
transnationalism, 38, 194–196, 222–227, 229, 239–249, 254. *See also* nationalism, tension with transnationalism
Trinidad and Tobago, 57, 111–112
Trobriand Islands, 55–56, 170, 188
Tsing, Anna, 195
Turkey, 147, 248. *See also* wrestling, Turkish oil
turner gymnastics, 42, 51, 82, 90, 144
Turner, Edith, 9, 271n5
Turner, Terence, 33–34
Turner, Victor W., 33–34, 59–165, 170, 186, 196
Tutsi. *See* Rwanda

United States, 57–60, 104–105, 118–125. *See also* baseball, in the United States; FIFA Soccer World Cup, 1994 United States; rugby, in the United States; schooling, in the United States; soccer, in the United States; women, in the United States
United Kingdom, 45, 53–57, 60–62, 98–99, 106. *See also* morality, in the United Kingdom; rugby, in the United Kingdom; schooling, in the United Kingdom
United Nations, 85, 200, 232, 234, 239, 299n22, 302n54
United Nations Educational, Scientific, and Cultural Organization (UNESCO), 234
USSR, 115–116, 130–133, 203. *See also* Russia
Uygurs, 208

van Gennep, Arnold, 161
Victorian sport ideals, 53–57, 61–62, 101
Virchow, Rudolf, 80
volleyball, 58, 131, 132, 142, 150, 193, 216–217

Waiwai, 4, 109
water polo, 203
Weber, Max, 99, 199
weightlifting, 146, 149
Wenner-Gren symposia, 159–161
Wenner, Lawrence, 205
West Africa, 241, 242, 244–245

West Indies. *See* Caribbean

Western civilization, 12–14, 16, 27, 66, 205

witchcraft, 76, 93, 112, 167–170

Wolf, Eric, 13

women, 24, 26, 36, 46, 60–61, 129–130, 144–145; and sport migration, 242, 247; in Argentina, 100; in Brazil, 144; in China, 89, 102, 148–151, 152, 215–217; in Eastern Bloc, 131–133; in Fiji, 115; in France, 104; in Germany, 215; in Japan, 146, 152; in Olympic Games, 129, 141–143, 144, 180; in Republic of Georgia, 146; in Sparta, 75; in Turkey, 147; in turner gymnastics, 144; in the United States, 61, 103, 130–131, 151. *See also* femininity; gender; masculinity; sex, testing; Women's Olympics

Women's Olympics, 144

World Anti-Doping Agency (WADA), 92–94, 95

World Health Organization (WHO), 224

World Rugby, 106–108

world's fairs, 172–174; 1851 Crystal Palace Exhibition, 18, 173; 1893 Chicago, 19; 1900 Paris Exposition, 173; 1904 St. Louis, 19–21, 51, 63, 81; 1908 Franco-British Exposition, 173

wrestling, 154; ancient Greek, 75; Indian, 50; Mexican, 162; Mongolian, 109; Senegalese 8*fig.*, 93–94, 112, 168–169; Turkish oil, 147. *See also* sumo

wushu, 4, 47–48

X Games, 182

yang sheng, 89

Yao Ming, 217

YMCA, 48–49, 57–62, 149, 153, 216

yoga, 84–86, 89

Young Men's Christian Association. *See* YMCA

Young, David, 24

zika virus, 224–225